DONNE,
MILTON,
AND THE END OF
HUMANIST
RHETORIC

■ ■ ■

Thomas O. Sloane

UNIVERSITY OF CALI
BERKELEY LOS ANGI

UNIVERSITY OF CALIFORNIA PRESS
BERKELEY AND LOS ANGELES, CALIFORNIA

UNIVERSITY OF CALIFORNIA PRESS, LTD.
LONDON, ENGLAND
© 1985 BY
THE REGENTS OF THE UNIVERSITY OF CALIFORNIA

Library of Congress Cataloging in Publication Data
Sloane, Thomas O.
  Donne, Milton, and the end of humanist rhetoric.

  Includes index.
  1. English poetry—Early modern, 1500–1700—
History and criticism. 2. Humanism in literature.
3. Rhetoric—1500–1800. 4. Donne, John, 1572–
1631—Criticism and interpretation. 5. Milton, John,
1608–1674—Criticism and interpretation. I. Title.
PR545.H86S58   1985   821'.009'384   83-24315
ISBN 0-520-05212-9

Printed in the United States of America

1 2 3 4 5 6 7 8 9

For Barbara

without whom not

Contents

List of Illustrations

Preface:
An Unsubtle Exordium

Donne was more the humanist than Milton. True, Milton articulated all those doctrines we associate with humanism: the revival of ancient modes of discourse, the praise of ancient authorities, a belief that poetry is morally efficacious and that we can acquire wisdom through interpreting texts. Donne was more the humanist because he was more the rhetorician.

Thus, the equation of humanism with rhetoric is the premise of my argument. I undertook this work mainly to explore some important and still active features of Renaissance writing. In doing so, I found it necessary to completely overturn the usual view of Donne and Milton, in which the former is considered a late scholastic, the latter a late humanist. If my argument, purpose, and conclusion are not enough—and for the reader I have in mind they probably aren't—perhaps I should note that I have also remained cognizant of certain intellectual currents, obscured of late and becoming ever more so, that yet run through the composition classroom. Anyone who teaches composition *and* literature—and who loves both—has a professional ancestry that is deeply rooted in the very sources of Renaissance humanism. For that reader, my work may reaffirm, and I hope clarify, our never totally irretrievable past. Here let me explain further the nature of my argument.

Since early in this century the rise of Donne's star has meant the decline, and at times the eclipse, of Milton's—which would seem to indicate that it is difficult to develop an enthusiasm for both poets simultaneously, so opposite do they seem. But I think the matter might be put somewhat differently: our failure fully to understand the ways in which Donne and Milton are truly opposite has led to a serious misunderstanding of humanism, to say nothing of the astronomical impact of that failure on literary fortunes.

Form is at the center of my attention and is a framework for my analyses. But I am no formalist. Much as I admire formalism, that critical approach almost as old as rhetoric, I do not offer these interpretations as a pure formalist might. Nevertheless, I have tried to apply a certain key formalist doctrine: that every work is to be grasped insofar as possible in its structural entirety; that we should center not on individual passages—such as Donne's difficulties with sustained prayer, or Milton's reinterpretation of Jerome's dream—but on the entire structure of a work, on how individual passages are encompassed and allowed to function within the whole. Pure formalists tend to carry this doctrine too far. Though all formalists insist that literary form is inseparable from its content, some purists claim that a literary work is actually its own little universe, self-contained and self-determined. Some go so far as to deny the emotional efficacy of a literary work, as if the perfection of form were all. Some—and these among the great formalists of our age—try to remove literature from the category of discourse altogether and place it among idealized aesthetic objects, art that somehow exists for its own sake.[1]

More than half a century ago, Kenneth Burke challenged these extreme positions with his concept of rhetorical form: the beauty of form is less important, he argued, than its strategic functions of arousing and then fulfilling expectations in an audience.[2] But rhetoric, the formalists believed, could be easily dismissed with this argument: a specific audience, then, they said, not the perfection of form, was for the rhetorical critic the *raison d'être* of the literary work. And that charge brought with it the ancient absurdities of hermeneutical skepticism, historicism, relativism: how can we reconstruct an audience? And how can rhetoricians understand an older discourse if they *cannot* reconstruct its audience? Isn't it therefore better to take form out of time, even our time? Burke's later efforts, through his "dramatistic pentad," to expand the concept of meaning so that speaker, audience, and occasion became formal constituents of meaning, have not laid the charges to rest. On the contrary, his attempts to restore rhetoric while preserving the best of formalism—such as, for example, his hypothesis that literature appeals to unchanging characteristics of human psychology—have only replaced charges of hermeneutical skepticism, historicism, and relativism with a newer charge: psychologism.[3]

Much as I admire Burke, I do not view form quite in the way he does. True, audience psychology was, most likely, as important to Donne and Milton as Burke insists it is to all artists. We know audience psychology was vitally important to Renaissance rhetorical theorists: humanists, at least, usually combined a discussion of how to arrange a discourse with a discussion of how to arouse various emotions in an audience. Form and the emotions of one's own audience are linked in humanist rhetoric. But we need not ignore our place in time either, or overlook the interval between our time and that of the text, or try to bridge the interval with notions of universal and unchanging audience psychology. The relationship I seek is between form and intention, another combination well known to Renaissance thinkers. What does the form—structure, organization, arrangement, *dispositio*—tell us about the writer's design on an audience? As every writer knows, giving an audience a clearly enunciated thesis is one thing; structuring a discourse is another—sometimes quite contradictory and disparate but always clarifying. Structuring is what a writer *does.* Thus, form is act, as Burke would say—or, as I prefer, form is *design* in the most specific, structuring sense and in the most general, intentional sense.

Obviously, the works I shall examine have outlived their occasions. But our approaches to them remain at least somewhat rhetorical. Though we are not their original audiences, we can yet recognize certain audience responsibilities, in these works as well as in us. An audience hears and judges, or reads in order to hear and judge. It would seem, then, that the initial aim of any approach should be to give discourse a hearing, both literally and forensically: we need to attend to the total work and "try" its argument, or at least try to grasp its intention.

I think this aim applies to reading all discourse, though I will admit it seems uniquely applicable to the argumentative nature of Renaissance writing. That nature, further, offers an audience two general, not necessarily discrete ways of proceeding: juxtaposing, or placing what we know alongside what we do not, and (in Burke's phrase) employing "perspectives by incongruity," or seeing one thing in terms of something that, to a greater or lesser extent, it is not. The first, in its humanist presupposition that knowledge (history especially) is meant to be used through imaginative participation, is not unlike what Milton thought of as becoming a "contemporary of time"; the second, in its elevation of the paradox as a mode of knowledge, resembles Donne's habit of using "contraries."[4] Together, these two ways of proceeding invite us as audience to compare similar as well as dissimilar things for the sake of their mutual illumination, and we shall start with these means, mainly because, as noted, we shall find something like them at work in the discourses we shall examine.

My analytical manner, in sum, is partly rhetorical and partly formalist, too, for I begin with the assumption that form is design, to be grasped as action but in its entirety. The mixture itself, though perhaps a curious result of my own critical temper, could be justified (I shall return to this point at the conclusion of the book) by the literary and critical history of the seventeenth century, when formalism first began making inroads into the purview of English rhetoric. In pursuing the analytical means I have mentioned—juxtapositions and perspectives by incongruity—through a rhetorical formalist manner of reading, we will, first, arrive at quite unconventional views of purpose in a funeral oration and in a radical pamphlet. Then we shall take a further look at this matter of form by setting before us two poems and trying, like formalists, to grasp the forms entire, but also, like rhetoricians, to view those forms as strategic in the speaker's intentional design.

Throughout this study, my view of a poem, like my view of any discourse, will be neither aesthetically pure nor historically innocent, and I shall continue to use juxtapositions and perspectives by incongruity. But at the conclusion of the first chapter I shall try to move beyond these fundamental means of analysis into certain humanist intellectual habits that produced if not discourse itself at least *voice* in discourse. These habits I shall name with a conceptual model Milton describes: the faces of Janus, each looking in an opposite direction. The directions are spatial (Roman Janus was the god of doors and gates); temporal, before and after in time (the first month in our year was named for this god); moral, one way religious, the other secular; and, above all, passionately argumentative: *pro* and *contra*. Milton calls the faces *"controversal"*—that is, "turned at once in two directions." The term, I think, more than any other names the habits of thought we seek—as *probable* best names the subject to which they were applied and as *voice* names the effect that they achieved, and still achieve.

The second chapter is a study of humanist rhetoric, the discipline of controversy, an historical study that, with the first chapter, forms the basis for the practical criticism in the second half of this book. I try to show in the third chapter that the best approach to Donne is through rhetoric, and in the fourth that the best approach to Milton is through formalism. A brief, tentative conclusion then follows.

So let me begin by admitting that in my juxtapositions and incongruous perspectives—studying "voice" by printed discourse, Donne by Milton and vice versa, or either by humanist rhetoric—the fit is not perfect. Nor is it meant to be. I am not seeking to revel in discrepancies, however, or to provoke contention, or to offer yet another study of literary irony. Rather, I seek to learn something practical about Donne, Milton, and humanist rhetoric by using, in all its naïveté, Milton's youthful pose as a "contemporary of time" and, in some of its sophistication, Donne's use of "contraries." To the extent that I gained my analytical method by reading Donne and Milton, I gained by the same means its efficient cause, a desire to find, at whatever ideological peril, not a few ideas of consequence.

I am grateful for the continuing support of the University of California Committee on Research and for a year's fellowship from the Guggenheim Foundation. To Art Quinn, Leonard Nathan, Bill Brandt, John Leopold, Jerry Press, Donna Gregory, John Gage, Carol Nathan; to Willis Salomon, Nancy Bradbury, Glen McClish, Kenneth Cardwell, Joel Loree; to Marc Cogan, Lois Bueler, Arlene Okerlund, Walt Cannon, Julia Watson; and to William McClung, Mary Renaud, Suzanne Lipsett, and two anonymous reviewers for the University of California Press I owe the best features of this book and some of the pleasure I took in writing it.

I

In Our End Is Our Beginning, and Vice Versa

As in all matters it is the beginning and the end which are most important, they held that Janus is the leader in a sacrifice, and derived the name from *ire,* to go. Hence the names *jani* for archways and *januae* for the front doors of secular buildings.

[Cicero, *De natura deorum,* ca. 45 B.C.]

I ask, "Who is Janus?" I get the reply, "He is the world." A succinct answer, to be sure, and a plain one.

[St. Augustine, *City of God,* ca. 416]

But, in a Morall sense, we may apply
This *double-face,* that man to signifie,
Who (whatsoere he undertakes to doe)
Lookes, both *before* him, and *behinde* him, too.

[George Wither, *A Collection of Emblemes,* 1635]

Literature is a kinetic art, but the physical form it assumes prevents us from seeing its essential nature, even though we so experience it. The availability of a book to the hand, its presence on a shelf, its listing in a library catalogue—all of these encourage us to think of it as a stationary object. Somehow when we put a book down, we forget that while we were reading, *it* was moving (pages turning, lines receding into the past) and forget too that *we* were moving with it.

[Stanley E. Fish, *Self-Consuming Artifacts,* 1972]

Brilliant

1

Two Speeches

We do not know how many people were there, or whether the day was dark or bright. The coffin may have been placed by the pulpit, close by, or somewhere in the transept, as the custom is today. The nave of St. Paul's—old St. Paul's, the Gothic cathedral that dominated the London skyline before the disastrous fire of 1666—stretched more than 350 feet westward from the pulpit, a cavern that could accommodate a crowd. There could have been hundreds of people in attendance, and probably were, all ranks and stations, all sorts and conditions, with the family and nobility seated while most of the others stood. Many—most, perhaps—were there to pay homage to the dead man, William Cockayne, former lord mayor of London and late alderman of Broad Street. Perhaps some were there solely out of a religious prompting, to meditate on death, which in this case appeared neither suddenly nor tragically, but came gradually, with warning, to close a long life of privilege and public service. Surely all anticipated the funeral sermon itself, to be delivered by John Donne, who at that time had been dean of St. Paul's for five years.

Though sermons did not hold the central place in Anglican service that they held in more radically "reformed" churches, this one was to be delivered by one of the most famous preachers in England. There is a curious irony here: John Donne, priest, became famous partly for his sermons, but he played a key role—largely through his sermons—in moving the Anglican church (he would have thought of it only as the "established" church) into the *via media* between the extremes of Catholicism and Protestantism, a position that tried to hold sermonizing and worship in balance. Nor does the irony stop there. This particular occasion—the funeral of Alderman Cockayne, 12 December 1626—was, certainly, profoundly worshipful. But for a number of reasons, important among them John Donne's contemporary reputation, it must have also had the characteristics—the excitement, the eager anticipation—of a public oration such as a classical epideictic, a commemorative speech designed to honor the dead and to affirm the community of the living. John Donne's reputation as an orator overwhelms the event now, and probably did then too, for at least some people.

3

Perhaps these ironies only confirm what a generation of literary critics have told us: irony is a key to seventeenth-century studies. But irony in the most general sense is simply a name for a certain conceptual or tonal discrepancy that arises when two ostensibly disparate things are juxtaposed—say, Donne's fame juxtaposed with William Cockayne's, or Donne's speech juxtaposed with this Anglican occasion, or with what we can reconstruct of the occasion generally. Another example, for that matter, might be the text of Donne's speech as we have it juxtaposed with an irretrievable, a forever unknown: what Donne actually did and said on this occasion. For the student (and, I suspect, for Donne too), irony often lies in juxtaposing evidence with conjecture, what we know with what we have surmised, particularly when the juxtaposing only makes the discrepancy evident. Irony, it would seem, often lies in us, in our total perception, and not necessarily in the thing we are looking at. Thus, irony can be simply another name for the effects arising from our analytical means of coping with uncertainties, such means as juxtapositions and perspectives by incongruity.

Of course, we must begin with what we have. And in dealing with this particular rhetorical event, what we have seems to be not very much. To repeat, just as we cannot know for certain how many people were present, we cannot know for certain precisely what Donne said on this occasion. From the little evidence we have about his delivery, it appears that he usually spoke not from manuscript but from notes. Though at times he must have prepared a manuscript in advance, he usually spoke extemporaneously, inverting an hourglass at the exordium and then moving toward his peroration as the sand began to run out—a dramatic device that might deceive us into thinking that the structure of his printed speeches was chronometrically imposed. Later, after delivery—days, months, and in one case eleven years—he prepared a manuscript version of what he thought he had said, or wished he had said, often spending many hours in "transcribing" a one-hour sermon.[1] Let us consider this matter for a moment, not because ironies pervade it but because it helps clarify our present relation to what Donne appears to have said on this occasion, and not because it will remove surmise but (perhaps) make the process self-conscious if only by iterating the obvious concerning letters, "literature," books, the physical form of printed sermons and poems, and our place in time and Donne's. However obvious the differences may seem, they challenge our casual assumptions about the nature of "rhe-

4

torical" as opposed to "poetical" form—for example, that the former is determined by its audience, the latter by its content.

In 1633, seven years after the Cockayne funeral oration and two years after Donne's death, the printer Miles Flesher published Donne's collected poems, including the secular poems that had made Donne famous at the turn of the century as a wit and libertine. These poems had circulated for decades in manuscript (and must have been known to more than a few in the audience at the Cockayne funeral), and they were the very ones that Donne, upon becoming "Doctor" (as Ben Jonson put it), claimed he wanted to destroy. One can only wonder, though, how earnestly he tried to destroy them, considering their ready availability after his death and the excellent state of some of the manuscripts (the 1633 edition remains the best guide we have to Donne's textual intentions). The sermons, ironically (so far as Donne's expressed will is concerned), were not published until 1640, 1649, and 1660, for the printing of all Anglican sermons in those decades collided with the rise and fall of the Puritans. At any rate, the printing history of Donne's works set the pattern in which most students continue to encounter them: first the poems—all the poems— and then the sermons.

However contrary to Donne's stated will, that pattern is surely an effective hermeneutic: "We cannot read Donne's sermons aright," his modern editors say, "without realizing that this preacher was essentially a poet."[2] Alas, those editors seem to conceive of poetry as something consisting largely of "rhythms and harmonies." Further, if it is true, as these editors state, that all Donne's sermons are one sermon, for he develops the same themes, ideas, and arguments in a characteristically Donnesque fashion, it may also be true that all his poem are one poem, for the same reason. Seldom do we read his secular poems for their secularity or his sacred poems for their devotional qualities, or either for their "rhythms and harmonies"; we read both for our delight in the movements of the man's mind and in his mastery of language. In the last century, Thomas De Quincey, in considering Donne's poetry, not his sermons, called him "the first very eminent rhetorician in the English literature."[3] In his sermons a poet, in his poems a rhetorician? In both he was both, I think, partly by virtue of his strategic use of juxtapositions and "contraries," associations and ambiguities, double visions and multiple perspectives—in short, in the movements of his mind as revealed in his mastery of language. De Quincey put the matter differently, and better: Donne was a skillful practitioner of the "older rhetoric," which De Quincey claims compelled both spectator and performer "to hang upon one's thoughts as an object of conscious interest, to play with them, to watch and pursue them through a maze of inversions, evolutions, and harlequin changes."[4]

Such might be the characteristics of the funeral sermon for Alderman Cockayne. Let us acknowledge that the form in which we have it may have been imposed later—but by a man who was recreating its utterance as a poet might. For *poet* we can just as easily, with a nod toward De Quincey, substitute the term *rhetorician*. At any rate, we can approach the sermon expecting to find in it something of the same experience we find in Donne's poems. Let us therefore read the sermon as we would (or should) Donne's poetry.

Donne announces his text, John 11:21: "Lord, if thou hadst been here, my brother had not died."[5] The text strikes a tone of despair, as we complete the implicit argument: but you were not here and therefore our brother is dead. In the familiar metaphors of Christianity, "brother" seems to refer directly to the dead man in the church before us. But those who know the Bible well could set the text immediately within the story of one of Christ's greatest miracles, the raising of Lazarus from the dead. We are centered on the grief and despair of Lazarus's sister Martha, the person who speaks in John 11:21. Those who have attended previous sermons by Donne and those, too, who have read his poems might ask *why* Donne has centered our attention on Martha's grief and despair. These same listeners might answer: to create double visions and multiple perspectives by juxtaposing Martha's grief and despair with our own.

Donne speaks first, after the text, of marriage. Again, the formal principle is juxtaposition:

> God made the first Marriage, and man made the first Divorce: God married the Body and Soule in the Creation, and man divorced the Body and Soule by death through sinne, in his fall. [p. 257]

Again, the metaphors of the family are the conventional metaphors of Christian doctrine. There is, perhaps, some comfort in the reassertion of those metaphors before a bereaved family—the actual family of Sir William and his "brothers" in the church: "As farre as a man is immortall, a man is a married man still," for the soul is married to the

6

body, the former to be preserved at death, the latter to be resurrected in Christ at the Final Day. However, it is our brother's dead body that is before us, and so naturally the preacher turns to a consideration of resurrection. The promise of a general resurrection was given in Christ, for he was All in All:

> They that are not faln yet by any actuall sinne, (children newly baptized) are risen already in him; And they that are not dead yet, nay, not alive yet, not yet borne, have a Resurrection in him, who was not onely the Lambe *slaine* from the beginning, but from before all beginnings was *risen* too; and all that shall ever have part in the second Resurrection, are risen with him from that time. [p. 258]

The passage both places Christ in time and takes him out of time, a favorite theme in this period and often enhanced, as here, by juxtapositions. This is also the treatment Donne wishes to give the text:

> Now, next to that great Propheticall action, that type of the generall Resurrection, in the Resurrection of Christ, the most illustrious Evidence, of the Resurrection of particular men, is this Resuscitation of *Lazarus;* whose sister *Martha,* directed by faith, and yet transported by passion, seeks to entender and mollifie, and supple him to impressions of mercy and compassion, who was himselfe the Mold, in which all mercy was cast, nay, the substance, of which all mercy does consist, Christ Jesus, with this imperfect piece of Devotion, which hath a tincture of Faith, but is deeper dyed in Passion, *Lord, if thou hadst been here, my brother had not dyed.* [pp. 258–259]

The movement, then, is from the general, Christ's Resurrection, to the specific, Lazarus's, and within the specific, the focus is on the momentary and "imperfect," Martha's passionate outcry. We are meant to keep all these elements in balance, however difficult, for Donne's argument depends upon shattering the confines of time and even the shackles of chronology—as if any moment were only a brief centering, perhaps an emergent occasion in which something essential is made evident in such a way that man's sense of time is either deepened or numbed. Form, as we shall see, is another restriction on thought and discourse, and it too will be shattered.

Now that we have completed a skeletal review of Donne's exordium, his introduction, let us try to catch up with his audience by reviewing here the biblical story from which he had drawn his text. For we know that in his juxtapositions Donne delights not simply in irony but in dramatic irony—which means, of course, that he makes certain assumptions about his audience's knowledge.

> Now a certain *man* was sick, *named* Lazarus, of Bethany, the
> town of Mary and her sister Martha.
> 2 (It was *that* Mary which anointed the Lord with ointment, and
> wiped his feet with her hair, whose brother Lazarus
> was sick.)

Already we find that the biblical story itself seems structured upon those rhetorical principles—multiple perspectives, temporal compression—we have noticed at work in Donne's sermon. St. John continues: the sisters Martha and Mary sent a message to Jesus, saying simply, "Lord, behold he whom thou lovest is sick." Jesus, who was then in Galilee, knew that the person referred to in this veiled speech was Lazarus, and he also seemed to know that the sickness was not "unto death, but for the glory of God, that the Son of God might be glorified thereby," and so he stayed where he was, for two more days. Then he decided to return to Judaea. As soon as Martha learned of Jesus's approach, she went to meet him and uttered the passage that is Donne's text. Jesus comforted her, however, by saying, "Thy brother shall rise again." She assumed—wrongly, as those of us who have read the story know—that Jesus referred to the Last Day, the general Resurrection. But Jesus answered her, "I am the resurrection, and the life: he that believeth in me, though he were dead, yet shall he live: And whosoever liveth and believeth in me shall never die. Believest thou this?" Martha responded, as if by rote, "Yea, Lord, I believe that Thou art the Christ, the Son of God, which should come into the world." She failed to grasp the meaning we have. As soon as Mary came to where Jesus was, she fell down at his feet and spoke the same words we heard earlier: "Lord, if thou hadst been here, my brother had not died." Then follows the miraculous raising of Lazarus from the dead.

Perhaps this much of the biblical story allows us to understand where Donne centered his audience's attention and what he might expect his audience to know. Not once does Donne retell the story, even in a fragmentary way, as I have done; rather, all his references to

8

the story assume the audience's prior and complete knowledge of it. Too, in reconsidering the biblical story we have seen at work certain juxtapositions through multiple perspectives, placing limited knowledge against deeper knowledge, short-sightedness against greater vision, all elements of a central strategy we call dramatic irony. The strategy, in turn, becomes part of Donne's larger, configurational strategy, one that extraordinarily complicates the formal arrangement of the sermon itself.

Having begun with metaphors of marriage and divorce, and having touched on his great theme, resurrection, Donne has returned to the words of his text and so completed his exordium in the space of one long paragraph. He has also, as is appropriate in an exordium, offered his thesis, Martha's "imperfect Devotion." What he will make of that thesis is suggested structurally, both by Donne's method of organization in this opening paragraph and by the biblical story to which he refers: he will probably develop his thesis by means of juxtaposition. The next part—the *divisio* itself—on the surface seems remarkably simple.

A *divisio* is the second formal part of a classical oration, or any speech structured along classical lines. The speaker, having introduced his subject, divides it into parts. In our copy of Donne's sermon, the section in which Donne accomplishes his *divisio* has been indicated by a marginal note. In fact, most discourse of this period openly displays its form through such devices as marginal tagging of the *divisio* and signposting throughout the text.

At first, the *divisio* of Donne's sermon seems clear and easy to keep in mind.

> This Text which you Heare, *Martha's* single words, complicated with this Text which you See, The dead body of this our Brother, makes up between them this body of Instruction for the soule; first, That there is nothing in this world perfect; And then, That such as it is, there is nothing constant, nothing permanent. [p. 259]

Donne's *divisio* actually extends through a long paragraph; I have reprinted only the first part, enough to indicate the apparent simplicity but actual complexity that pervades Donne's rhetoric. One might expect that Donne will divide his sermon into two parts, the "Text which you Heare" (imperfect) and the "Text which you See" (impermanent)—and so he does, to a certain extent. But, as the *divisio* suggests, the two parts are actually indivisible, for the two texts are, if not one, then "complicated," as he says. The overall form, as it turns out, has a skeletal arrangement something like this (here I use for the two major heads terms that Donne does not introduce until the latter half of his speech, and I have tried to show the complication of the texts through Donne's subtle shifts in emphasis, marked by italics):

I. Doctrine of Mortification [*the text which you hear* and the text which you see]
  A. Nothing in this world is perfect
    1. The weakness of man's best actions
    2. The weakness of Martha's action
    3. God's goodness in accepting our imperfect sacrifices
  B. Nothing in this world is permanent
    1. The transitoriness, in general, of all temporal things
    2. The putrefaction of God's masterpiece, the body of man
    3. The goodness of God in offering even to man's body a glorious state
II. Consolation [the text which you hear and *the text which you see*]
  A. *In vita*
  B. *In morte*
  C. *In funere*
  D. *In resurrectione*

Something significant is said about form itself in this usage: it too is an imperfect and impermanent, and very human, imposition upon the possibilities of truth.

To the Ramists, for example, the dominant logical and rhetorical theorists of Donne's day, Donne's organization would appear confusing, ambiguous, and unnatural. The Ramists placed a premium on stark simplicity and formal confidence. But Donne's overall movement, from general considerations to the life and death of Sir William, and Donne's indivisible divisions (the not only indivisible but continually visible presence of the second text lends another level of irony to the first) themselves constitute a virtual critique of anyone who would use form with confidence and simplicity. Moreover, how could Donne on the one hand argue that our knowledge, or action, is imperfect and impermanent, and on the other speak with formal simplicity and confidence about such matters?

Furthermore, even if we were tempted to accept the above outline as a clear statement of Donne's organization, we would find the actions of his mind in the speech itself to be so complicated that they render any such attempts to diagram his form insignificant and oversimplified. Though he sets the main heads of Part I before us in his *divisio,* another, tripartite organization plays against an orderly arrangement of those heads—as if Donne set up a particularly complicated theme and then almost immediately played a counterpoint or variation on it, an effect like the one called musical "division" in the seventeenth century. "So have you the frame set up [the texts], and the roomes divided [I, II]; The two parts [A and B of I] and the three branches of each; And to the furnishing of them, with meditations fit for this Occasion, we passe now." The later tripartite "division" is similar to, but decidedly not identical with, the "three branches." This structure could further thwart the audience's expectations and confuse the reader, except that it seems to show that the speaker's skepticism—the very soul and subject of his argument—pervades his use of discursive form. His construction is not necessarily an assault on form, but a use of it to the meager extent that it suffices. In sum, in spite of its announced form, the speech itself is not easy to follow; the audience must grapple with form. These difficulties only dramatize Donne's point, which ultimately centers in the acknowledged discrepancy between human truths and eternal verities.

Skepticism is the mood wherein the first room is furnished:

> In entring upon the first branch of our first part, That in spirituall things nothing is perfect, we may well afford a kinde of spirituall nature to knowledge; And how imperfect is all our Knowledge? What one thing doe we know perfectly? Whether wee consider Arts, or Sciences, the servant knows but according to the proportion of his Masters knowledge in that Art, and the Scholar knows but according to the proportion of his Masters knowledge in that Science . . . And if there be any addition to knowledge, it is rather a new knowledge, then a greater knowledge; rather a singularity in a desire of proposing something that was not knowne at all before, then an emproving, an advancing, a multiplying of former inceptions; and by that meanes, no knowledge comes to be perfect.   [p. 260]

The argument sets the tone for the entire oration and, I think, its use of form: humane learning, like form, is insufficient, unequal to our striving. Yet Donne will grapple with form, as he grapples with knowledge, not changing or "reforming," but using what he has for all it's worth. In this case, form has considerable value in the communication of emotion, both grief and comfort.

Soon after the passage on knowledge, Donne introduces the tripartite variation, or counterpoint of the announced form:

> We consider this therefore *in Credendis,* In things that we are
> bound to Beleeve, there works our faith; And then, *in Petendis,*
> In things that we are bound to pray for, there works our hope;
> And lastly, *in Agendis,* In things that we are bound to doe, and
> there works our charity; And there is nothing in any of these
> three perfect. [p. 261]

Faith, hope, and charity work against, though not in disharmony with, the orderly development of Donne's argument. Moreover, in each part of this triadic variation, Donne condemns the confidence and assurance of the Puritans, who are not skeptical enough, whose faith, hope, and charity blithely ignore the eternal verity that there is "nothing, nothing in spirituall things, perfect in this world."

Perhaps we should pause to note that in the center of his triadic variation Donne shapes an argument that has subsequently become famous; the passage is developed out of his condemnation of the "extemporall" prayers of "our new men," who have rejected out of hand the traditional forms of prayer. Here is another complex of ironic juxtapositions: Donne is, most likely, sermonizing extemporaneously, though in a service that holds steadfast to the use of uniform, now printed prayers; but in the midst of his sermon, having condemned the impromptu praying of the Puritans, he describes vividly the travails of an Anglican divine at private prayers:

> I throw my selfe down in my Chamber, and I call in, and invite
> God, and his Angels thither, and when they are there, I neglect
> God and his Angels, for the noise of a Flie, for the ratling of a
> Coach, for the whining of a doore; I talke on, in the same pos-
> ture of praying; Eyes lifted up; knees bowed downe; as though I
> prayed to God; and, if God, or his Angels should aske me, when
> I thought last of God in that prayer, I cannot tell: Sometimes I

12

finde that I had forgot what I was about, but when I began to forget it, I cannot tell. A memory of yesterdays pleasures, a feare of to morrows dangers, a straw under my knee, a noise in mine eare, a light in mine eye, an any thing, a nothing, a fancy, a Chimera in my braine, troubles me in my prayer. So certainely is there nothing, nothing in spirituall things, perfect in this world. [pp. 264–265]

The next branch of the first part, "the weakness of Martha's action," is totally organized in terms of faith, hope, and charity, the triadic variation of his announced form. Here the extraordinary complications of Donne's speech become most evident, turning on a lesson about placing too much faith in corporal reality, what we can see and touch. In Donne's discourse, everything tends to echo everything else in the discourse; the following has striking echoes of the passage on prayer:

This then was one weaknesse in these Sisters faith, that it carried them not up to the consideration of Christ as God; And then another rose out of that, That they insisted so much, relied so much, upon his corporall, and personall presence, and promised themselves more from that, then hee had ever given them ground for; which was that which Christ diverted *Mary* from, when after his Resurrection manifesting himselfe to her, and shee flying upon him with that impatient zeale, and that impetuous devotion, *Rabboni, Master, My Master,* Christ said to her, *Touch mee not, for I am not ascended to my Father;* that is, Dwell not upon this passionate consideration of my bodily, and personall presence, but send thy thoughts, and thy reverence, and thy devotion, and thy holy amorousness up, whither I am going, to the right hand of my Father, and consider me, contemplate mee there. S. *Peter* had another old distemper of another kinde, upon the personall presence of Christ; He was so astonished at his presence in the power of a Miracle, that he fell downe at his feet, and said, *Depart from me, for I am a sinfull man, O Lord.* These Sisters longed for him, and S. *Peter* longed as much to be delivered of him; both out of weakness and error. So is it an error, and a weaknesse to attribute too much, or too little to Christs presence in his Sacraments, or other Ordinances. [p. 267]

13

The lesson is that any corporal manifestation of our faith, even the actual presence of Christ's body in the Sacraments, is to be treated with some diffidence. Here we approach, again, the core of Donne's skepticism. This is neither idealism nor doubt, but diffidence—especially toward anything tangible, substantive, or human, such as a church, a Bible story, a sermon, or discursive form; and at the same time toward anything that is somehow *not* approachable through the tangible, substantive, and human. That is our dilemma and the necessary cause of spiritual travail. Truth, or for that matter error, is not unmixed, nor are our means of apprehending either. For the sake of our understanding, let us therefore juxtapose elements—Martha's grief with the outcome of Lazarus's story, Mary's grief and impetuousness here with these qualities in the story of Christ's Resurrection, Martha's and Mary's human imperfections with Christ's greater mastery, Mary's "passionate consideration" with Peter's "distemper of another kinde"—and let us always draw what lessons we can from these juxtapositions (as Donne does, here and throughout the sermon, in many of the parts we are leaving unquoted), but let us never assume that any of our perceptual strategies or grids actually *contain* the truth. Donne seems driven to make that point. Thus, to return to the sermon, the tasks of faith, hope, and charity are ours in a world whose imperfections presume upon God's mercy.

Also presuming upon God's mercy is the impermanence of this world (Part I.B):

> I need not call in new Philosophy, that denies a settlednesse, an acquiescence in the very body of the Earth, but makes the Earth to move in that place, where we thought the Sunne had moved; I need not that helpe, that the Earth it selfe is in Motion, to prove this, That nothing upon Earth is permanent; The Assertion will stand of it selfe, till some man assigne me some instance, something that a man may relie upon, and find permanent.   [p. 271]

Yet Donne had, as we know, used the "new Philosophy" for that very purpose in his anniversary poems, written just fifteen years before, to commemorate the death of the young Elizabeth Drury—two poems of only three which Donne, living, had allowed to be published.[6] Donne's mention of the "new Philosophy" here in his sermon is in the form of a rhetorical *praeteritio,* a dismissal that nonetheless echoes in the minds of the audience and may be used by them to prove the

orator's case. The move fits well his formal dramatic irony, constantly
placing the audience in a position of—ostensibly—greater knowledge, but forcing them continually to question the truth even in that
knowledge.

The second part of Donne's first room is easier to prove, as his
praeteritio indicates. Donne passes quickly from this second part (I.B)
to the second room of his "frame":

> And since we are in an action of preparing this dead Brother of
> ours to that state, (for the Funerall is the Easter-eve, The Buriall
> is the depositing of that man for the Resurrection) As we have
> held you, with Doctrine of Mortification, by extending the
> Text, from *Martha* to this occasion; so shall we dismisse you
> with Consolation, by a like occasionall inverting the Text, from
> passion in *Martha's* mouth, *Lord, if thou hadst been here, my
> Brother had not dyed,* to joy in ours, *Lord, because thou wast here, our
> Brother is not dead.*   [p. 273]

The two sections of the "frame," then, are rooms named Mortification and Consolation, and Donne's method of proceeding is by means
of "inverting the Text." But, again, that apparent simplicity denies
the true complexity of movement, which De Quincey might call "a
maze of inversions," including, as I have suggested, a theme and variation, a musical division. In simplest terms, these are juxtapositions,
and their use is at the center of Donne's art as poet and preacher: two
texts are juxtaposed, Martha's words and the dead body of our
Brother, but each is only a line in a much greater story; juxtaposing
line and story is like juxtaposing "now" and "then," or vice versa.
Dramatic irony—whether in the first story of Martha's weakness and
failure to understand or in the juxtaposition of a line from that story
with the corpse of our dead Brother—may be a means of knowledge,
but it only enhances our skepticism: how can we truly know? when
do we have the full story? Appropriately, the questions are somewhat—
but not fully—muted as we approach the final room, the Consolation.

This second, and smaller, room in the oration consists of four long
paragraphs (marginally tagged *in vita, in morte, in funere,* and *in resurrectione*), ostensibly reviewing Sir William's life, his death (especially his last
actions and words), his funeral (a lesson on proper Christian burial),
and his resurrection (in which all believers shall participate, with
Christ). There would seem to be no skepticism here. Indeed, when

15

these paragraphs were later abstracted from the sermon as a kind of "character," a genre widely popular in Donne's day, Sir William emerged as a paragon of Christian living and dying.[7] But some members of Donne's audience must have known all too well that the orator was struggling with a very real, a very human problem: that Sir William's character did not perfectly fit the mold of conventional praise.

Only five years earlier, Sir William's scheming and use of his influence with King James had provoked a great trade crisis, so great, Sir Edwin Sandys said in 1621, that it made mere "Trifles" of "all the Grievances of the Kingdom."[8] In a sense, Sir William had merely attempted to advance the fortunes of his own organization of cloth merchants, who by law had to export finished cloth (dyed and prepared) while others profitted by being allowed to export unfinished goods. Donne tries to put the best face on the matter, first constructing an ethos, or persona, for himself as someone aloof from commercial matters:

> You have, I thinke, a phrase of Driving a Trade; And you have, I know, a practise of Driving away Trade, by other use of money; And you have lost a man, that drove a great Trade, the right way in making the best use of our home-commodity.   [p.274]

Perhaps Sir William's motives were good, to enhance domestic manufacture. But his methods, which can only be called scheming, proved disastrous. Though Donne does not ignore the issues, neither does he make them explicit, and he places such careful tonal control on the matter[9] that even his reporting the king's praise of Sir William is secure from controversy:

> I have sometimes heard the greatest Master of Language and Judgement, which these times, or any other did, or doe, or shall give, (that good and great King of ours) say of him, That he never heard any man of his breeding, handle businesses more rationally, more pertinently, more elegantly, more perswasively.
> [p. 274]

Traditionally, the duty of a Christian orator at a funeral is to comfort the survivors by allowing them to believe that the deceased was "saved," that he went to heaven. The final four paragraphs perform that duty, and if they convince, they do so partly by convention and ritual and partly by an exercise of will. Reasoning is not Donne's chief

16

mode of persuasion in this sermon: emotional appeals, pathos, seem to be. Misleading passion, like Martha's, is to be avoided, but the world's asymmetry necessarily provokes our passion, in which and through which we look for comfort. *That,* it seems, is the drama of Donne's homily. Significantly, the final four paragraphs, with their conventional and willed attempts at comfort, only increase our sense of asymmetry. In juxtaposing the two "texts," Donne discusses the latter in an organization (*vita, morte, funere, resurrectione*) that does not correspond to any feature whereby the parts in the first room of the "frame" were "furnished." The second room, "Consolation," is formally distinct. It becomes juxtaposed to "Mortification" only through will—that is, through our faith, hope, and charity. This trinity of will receives a kind of formal recapitulation at the very end of the sermon, the peroration, wherein, looking again for form, we find that only the triadic variation is echoed, as if it were the only formally significant feature of the entire discourse:

> But that which *Moses* said to the whole Congregation, I say to you all, both to you that heare me, and to him that does not, *All ye that did cleave unto the Lord your God, are alive, every one of you, this day:* Even hee, whom we call dead, is alive this day. In the presence of God, we lay him downe; In the power of God, he shall rise; In the person of Christ, he is risen already. And so into the same hands that have received his soul, we commend his body; beseeching his blessed Spirit, that as our charity enclines us to hope confidently of his good estate, our faith may assure us of the same happinesse, in our own behalfe; And that for all our sakes, but especially for his own glory, he will be pleased to hasten the consummation of all, in that Kingdome which that Son of God hath purchased for us, with the inestimable price of his incorruptible blood. *Amen.*   [p. 278]

There is no true, but only ostensible, balance, symmetry, or perfection in life, in the world, or in arguments. The only verities seem to be the experiences of charity, hope, and faith.

Considering what the sermon comes to, we might suppose it offers another example of Donne's Augustinianism, his debt to the Church Father who acknowledged the full range of human emotions and emphasized the power of will. Unquestionably, St. Augustine's influence is present. But by studying Donne's use of discursive form and letting that be our index of intention, we find another kind of focus, one that is uniquely Donne's.

A central epistemological issue in this oration—and, I think, in Donne's work generally—is the problem of trying to grasp a sensed, immutable truth with mutable, human instruments of perception and analysis.[10] The oration is sometimes prized largely as a collection of famous passages, many of which are reprinted in this discussion—as if its total structure were a setting for what De Quincey called, in speaking of Donne's unfinished "epic," *Metempsychosis,* "massy diamonds." Donne's modern editors find the sermon "full of memorable passages." But when we try to determine how all these passages relate to each other in something other than a merely conventional way, we find no clear, tightly organized discourse. That is to say, the memorability of the sermon does indeed lie in various, separable passages that accumulate, and perhaps overwhelm, strung together as they are in a form dictated not by "content" (except, possibly, insofar as its asymmetry mirrors the asymmetry of the world) but by convention, ritual, and will. Thus, Donne's use of form is pervaded by his skepticism—that is, his diffidence—concerning the efficacy of form in capturing truth. Certainly form is efficacious in stirring emotions; indeed, form would seem more appropriate to emotions than to reason. In its detachability and partiality, its variableness, and its deference to conventions and will, form is like the "lattices" of our eyes (as Donne calls them in *The second Anniversary*), through which we "peepe" at truth in this life, where it is our portion to learn "by circuit" and to discern by "collections."

■ ■ ■

Eighteen years later, John Milton delivered a speech quite different from Donne's. One difference is that Milton's speech appeared only in print. It was never presented orally, though he calls it a speech and at times appears to imagine that it is being spoken: "the very sound of this which I utter." But the rhetorical, or humanist, traditions in which Donne and Milton were educated made few compositional distinctions between spoken and printed forms, though most humanists were enchanted with the latter as a means of communication—as a means, for that matter, of "eternizing" their ideas and emotions. *Areopagitica: A Speech of Mr. John Milton for the Liberty of Unlicenc'd Printing to the Parliament of England* was loosely modelled on a speech by Isocrates (355 B.C.) to the Areopagus, and Isocrates' speeches—all of them, so far as we know—were not delivered orally in person but were transmitted in manuscript and read by citizens of Athens. There are several reasons why Milton chose this mode of delivery—beyond the obvious one, of gaining an audience when an appearance in Parliament would have been denied. Some of these reasons we must explore later.

The expressed intention of the *Areopagitica* seems disarming in its ingenuousness. The title, as we have noted, actually identifies the speaker, the thesis, and a specific audience.[11] Below the title, five lines from Euripides' *The Suppliants* are printed, first in Greek, then in English:

> This is true Liberty when free born men
> Having to advise the public may speak free,
> Which he who can, and will, deserv's high praise,
> Who neither can nor will, may hold his peace;
> What can be juster in a State then this?

These lines are not exactly a text, in the way the biblical passage served Donne as a text. They are rather what a rhetorician might call *ethos moves*, with a pathetic appeal: they establish the speaker's character (ethos) as a student of ancient wisdom and offer the audience (pathos) a role, too, as members of a free and just community. Of course, the title also makes these moves. Parliament becomes likened to the Areopagus, a body of wise and learned judges to whom Isocrates addressed his appeal for the reforming of Greek democracy. Moreover, the Areopagus was only Isocrates' specific audience, the men of Athens his general one, and Parliament too was only Milton's putative audience, for print allowed him to reach a wider one, both in his time and beyond. Could his intention, too, have been wider than the one announced on the title page? To answer that question, we shall follow the same method we used in examining Donne's oration, letting form be our major guide to intention.[12]

Having noted that Milton begins with an ethos move, let us begin by recalling that Milton's ethos was directly involved in the considerations that produced the very law whose repeal he now urged.

In 1644, the year in which *Areopagitica* was published, Milton's fame as a poet was considerably less widespread than his fame as a pamphleteer who supported radical Protestant causes. His poem "On

Shakespear" had been published in the Second Folio (1632); two years later his masque *Comus* had been performed and then three years after that (1637) it was published; and in 1638 his "Lycidas" was published in a volume of singularly undistinguished work. These few poems were possibly known by friends and some members of the literati; some of these same people also might have known of the few other unpublished poems that gave clear evidence of developing genius. But the public at large knew Milton best as a writer of pamphlets: five had been printed attacking the Anglican prelacy, in one of which Milton made public his desire to write—eventually, once the call to reform the church had been answered—a great English epic.

Then, in 1643, not simply fame but notoriety, even among his supporters, came with the publication of his pamphlet *The Doctrine and Discipline of Divorce*. The pamphlet was shocking in its time, though we can see that its thesis is profoundly consistent with Milton's general rhetoric, stance, mode of analysis and argument, and characteristic themes. Man is most man, least animal, when he exercises his reason. To choose, to make a choice, is to exercise reason. So is interpreting texts. The real shock came in this part of his thesis: Christ's teaching that no man should divorce his wife except on the grounds of her having committed adultery does not cancel the Mosaic law that allows divorce on grounds not unlike the modern one we call "incompatibility." For, Milton reasons, Christ's teaching must be read in its context (again, the humanist travels through texts as a contemporary of time as Donne did, in his reading of line and story), and understood both within the total body of the Bible, including the Old Testament, and through the unique qualities whereby man, as we have noted, becomes most man. Context, text, and use or consequence are Milton's hermeneutic triad. Inevitably, however, the reasons Milton himself advanced were less carefully attended to than the import of his argument: his audience could see all too clearly (or if they could not, the politically powerful would see for them) that Milton would rather freely allow divorce, and that he regarded marriage not as a sacrament but as a civil contract. The import of the argument was quite disturbing to those Presbyterians who were seeking to become the new establishment and to consolidate their gains by becoming in the eyes of the public not radical reformers but true conservatives. The pamphlet had to be denounced—as it was, most vigorously, just two weeks after its appearance. A Presbyterian divine, Mr.

Herbert Palmer, delivered in Parliament a denunciation of the heresy of divorce, calling Milton's pamphlet "a wicked book" and "uncensored, though deserving to be burnt."[13]

True, the pamphlet was uncensored. *The Doctrine and Discipline of Divorce* had been published in open violation of a law that was then only a few weeks old. Parliament, led by the Presbyterians, had enacted an ordinance for the licensing of the press on 14 June 1643. Proper persons were to be appointed from whom a publisher had to secure license to print. (The new law was a Presbyterian version of the Anglican licensing law of 11 July 1637, which virtually gave the sole power of imprimatur to Archbishop Laud.) In the early stages of the revolution, censorship had been left largely to the wardens of the Stationers Company, and regulation was ineffectual: only seventy-six books were registered in 1642 though more than seven hundred items appeared, and a similar proportion obtained in the first six months of 1643.[14] Milton was cited by name among the pamphleteers whose open defiance of regulation provoked the need for a new licensing ordinance. But no sooner had that ordinance appeared than Milton flaunted it again, this time with the most shocking pamphlet of all. The *Divorce* pamphlet appeared anonymously in August 1643. When the second edition appeared, on 2 February 1644, the author dropped his thin mask of anonymity and spoke directly in a preface to the "Parliament of England with the Assembly": "Truth," Milton says in a statement that seems at the center of his rhetoric (as it does not quite of Donne's), "is as impossible to be soil'd by any outward touch as the Sunbeam. . . ." Later we shall take another look at this concept of truth. Let us note here that, when it came to the—again, unlicensed—publication of *Areopagitica* in 1644, his putative audience could not have been more hostile, nor could many in his reading public have had a less favorable view of his ethos.

Ancient rhetoricians had advised that when one is faced with a situation like this—a hostile audience, a damaged ethos—the exordium needs particular consideration. Not an especially profound lesson. The strategy rhetoricians advised seems to match that lesson in profundity: use a "subtle" or "insinuative" exordium; that is, if a thesis is likely to be shocking, antagonistic, or repellent to an audience, its introduction can be postponed somewhat, until the audience has been placed in a receptive mood. But Milton does not do that. He has already announced his thesis on the title page. He does, however, follow standard rhetorical advice in trying to use his exordium to soften up at least his putative audience through further moves in ethos and pathos. But the tactic seems to result in some of Milton's most awkward and jarring prose:

> They, who to States and Governours of the Commonwealth direct their Speech, High Court of Parliament, or wanting such accesse in a private condition, write that which they foresee may advance the publick good; I suppose them as at the beginning of no meane endeavour, not a little alter'd and mov'd inwardly in their mindes: Some with doubt of what will be the successe, others with feare of what will be the censure; some with hope, others with confidence of what they have to speake. And me perhaps each of these dispositions, as the subject was whereon I enter'd, may have at other times variously affected; and likely might in these formost expressions now also disclose which of them sway'd most, but that the very attempt of this addresse thus made, and the thought of whom it hath recourse to, hath got the power within me to a passion, farre more welcome then incidentall to a Preface.   [pp. 486–487]

However, though the speaker has confessed his own passionate involvement in the topic, pathetic appeals depend, as the exordium continues, largely on dispassionate praise and rather stilted prose. The praise echoes the lines from Euripides, as Milton argues that Parliament will surely in its wisdom grant true liberty and allow him to speak freely. Of course, if it does, his case is won. But Milton takes no Donnesque delight in exploiting this situational dilemma. Moreover, speaking freely is not the real issue in this argument, just as Milton's intention is not truly polemical, as the form itself will indicate.

Thesis and *divisio* come next; then a striking shift in style occurs. The thesis is expressed simply: Parliament should judge "over again" its order to license printing. The speech itself is described as a kind of "homily"; however, though Milton does not use precisely Isocrates' pattern, the oration is as much deliberative as sermonic (he is, after all, addressing a deliberative body distinctly religious in character). The *divisio* is also quite simply set forth. No marginal note tags the passage as *divisio;* Milton lists his arguments, then signposts them throughout his discourse. Again, form is salient. The thesis will be supported by four arguments: (1) the inventors of licensing are people whom Parliament loathes; (2) God, for discernible reasons, "left arbitrary the dyeting and repasting of our minds"; (3) the ordinance will not suppress those books that Parliament intends mainly to suppress; but (4) it will discourage all learning and so put an end to the discovery of yet further wisdom in religious and civil matters. The order of these four parts seems somewhat arbitrary. Yet Ciceronian rhetoric, as Milton well knew, had articulated an ancient, traditional wisdom for arranging materials in an oration: on the basis of what you know about your audience, it said, arrange your arguments in the pattern of stronger, strong, strongest. The least strong argument might be the second one; of the four, it is most vaguely expressed in the *divisio*. Milton merely describes this second argument as "what is to be thought in generall of reading, what ever sort the Books be"; I have amplified the statement of the argument with words that appear later in the speech. As we review these parts, let us keep the Ciceronian advice in mind.

But first let us note here the shift that occurs in style with the shift from the *divisio* to the first argument. Compare this passage with the one quoted earlier, from the exordium:

> And yet on the other hand unlesse warinesse be us'd, as good almost kill a Man as kill a good Book; who kills a Man kills a reasonable creature, Gods Image; but hee who destroyes a good Booke, kills reason it selfe, kills the Image of God, as it were in the eye. Many a man lives a burden to the Earth; but a good Booke is the precious life-blood of a master spirit, imbalm'd and treasur'd up on purpose to a life beyond life. 'Tis true, no age can restore a life, whereof perhaps there is no great losse; and revolutions of ages do not oft recover the loss of a rejected truth, for the want of which whole Nations fare the worse. We should be wary therefore what persecution we raise against the living labours of publick men, how we spill that season'd life of man preserv'd and stor'd up in Books; since we see a kinde of homicide may be thus committed, sometimes a martyrdome, and if it extend to the whole impression, a kind of massacre, whereof the execution ends not in the slaying of an elementall life, but strikes at that ethereall and fift essence, the breath of reason it selfe, slaies an immortality rather then a life.   [pp. 492–493]

Did the awkwardness in the style of Milton's exordium come from his having paid too much attention to the rhetoricians? He knew the traditional function of the exordium, as his youthful First Prolusion indicates, but Milton's knowledge of rhetorical theory is not and can hardly be in question. Had he spent too much effort in striving to please his putative audience? Did the later eloquence come from his forgetting that audience in order to concentrate on his subject alone? If so, does the shift in style further come about because Milton has a subject, or object, beyond the one he declares: to demonstrate that reason, truth, is available in every man's discourse, even in the discourse of a man you have reprimanded who is offering a book in a manner you have outlawed?

That last conjecture places Milton's rhetorical form in a certain perspective: form may be less significant, and is probably less efficacious, than the character of the speaker, the "Milton" glimpsed or heard through that form. Perhaps therein lies Milton's real skillfulness. Initially Milton's ethical appeals depend largely upon his implicit identification of himself with Isocrates and upon his explicit characterization of himself as speaking "from the industry of a life wholly dedicated to studious labours," abundant evidence of which is available throughout the speech. These appeals, however, are only the bare outlines of ethos, which the speech itself completes through action; the speech, that is, not only tells but shows the speaker's ethos. And if the speaker's ethos is his true subject, then the bold flaunting of an antagonistic thesis to a putative audience is an entrance only, an attention-getting one certainly, and the book itself, as suggested, is a dramatization of his *ethical* action.

Throughout his first argument, Milton becomes a contemporary of time, a student the results of whose labors are set before us, showing that from ancient Greece through the Inquisition and later to "our inquisiturient Bishops, and the attendant minorites, their Chaplains," the inventors of licensing were exactly the sorts of people Parliament now abhors. But, he suggests, some may argue that though the inventors were bad, the thing itself may still be good.

The imagined objection leads him to his second argument—perhaps the least strong—concerning (again, the matter is vaguely put) whatever is to be thought in general of reading all books. Yet this part, *we* quickly realize, contains the very core of Milton's philosophy:

24

Good and evill we know in the field of this World grow up together almost inseparably; and the knowledge of good is so in-
volv'd and interwoven with the knowledge of evill, and in so
many cunning resemblances hardly to be discern'd, that those
confused seeds which were impos'd upon *Psyche* as an incessant
labour to cull out, and sort asunder, were not more intermixt. It
was from out the rinde of one apple tasted, that the knowledge
of good and evill, as two twins cleaving together, leapt forth
into the World. And perhaps this is that doom which *Adam* fell
into of knowing good and evill, that is to say, of knowing good
by evill. As therefore the state of man now is; what wisdome can
there be to choose, what continence to forbeare without the
knowledge of evill? He that can apprehend and consider vice
with all her baits and seeming pleasures, and yet abstain, and yet
distinguish, and yet prefer that which is truly better, he is the
true warfaring Christian. I cannot praise a fugitive and clois-
ter'd vertue unexercis'd & unbreath'd, that never sallies out and
sees her adversary, but slinks out of the race, where that immortall garland is to be run for, not without dust and heat. Assur-
edly we bring not innocence into the world, we bring impurity
much rather: that which purifies us is triall, and triall is by what
is contrary.   [pp. 514–515]

This philosophy is at the heart of the *Divorce* pamphlet. It is also at the
heart of *Paradise Lost,* for that matter. This passage captures the very
essence of Milton's own role in *Areopagitica,* and throughout his life, as
a "warfaring Christian." Perhaps Milton did not follow Ciceronian
advice on arrangement, or perhaps the *third* of his four arguments is
the weakest. At any rate, if this second argument is at the heart of his
philosophy, why is it not located last, in the rhetorically strongest
position? There is another possibility, one that mutes this question
and leads us back to our earlier conjecture: the location of this argument may be strategic in allowing Milton to dramatize himself early
enough in his discourse to reveal his true subject and method.

For as he is in the process of developing this second argument, the
third argument seems suddenly to force its way into his speech: "See
the ingenuity of Truth," he exclaims as he discovers that he is into his
third argument before he has quite finished with the second, "who,

when she gets a free and willing hand, opens herself faster, then the pace of method and discours can overtake her." Of course, it is his particular purpose and true method, as I have suggested, to show that truth is both accessible through and operative in this discourse. Yet *method* as Milton uses it was a technical term in his day, pertaining to discursive form, above all to a systematic and reasoned exposition of an idea. Even my attempt to be systematic, he says, is outpaced by truth herself. This exclamation is profoundly indicative of Milton's attitude toward discourse, and we shall need to keep it constantly before us. Note here, though, that if Milton's character as glimpsed through this exclamation is his true subject, it, and not his declared thesis, *has* been strategically postponed. And the strategy would seem aimed as much at a once *and* future audience as solely at a group of Milton's contemporaries.

The third argument is "That this order of licensing conduces nothing to the end for which it was fram'd. . . ." However, before fully opening the argument, he must return to the imagined objection offered earlier, the one that led him into his second argument: that though the inventors be bad the thing itself might be good. This objection he answers now, by repeating and completing the ideas begun in his second argument:

> Impunity and remisenes, for certain are the bane of a Commonwealth, but here the great art lyes, to discern in what the law is to bid restraint and punishment, and in what things perswasion only is to work. If every action which is good, or evill in man at ripe years, were to be under pittance, prescription, and compulsion, what were vertue but a name, what praise could be then due to well-doing, what grammercy to be sober, just, or continent? Many there be that complain of divin Providence for suffering *Adam* to transgresse, foolish tongues! when God gave him reason, he gave him freedom to choose, for reason is but choosing; he had bin else a meer artificiall *Adam*. . . .   [p. 527]

The thing, licensing, itself is bad, for it restricts our reason, our God-given freedom to choose. The answer fuses the second and third arguments. Earlier came a passage that seems to be the heart of his third argument:

> If we think to regulat Printing, thereby to rectifie manners, we must regulat all recreations and pastimes, all that is delightfull

26

to man. No musick must be heard, no song be set or sung, but what is grave and *Dorick*. There must be licensing dancers. . . . It will ask more then the work of twenty licencers to examine all the lutes, the violins, and the ghittarrs in every house; they must not be suffer'd to prattle as they doe, but must be licenc'd what they may say. [pp. 523–524]

The point of the third argument is that the ordinance is a practical impossibility, a reason Milton, as it were, harps on: "This office will require the whole time of not a few overseers, and those no vulgar men . . . [C]onsider . . . the quality which ought to be in every licenser."

Fourth, "I lastly proceed from the no good it can do, to the manifest hurt it causes, in being first the greatest discouragement and affront, that can be offer'd to learning and to learned men." In this argument, Milton's ire seems fully roused, as in the rhythm of the following:

When a man writes to the world, he summons up all his reason and deliberation to assist him; he searches, meditats, is industrious, and likely consults and conferrs with his judicious friends; after all which done, he takes himself to be inform'd in what he writes, as well as any that writ before him; if in this, the most consummat act of his fidelity and ripenesse, no years, no industry, no former proof of his abilities can bring him to that state of maturity, as not to be still mistrusted and suspected, unless he carry all his considerat diligence, all his midnight watchings, and expence of *Palladian* oyl, to the hasty view of an unleisur'd licencer, perhaps much his younger, perhaps far his inferiour in judgement, perhaps one who never knew the labour of book-writing; and if he be not repulst, or slighted, must appear in Print like a punie with his guardian, and his censors hand on the back of his title to be his bayl and surety, that he is no idiot, or seducer, it cannot be but a dishonour and derogation to the author, to the book, to the priviledge and dignity of Learning. [p. 532]

The speech is only about half finished. The remainder is a tripartite amplification of this fourth argument, with returns and excursions back into the first three arguments. There are repetitions of themes, certainly:

Henceforth let no man care to learn, or care to be more then worldly wise; for certainly in higher matters to be ignorant and

slothfull, to be a common stedfast dunce will be the only pleasant life, and only in request.   [p. 535]

So much the more when as dettors and delinquents may walk
abroad without a keeper, but unoffensive books must not stirre
forth without a visible jaylor in thir title.   [p. 536]

This is not, Yee Covnants and Protestations that we have made,
this is not to put down Prelaty, this is but to chop an Episcopacy,
this is but to translate the Palace *Metropolitan* from one kind of
dominion into another, this is but an old canonicall slight of
commuting our penance.   [pp. 540–541]

Too, the fourth argument contains some of the most famous passages
in the work, in their patriotism, in their respectful references to Francis
Bacon, in their mention of Milton's own visit to Galileo, and (to us) in
their anticipation of Milton's later charge that new Presbyter is but old
priest writ large. Pathetic appeals are, appropriately, strong in this development of the fourth argument, which virtually summarizes Milton's case—perhaps nowhere stronger than when he insists that, ostensibly contrary to his argument, all books should be published without
imprimatur *but* all books advocating "popery" should be banned. I
think, however, this is neither an inconsistency nor a catering to the
values of his audience, but rather logically a part of his theme of liberty:
freedom cannot tolerate the advocacy of its overthrow.

And now that we are speaking of discrepancies, let us note that in
one significant respect *Areopagitica* was a rhetorical failure. The licensing ordinance was not repealed, was not even seriously reconsidered; in
fact, even stronger efforts were made to put teeth into the imprimaturs.
However, in calling the pamphlet a failure we have assumed that its
rhetorical intention lies in Milton's stated thesis. But, as our review of
Donne's oration has suggested, an examination of discursive form can
modify the stated thesis: form is a *doing,* a thesis is a *saying;* the two may
not be the same and so should be considered together for an estimation
of intention. In advancing his thesis that the ordinance should be repealed, Milton has said a great deal about how books are written and
read, and about what sort of person writes books—arguments that certainly reflect upon us, his readers; upon Milton, the writer; and upon
the book we are reading. The fourth argument, which is the best writ-

28

ten and is in the traditionally strongest location, may be strongest in Milton's view because of his own passion: significantly, it sees the ordinance as an attack on learning, the very life-blood of Milton's kind of engaged intellectual, or "warfaring Christian," who acquires virtue through ideological encounters. For us, too, the fourth argument is the strongest in its function of making the speaker's true subject explicit. Coming after the initially "studious" characterization of the speaker and after our glimpse of him at work in trying to outpace ingenious Truth, the argument fully realizes the speaker's ethos and, as he would surely wish, makes it exemplary.

Another view of form confirms our conjecture regarding intention. Milton's four arguments could be thought of in dichotomous terms. The first two arguments might be grouped under one head as setting forth the historical background of the issue and the philosophical framework of the present thesis. The second grouping, of the third and fourth arguments, specifically applies this background and philosophy to the ordinance in dispute and anticipates its evil effects. The arrangement, thus, looks more Ramistic than Ciceronian. But the overall structure of the speech—exordium, thesis, *divisio, narratio,* development (proof, refutation, and digressions), and finally peroration—can just as easily be viewed as Ciceronian with a slight redistribution of arguments. Milton, like Donne, may be fusing several rhetorical traditions. But there is a difference. Let us, before proceeding to Milton's peroration, consider one major difference that I have already touched on several times: truth is present in Milton—by his view, almost unavoidably so, however much she may seem to exceed his rhetorical grasp.

Of course, to prove Milton's confidence in the proximity of truth by contrasting that confidence with Donne's skepticism is an easy matter, and ultimately an empty one unless we understand the unique qualities and unique rhetorical force of each. Donne, we have seen, does little to disturb tradition, whether in church doctrine or in discursive form; the attitudes of the *via media* are constituent of his very ethos. But Milton seems to find little point in maintaining tradition; he would not only *use* it but *alter* it when necessary to free man. This is hardly *via media* thinking. If the point is not already evident from my review of *Areopagitica,* consider Milton's confident revision in that work of the story of St. Jerome's dream. According to tradition, St. Jerome had a dream, or vision, brought on by a fever, in which he

29

was dragged before a judge, who asked him what he was. "A Christian," Jerome replied. "You are lying. You are a disciple of Cicero, not of Christ; for your heart is where your treasure is." Jerome was then flogged, but he pleaded with the judge and swore, "Lord, if ever again I possess worldly books, if ever I read them, I shall have denied You."[15] The traditional interpretation is that the judge is Christ. Milton, however, puts a different face on the matter:

> . . . the Divell whipt St. *Jerom* in a lenten dream, for reading *Cicero;* or else it was a fantasm bred by the feaver which had then seis'd him. For had an Angel bin his discipliner, unlesse it were for dwelling too much on Ciceronianisms, & had chastiz'd the reading, not the vanity, it had bin plainly partiall; first, to correct him for grave *Cicero,* and not for scurrill *Plautus* whom he confesses to have bin reading not long before; next to correct him only, and let so many more ancient Fathers wax old in those pleasant and florid studies without the lash of such a tutoring apparition. . . .   [p. 510]

Thus, Cicero and most ancient learning are saved by a steadfast belief in justice, and in reasoning about justice, nor is much damage done to that teaching that troubled the humanists: put nothing before God. The exercise shows us what reason can do even at the expense of deflecting mainstream tradition. It is Donne's skepticism that seems to keep him in the mainstream, as it is Milton's confidence and emphasis on *use* that seem to keep him out of it. In this way, the latter appears more the humanist, a controversion of my own thesis, which I shall let stand for the present.

Too, in comparing these speeches by Donne and Milton I may have opened myself to charges that they do not fall within the same rhetorical genre. Donne's speech is commemorative, epideictic. However, the person we find celebrated in that speech is not Alderman Cockayne but to a significant extent *Donne,* who dramatizes for us first the impact of the text on his own devotional life and second what he, as the most famous Anglican orator of his day, can say about that other text there in the coffin before him. Might something of the same be true of Milton's speech? Might it, too, be commemorative— or more epideictic than deliberative?

Consider Milton's isolation. In 1644 he was at the forefront of the rebel Protestants,[16] and in times of revolution the avant-garde can be dangerously out of step. In fact, the little effect Milton's pamphlet had on its immediate surroundings may be the result of planned neglect by those rebels who kept in step and based their moves less on a belief in the prevalence of truth than on a hard knowledge of the efficaciousness of propaganda. Even among the most advanced rebels, Milton was isolated. Walwyn seems his closest ally in matters argued in the *Areopagitica,* and his most likely precursor in such matters as freedom of the press or the inevitable triumph of truth. But, compared with Milton's, Walwyn's arguments "pale like candle gleams in the noonday sun."[17] Milton stood apart from his times, even when those times were involved in making changes of which he most profoundly approved.

Earlier I mentioned that *Areopagitica* may be a dramatization of its true subject, or argument, and that herein may lie the genius of its maker. It appeared unlicensed, in print, and offered the reader the opportunity to follow the tracks of a studious man who stumbles once in his effort to keep up with the advances of truth ("See the ingenuity of Truth . . ."). One of the premises of the work is that a book is not simply "a reasonable creature" but "reason itself." The work, then, virtually proclaims itself the voice of flawed, fallen man engaged in one of the highest acts of his manhood, sending forth the actions of his reason for the benefit of other men. Through one perspective, it might appear, as I suggested, that history has played a joke on this speaker: truth, as he saw it, did not prevail; in fact, his case failed abominably—it was not adopted by the revolutionary leaders, and even stricter licensing laws were eventually passed. But by that token, Isocrates' written speeches failed, too—so much so that one historian has conjectured that, given Isocrates' evident political opportunism, he must have prepared his speeches largely as advertising for his own academy.[18] Let us acknowledge that the view is at least heightened, if not caused, by our retrospectivity. Perhaps Milton was advertising, too—if not his own academy (though he did draw a meager salary as a tutor), then perhaps himself. He knew he was isolated; he knew his reputation in Parliament. He surely knew no amount of praise would soften his audience. He was confident that there was truth in the *Areopagitica;* that we still find truth in it confirms his confidence and proves his case, to a degree.

But in dramatizing its argument, the pamphlet also—above all— advertises Milton, not "sells" in the crass modern meaning of advertising, but heightens the public awareness of a man of rare abilities destined for greater things. Milton's conscious intention may have been the dramatization of his point about truth. But the pamphlet itself presents him, then as now, in a clearly public role, in an ethos responsive to his vocation as a great English poet. The pamphlet gives us that voice and, almost like a courtesy book, it went forth to demonstrate what a man in those times must do, how he must behave—a man, that is, like Milton, who is confident that truth is in our midst, a man of destiny whose character is always implied in some of the most emotionally charged passages, such as this one near the peroration:

> For when God shakes a Kingdome, with strong and healthfull commotions to a generall reforming, 'tis not untrue that many sectaries and false teachers are then busiest in seducing; but yet more true it is, that God then raises to his own work men of rare abilities, and more then common industry not only to look back and revise what hath been taught heretofore, but to gain furder and goe on, some new enlighten'd steps in the discovery of truth. [p. 566]

Implicit in this truly thematic passage is the figure of Janus, "with his two *controversal* faces," as Milton puts it earlier in another passage, in which he exhorts his audience with his *stated* thesis:

> And now the time in speciall is, by priviledge to write and speak of what may help to the furder discussing of matters in agitation. The Temple of *Janus,* with his two *controversal* faces, might now not unsignificantly be set open. [p. 561]

The figure pervades much of Milton's conceptualizing in this speech: the faces are *"controversal"* (here let us remind ourselves that with Milton too we are reading the prose of a poet)—that is, looking backward as well as forward, or in opposite directions, *pro* as well as *contra,* warring, agitating, stirring up in liberty ("the nurse of all great wits") opinion, which "in good men is but knowledge in the making." Controversy is our means of knowledge, the controversy of turning in two different directions and juxtaposing modes, manners, means, opinions. We do this not only to look back but to revise and so look forward. And truth, immutable truth, *will* be discovered in the process, of that there can be no doubt. Such is the moral stance, the ethos, the character of Milton, uttered in every argument.

That *Areopagitica* may have been designed to advertise that ethos to

32

the world is further indicated by the nature of the peroration. Like the exordium, it is addressed directly to its putative audience, but without any of the awkward prose we found in the earlier place, perhaps because here passion, not rhetorical rules, governs. The peroration is brief, encompassing two paragraphs; morally threatening, in suggesting that the framers of the ordinance had themselves broken the earlier Anglican licensing law; and exhortative, urging the repeal of the ordinance. The specificity and the size of the peroration—for that matter, the amount of space given directly to the issue in question, both here in the peroration and *throughout* the speech—show us that something else, much more, is Milton's design.

How humanist is the ethos of that design? Certainly all Milton's expressed opinions seem thoroughly humanist, as we have noted throughout; these opinions, as I have suggested, can be summarized and emblematized by the controversial faces of Janus. Yet controversy meant something to the humanists that it did not quite mean to Milton. That other meaning is motivated by different attitudes toward truth and its accessibility. Those attitudes have everything to do with the use and flexibility of discursive form in practice, and they are ultimately more akin to Donne's skepticism than to Milton's confidence.

Two Poems

Donne's poem "Goodfriday 1613. Riding Westward," especially in view of its title, would seem largely autobiographical. A specific date is mentioned as well as a specific event; indeed, the titles of some manuscript versions are even more explicit—for example, "Mr. J: Dun goeing from Sr. H:G: on good fryday sent him back this Meditacion, on the Waye."[19] But Donne never viewed his own biography as either unique or extraordinary; he was, as he put it in an often memorized passage, "involved in *Mankinde*." Though he was apparently literally riding westward during the creation of the poem, so is all mankind riding westward, moving toward death. The first lines, therefore, speak not of Donne, nor of the occasion, but of "man." The first lines, too, introduce the subject of form, though they seem to talk of spheres.[20]

Goodfriday 1613. Riding Westward

Let mans Soule be a Spheare, and then, in this,
The intelligence that moves, devotion is,
And as the other Spheares, by being growne
Subject to forraigne motions, lose their owne,
And being by others hurried every day,   5
Scarce in a yeare their naturall forme obey:
Pleasure or businesse, so, our Soules admit
For their first mover, and are whirld by it.
Hence is't, that I am carryed towards the West
This day, when my Soules forme bends toward the East.   10
There I should see a Sunne, by rising set,
And by that setting endlesse day beget;
But that Christ on this Crosse, did rise and fall,
Sinne had eternally benighted all.
Yet dare I' almost be glad, I do not see   15
That spectacle of too much weight for mee.
Who sees Gods face, that is selfe life, must dye;
What a death were it then to see God dye?
It made his owne Lieutenant Nature shrinke,

It made his footstoole crack, and the Sunne winke.   20
Could I behold those hands which span the Poles,
And tune all spheares at once peirc'd with those holes?
Could I behold that endlesse height which is
Zenith to us, and our Antipodes,
Humbled below us? or that blood which is   25
The seat of all our Soules, if not of his,
Made durt of dust, or that flesh which was worne
By God, for his apparell, rag'd, and torne?
If on these things I durst not looke, durst I
Upon his miserable mother cast mine eye,   30
Who was Gods partner here, and furnish'd thus
Halfe of that Sacrifice, which ransom'd us?
Though these things, as I ride, be from mine eye,
They' are present yet unto my memory,
For that looks towards them; and thou look'st towards
          mee,   35
O Saviour, as thou hang'st upon the tree;
I turne my backe to thee, but to receive
Corrections, till thy mercies bid thee leave.
O thinke mee worth thine anger, punish mee,
Burne off my rusts, and my deformity,   40
Restore thine Image, so much by thy grace,
That thou may'st know mee, and I'll turne my face.

Our subject is *form,* whose meaning in the seventeenth century
ranged from something as tangibly specific as a shape, a triangle or a
sphere, through something as mixed in tangibility as the "forms" in a
sacrament or as the structure of an oration, to something as intangible
(to most philosophers, at least) as the human soul. We must pause for a
moment before reviewing the poem to consider this range of meaning.

The Aristotelians (that is, the scholastics), talked about form as one
of the four "causes"—say, the four forces that produced man: the
efficient (God), material (body), formal (soul), and final (salvation).
God made man out of dust and embued him with a soul wherewith he
could find the means of salvation. Perhaps it is simpler to think of
these causes as operative in the production of a statue: the sculptor is
the efficient cause, stone is the material cause, shape and identity are
the formal cause, and artist's intention, or end, is the final cause. The

formal cause, then, would seem to have something to do both with what a thing is, or what uniquely distinguishes it from other things, and with how it is constituted.

Separating any one cause from the others might seem virtually impossible. Nonetheless, toward that effort the period used several ways of grouping the causes: for example, as "external" (efficient and final—the sculptor and his predetermined end, which exist "outside" the statue) and "internal" (material and formal—the stone, shape, and identity, which inherently constitute the thing itself); or as those causes that precede the created object (the efficient and material—the sculptor and the stone, which were *there* before the statue was) and those that do not (the formal and final—the statue itself and its end, the latter pertaining in this case only to the artist's fulfilled intention).

Such groupings probably provoked more problems than they solved. The Platonists and Augustinians, for example, took issue with both the groupings described above, and insisted that the formal cause is actually external and preexistent, as a Form, or Idea, that is antecedent to the created object, itself only a shadowy representation of great, metaphysical "realities." But, in some deference to these other-worldly (and doubtfully humanist) thinkers, we might summarize the characteristics of the formal cause by noting that it is a unique, distinguishing feature of a created object, a constitutive force that binds all parts to a single purpose, and an internal element that may or may not have preceded the object itself and that is partly at least externally perceptible (as in the shape, behavior, or attitude of the created thing).

The seventeenth century used yet another, and simpler, category (also inherited from its scholastic past), this one containing the "formal cause" alone: it was considered as both "outer" (shape or aspect) and "inner" (nature or "temperament"). In this category, form encompassed the appearance of a thing as well as the evidence its appearance gives of creator's purpose and will. This view of the formal cause means *arrangement,* or *dispositio*—to put the matter in rhetorical terms and so provide an ultimate summary—and it invites a consideration of final cause, end, or intention, whether we are speaking of the causes of a human being, a statue, a speech, or a poem.

Donne opens his poem by playing on the rich ambiguity of the term *form,* suggesting that man's soul (a form) be regarded as if it were in the shape of a sphere (an outer form), and, like heavenly spheres, as falling under the influence of other motions and so failing to follow its own natural course, or inclination (an inner form). Characteristically, Donne plays on the full range of meaning not only in a concept but in all the words used to express that concept—in this case, soul, shape, and nature, all relating to form. His use of the phrase "Soules forme" has that metonymic complexity Donne loves (it is almost like saying "form's form").[21]

I shall continue to pay attention to what Donne and Milton say about form, but their speculations will be useful mainly insofar as they clarify attitudes toward *discursive* form—any recognizable structuring of words (a figure of speech, a stanza, an oration). At the end of this section, I will summarize the various meanings of the term we encounter in Donne's poem and in Milton's. But we must keep in mind from the outset a further distinction in the concept, as will become increasingly clear throughout this study. This distinction is between two profoundly contrary ideas about form, including discursive form: one idea makes form analytically separate from matter but closely tied to creator's purpose; the other fuses form, matter, and purpose. These two ideas are far more significant for our study than the other philosophical distinctions reviewed above, though they are related to a philosophical argument about the separability, in particular the conceptual separability, of form from other elements in a created object. They center on the extent to which form, though closely linked with creator's end, is itself a product of the material cause. The first idea about form is both dualist (that is, separable, the duality being form and matter) and rhetorical; we encounter it immediately in Donne's poem. The second idea, which I shall attempt to articulate fully in the final chapter of this book, on Milton, is monist and formalistic. The first idea tends to be fully in accord not simply with the detachability of discursive form but also with a rhetorical epistemology: form, as a thing to be known, is always suppositional; it is in controversy, and must be argued for. That would seem to be the idea about form with which Donne begins his poem.

It is significant that a poet as conscious as Donne would introduce the concept of form in his "Goodfriday" poem in the language of a geometrical theorem: "Let . . . then." But note that for Donne's original audience the matter arranged in that linguistic form is itself controversial. According to conventional cosmology, each of the heavenly spheres, in which were situated the (then considered) five planets, the sun, and the moon, was governed by an intelligence—an angel, Christian philosophers called it. An intelligence /angel directed the movement of each sphere, whose shape though translucent and invisible to us was perfectly described for us by the planet itself (the movement below our horizon had to be imagined). In the spheres' differing velocities of movement, they made a kind of music, the "music of the spheres"; though not audible to human ears, the music was a further feature of the heavenly harmony in a planned and governed universe. The concept, Donne well knew, was considered fanciful and old-fashioned in his post-Copernican age; the scientists of the "new Philosophy" were, in fact, continuing to wipe out all vestiges of this old belief, in which a flat earth hung suspended in space at the center of the stars, as God's "footstool." Note, however, that Donne does not *declare* the similarity between man's soul and a heavenly sphere. Rather, he asks us—indirectly, at least, perhaps asking himself most directly—only to imagine for the nonce that such similarity exists. And he places this initial, fanciful disquisition of "form" not in the "put-case" suppositions of a lawyer, but in the language of a geometer: "Let . . then . . ." But this does not diminish the fantasizing one bit; on the contrary, it enhances it and so clarifies Donne's stance toward form.

The first English geometry, published forty years earlier, had waxed enthusiastic about the uses of the "Let . . . then" or "Suppose . . . then" geometric theorem:

> Suppose that there be two triangles ABC and DEF, hauing two sides of the one, namely AB, and AC, equall to two sides of the other, namely to DE and DF, the one to the other, that is, AB to DE, and AC to DF, hauing also the angle BAC, equall to the angle EDF. Then I say the base also BC is equall to the base EF. . . .[22]

If you grant the supposition, then your conclusion is certain, for your mode of proving relies neither upon "probable argument," as rhetoric does, nor upon the evidence of the senses.[23] Little wonder that mathematics was rapidly becoming the language of the new science. But suppose that the arguer did not ask you merely to grant the supposition. Suppose he proceeded as if his supposition were true, as if its

form—that is, the numbers and shapes we see before us—were profoundly indicative of the divine order of things; then the language of
mathematics becomes the language of wisdom itself and the means
whereby we look on beauty bare:

> O comfortable allurement, O rauishing perswasion, to deale
> with a Science, whose subiect, is so Auncient, so pure, so excel-
> lent, so surmounting all creatures, so vsed of the Almighty and
> incomprehensible wisdome of the Creator, in the distinct crea-
> tion of all creatures. . . . [sig. ★i]

Such formalist certainty and positivism, we can see, clashes with
what we know already about Donne's views of form. The outcry is
John Dee's, in an apologetical preface to that first Englishing of Euclid's geometry mentioned earlier. The enthusiasm of an apologist,
particularly one so controversial as John Dee, should be taken for no
more than what it is. Nonetheless, the chords of Dee's theme were still
sounding in Donne's day, and were to continue, and to build to a cre-
scendo, in part an ironic legacy of the humanism that is a subject of
this book. It is good to let these chords echo as we consider Donne's
poem, whose opening confronts and shatters what Dee would call the
"marvelous neutrality" of mathematical reasoning.

Further, the poem continually asserts limits to the efficacy of all
man's instruments, including his willed use of form even in petitioning
for grace, even in shaping a poem. The geometrical orderliness, the
tonally relaxed clarity, of the first ten lines is rapidly displaced in the
speaker's acknowledged inability to face the Crucifixion. Christ, the
greater Form, is not present in this poem. Nor is he centered: if he is
Jesus of Nazareth dead on the Cross, he is also God, the *primum mobile,*
the first mover of the spheres, who inhabits and gives life to the universe—and who was born of Mary. The multiple perspectives following the first ten lines reveal a speaker trying to grasp the (for him)
ungraspable, and sound like a tonal variation, a *division,* upon the formal regularity of the first ten lines. Tonal discords sound throughout
the center section. Donne, in his anguish, is "almost . . . glad." The
withering of nature, the earthquake and darkness that accompanied the
Crucifixion, are belittled: God's place is the greater universe after all;
man inhabits the mere earth (an echo, perhaps, of the most frightening
implications of the new, Copernican philosophy). Again, as in the ser-

mon, the juxtapositions are formally significant and threaten any simple view of poetic order or logical progression; poetry and logic, after
all, are only human instruments of form.[24]

The body of Christ is mentioned first in two lines at the mathematical center of the poem (lines 21 and 22), and his presence, so argues an excellent critic, produces a spiritual change in the speaker, a
meeting of contraries.[25] But surely someone who only sees the poem
and does not hear it as well, someone who measures its center mainly
by counting its lines, could locate the Second Person at such a conjectural fulcrum. What I hear in the poem is not a meeting of contraries,
but the speaker's anguish at the collapse of will and the limits of man's
own doing. God's "apparell" is "rag'd and torne"; the blessed Virgin
is "Gods Partner"—the contraries do not avoid either violent or blasphemous extremes. But their violence and blasphemousness only
demonstrate the limits of man's use of form as a means of apprehending. Man's use of form, too, is that "deformity" that Christ must
"Burne off." In the final lines, from 33 to the end of the poem, something like the formal regularity of the opening is heard again—not a
restoration, but rather a turning to the attempted forms of confession
and prayer.[26] Again, the speaker's own dramatic situation, riding toward the West, is mentioned. Though he faces West, his memory,
which Elizabethan psychology located in the hindmost part of the
brain, faces East. Christ himself may be located in the East, but as a
Cruciform that looms above the horizon and that is ultimately, in the
speaker's closing words, fused with the God of Genesis, the maker of
man in his own image. In our end is our beginning, to echo a paradox
(Mary Stuart's motto)—*only* our beginning, one might say, considering this poem.

At the center of the poem—early, late, throughout—is Donne as a
curiously Janus-faced man. One face, of will, turns away from Christ.
The other, of memory, looks toward him. This is a "controversal"
position that normally delighted the humanist, for it allowed him to
apply a mode of thought that was unique to the rhetoric he offered as
an alternative to philosophy. In Donne's poem, the prominence of the
will and its freedom would surely excite the humanist, just as the
prominence of memory and its urgency would excite the Platonist
and Augustinian. But the dominant mood is torment. From the first
lines of the poem, the speaker experiences pulls in opposite directions. Then Janus, the god of doors and of setting forth and the em-

blem of controversy in Milton, is made explicit as a final, paradoxical expression of the speaker's inability to act—perhaps the ultimate humanist horror—within which the poem's *present* is defined.

It may be significant to note that the poem is written in couplets and in iambic pentameter, a poetic form that a century later was to become suffused with confidence and applied to the purposes of poets in the Age of Enlightenment. From our perspective, the contrast sharpens our view of Donne's use of all forms, "inner" as well as "outer," throughout the poem: neither abandoned nor revised but used to the extent they suffice.

John Carey, in his recent book on Donne, has offered this poem in evidence of a quality that he finds characteristic of Donne's entire life and career: his lust for power. In this poem Donne is riding westward, through Warwickshire and Shropshire, yet he obliterates the landscape, with its birds, trees, and people, in order to move onto a cosmic plane where there are only two figures, Donne and Christ. "This titanic management of space," Carey argues, "spreads through Donne's poetry. His eyes are receptacles for oceans . . . as for his love, seismic convulsions are not vast enough to figure it. . . . The geography of the poems combines with their other dynamic features to make them the most enduring exhibition of the will to power the English Renaissance produced."[27] I disagree with most of this argument, and especially with the part that makes Donne's work an "enduring exhibition of the will to power," which I should rephrase somewhat to make it more nearly fit the conclusion that follows from my own examination of Donne's discourse: his poems exhibit the power of will. The point of "Goodfriday 1613" is to exhibit the defacement and limitations of that power, even in the poem's dazzling management of geography. Discursive form is an outward, audible, and visible sign of the will to power—but *in this case* it is turned on itself. All form, being suppositional, is *too* evanescent. Something greater is needed—beyond supposition, beyond rhetoric, and beyond Donne, too.

■　■　■

Will, power, form, and effacement are subjects of Milton's "Nativity Ode," a celebration of Christ's birth. Moreover, as in Donne's poem about Christ's death, in Milton's poem the Savior is not realized. Indeed, a special characteristic, and part of the beauty, of Milton's poem is its anticipation of Christ's personhood. In a sense, the two poems, Donne's and Milton's, are mainly about their speakers. Both actually center on the speakers of the poems' words and their experiences and emotions. But there are vastly more important differences—chief, for our purposes, are those discernible in the speakers' attitudes toward form.

In retrospect, we call this poem by Milton an *ode*. However, the poet, or his persona, does not announce that form until the third stanza. The first four stanzas constitute a kind of exordium for this long (twenty-seven stanzas) poem:[28]

On the morning of Christs Nativity.
Composed 1629.

I

This is the Month, and this the happy morn
Wherin the Son of Heav'ns eternal King,
Of wedded Maid, and Virgin Mother born,
Our great redemption from above did bring;
For so the holy sages once did sing,   5
    That he our deadly forfeit should release,
And with his Father work us a perpetual peace.

II

That glorious Form, that Light unsufferable,
And that far-beaming blaze of Majesty,
Wherwith he wont at Heav'ns high Councel-Table,   10
To sit the midst of Trinal Unity,
He laid aside; and here with us to be,
    Forsook the Courts of everlasting Day,
And chose with us a darksom House of mortal Clay.

III

Say Heav'nly Muse, shall not thy sacred vein   15
Afford a present to the Infant God?
Hast thou no vers, no hymn, or solemn strein,
To welcom him to this his new abode,
Now while the Heav'n by the Suns team untrod,
    Hath took no print of the approaching light,   20
And all the spangled host keep watch in squadrons bright?

IV

See how from far upon the Eastern rode
The Star-led Wisards haste with odours sweet:
O run, prevent them with thy humble ode,
And lay it lowly at his blessed feet;   25
Have thou the honour first, thy Lord to greet,
    And joyn thy voice unto the Angel Quire,
From out his secret Altar toucht with hallow'd fire.

The next section of the poem, which I shall review shortly, is sub-
titled "The Hymn." A hymn, of course, is simply a religious ode. But
observe that Milton allows his generic intentions to unfold in the
course of the poem, though literary history has revised his strategy:
we usually call the poem "The Nativity Ode," as if that were Milton's
title, and often rank it with other attempts to "English" the ode, such
as those by Spenser and Jonson. But, to be time's true contemporary,
what we must do in our retrospectiveness is move back in time imagi-
natively, starting with whatever we have learned about history or a
poem, and then move forward through the discourse itself, allowing it
to work on us as *it* unfolds in time. Too, retrospectivity is dramatized
for us in both of these poems, as if the prior question were, How do I
at this moment come to terms with—face without defacing, define
without delimiting—a great event in the past?

Present and past are juxtaposed in Milton's title and stated in the
opening stanza: this *is* the morning on which Christ *was* born. The
perspectival paradox is neither displayed nor emphasized. Nor is
much violence done to the concept of form in the second stanza, the
contrast between Christ's preexisting "glorious Form" and his incarnation. Further, Milton in the third line is no less paradoxical in his
reference to Mary than was Donne; but the latter does a kind of tonal
violence to conventional reverence, whereas Milton creates a smooth
chiasmus, a rhetorical X, not unknown in the Psalms, which Milton
believed were great sources of poetics. Thus, Milton's poetic form,
here and throughout the hymn, manages and controls the tone without threatening, as in Donne, to disintegrate.

The third stanza is in the form of an apostrophe—a turning from
one's audience to address an imaginary person. But the fourth stanza
seems addressed not so much to the muse as to Milton himself, the
poet—or the muse embodied in the poet—for the former is already

"Heav'nly" and has a "sacred vein," the latter has only a "humble ode" and seeks to join his voice with the "Angel Quire," or even, as line 28 indicates, to speak in prophetic tones. Note, too, what has happened to time in these stanzas: Christ *is* the "Infant God" and the Wise Men are approaching; the poet wishes to arrive before they do, gaining the first "honour" with (a moderated paradox) his "humble" ode, not only placing that ode at the feet of the Infant but also somehow at the same time joining his voice with the angels whose hymn *announced* the moment of birth.

As I read the poem, certain formal qualities—perhaps the metrical regularity, the steady use of the Alexandrine with its Spenserian closure, the echoes in sound and syntax ("Say . . ." "See . . .")—achieve that tonal control I mentioned earlier; that is, they continually free me from the paradoxes without allowing me to ignore them. And when I try to dramatize the scene, as in the fourth stanza, which defies dramatization, I am led inexorably to imagine Milton offering the song as an act of devotion in the predawn cold of Christmas, 1629. I could justify that latter reading by thinking of the stanzas as a kind of rhetorical exordium, the first part of any public discourse, whose function is to offer the audience a contract concerning subject, speaker, and the form of the discourse: the subject is the Nativity, past and present; the speaker is a poet, in this case a public poet, a maker of odes and hymns, who aspires to prophethood (his lips "toucht with hallow'd fire"); and the *divisio,* or formal contract, is dramatized for us as a kind of double vision, with a focus on the past (the moment of Christ's birth) and on the future, both involved in the present act of shaping a song about that moment. As Rosemond Tuve remarked about this poem, it "celebrates the meaning of the Incarnation not only in history but after history is over, an event both in and not within created nature, a peace both in and not within created time."[29] Correlatively, we readers find Milton declaring his intentions to produce the poem that is already before us; in taking that object and turning it into an act, as we do when we read, we too bring the past and the future into the present. The exordium makes us aware of changes in time and in mode of address, and thereby focuses our attention on these shifts and changes as they occur in the succeeding hymn. In sum, the exordium makes us aware of product and process. These awarenesses become, in effect, our poetic contract.

The first eight stanzas of the hymn are pervaded with a remarkable stillness.

The Hymn

I

It was the Winter wilde,
While the Heav'n-born-childe,   30
    All meanly wrapt in the rude manger lies;
Nature in aw to him
Had doff't her gawdy trim,
    With her great Master so to sympathize:
It was no season then for her   35
To wanton with the Sun her lusty Paramour.

II

Onely with speeches fair
She woo's the gentle Air
    To hide her guilty front with innocent Snow,
And on her naked shame,   40
Pollute with sinfull blame,
    The Saintly Vail of Maiden white to throw,
Confounded, that her Makers eyes
Should look so neer upon her foul deformities.

III

But he her fears to cease,   45
Sent down the meek-eyd Peace,
    She crown'd with Olive green, came softly sliding
Down through the turning sphear
His ready Harbinger,
    With Turtle wing the amorous clouds dividing,   50
And waving wide her mirtle wand,
She strikes a universall Peace through Sea and Land.

IV

No War, or Battails sound
Was heard the World around:
    The idle spear and shield were high up hung;   55

The hooked Chariot stood
Unstain'd with hostile blood,
   The Trumpet spake not to the armed throng,
And Kings sate still with awfull eye,
As if they surely knew their sovran Lord was by.   60

V

But peacefull was the night
Wherin the Prince of light
   His raign of peace upon the earth began:
The Winds with wonder whist,
Smoothly the waters kist,   65
   Whispering new joyes to the milde Ocean,
Who now hath quite forgot to rave,
While Birds of Calm sit brooding on the charmed wave.

VI

The Stars with deep amaze
Stand fixt in stedfast gaze,   70
   Bending one way their pretious influence,
And will not take their flight,
For all the morning light,
   Or *Lucifer* that often warn'd them thence;
But in their glimmering Orbs did glow,   75
Untill their Lord himself bespake, and bid them go.

VII

And though the shady gloom
Had given day her room,
   The Sun himself with-held his wonted speed,
And hid his head for shame,   80
As his inferiour flame,
   The new-enlight'n'd world no more should need;
He saw a greater Sun appear
Then his bright Throne, or burning Axletree could bear.

VIII

The Shepherds on the Lawn,   85
Or ere the point of dawn,
   Sate simply chatting in a rustick row;

Full little thought they than,
That the mighty *Pan*
    Was kindly com to live with them below;   90
Perhaps their loves, or els their sheep,
Was all that did their silly thoughts so busie keep.

The silence is broken, in stanza IX, with a music that is first heard
by the shepherds, as in the Bible story. During the quiet of the first
eight stanzas, the verb tenses are all past (except for those in VI).
Then, with the music of IX, a prolonged shift to present tense is
made, which extends, with some variation, throughout the remainder
of the poem: the Star of Bethlehem appears now (in XI) and the Babe
lies in his infancy now (in XVI). The most important variation in
tense occurs in XII, but here the speaker changes his mode of address.
Up to that stanza, he had been speaking as a narrator of great events,
but now, in XII, he speaks as a contemplator, a shift the exordium has
already prepared us for, a self-awareness. In fact, the center section of
the hymn, XII–XVI, calls our attention to the singer as he contemplates the materials of his story—one element in particular, music.

IX

When such musick sweet
Their hearts and ears did greet,
    As never was by mortall finger strook,   95
Divinely-warbled voice
Answering the stringed noise,
    As all their souls in blisfull rapture took:
The Air such pleasure loth to lose,
With thousand echo's still prolongs each heav'nly close.   100

X

Nature that heard such sound
Beneath the hollow round
    Of *Cynthia's* seat, the Airy region thrilling,
Now was almost won
To think her part was don,   105
    And that her raign had here its last fulfilling;
She knew such harmony alone
Could hold all Heav'n and Earth in happier union.

XI

At last surrounds their sight
A Globe of circular light,   110
    That with long beams the shame-fac't night array'd,
The helmed Cherubim
And sworded Seraphim
    Are seen in glittering ranks with wings displaid,
Harping in loud and solemn quire,   115
With unexpressive notes to Heav'ns new-born Heir.

XII

Such Musick (as 'tis said)
Before was never made,
    But when of old the sons of morning sung,
While the Creator Great   120
His constellations set,
    And the well-ballanc't world on hinges hung,
And cast the dark foundations deep,
And bid the weltring waves their oozy channel keep.

XIII

Ring out ye Crystall sphears,   125
Once bless our human ears,
    (If ye have power to touch our senses so)
And let your silver chime
Move in melodious time;
    And let the Base of Heav'ns deep Organ blow,   130
And with your ninefold harmony
Make up full consort to th' Angelicke symphony.

XIV

For if such holy Song
Enwrap our fancy long,
    Time will run back, and fetch the age of gold,   135
And speckl'd vanity
Will sicken soon and die,
    And leprous sin will melt from earthly mould,
And Hell it self will pass away,
And leave her dolorous mansions to the peering day.   140

XV

Yea Truth, and Justice then
Will down return to men,
    Th'enameld *Arras* of the Rainbow wearing,
Mercy set between,
Thron'd in Celestiall sheen,   145
    With radiant feet the tissued clouds down stearing,
And Heav'n as at som festivall,
Will open wide the Gates of her high Palace Hall.

XVI

But wisest Fate sayes no,
This must not yet be so,   150
    The Babe lies yet in smiling Infancy,
That on the bitter cross
Must redeem our loss;
    So both himself and us to glorifie:
Yet first to those ychain'd in sleep,   155
The wakefull trump of doom must thunder through the deep.

XVII

With such a horrid clang
As on mount *Sinai* rang
    While the red fire, and smouldring clouds out brake:
The aged Earth agast   160
With terrour of that blast,
    Shall from the surface to the center shake,
When at the worlds last session,
The dreadfull judge in middle Air shall spread his throne.

XVIII

And then at last our bliss   165
Full and perfect is,
    But now begins; for from this happy day
Th' old Dragon under ground
In straiter limits bound,
    Not half so far casts his usurped sway,   170
And wroth to see his Kingdom fail,
Swindges the scaly Horrour of his foulded tail.

The music at Christ's birth was like the music of the Creation. So caught up in that similarity, the singer standing "now" at the moment of that birth appeals to the spheres, in an apostrophe (XIII), to sound the music that will restore the Age of Gold—then he reverses himself, but not dramatically, in XVI, as if he were recalling then the true import of the birth. The reversal is not dramatic because the Age of Gold pales when compared with the events of Creation and birth, keynotes sounded in XII. The appeal to classical traditions—to the idea of the four ages of man, Gold, Silver, Bronze, and our present age, Iron—however deeply expressive of man's desire and hopes, must give way to God's will as revealed in human history. The echo of Vergil's eclogue in XIV, often seen in Milton's time as an eloquent if unformed and pagan hope for true revelation, limits the stature of the singer's own hope in these lines. "Fate" of XVI is not Fortuna but God's will, and the speaker at that point, standing in the presentness of Christ's birth, looks not backward to the Age of Gold but forward to the end of history. Verb tenses shift to the future, then back to the present again in XVIII, with its echo ("this happy day") of the first line of the exordium.

The remainder of the poem stays within the fictive present of the story of Christ's birth—which is also the poet's, and our, fictive present—and draws within it echoes, often contradictory, of key-notes sounded earlier.

XIX

The Oracles are dumm,
No voice or hideous humm
    Runs through the arched roof in words deceiving.   175
Apollo from his shrine
Can no more divine,
    With hollow shreik the steep of *Delphos* leaving.
No nightly trance, or breathed spell,
Inspire's the pale-ey'd Priest from the prophetic cell.   180

XX

The lonely mountains o're,
And the resounding shore,
    A voice of weeping heard, and loud lament;
From haunted spring, and dale

50

Edg'd with poplar pale,   185
    The parting Genius is with sighing sent;
With flowr-inwov'n tresses torn
The Nimphs in twilight shade of tangled thickets mourn.

XXI

In consecrated Earth,
And on the holy Hearth,   190
    The *Lars,* and *Lemures* moan with midnight plaint;
In Urns, and Altars round,
A drear, and dying sound
    Affrights the *Flamins* at their service quaint;
And the chill Marble seems to sweat,   195
While each peculiar power forgoes his wonted seat.

XXII

Peor, and *Baalim,*
Forsake their Temples dim,
    With that twise batter'd god of *Palestine,*
And mooned *Ashtaroth,*   200
Heav'ns Queen and Mother both,
    Now sits not girt with Tapers holy shine,
The Libyc *Hammon* shrinks his horn,
In vain the *Tyrian* Maids their wounded *Thamuz* mourn.

XXIII

And sullen Moloch fled,   205
Hath left in shadows dred,
    His burning Idol all of blackest hue,
In vain with Cymbals ring,
They call the grisly king,
    In dismall dance about the furnace blue;   210
The brutish gods of *Nile* as fast,
Isis and *Orus,* and the Dog *Anubis* hast.

XXIV

Nor is *Osiris* seen
In *Memphian* Grove, or Green,
    Trampling th' unshowr'd Grass with lowings loud: 215

Nor can he be at rest
Within his sacred chest,
    Naught but profoundest Hell can be his shroud;
In vain with Timbrel'd Anthems dark
The sable-stoled Sorcerers bear his worshipt Ark.   220

XXV

He feels from *Juda's* Land
The dredded Infants hand,
    The rayes of *Bethlehem* blind his dusky eyn;
Nor all the gods beside,
Longer dare abide,   225
    Not *Typhon* huge ending in snaky twine;
Our Babe to shew his Godhead true,
Can in his swadling bands controul the damned crew.

XXVI

So when the Sun in bed,
Curtain'd with cloudy red,   230
    Pillows his chin upon an Orient wave,
The flocking shadows pale
Troop to th' infernall jail,
    Each fetter'd Ghost slips to his severall grave,
And the yellow-skirted *Fayes*   235
Fly after the Night-steeds, leaving their Moon-lov'd maze.

XXVII

But see the Virgin blest,
Hath laid her Babe to rest.
    Time is our tedious Song should here have ending:
Heav'ns youngest teemed Star   240
Hath fixt her polisht Car,
    Her sleeping Lord with Handmaid Lamp attending,
And all about the Courtly Stable,
Bright-harnest Angels sit in order serviceable.

The silence of XIX is like the silence of the first section of the hymn, but it is a dumbness, not an anticipation. The sounds that are introduced in XX and that build in intensity through XXIII are discordant, not harmonious. And as the pagan gods and false idols desert the earth, light and darkness are again—as in the first Creation and as in the early parts of this hymn—divided. Pagan myths, however, are not all erroneous and may be serviceable to the Christian prophet (the sort of Christian prophet who, fifteen years later, was to write the *Areopagitica*), as the final couplet of XXV indicates, with its glance at the legend of the infant Hercules. Stanza XXVI announces the dawn. The final stanza closes the poem, in the present—a present suffused with neither silence nor sound but with a sense of tremendous power, waiting and approachable.

The attainment of that final stasis, that realization of supreme power, would seem to be the point of the poem. Yet, when we compare the final stanza with the first, whether of the exordium or of the hymn, it is obvious that we have moved no very great distance: in spite of the final realization of power, there are no marked differences in tone. This is not a self-consuming artifact, however, nor is the circularity of the apparent journey meant to be symbolic (of eternity, or even of the lesson that in the end is our beginning): the complicated form indicates that it is not the destination but the nature of the journey itself that is the point of the poem.

A line of argument, tone, action, or perspective is introduced, then a variation is played on it by means of dividing the whole. Indeed, division seems an important principle of form. We have seen divisions introduced in the exordium. We have also seen divisions made of elements in the first section of the hymn. Above all, divisions are made in the concept of time: past, present, future are divided, and then brought together in the final stanza, where the word *time* is spoken, like a revelatory act, embodying all the temporal and musical elements of the hymn. We are not invited to "see the Virgin blest"; we are exhorted to do so, as in the peroration of a discourse, with its return to the exordium, the only other place in the poem where the Virgin is mentioned. Our movement forward in time is only ostensible—it does not, to use a modern cliché, tell the whole story.

Moreover, the story, as the form indicates, is not the story of Christ's birth. Rather, it is the story of preparing one's heart, mind, and soul for the realization of that birth. One might continue this line of argument and pursue its devotional implications: the poem, like Donne's, is a meditation, although, unlike Donne's, it is offered in explicit awareness of its public. But I wish to pursue another line: the formal principle of the work is neither the generic choice nor division. It is, rather, the character of the speaker—Milton, the self-created public poet—whose dramatized actions provide the shape and are themselves the intention of the work.

Consider the poet's confident use of forms. For Milton, all forms—even conventional forms, such as the Nativity story—seem to have a truth. (Donne, by contrast, finds it necessary to grapple with truth, any truth, and in dubious battle.) The outer form of the ode blazons its "publication": an explicit use of genre—ode, hymn—always gives a poem a public dimension, an awareness of a tradition and a public for that tradition. But the ode's more significant and inner form lies in the progression of the poet's actions, addressing an audience, apostrophizing, narrating, contemplating, juxtaposing forms (fulfillment of pagan time, fulfillment of Christian time) with little anxiety as to their inherent truth. Paradoxical as it seems, my point is that action freed from formal considerations is the principle of form in this poem, whereas with the Donne poem the principle is action chained to formal considerations.

Outer and inner form are one in their public nature. In Milton we observe the poet in a clearly definable role: he is not all men, nor that "I" through which Donne seeks to become all men, but a public poet, a Christian rhetor—an imaginative construct, like the poem itself. That a poet would assume an explicitly public role was still somewhat extraordinary in this period, when poets preferred a certain shyness or coyness, transmitting their poems among friends or to a coterie, or offering their poems as acts of private communication, as Donne did (except with the two anniversary poems), or at the most playing the public role of cavalier-poet, as Waller did. Perhaps it was Spenser of the *Epithalamion* and the *Prothalamion* who pointed the way Milton was to follow. In this poem, at least we see Milton clearly emerge, early in his career, with a poetic ethos that is overtly public and explicitly persuasive. Later, when he placed this poem first in his collected edition of 1645, he offered a clear signal to the public that in this poem he had found his role, his voice, one he was to use with some modulation throughout his major works.[30] The point of "The Nativity Ode" became for Milton that action the poem still performs, to make us hear his uniquely prophetic voice. I find neither overweening pride nor vanity in this intention. The urgency as well as the difficulties of getting that voice heard provide, as we have earlier suggested, a context for the *Areopagitica* and for reading it as self-advertisement.

Our topic in this section is discursive form. *Discursive form,* as I noted earlier, means any verbal experience whose shape we can recognize (a rhyme scheme, an exordium, stories of Christ's birth and death, an argument, a comparison, a poem). When dealing with these verbal forms, we have also had to recognize the presence of intangible forms, certain attitudinal or actional configurations: we become aware of the shape and purpose of Donne's emotions in the "Goodfriday" poem, and of Milton's actions in the ode. Moreover, intention seems allied with discursive form, whether tangible or intangible, particularly when we think of intention as both a *saying* and a *doing.* Thus, in speaking of discourse, we have become involved in the use of a concept not unlike that complicated use of *form* in the seventeenth century, where its meaning ranged from tangible shape to human soul. Whether in rhetoric or in philosophy, *form* was usually allied with intention, end, or final cause—but, as was suggested, significant differences, both in rhetorical practice and in philosophical thought, lay in the extent to which form was believed to be separable from *matter.*

So much by way of summary. A related subject deserves summarizing, too, before we proceed: our initial analytical instruments of form, juxtaposition and perspectives by incongruity.

There are two basic forms of juxtaposition, as the poems we have examined suggest. Like may be posed with unlike, wherein dissimilarities are emphasized in order to heighten those few similarities that might be possible. For example, a soul is imagined to be a heavenly sphere; these two seem vastly unlike, except that the soul is *meant* to be perfect, while the sphere, by being circular, *is* perfect, and the soul is meant to be guided by intelligence while the sphere (at least in one convention) is so guided. In Donne, it is dissimilarity that reaches us first, as if the speaker were most aware of an incoherent world, in which truth had to be pieced out of contraries and otherness.

The other basic form of juxtaposition is the posing of like with like, sometimes for purposes of contrast. For example, the two silences in the ode are superficially alike, though their differences (hushed anticipation, stricken dumbness) are greater by far. The mind is neither strained to construct a phylum in which these silences may be classed nor awed at the differences between them. The mind is not snared by forms. Too, like may be posed with like because one adumbrates or is a type of the other: Hercules prefigures Jesus (cf. stanza XXV).

Donne's juxtapositions almost always involve contraries, or perspectives by incongruity. The juxtaposed elements do not seem to belong together, and a considerable amount of mental contortion and ingenuity are required, on our part as well as Donne's, to make them fit—often we discover later, as we do in the "Goodfriday" poem, that whether the elements fit together or not, their emotional effects are the same. Milton's juxtapositions presuppose a coherence shared with his reader: the juxtaposed elements have a relationship that does not need to be argued for and that can be assumed. In the "Nativity" poem, the coherence lies in the poet's and the implied reader's view of time. The light that appeared at Christ's birth dividing the darkness is the light that appeared at the moment of the world's creation and that will reappear at the moment of the world's dissolution. It is also the light sought through the poem's creation, as the poet looks backward and forward and prepares his heart to face the dawn of Christmas, 1629. In Donne's poem we are continually released from some forms—such as the soul / sphere juxtaposition—into an emotion whose shape is embodied by the total poem; thus, we are never released from form.[31] In Milton's poem we are never caught up in form to begin with but continually proceed through forms to the actions they embody, the actions of the poet-prophet. Thus, critical formalism, which received tremendous impetus in our day from a resurgence of interest in Donne's poetry, would seem well founded, for Donne keeps us where the formalist thinks we should be kept, within the form of the poem itself. Milton takes us outside the text, to join in another fictive creation, the poet-prophet. But I shall suggest, at the end of this book, that it is Milton's poetry that is genuinely formalistic.

My views are, of course, enforced by my own juxtapositions and incongruous perspectives. As we juxtapose Milton with Donne, and look at either from the other incongruous perspective, differences between the two, although they are only differences in degree, are sharpened into contrasts. I have already mentioned certain formal contrasts. In the next section I shall try briefly to take our study one step beyond the formal, into contrasts in the kinds of thinking the discourse of each represents. Again, we shall find the differences are largely matters of degree—but in these posited contrasts we shall find the final vestiges of humanism's unique mode of thought.

Janus Academicus

"The Nativity Ode" reminds all critics that a discourse has a history and exists in time, even for the poet: Milton, too, saw its meaning and significance in a broader if not different light in 1645 than he could have in 1629. I have not tried simply to dismiss questions concerning the critical pitfalls of historicism or relativism in revisiting Donne and Milton. I have tried, rather, to insist on hermeneutical perspectives that would not have been unknown to them, entranced as men of that time were with print and the survivability it gave discourse. A poem or a speech, if printed, outlives its moment and audience and yet remains within its occasion as well.

The critical paradox inheres, to a certain extent, in Milton's advice to become a "contemporary of time." But the paradox itself is best captured in another emblem, also in Milton. Reading and interpreting seem by their very nature Janus-faced, necessarily so, in the sense of looking before and after. When we *read* we anticipate the completion of something, for we assume the thing we read has a completeness, and we acquire certain expectations as well, such as those provoked by suspense or the movement of argument or the patterning of prosody. As we anticipate completion and acquire expectations, we also carry with us the memory of what has been accomplished in the work so far. (St. Augustine, we shall see, expressed this phenomenon eloquently.) When we *interpret* we look at the work as a unit in the writer's career, again looking before and after, and as a unit created perhaps centuries ago but still somehow eventful within our own moment as well. Even our critical writing is suffused with eventfulness and presentness: in this or that passage, we say, Donne "argues. . . ," "claims . . . ," "uses . . ."—as if the action were revisitable, not only in our time but through the time it takes us to read the "passage" itself.

Moreover, both of my earlier, always overlapping approaches can now collapse into the Janus emblem. Janus is himself a juxtaposition, of two directions, and this Roman god of doors and gates, of beginnings, of setting forth suggests multiple, even incongruous perspectives, looking backward and forward. For the writings of Donne and Milton, the emblem is meaningful and complex.

In particular, Janus is significant in two major ways for the critical work of this book: the temporal one just noted, and an analytical one involved with rhetoric as a mode of thought. In proceeding toward the second, it might be wise to note the way in which the temporal significance alone controverts certain modern attitudes. Partly because the Janus idea—as in *Janus-faced*—seems to stand in an uncertain relation to truth, as does *rhetoric,* these words mean, for some of us, deceitful and "two-faced." But in this we are perhaps being misled by our own retrospectivity. Renaissance emblematic traditions reveal quite a different attitude. For example, Cesare Ripa's *Iconologia* pictures a dramatic contrast between being two-faced, which is *fraud,* and being of two minds, which can be *prudent* (see Figures 1 and 2). Only the latter is the true Janus, and its significance of "prudence" is, as suggested earlier, dependent upon giving each face a temporal aspect: one is time past, the other time future. In a Florentine coin (see frontispiece), the temporal aspect is depicted by showing one face old, the other young. The juxtaposition suggests a lesson in prudent behavior: to the present, the past brings precedents and the future offers consequences. Titian, whose *Allegory of Prudence* was identified by Panofsky, turned the Janiform into an explicit representation of Ciceronian *prudentia* (see Figure 3), showing the present (intelligence) between the past (memory) and the future (foresight).[32] Related in pattern and inherent in the Janiform conception itself is yet another kind of thought, which Milton captures precisely in the word he applies to the heads of Janus, *"controversal."* It is a word that also, of course, captures a dominant characteristic of the age of Donne and Milton. But it is a word, too, that is as Ciceronian as *prudence* and that, further, denotes the single most important concept in humanist rhetoric.

It has become a commonplace to say that controversy was a way of living and a way of perceiving in the English Renaissance, that people then lived amidst so much controversy (the agon out of which our modern age was born) that it became a mode of thought and a means of shaping discourse. Though the matter is more divisive, as I shall suggest, and much more specific, nonetheless such a view gives Donne's argumentativeness a wider causality than his training in casuistry and the law, and gives Milton's ostensibly adversarial poems *(Paradise Regained, Samson Agonistes)* a greater context than his rhetorical education and experience as a revolutionary. Controversies there were indeed: between sciences and the arts, the religious and the secu-

Figure 1. Fraud. From Cesare Ripa, *Iconologia* (Rome, 1603), p. 174.

lar, the monarchy and popular representation, even on the most abstract level between the uniform and the individual (later to be represented in tensions between the "classical" and the "romantic").

But *controversy,* or *controversia,*[33] is a technical term in rhetoric, one that is perfectly expressed in the Janus emblem. For it too means, essentially, *turned at once in opposing ways,* signifying debate, division, contest, trial. *Controversia* presupposes a question in contention, one with (at least) two sides, and anyone who would think controversially must give some thought to *both* sides. Two directions are always implied, such as *pro* and *contra,* or affirmative and negative, or prosecution and defense. But the directions exist simultaneously—as in the

Figure 2. Prudence. From Cesare Ripa, *Iconologia* (Rome, 1603), p. 416.

heads of Janus, a simultaneously dual directionality that, as Milton
perceived, signifies a certain mode of thought in intellectual combat.
Unlike prudence, dependent not so much on two directions in *time* as
on two directions in *arguments,* this mode of thought is, I believe,
thoroughly humanist. As a mode of thought, *controversia* belongs
within *inventio,* the first of rhetoric's five traditional parts: often called
"prewriting" by modern composition teachers, *inventio* is the means
whereby arguments are discovered, whether one is reading or getting
ready to compose a discourse.

In ancient rhetorical *inventio, controversia* was primarily associated
with probable matters, questions that could not be resolved with any
degree of certainty. For these matters *controversia* became a means

Figure 3. *Allegory of Prudence,* Titian's triple portrait of himself, Orazio Vecellio, and Marco Vecellio. Reproduced by courtesy of the Trustees, The National Gallery, London. The trifold temporal aspect gives the portrait the appearance of a Renaissance Janiform (see frontispiece and Figure 2), in which a prudent moderator or *iudex* has been placed between the past and the future or between any oppositional dualities. So viewed, the painting brings the conceptualizing processes in both *prudentia* and *controversia* to a formal completion.

whereby one could arrive at some truth, by judging which side had the better arguments. Of course, for the skeptic *all* matters are, at best, probable matters. Moreover, the very method of controversy—examining, arguing, juxtaposing evidence with contrary evidence, challenging—itself actually extends the purview of the probable, or tends to. The ardent debater wants to question every assertion and holds no truths to be self-evident. It is little wonder that in the history of Western education it was the skeptics, the so-called Academics, who insisted that all students learn how to debate both sides of every question. The educational strategy could foster their philosophical view, for the procedures of debating are themselves productive of controversy as a mode of skeptical thought. In that regard, we might note that war was associated with the *temple* of Janus,[34] and though combat, intellectual combat, is of the essence in rhetoric, to understand humanist thought we must relocate Janus's temple from the Roman forum to Cicero's Academy.

Controversia was taught in logic, or dialectic, as well as in rhetoric, and it makes of both two great arts of disputation. But rhetoric, unlike logic or dialectic, puts the controversy between people, not simply between ideas. Rhetorical controversy is on the earthy level of practical affairs and consequence, not on the ethereal level of metaphysical speculation. And to logic's almost exclusive emphasis on the mind, rhetorical *controversia* restores the body, with its passions and its faculty of imagination. Significantly, humanism itself lasted only so long as rhetorical theories offered instruction in how to think by means of controversy—a change that occurred in England toward the close of the sixteenth century.

It was largely the mentalism and the dogmatism of the scholastics that the humanists abhorred. So they fastened on rhetoric as a surrogate philosophy and welcomed the extensions of its full-bodied controversial thinking into as many questions as possible. "Prove all things; hold fast to the good," St. Paul himself said, in a passage Milton was fond of quoting. Place all things in controversy, and find truth by judging arguments. Truth, for the humanist, for the rhetorician, is always verbal. So is living, for that matter (and here St. Paul is left well behind). All things that are to be proven are thus *in* the *studia humanitatis,* the *bonae litterae,* the "literary culture" that the humanists sought to promulgate, the world of the probable.

That world is in action in Donne, more in his early poems than in his mature discourse, and more generally than in Milton. Donne in his sermon and poem does indeed *sound* more nonhumanist than Milton in his speech and poem. The former is pessimistic, the latter optimistic—which may only be another way of noting Donne's comparative skepticism. But it is that skepticism—itself inhering in and fostering the world of the probable—that partly makes Donne more the humanist. For Donne the only available truth frequently lies in our means of composing language about it (here his skepticism became compounded, for, as we have seen, he could be too diffident—in nonhumanist ways—about the efficacy of language, of all human instruments). For Milton truth was somewhat more readily available (here his optimism became compounded, for at times he seemed certain that immutable truth was within the grasp of human apprehension).

All these statements, however, express extreme positions, and do so too soon. Perhaps it will suffice to say at this point, as we did at the outset, that Donne's *practice* is humanist, as Milton's *pronouncements* are. Consequently, the latter articulates principles that help uncover the strategies of the former. Indeed, one of Milton's special powers was to raise humanist ideas to the level of eloquence, as in his call to open now the temple of Janus, with his two controversial faces. For the present, that call well expresses perhaps the only sure point reached in this study.

II

Rhetoric in Controversy,
and Vice Versa

In all human decisions and actions there is always a reason for doing the opposite of what we do, for nothing is so perfect that it does not contain a defect. Nothing is so evil that it does not contain some good, just as nothing is so good that it does not contain some evil. This causes many men to remain inactive, because every tiny flaw disturbs them. They are the overconscientious, awed by every minute detail. That is no way to be. Rather, having weighed the disadvantages of each side, we should decide for the one that weighs less, remembering that no choice is clear and perfect in every respect.

[Francesco Guicciardini, Recordo #213, ca. 1530]

The ironist is essentially *impure,* even in the chemical sense of purity, since he is divided. He must deprecate his own enthusiasms, and distrust his own resentments. He will unite waveringly, as the components of his attitude, "dignity, repugnance, the problematical, and art."

[Kenneth Burke, *Counter Statement,* 1931]

Erasmus

Lawyers, more than clergy or the religious generally, sparked humanism, fanned it into flames, and kept it going. Many of the leading humanists in both Italy and England were trained in civil law. The movement itself, moreover, was fueled by the revived work of that ancient lawyer, Cicero. But transmission of the flame was the achievement of the monk Erasmus, who believed that humanism illuminated a certain *modus vivendi* not incompatible with Christianity.

On a trip across the Alps, Erasmus began to compose the first document we are to examine. Document is a misnomer; poetry might be equally extreme but less inexact. For Erasmus saw himself as conveying the benefits of literature—*bonae litterae*—to northern intellectuals, and by the phrase he meant the reading of ancient pagan poets and playwrights, and even a philosopher or two, along with learning grammar and rhetoric as well as Greek and Hebrew (knowledge of Latin was assumed). *Moria*—as Erasmus referred to his discourse *The Praise of Folly* (whose Greek title is *Moriae Encomium*)—reflects the tone and range of his educational reform. Significantly, *Moria* is in the form of a Latin oration, a species of the classical genus epideictic, or demonstrative, which also includes such public performances as Donne's funeral oration. Like its author and the humanism he transmitted, the *Moria* is ambiguous, formally complex, and *vocal* in the best sense—that is, poetic.

The *Moria* is spoken by a woman named Folly. She is an embodiment of a kind of muse or other traditionally female and therefore nonrational spirit. She appears in academic garb but wearing a fool's cap, with ears and bells (at least, as Holbein has represented her in drawings that accompany many editions), and her audience, like Erasmus's, is learned men.

Erasmus saw humanism as an intellectual enterprise, a movement to be carried on by the learned elite: at the outset there was nothing democratic in humanism, nor anything specifically designed to benefit the common man. The classic spirit was to be introduced not among all the people but among those upper classes who already had Latin. Erasmus's plan was to infuse their learning with certain ancient, fundamentally literary attitudes; within the circle of the learned elite, he would—as Huizinga put it—make "current the classic spirit."[1]

Erasmus was no popularizer, that is, and of course he was no Luther, either. The reform he proposed was extraordinarily subtle and consisted mainly in the adoption of certain attitudes, fully represented by the humorous character of Folly. For some members of his audience, Erasmus may have made a tactical error in presenting his subject ironically, through giving it a ludic treatment. The work has not been widely understood. The clergyman Dorp, for example, who had only a partial understanding of the work, felt compelled to reject it. But the lawyer More grasped the work fully and treasured it. So far as we are concerned, the ludic treatment, which as we shall see is rhetorically essential to Erasmus's thesis, may actually be the source of the work's ongoing readability. "For only when humor illuminated that mind did it become truly profound," states Huizinga, perhaps somewhat unfairly. Humor made the work unique—"in the *Praise of Folly*," Huizinga continues (p. 78), "Erasmus gave something that no one else could have given to the world"—and in that uniqueness it continues to find readers, and continues to appeal to us as something other than a mere relic from the past.

Humor, the ludic spirit in the work, is its whole point and, if humor is the cause of the work's immortality, it is also the cause of some readers' bafflement, certainly among Erasmus's intended audience. To make the humor artfully plain, Erasmus relied on certain tactics such as the use of a mask, a frame provided by the voice of Erasmus himself, and the conventions of the encomium; these are meant to provide a distance. However, these tactics blur and at times become opaque, and thus the distancing is highly variable. Some of Folly's opinions are extreme, and easily dismissable. But some are close to Erasmus's values. Trying to figure out what to do about the distancing and what to make of those arguments that seem more trenchant than dismissable will utterly baffle some readers, especially those who insist upon clarity, coherence, and consistency—and who are most in need of the very reform Erasmus seeks through Folly to work. Yet he knew he could not reach those readers whose ears, as he describes them, "admit nothing but propositions, conclusions, and corollaries"—philosophy rather than literature. But the work is not a tactically simple one even for those of us whose ears are not stuffed with philosophy. For example, the conclusion of the work, where the tone becomes somewhat less ludic and more earnest, advances a value that is not only antiliterary but anti-intellectual. "Simplicity" is Folly's word for the value, and if advanced it would rid the world of the very thing—literacy—on which humanists were staking their careers.

In the best modern translation of the work, Clarence H. Miller points out that "no other brief, integral work of Erasmus condenses the humanists' program for educational, religious, and theological reform better than the *Folly,* especially if we read it in conjunction with Erasmus's defensive letter to Dorp and More's even longer, more profound defense of the *Folly* and Erasmus's projected Greek New Testament (both composed in 1515)."[2] But as a document offering a condensed version of the humanists' reform, the *Moria* is less significant, I would suggest, than it is as a kind of poem embodying certain attitudes, as I mentioned earlier, attitudes that motivate humanist reform and that would, eventually, crumble walls where Erasmus proposed to put doors and windows. In that latter regard, Huizinga (p. 52) has made a similar point about Erasmus's *Enchiridion,* which advanced the doctrine of Christian liberty: "Erasmus did not apply it [liberty] here in a sense derogatory to the dogmatics of the Catholic Church; but still it is a fact that the *Enchiridion* prepared many minds to give up much that he still wanted to keep." To anticipate a point I shall make later, the *Moria,* like all humanist discourse, has "voice," it presents a character in action; in this case, as in most, the character is full of contraries and inconsistencies involved in a lively speaking situation. Revealing these contraries and inconsistencies was as necessary to humanist reform as it was ultimately fatal to humanism generally.

Erasmus called the *Moria* not only an encomium but also a *jeu d'esprit,* a declamation, a satire. The work is all these things, just as the speaker is Erasmus and a woman, an academic and a fool, a muse and an orator. Like many works with the greatest potential for being misunderstood, it is ironic. It used indirection before a learned world many of whose members were deeply fearful that their integrity and professionalism, not to say their prerogatives, were threatened by the slightest deviance from orthodoxy. But irony and indirection are marks of the very attitudes Erasmus wished to demonstrate, all of which in turn have their source in that Janus-like habit of mind called *controversia,* or controversial thinking. Imagine a continuum: black-and-white thinking, or either-or thinking (either he means it or he doesn't, either he's for us or against us) is at one end, true humanist *controversia* is at the other. Only the latter allows for division, even self-division, without destruction—or it should. Only the latter can be undogmatically anti-dogmatic. But the communication of these attitudes is complex and risky, and the central interpretive problem in reading the *Moria,* whether in our century or in Erasmus's, is intention.

Let us approach the question of intention first by using one of Erasmus's favorite avenues, *ad fontes,* or return to the sources.

In July 1509, Erasmus left Rome to return to England. Stimulated by his talks with the Italian humanists and angered by his contact with the Church establishment, he began composing the *Moria.* The idea was suggested by the name of his closest friend and intellectual ally in England, Thomas More. So much Erasmus tells us in his prefatory letter. Obviously, there seems from the outset no intention to *impugn* folly, this More-ia. Rather, as Erasmus notes in his letter, his intention was to adopt a favorite stance of More's, that of Democritus, the laughing philosopher, who made the only response possible to man's incorrigible foolishness. Too, Erasmus was deeply concerned—this he tells us not in his letter but in other documents, some of which we shall review later—about the paganism in Italian humanism; nonetheless, he was convinced that rightly used humanism could restore a fuller and deeper Christianity, which he claimed is the intention pervading all his works, the *Moria* in particular.

Erasmus completed the encomium at More's home in London. It was published first in 1511, in an unauthorized edition. Then Erasmus revised and augmented the work in seven separate editions from 1512 to 1532. Although the first English translation was published in 1549, the intention itself is left somewhat unfulfilled if the work is not read in Latin, partly because it was directed, as was much of the humanist educational reform, toward a graceful use of that language.[3] There is, moreover, no document in the early sixteenth century—at least, no document that continues to be read and valued—that makes such an extensive use of *punning.* The title itself is a pun; the work praises folly and is also a *praise* spoken by Folly. English, regardless of the grace and accuracy of the translation, cannot capture the puns throughout the oration. The work shows the surprising plasticity of Latin (surprising, at least, to those of us who learned the language centuries after the later humanists killed it off). Too, the work takes flights into Greek and at one point into Hebrew—appropriately, considering Erasmus's insistence that knowledge of these three languages is essential to a humanist study of the Scriptures. The important letter to Dorp might be considered formally a part of the discourse. From the first the *Moria* provoked an outcry: the learned Erasmus was shaking the very foundations of learning. The ones who cried loudest were those, like Martin Dorp, who either did not see or could not appreciate the irony of the work, and so read it all too literally. Erasmus's answer to Dorp (1514) was printed with most of the major editions of the *Moria* during Erasmus's lifetime.

Let us now attempt an analysis of the work itself. Any analyst might wish that Folly would stand still, but she will not. She cannot. She turns this way and that. She laughs and gesticulates (at one point makes an obscene gesture); in short, to use a word we have lost, she *tergiversates*. Her relation to Erasmus is the crucial point. It is he who controls the form she so blithely liquidates and negotiates and who could make the irony stable. "Moriae Encomium," Erasmus announces in Greek on the title page, and then continues in Latin, "id est Stultitiae laudatio." But Folly herself cannot resist cutting "the rhetoricians of our times" who sprinkle some Greek among their Latin to show that they are bilingual—a characteristic they share with the horseleech (p. 14), which her contemporary science claimed had two tongues. The author's name, many title pages announce, is "Desiderius Erasmus Roterodamus." Later, Folly pokes fun at authors whose "full names with all three parts are there to be read on all the title pages—especially when those names are foreign and sound like the strange words of a magician's spell" (p. 83). And in the center of this work, whose artificiality is heightened by a frame in which Erasmus speaks in his own voice first to Thomas More and last to Martin Dorp, Folly (Erasmus's all but transparent mask) proclaims, "Nature hates disguises, and whatever has not been spoiled by artifice always produces the happiest results" (p. 52). The work flouts the reader's tendency to turn complex irony into simple either-or thinking. And readers who do so miss the work's most central point.

Because Folly will not stand still, the only way to reproduce the work's form—and capture its point—is to read it aloud, even in English. The elusiveness of the tone diminishes when the liveliness of the work is preserved in a form that conveys, as does Folly herself, an evanescent and self-indulgent mood. To attempt to outline the work is an exercise in futility, like trying to track the flight plan of a bee.

Ironically, a modern editor of the *Moria* who has contributed significantly to our knowledge of Renaissance rhetorical theory has provided an outline of the work that only substantiates the preceding observation.[4] The simplest outline is best.[5] Folly, like Donne in the works we have touched on, uses form with no notion that it will capture truth and, like Milton in other works we have touched on, continually retreats from an occupation with form to direct attention to ethos. In that latter regard, it is noteworthy that Erasmus himself grouped the *Moria* among those works of his "which contribute to the building of character."[6]

There are, in effect, two exordia. The first is Erasmus's dedication to More in a prefatory letter. The second is the opening of Folly's oration, after Erasmus announces, "Stultitia loquitur." Both exordia attempt to clarify intention. Erasmus attempts to do so by placating the reader who will be offended by his levity: he points out that he is simply following a tradition set long ago by classical poets and playwrights. But he cautions that the true delight of his work lies in his effort to treat a trifle in a way that is not itself trifling: "my praise of folly is not altogether foolish" (p. 4). Folly's exordium claims that she has only one intention, to praise herself. And in this she will follow the sophists. Just as Erasmus will follow the tradition of poets and playwrights, Folly herself will follow the tradition of ancient rhetoricians—not just any ancient rhetoricians but the sophists, the most maligned of the bunch, who have been assigned to perdition in the history of rhetoric by philosopher-rhetoricians such as Aristotle and Plato. The need for her praise is simple, she asserts: she's been neglected. So have the sophists. And, in view of her benefits to mankind, *somebody* should praise her. *Divisio* should come next. But Folly declines to divide, again for a simple reason: the oration is about herself and she cannot be either divided or defined. After all, she is there before us, speaking plainly, simplicity itself: "I never wear disguises, nor do I say one thing and think another" (p. 13). (Folly's declining to divide herself is, thematically, significant. Keeping the two exordia before us, we see that she is a division of Erasmus himself; we shall return to this point later.) Finally, she establishes her ethos with her genealogy, upbringing, and companions. "Genus, educatiõem, & comites, audistes."

Obviously, with the use of summaries, sign-posting, and transitions, Folly has employed *some* division and definition. Indeed, the body of her oration may itself be divided into two broad parts, the benefits she confers or the claims she makes in her behalf and the substantiation of those claims through examples and authorities. Nonetheless, the progression through the argument is almost freely associational. For example, the benefit "never to think" leads to talking about "eternal youth," which leads to talking of gods—then back to mortal man and the two sexes. The very first claim Folly offers is "life itself"—that is, the folly in the sex act, in making a baby: the wise man must come to Folly if he wants to be a father. The bawdiness of the jokes and innuendoes here contrasts with the conclusion of Folly's speech, where she speaks with not quite the same degree of irony concerning religious ecstasy.

All Folly's benefits may be summed up in a single word: illusion. It is illusion that relieves the "taedium vitae." It is illusion that is the source of all our pleasure. The need for illusion shows that our life is a deception, a disguise. All human affairs "have two aspects quite different from each other."

> Hence, what appears "at first blush" (as they say) to be death, will, if you examine it more closely, turn out to be life; conversely, life will turn out to be death; beauty will become ugliness; riches will turn to poverty; notoriety will become fame; learning will be ignorance; strength, weakness; noble birth will be ignoble; joy will become sadness; success, failure; friendship, enmity; what is helpful will seem harmful . . .   [p. 43]

But this double nature is a given, not a cause for despair or nihilism, nor a reason to join the stoics. It is a reason, though, carefully and self-consciously to maintain the illusion—a game the philosophers believed the sophists were quite good at.

Throughout the oration it becomes clear that Folly's chief enemies are the stoics,[7] by extension all philosophers or theologians who deny the fundamental human condition, that successful living depends upon illusions or that man is one part mind to nine parts body, who in effect offer merely an illusion but in the name of truth. The extreme rationalism and the airy abstractions of schools of philosophy and theology, best represented by the stoics, are "useless in the ordinary affairs of life" (p. 36). Man cannot live by reason alone. Thus, the adversaries are, on the one hand, Folly as a sophist with her friends the skeptics ("the Academics, the least arrogant of the philosophers,"

p. 71) and, on the other, the stoics and other rationalists and literalists, serious men. The battle would seem to be between the antidogmatic and the dogmatic; but, as Folly would be the first to perceive, even antidogmatism can become a dogma, and therefore the best philosophical position toward all dogma is diffidence. However, to pursue this point would amount to unravelling Erasmus's purposefully intricate thread. The only point that needs stressing here is the remoteness of stoicism and the nearness of skepticism to the saving attitude that the *Moria* dramatizes.

In order to advance her case, Folly must also admit the nearness of *Philautia,* her closest companion, self-love. Self-love is a Christian sin, true; but worry on this score is neutralized by Folly's ostensible simplicity—and by her pre-Freudian argument that love of others may not be possible without love of self. The simplicity of calling self-love a sin is overwhelmed by Folly's own simplicity. Again, as throughout, certitude is the bête noire, properly so for an adversary of rational order.

But Folly, among her hundreds of tergiversations, does not completely abandon order. In fact, she makes frequent references to order, all to emphasize intention and tone.[8] And, for the same purpose, she will divide. One division in particular is crucial so far as Folly's conclusion is concerned. There are, Folly asserts, two kinds of madness: that which is sent up from the underworld and that which is a "pleasant mental distraction" (p. 57). Before we reach her conclusion, however, she takes us through a description of the latter (including different sorts of delusions and illusions) to the confirmation of her claims. This confirmation, we noted earlier, consists of various examples and authorities. The examples are divided into individuals and classes, such as grammarians, poets, rhetoricians (who belong to Folly's party, "though they do indeed put up a false front by their specious alliance with the philosophers"; p. 81), lawyers, dialecticians, philosophers and theologians (most of whom, as noted, offer only illusions while claiming to offer truth), "religious" and "monks" and preachers, kings and courtiers, popes, cardinals, bishops, and priests. Most of these are fools without knowing they are; the notable exceptions are the rhetoricians, who know they are fools because they actually incorporate folly into their art by insisting upon the persuasiveness of laughter. Of all these individuals and classes, it is, as we might

74

suppose, the theologians who receive the brunt of Folly's own barbed laughter. Folly largely cites authorities from Scripture to substantiate her case, and this discussion inexorably leads her back to the theologians and their absurd warping of the holy writ, especially the gospel. This, in turn, ultimately leads Folly to her supreme example (here as in all parts of her speech, the lines set up in a division are seldom maintained, so that having proceeded from "example" to "authorities," Folly blithely shuttlecocks from one to the other). Her final example is the kind of madness that most particularly marks the Christian religion. Here she moves onto dangerous ground indeed.

This madness would seem to be part of the previous division. The previous division, however, was made largely for the sake of talking about "pleasant mental distraction." But this concluding condition is more than a distraction. It is a kind of madness associated with Christian piety and utterly inaccessible to the ordinary man. To begin with, Folly remarks, "you see how those first founders of religion were remarkably devoted to simplicity and bitterly hostile to literature" (p. 132). This observation, considering that Folly is a spokeswoman for the learned Erasmus, whose life was spent in resuscitating literary education, would seem to move the discussion onto the level of lying and duplicity, as if Folly were voicing opinions directly contrary to Erasmus's. But here, as elsewhere, the matter is not so simple. The tone changes. Indeed, the final third of the oration becomes increasingly serious, leading to the ultimate folly, which is religious ecstasy. Nonetheless, this final matter is perfectly (to use Folly's word) consistent (which is neither her word nor her admitted value) with the entire argument: religious ecstasy is irrational, involves the total person—heart, mind, body, soul, passions, and reason—and cannot be reduced to syllogism and dogma. This was the part of the work that most offended the theologians, and caused Erasmus to rise to Folly's defense in his letter to Dorp:

> Read the passage again, I beg you, and pay close attention to the stages of the argument and the gradations of language leading up to the statement that heavenly happiness is a species of madness. Also, notice the words I use to express that idea. You will see that, far from giving any offense, what is written there would actually delight truly pious ears. [p. 157]

As for my development of it, is there anything at all which is not expressed with piety and prudence and with even greater reverence than is suitable to Folly? But in this passage I preferred to be a little negligent of decorum than to fall below the dignity of the subject matter. I preferred to offend against rhetoric than to violate piety.   [p. 160]

Indeed, Erasmus's letter to Dorp is a more extensive peroration than the one Folly herself provides. Hers is largely a refusal to provide a peroration—since the purpose of such a device is to summarize the speech for the refreshment of the auditors' memory and she does not seek auditors who *have* memories. Folly, as we noted earlier, is meant to be a mood, an evanescent one but healing. "Therefore," she says in her famous conclusion, "Quare ualete, plaudite, uiuite, bibite, Moriae celeberrimi Mystae"—"Therefore, farewell, clap your hands, live well, drink your fill, most illustrious initiates of Folly" (p. 138). The final Latin address may be rendered literally as "Fool's celebrated priests." Even when that English rendering is heard rather than seen, it indicates some of the plasticity of the language throughout, as if we were being called first fools, then Fool's servants. The final Latin word indicates, too, the plasticity of Folly's intention, now praise, now initiation into holy mysteries.

Earlier I referred to the work as being indirect. Perhaps now we might think of that indirection as being something like the action of buckshot: some hit the mark directly but none exactly *miss*. Or, as Erasmus says in his letter to Dorp, Folly's critique "was stated in such a way as to apply to everyone and therefore to no one, unless somebody should willingly claim it for himself" (p. 146). As noted, this letter might be considered a second peroration. But the reader does not progress very far before wishing the letter had some of Folly's simplicity For example, Erasmus claims that he used Folly as a persona because he had set out to do "something improper": "just as Plato's Socrates covers his face when he proclaims the praises of love, so too I assumed a mask to play this part" (p. 145). The comparison is misleading. Socrates later in that dialogue *(Phaedrus)* repudiates the opinions he uttered behind the mask, but Erasmus in his letter to Dorp affirms several of Folly's points—in particular, as we noted, her point about religious ecstasy. And *that* is a curious affirmation. Erasmus throughout his life insisted he was a man of peace, but the peace

76

that the *Moria* offers is not the conventional Christian one—which was usually a dull sort of contemplative homeostasis. *Moria*'s peace is, instead, a divine transport. Erasmus, of course, was no mystic. Nonetheless, he saw in mysticism a way to Christianize Folly's point: religion is too "contaminated with Aristotle" (p. 155); Christ and the Apostles really did "have a certain infirmity, a sort of concession to our emotions, which, by comparison with the eternal and pure wisdom of God might seem something less than wise" (p. 157). To return to a true Christianity—his only purpose, he insists—we must, to use a modern phrase, get back in touch with our feelings, to lead that more abundant life that Christ offered. And the way to do that is through *bonae litterae,* through literary culture.

But literary culture, as the *Moria* makes abundantly clear, leads to controversial thinking that is stressful to established dogma—or, better, to the established dogmatic. That shift in tone at the conclusion of the *Moria* and its ostensibly simple, direct praise of religious ecstasy are efforts to Christianize controversial thinking, to show that *controversia* does not necessarily strain dogma to the point of shattering it or to the point of adopting atheism (in a dogmatic age the only conceivable alternative to Christianity). That effort to challenge dogma, to confront staid rationalism with unstaid emotionalism, all without turning one's back on the Scriptures or on the Catholic Church, pervades Erasmus's writing. If anywhere, it is in his direct, less literary writing, such as his later arguments with Luther, that his controversial thinking comes close to stretching the limits of belief, and to requiring a choice. In his dispute with Luther on the nature of the will, Erasmus constructs an argument and makes a move, both of which are typical of the aforementioned effort:

> . . . I have always preferred playing in the fairer field of the muses, than fighting ironclad in close combat. In addition, so great is my dislike of assertions that I prefer the views of the sceptics wherever the inviolable authority of Scripture and the decision of the Church permit—a Church to which at all times I willingly submit my own views, whether I attain what she prescribes or not.[9]

As I noted earlier, skepticism, folly, and rhetoric are one side of the coin; on the other are stoicism, reason, and philosophy. It is literary culture—humanism, in short—that gives us the coin in the first place, with both of its sides, or so Erasmus thought and hoped. Humanism was to be corrective, expansive, and deeply and broadly Christian.

Erasmus saw clearly that what had happened in Italy in the Quattrocento was not what seemed to be, and to some people still seems to be, merely a scholarly incursion into pagan manuscripts. On the surface, the humanists might not appear terribly threatening to anyone. Their revived Latin grammar and rhetoric seemed only to stimulate philology, resulting in a new purity of style, or ornamental writing, that led to graceful imitations of ancient masters. The reform seemed largely antiquarian in interest—and for many interpreters, including not a few of our own contemporaries, it remained so. Humanism was simply a refined method of editing and teaching the ancient manuscripts. But the enterprise itself and the discourse it offered inculcated an attitude that shattered the dominance of any severe, confined, and limited mode of reasoning. By the very nature of their work, the humanists offered a philosophical alternative. It was not simply that the humanists revived a host of pagan philosophers and poets whose works had to be made acceptable to Christian readers—though that task was never far from their concerns. Nor was it simply that debating both sides of a question was born anew—ancient *controversia* had been formalistically perpetuated in theological dialectics and other Church-infused disputation, and had recently (in the sixteenth century) become dramatically ritualized in one of the Church's most solemn ceremonies with the presence of a "devil's advocate." It was that the work of turning to the past for the sake of augmenting the present placed an emphasis on the practical application of wisdom and scholarship. In reviving rhetoric for the sake of practically applying both wisdom and scholarship, the humanists were offering instruction in a different *controversia,* a mode of thought that is premised on uncertainty and that acknowledges epistemological diversity.

Ad fontes—back to the sources—is what Erasmus called his hermeneutic. His method of interpreting the Scriptures was to make use of historical philology, a neutral enough procedure, it might seem. He would take into consideration all the texts, not only the codices but also the references in the Church fathers, using texts and commentaries, corrections, emendations, and above all superior knowledge of the original languages—Latin, Greek, and Hebrew. Again, the procedure seems hardly revolutionary. The true theological revo-

78

lution, as we shall see shortly, was enunciated in the translation he provided of the New Testament and his commentaries thereon. But the wellsprings of that revolution lay in his method of reading the Scriptures: textual criticism, we would call it today, in both its senses of establishing the authenticity of and interpreting a text. His method of interpretation, as so incisively described by Aldridge, is clearly rhetorical: "One comes nearer to perceiving the sense of Scripture if he considers not only the situation and what is said, but also by whom it is said, to whom it is said, the words that are said, what time, what occasion, what precedes and what follows."[10] This is the rhetorician's view of language, not the view of those theologians whose ears "admit nothing but propositions, conclusions, and corollaries." It is a view that sees discourse as someone's behavior, the action of a character or ethos.

Nowhere are this view and its profound implications more clearly grasped than in Erasmus's Latin translation of St. John 1:1, "In the beginning was the Word," *in principiam erat verbum.* For *verbum* the Greek word was *logos,* but in Erasmus's Latin the word became not *verbum* but *sermo: in principiam erat sermo.* Christ was not a word to be contemplated, as Augustine and most Church fathers had described him. He was, rather, God's oration—word in the sense of an entire speech.[11] In English we can translate *sermo* as "sermon" (our word comes from it) so long as we keep in mind that the message of this sermon can be neither paraphrased nor abstracted; its meaning is itself. What was to be contemplated if anything was not iconographic but actional, Christ's entire life and ministry. *Logos* was not to be objectified but to be regarded as it is in the rhetorical tradition, as the verbal aspect of a speaker's total transaction with an audience. The speaker, in this case, is God, whose oration is Christ, and we are—evermore—the audience.

This view of Christ is broad as well as actional. But, of course, Erasmus's case for the revival of pagan learning, for literary culture, itself required a broader view of the Savior. One way in which Erasmus established that broader view was to argue that Christ drew all things into himself, including not only our passionate natures, such as anger, humiliation, and suffering, but pagan literature as well:

> It was he who willed that the Golden Age in which he had chosen to be born was to be sovereign over all epochs which came

was there literary culture before humanism?

before or followed after; it pleased him that whatever existed in nature should be put to use for increasing the happiness and glory of that time. He himself promised that this should be done: "I, if I be lifted up from the earth," he says, "will draw all unto me." Here it seems to me that he most aptly uses the word *traho,* "I draw," so that one may understand that all things, whether hostile or heathen or in any other way far removed from him, must be drawn, even if they do not follow, even against their will, to the service of Christ.[12]

A further implication is clear: the imitator of Christ—he who has consciously chosen to follow the Savior—must do likewise, and draw all things into himself, acknowledging not simply that good and evil are inextricably mixed in this life but that some truths lurk even in those contrary features of his own personality that he might wish to deny. Folly cannot be divided, but we can, and she is part of us. Erasmus's Christology as well as his efforts to promulgate an expansive literary culture underpin the *Moria*'s intention. Thus, we read that discourse best when we see it as the dramatization of an attitude—a necessarily unparaphrasable and indivisible one:

> If our object is to shield ourselves from being the cause of evils which patently exist, why not heap everything which goes wrong in the lives of mortals on the head of Homer's Ate, just as Agamemnon does, in the same poet, and Jupiter, and just as the common run of Christians do when they blame the devil as the author and instigator of anything they contrive by their own folly? Once we have allowed the opening of a window like this, what is to prevent the rake blaming his youthfulness, the miserly niggard his age, the climber the ways of Fortune, the irascible man his physical constitution?[13]

The quotation is not from the *Moria* but from *The Antibarbarians,* as was the preceding quotation. *The Antibarbarians* is another work by Erasmus that dramatizes the very attitude it seeks to inculcate. But in this case that attitude is much more explicitly and directly aimed at establishing a literary culture. The barbarians are of three sorts: yokels, who know nothing or care nothing for learning; others who scorn the classics as anti- or non-Christian; and finally those who try to revive learning but who have little respect for it or little skill in editing. The second group gets the largest share of criticism. And, significantly, a synonym for all these barbarians is *antirhetoricians*.[14] The learning most in need of revival is literary, and rhetorical.

The work is a discourse among five learned men in the open air, in a setting they acknowledge to be not unlike Plato's Academy. Erasmus himself is one of these men. Though the principal speaker is a man named Batt, all, like Folly, are masks of Erasmus himself. Significantly, Batt is hot-headed, emotional, and contemptuous of the stoics, but he is such a hater of the barbarians that "meeting with them often made him vomit or go hot with rage" (p. 27). Such a character would be the most interesting speaker of the five. But Batt's passionate nature is thematically significant as well, for his arguments, though directed against the antirhetoricians, are accordingly opposed to a life of reason and logic, or to any life that is static and prizes contemplation. Batt's argument in defense of classical learning is a precursor of Milton's in the *Areopagitica*. In both cases, the problem and the solution are the same: error is not evil for it is never unmixed; pagan wisdom, however seductive (and here Batt is more Erasmian than Miltonic), leads to Christ; Christ, in drawing all things to himself, resolves the controversy into utter simplicity (the simplicity that Folly will later praise).

Thus Erasmus had a vision whereby the humanist program, regardless of its pagan overtones, might succeed: "a classical world illuminated with the Christian faith."[15] Within that vision controversial thinking, even skepticism and the contraries of pagan and Christian are not destructive divisions. All meet in infinity—that is, in Christ. Erasmus tried to fuse the pagan and the Christian worlds

> into one by the power of his belief in truth, and that truth was Christ. No form of truth can harm the cause of truth, and all truth is valuable in itself, because truth is one. It would have seemed sufficient to Erasmus to quote the word of Christ, *Ego sum veritas*.[16]

But all meet in a controversial, a rhetorical, view of Christ, as *sermo* not *verbum*.

At the outset of this discussion, I suggested that the *Moria* corresponds to Donne's funeral oration (both are species of the same rhetorical genus); now I have suggested that *The Antibarbarians* corresponds somewhat to *Areopagitica*. But far more dramatic differences

81

remain. Erasmus used masks for his strongest arguments, preferring to remain not exactly aloof but in a position of moderator—a Christ-like position. The Erasmus who appears in both discourses could live in this world in a way that Folly and Batt could not. At least, he thought he could.

Among Erasmus's most painful experiences was the unavoidable confrontation with Luther on the nature of the will. It is in that confrontation that Erasmus says, using a tactic that is death to any debater, "I like moderation best."[17] Luther, with a rather different conception of Christ and man and a totally different hermeneutic, won the battle. As Aldridge puts it,

> Luther appreciated and used the philological method that Erasmus developed from *ad fontes,* but Erasmus' use of the term itself was too broad for Luther, since he considered the Scriptures as the only true source. *Sola Scriptura* was to become the by-word of the Reformation, not the *ad fontes* of Erasmus.
>
> [p. 37]

Erasmus thought he had found that catholic point where all differences dissolve and moderation is possible. But the way *to* that point—and the point itself, Christ as Erasmus saw him—were apparently too broad for most men to travel or imagine. What looks like breadth from one angle appears from another to be a stirring of antagonisms. Late in his life, Erasmus was forced from his always tenuous position of moderation: the world that the humanists themselves stirred up demanded that a man *choose,* and Erasmus, not surprisingly, chose the Church, the whole Church, and nothing but the Church. To try to stand on moderation while at the same time reviving a system of thought that thrives on controversy reflects the paradoxical nature of humanism in its efforts to create breadth within established boundaries, and Erasmus's career shows the inevitable outcome of that stance in that world at that time. But it is his writings that most concern us here.

Erasmus's greatest *theoretical* contribution to rhetoric in England was not a work on argumentation but a work on style, *De duplici copia verborum ac rerum commentarii duo,* first published in 1512. The *Copia* is designed to teach boys abundant Latin style in two ways, through copiousness of expression and through copiousness of thought, or invention. Into the former fall most of the figures of speech, such as metonymy; into the latter fall such methods of analysis as division. The overall purpose of the book is put simply, "to turn one idea into more shapes than Proteus himself is supposed to have turned into."[18] The purpose is fulfilled, abundantly, as when Erasmus shows that the sentence "Your letter pleased me mightily" can be restated in one hundred and fifty different ways, or that "always, as long as I live, I shall remember you" can be restated in two hundred ways. The latter includes "I shall myself depart from the living before More departs from my memory," a variation stimulated not only by Erasmus's close friendship with More but also by the association of More with *mori,* "die." The variation is meaningful, of course, only when the person addressed or thought of is named "More." But the real point is that language is echoic, plastic. Quintilian called language a ball of wax that can be molded into one shape after another. For Erasmus, however, the shapes themselves are associational; they are related to one another in ways caused by the reverberation of words—even in several languages (More, *mori, moria*)—in the mind. Language itself reflects the diversity and variety that is in life, or should be. *Copia* remained one of the single most important works on rhetoric in English education through at least the first half of the sixteenth century—a fact that is less significant, perhaps, than the emergence of the work as the most readily identifiable rhetorical offspring of the father of northern humanism.

Let us at this point summarize the characteristics of that humanism as touched on so far in this discussion. Primary is what I have called controversial thinking. Equally important is what Erasmus calls "literary culture." Both of these elements—the former involving the acknowledgment, even the exploitation, of contraries, the latter involving modes of persuasion that do not depend upon reason alone—do not simply presuppose but delight in a fluid and changeable world of men in action, as in the *Copia,* or the *Moria,* or the *Antibarbarians.* The instability of language was to be revelled in, not fretted over. That language is plastic was shown in puns and in verbal ironies. But this plasticity, this nominalism, was no more cause for despair than the contrarieties of living in a fluid and changeable world. The safeguard against intellectual anarchy, the center that holds the varied and variable world of learning together is Christ, particularly the humanity of Christ, vividly embodying as it does the plan of God (in Genesis) to create man in his own image and likeness and dramatically serving to fuse such contraries as the divine and the mundane, the sacred and the secular, the Christian and the pagan. Of course, Christ himself in the Erasmian view is actional, *sermo* not *verbum*—or, as he calls Christ in the *Ratio,* "Proteus."[19]

This Erasmian Christ is both Proteus and a Moderator, just as Erasmian controversial thinking looks in two directions and yet returns to a mediatory position. In discourse, this thinking produces a strategy of indirection—irony, we might call it, or *via diversa.*[20] Under whatever name, its purpose is to involve the reader, to get the reader's mind to move, to become active, to open to him various alternatives while placing him in a moderating position where, ultimately, superficial differences between alternatives dissolve. Such, moreover, as Elizabeth McCutcheon has shown, is precisely the effect of Thomas More's *Utopia,* as seen best in More's use of the rhetorical figure *litotes* (affirming one matter by denying its contrary—for example, "not unmindful"—a figure that by its nature is Janus-like, or controversial, for it looks in two directions at once):

> the figure becomes, ultimately, a paradigm of the structure and method of the book as a whole, echoing, often in the briefest of syntactical units, the larger, paradoxical and double vision which will discover the best state of the commonwealth in an island called Noplace.[21]

The *Moria* itself begins with a *litotes* that brilliantly sets the tone and stance of the entire work: "I am not unaware of how bad Folly's reputation is, even among the biggest fools of all" (p. 9). The Latin is more effective: "neque enim sum nescia, quam male audiat stultitia etiam apud stultissimos." Folly compounds the effect with her play on the words *stultitia* and *stultissimos,* a rhetorical *polyptoton* (a figure exploiting different forms of the same word), which turns the *litotes* back on itself: Folly is and is not among the biggest fools who are and are not aware. In some discourse—for example, the Anglican prayerbook—*litotes* can be used primarily for emphasis. But in the hands of More and Erasmus, this device can be used for the larger and more profoundly humanist purposes of ambiguity, paradox, irony, and double vision: to acknowledge that most questions have more than one side—and, above all, to get the reader to acknowledge that, too. Such is not an infrequent result when the mind moves to moderate a *litotes,* to reconcile irony, to deal with the overwhelming plasticity of language, or to find meaning in a discourse—or a world—rich with possibility.

Humanism

Humanism was an intellectual movement that had assumed the all but impossible task of expanding man's ideas not so much by reformation as by acknowledging diversity within given forms. For this task the humanists found their appropriate instruments in rhetoric—specifically, in controversial thinking and in literary culture.

Both Erasmus's opening and closing arguments in *The Praise of Folly* illustrate the humanist stance and manner. I have spent some time discussing Folly's final example, religious ecstasy, but her first example—the inescapable foolishness of sex—is an equally clear argument for humanism. Not only is the point of this first example echoed in the last, but this example also serves initially to specify Erasmus's true thesis and opposition.

To begin with, the sex act, because it is not only foolish but picturesquely so, allows Folly to claim that folly is the source of life itself. Without folly there can be no life, no babies. Even a stoic who wishes to become a father must put aside his image of himself as a dispassionate wise man—put aside, that is, what Folly calls his "iron clad principles"—and engage in an act that is emotion-laden and irrational, or, in short, foolish. The stoics, vulnerable on this point, were a synecdoche for the opposition. Erasmus, like Cicero, believed that the stoics were not active, participatory, emotional, or for that matter *imaginative* enough.

Sex is also an application of Erasmus's *ad fontes* principle, this time to life rather than to scholarship. This application is almost literal, for *ad fontes* means "to the sources" or, literally, "to the fountains," and Folly's research takes us right to the genitals. *These* fountains, she knows, will elicit some titters and embarrassed shuffling of feet ("the human race is propagated by the part [of our anatomy] which is so foolish and funny that it cannot be mentioned without a snicker"; p. 18). The subject itself was one that could rattle the theological superstructure by pointing up the difference between life as it is lived and life as it is talked about by philosophers. A fundamental question was blunted: what do we do about the urgent desires of the flesh? The stoical answer—mortify them—became an easy target for the humanists, who could claim that the answer would eventually remove the means whereby life itself is propagated and continued. Indeed, the word *mortify* has death (*mors*) within it. And what do we do about sensation generally? Again, the stoical, traditional, and monastic Christian answer advised mortification. Sensations, after all, belong to the animal, or fleshly, part of our being, and we should follow the lead of the spirit, our rational, immortal souls. But, then, said the humanists, shall we rule out whatever access to wisdom or peace is provided by religious ecstasy? Thus, in Folly's beginning is her end, and vice versa.

However, Erasmus's intention in *The Praise of Folly* is not to rip away illusions. After all, the *Moria* is itself an illusion about illusions. Some are necessary, all are foolish. That is Folly's point, and that is the drama of the work. In this ironical tour de force, Erasmus tries to get man to adopt a more complicated idea about himself, but certainly not at the expense of tossing out the necessarily illusory nature of thought itself. Language was the humanists' material and their stage: a little make-up, a different costume and—lo!—the foolishness of sex reappears as divine ecstasy. Language is as ambiguous as life, and because for the humanists language *is* life, the proposition is self-confirming. Language and life, that is, have a richness, an ambiguity, and a vital illusoriness beyond anything dreamed of in most philosophy and theology.

I began these remarks with a definition of Renaissance humanism, based largely on our examination of Erasmus. In this section, we shall keep that definition in mind as we consider a significant and most recent development in modern studies of humanism: many scholars now equate humanism with the revival of rhetoric. We have seen Folly's thought move in rhetorical—that is, controversial—ways while trying to avoid anarchy at one extreme and dogmatism at the other. And we have noted Erasmus's contribution to rhetorical theory. Indeed, all humanists were teachers of rhetoric or writers on it. That would seem to be their common denominator. Once scholars grasped that simple fact, many disagreements about the essential identity of humanism were somewhat lessened.

But we need to consider further the philosophical implications of the movement's centering on rhetoric. Simply by virtue of rhetoric's nature as a repository of instruction in persuasive strategies—means of jockeying to advantage and scoring points—rhetoric is the least innocent of all humane arts. It may not be *programmatically* subversive. But rhetoric became so when it was viewed, as it was in the Renaissance, as an alternative to traditional modes of thought— especially to scholastic dialectic, which had dominated the intellectual scene for centuries. Rhetoric, even when restored merely for the sake of improved Latinity, could not avoid having philosophical implications. But rhetoric, too, like humanism, insisted not on the reformation of knowledge but on the *use* of *available* knowledge.

Rhetoric as a mode of thought is the subject of this entire chapter, for which the first two sections are largely introductory. The chapter's thesis is this: rhetoric may have failed as an alternative to philosophy, but in its intellectual affinities with the all but impossible task of humanism, rhetoric succeeded in humanism's great desideratum, the artistic creation of adept personhood. That is, rhetoric showed us how, through its controversial mode of thought, to create *voice* on paper, how to create in writing the sense of a person speaking. This in turn fulfilled not the all but impossible task of humanism but a desideratum inherent in it: the self-creation of an effective personality. This desideratum is potentially blasphemous and prideful, of course, and the Augustinians were ready to chastise all who would parody the Creator or who would become occupied with anything, such as art, not directed toward God. But the rhetorical achievements of the humanists, as we shall see in the final section of this chapter, were accomplished not only in spite of the Augustinians but even in spite of themselves. In this section I shall describe certain general intellectual, or philosophical, affinities between humanism and rhetoric—in particular, rhetoric's close alliance with diversity, the very purpose of the humanist intermingling of controversial thinking and literary culture.

Stoicism and Augustinianism were, according to William Bouwsma, "two faces" of humanism in the Italian Renaissance.[22] The stoic "face" held that the universe is governed by reason and order and that man must pattern his own behavior after that serenity. The Augustinian "face" held that philosophy should begin not with the universe but with man himself, and it saw that stoic control over the emotions posited not rationality but a certain inauthenticity: the unemotional man was obviously not a full being. Moreover, for the Augustinian position, ultimate truth "is mysterious, beyond rational comprehension, and therefore first planted in the heart by grace, not discovered by the mind" (Bouwsma, p. 42). The stoic "face" was ra-

87

tional and withdrawn, the Augustinian emotional and engaged. Bouwsma calls these two positions "ideal," for the actual humanist fell midway between the two, at times looking like a stoic, at times like an Augustinian.

Janus again. The twin impulses, we shall see, set a pattern for the later English humanism. The faces are controversial, turned in opposite directions, each with a correlative and acceptable alternative: the *vita contemplativa* and the *vita activa,* the quiet inner search for peace through redemption and the engaged life of religious and political activism. One might think that if rhetoric is of the essence of humanism, the choice would be simple: the *vita activa.* But humanists could not so easily choose between the two. As I remarked earlier, humanists were not reformers—except in the way most pedagogues are, as *in*formers, more nearly, than *re*formers. But the *vita contemplativa* veered inexorably toward stoicism, and the stoics were on the whole too rational, too denying of body and flesh for most humanists. However, the stoics *did* place a premium on man's sufficiency, whereas the Augustinians constantly insisted on man's dependence upon God—a quality that would force most humanists, given the choice, to veer back toward the stoics again.

Stoicism is bloodless, emotionless, and bodiless, for the stoics believed that truth was immanent, and thus had merely to be presented to the mind for the reason to acquiesce and the will to act. Many humanists—Erasmus and Cicero included—attacked the stoics repeatedly on this point. But Augustinianism is equally antagonistic to rhetoric. Neither the stoics nor the Augustinians would allow rhetoric its processes of thought, and without these processes of thought (without *controversia*) both rhetoric and humanism disintegrate. Thus, both faces turn away from the center, and woe to the man who finds himself there—which is the position the humanists tried to hold. At the same time, both faces looked like humanism, the stoic with his emphasis on man's self-sufficiency, the Augustinian with his emphasis on man's body.

It was their particular brand of skepticism that presented the humanists with their many moral and theoretical problems and that in effect kept them in the center I've tried to describe. Skepticism is always a difficult position to maintain, especially in an era when strong commitments are called for. One keeps falling away from skepticism to face in a stoical or Augustinian direction. Cicero had that problem; though Augustinianism wasn't an alternative, he always had difficulty disentangling himself from the stoics. Like all humanists, he did battle with the stoics only to leave himself wide open to cooption by the (in his case, later) Augustinians.

Cicero's brand of skepticism is at the core of humanism, I think. In fact, calling it *Ciceronianism* or even, as both Cicero and Augustine did, *Academicism* might even be preferable, considering the modern connotations of the word *skepticism*. For Cicero's position is not denial or nihilism or atheism, but rather emotional and intellectual diffidence; it is—ideally—the most complex knotting of contraries we can imagine. The Ciceronian Academic can know truth only provisionally; that is, he knows truths, not truth. He must explore each case, like a case at law, anew, proving or disproving charges and reaching a decision based both intrinsically on the merits of the case and extrinsically on whatever prior agreement, such as law, is applicable to the matter. Ciceronians say not that truth does not exist but that it cannot be known with anything like rational certainty. But once truth has been arrived at, discovered—or, as rhetoricians say, "invented"—it can be argued for, tooth and claw, the way lawyers do.

This skepticism is pervaded with some confidence in man's own powers (like stoicism), and once it has arrived at a truth it can urge that truth upon man's will (like Augustinianism). Thus, if humanism has a center, it is a center formed by a joining of these two Janus faces. This is a skeptical observation, and one skeptically expressed perhaps, but I think it represents an important way in which rhetoric (whose *controversia* has been characterized as a "lawyer's logic") and the movement we have for centuries called humanism can be intellectually linked. That modern scholars now acknowledge that linkage is, as I have noted, a recent development. As we began our studies of the Renaissance, even when we were seeking to determine if there *was* a Renaissance, a question existed as to whether a new philosophy of man had arisen in the period. Writers on the subject, notably philosophers and historians, agreed that some *change* had occurred in the period we call the Renaissance. But opinions differed as to the nature and degree of that change—as to whether the Renaissance truly marked a radical shift, particularly along philosophical lines, from the past. Philosophers tended to argue that a radical shift had occurred, while historians held that a continuity existed with mini-renaissances that had occurred in the preceding centuries. It was the philosophers who were first to answer the question, and they talked about radical shifts in man's view of himself, his society, and his traditions.

More than one hundred years ago, Jakob Burckhardt argued that so profound a philosophical change had occurred in man's view of himself that the Renaissance marked a decisive break with the Middle Ages. In Burckhardt's argument, moreover, the philosophical view he described had little to do with the rebirth of rhetoric, which he dismissed simply as "the Greek tongue" that continued to wag long after the passing of Greek culture.[23] Ernst Cassirer continued the Burckhardtian theme and, for many readers, clarified the philosophy associated with the Renaissance as one placing a new emphasis on secularism and individualism.[24] Rhetoric did not enter the picture in any significant way until the writings of our distinguished contemporary philosopher Paul Oskar Kristeller, who was the first to argue for the prominence of rhetoric in the Renaissance and the first to point out that common denominator of which I spoke earlier. But for Kristeller, as for most philosophers, rhetoric could not be a philosophical alternative, for it seemed to be no more than a method, a way of doing something, such as composing or interpreting discourse. Presumably, the ideas to be composed or interpreted were determined by other means. Rhetoric, thus, could have no philosophical implications. At the heart of the Renaissance, Kristeller argued, was the rebirth of the *studia humanitatis*, no concerted philosophical movement but a cultural and educational enterprise whose chief concerns were rhetoric, scholarship (especially textual criticism and philology), and literature.[25] Thus we have it: Renaissance humanism was either a philosophical movement in which rhetoric was a curiosity or it was an intellectual enterprise with no philosophical implications but in which rhetoric was at best a scholarly instrument, at worst a "trivial" discipline.

It was the intellectual historians who cut across these distinctions.[26] Many of them argued that although the Renaissance continued certain humanistic ideals of preceding epochs, it was truly marked by the cultural and philosophical prominence of rhetoric. William Bouwsma's interpretations of the period, for example, differ profoundly from Kristeller's. In Bouwsma's view, the uniqueness of Renaissance humanism lies in its repudiating traditional ways of systematic thought as irrelevant. For this opposition, he argues, the humanists found no alternative quite so well suited as rhetoric.[27]

Significantly, as my earlier statements might lead us to expect, there was a mutual attraction between humanism and the study of law. Many studies have probed the relationship of the two.[28] But where humanism and the legal profession are truly linked, it seems to me, is in their equal enthusiasm for rhetorical *controversia*. Erasmus was deeply influenced by the study of jurisprudence, and as for his friend More, Richard Schoeck has put the matter eloquently: "in the flowering tree of More's thought, the legal roots are so intermingled with the humanistic that we could not cut the one kind away without killing the other. This is as true of the pre-*Utopia* as of the post-*Utopia* More."[29] This does not simply mean that legal training "takes"—that once you're a lawyer, you're always a lawyer. Rather, it means that there was something deeply characteristic of humanism that blended well with legalistic modes of thought. Both find a mutual center in the discipline of rhetoric,[30] a center that should become increasingly clear as our study proceeds.

Moreover, Bouwsma's point is not simply the negative one that rhetoric became the humanists' alternative by default. One of his primary points is that the significance of Renaissance humanism lay in its bringing to consciousness certain conflicts in Western traditions. For Bouwsma, humanism is in effect a nexus of contraries, with none neglected or denied and all brought to consciousness. But that very nature, it seems to me, is the counterpart if not the consequence of rhetoric as a philosophical position: it encourages "controversial thinking," which can only proceed by acknowledging the rights of all parties in a dispute, a feature of rhetoric too often ignored in efforts to disparage its simple adversarial nature. If all parties do not have rights, there can be no controversy.

Furthermore—and here Bouwsma's interpretation directly addresses the incorporation of rhetoric into humanism—he goes on to point out that the humanists in their arguments with traditional philosophers, especially the rational theologians, encouraged a shift of emphasis from the reason to the feelings and will as man's most significant operative principle:

> For Petrarch, man seems no longer primarily an intellectual being but a complex mixture of thought and passion, and man's relation to the world and the full realization of his potentialities depend, however ambiguous the process, not on his reason

91

alone but even more on his feelings and will, access to which is provided not only by logic but by rhetoric.[31]

Recall the definition of humanism with which this section begins. An attitude toward experience, humanism involved a turning in love toward the things of this world. Although it was not exactly a secularizing of thought, humanism nonetheless placed emphasis on the *diversity* of things as well as on the *uniqueness* of things—and in the midst of such vastness and complexity the attitude began if not exactly to accept *uncertainty* at least no longer to fear it. In this latter regard, the humanists found themselves anticipated not only by the classical poets but also by the classical orator and theorist Cicero, the Roman lawyer who kept the "Greek tongue" wagging.

Moreover, a certain boldness toward diversity and uncertainty is an attitude that, besides connecting with several we have already noted, can be antagonistic to any philosophy (whether stoic or scholastic) that flattens man to a single dominant dimension, reason. Humanists, and rhetoricians, recognize that man is a composite of reason and emotion—that he has a body and is, essentially, imaginative. In the imagination, reason and emotion meet, to influence the will. In fact, we might say that Erasmus was really proposing that man attain the good life by placing imagination in the service of reason to better move the will—a proposal that was directly reversed, as we shall note later, by the nonhumanist reformer Francis Bacon. Thus, even in their shift of emphasis from reason to will, humanists were diversifying traditional faculty psychology, not by reforming it but by encouraging man to value formerly disparaged faculties. One point in all this diversifying was to force man into *full consciousness* of the mind and its means of choice.

Montaigne makes a similar point. He states, in the translation John Florio published in 1603,

> No quality is so universall in this surface of things, as variety and diversity.... There is but little relation between our actions, that are in perpetual mutation, and ... fixed and unmoveable laws.... Histories teach me, how much more ample and diverse the World is, than either we or our forefathers could ever enter into.... *The greatness of the mind is not so much to draw up and hale forward, as to know how to range, direct and circumscribe itself.*[32]

There is a correlative to this delight in diversity, with its impulse toward self-knowledge and conscious adaptation, and it amounts to a resistance to coercion. Though the humanists did not seek reformation and revolution, they did teach an abhorrence of coercion—as Hannah Arendt brilliantly points out in interpreting one of Cicero's statements:

> What Cicero in fact says is that for the true humanist neither the verities of the scientist nor the truth of the philosopher nor the beauty of the artist can be absolutes; the humanist, because he is not a specialist exerts a faculty of judgment and taste which is beyond the coercion which each specialty imposes upon us. This Roman *humanitas* applied to men who were not free in every respect, for whom the question of freedom, of not being coerced, was the decisive one—even in philosophy, even in science, even in the arts. Cicero says: In what concerns my association with men and things, I refuse to be coerced even by truth, even by beauty.[33]

Once more, the humanist attitude—not only in its delight in diversity but also in its abhorrence of coercion—connects with that "controversial thinking" that is the very soul of rhetoric. No one can be coerced who practices, and preaches, an inherently skeptical doctrine of analyzing any issue from *pro* and *contra* standpoints, who thinks with his body as well as his mind, who revels in contraries and ambiguities, who delights in verbal irony, who is, in Richard Lanham's words, the "homo rhetoricus," the diametrical opposite of the "homo seriosus."[34] Trinkaus's history offers much the same point: "the fact that a man is a humanist, i.e., a rhetorician, doesn't necessarily mean that he is not serious about the idea he presents, although, of course, on occasions he may not be."[35] You cannot coerce a man who will not stand still, keep quiet, or refrain from laughter.

Let us shift our attention somewhat to consider the general nature of humanism's intellectual ally, rhetoric—I mean, in particular, Ciceronian rhetoric, which attracted the humanists. Later, in my essay on Cicero, I shall examine the specific nature of rhetorical *controversia*.

The aim of Ciceronian rhetoric is always the task at hand, centering on a specific audience at a certain time and place. Audiences and occasions were divided into three broad kinds or genres: a forensic situation, as before a court of law, in which one tries to persuade the judges about the truth of a certain past event (a crime was or was not committed; or, if it was committed, one's client didn't do it or did it under extenuating circumstances); a deliberative situation, as before Parliament or a committee, in which one tries to persuade the auditors to adopt a certain policy or pass or rescind a certain law; and, finally, an epideictic situation, such as a funeral, dedication ceremony, retirement dinner, worship service, or even seduction, in which one tries to shape the audience's attitude toward something or someone—which may, of course, in turn lead them to pass judgment or take action. The three genres are broadly distributed into three time zones: the past, the future, and the present. Further, communication itself was usually divided into three aspects: teaching, pleasing, and moving. One told people something that they didn't know and convinced them of it; one put them in a good mood; and one got them emotionally involved in one's subject. That is, to persuade, whether in a forensic, deliberative, or epideictic situation, one had to do all three things—teach, please, and move.

And one succeeded not simply by appealing to someone's reason. There were, again, three major forms of appeal. Or, better, there were three major ways to confirm a case: through reason, through a kind of moral force, and through the audience's emotions. These tended to be distributed according to the three major components of the rhetorical act: the speech, wherein any reason at work in the situation—if there was any at all—was to be heard; the speaker, whose character had to be attractive to an audience and give them the assurance that the speech had been fashioned by a person of good morals; and the audience, whose own character and self-interest were the source of emotions to be activated by the speaker. All three—usually called, from Aristotle, logos, ethos, and pathos—did the job of persuading, of reaching the imagination, engaging the feelings (activating the emotions), and moving the will.

Consider, then, that logic, or appeal to reason, was at best one-third of the total process. The speaker's character itself was to be *used*. So were the audience's emotions. Now the speaker's character was a variable thing—an appearance he was to don, or a role he was to play for the sake of his argument. We have seen Donne be very careful about his ethos in the funeral oration—as, fundamentally, a religious man aloof from the world of business. We've seen Milton in the *Areopagitica* adopt the role of a scholarly, retiring man provoked to ire

94

by the licensing law. To ask which is the "real" Donne or which the "real" Milton is to ask an irrelevant question so far as rhetoric is concerned (no wonder the Romantic or anyone who seems to value "sincerity" abhors rhetoric). The important question centers in decorum and probability: was the role appropriate to the situation and did it fit the speaker's intention and the audience's expectations?

Since the emotions are important instruments of the orator's case, the rhetoricians kept alive for centuries a certain practical interest in man's emotional make-up, using what seemed to be true of man's nature as taught in the traditional wisdom about his "faculties": reason, will, and memory as parts of his mind; imagination and passions as faculties of his body. Man, in sum, was a duality, of usually warring natures. The phenomenon engaged the theologian. The rhetorician's interest was more practical: the orator had to know how to use the various emotions, or passions, that were likely to be in his audience as well as in himself. Rhetoricians went about teaching those emotions in a typical way—a way typical of rhetoricians and a way that divided the audience members into types. Traditional wisdom taught that emotions arise from self-interest, and thus the emotions of aristocrats differ from those of slaves, those of women from those of men, those of old men from those of young men. Aristotle began this kind of categorizing. His student Theophrastes continued the effort and formed a tradition that flowered in the Renaissance, with a host of short sketches of various kinds of people, called "characters." (I referred to these in my study of Donne's sermon.) Again, in rhetoric as in humanism, the emphasis is on the practical application of what is available.

Given the humanist perspective in which man's rational nature was viewed as only part of what in him determines his opinion and action, it is significant that the rhetorical act itself is regarded as, at most, one-third rational. We must keep in mind that the conceptual model of rhetoric is public speaking, oratory. Oral delivery is therefore an important part of the rhetorical composition process, as are style and the temporal order in which the audience is led through one's arguments. Cicero divided these parts more or less discretely: into *inventio,* the discovery and analysis of arguments; *dispositio,* the arrangement of material; *elocutio,* the style of speaking; *pronuntiatio,* oral delivery; and *memoria,* the lodging of something in memory, one's own and that of one's audience. Efforts were made to transfer this entire speech process to the writing process—with some difficulty, but always with one significant effect: writers as well as speakers were taught to analyze their tasks and think about what to say by imagining their own speaking roles (their voices) and the kinds of responses they were likely to elicit from their specific audiences. That is—and this is shocking to many people—one actually analyzed a matter not simply in terms of logic, but also in terms of who he was or who he could seem to be and in terms of the kind of audience before whom he was to speak. Rightly viewed, this process constantly kept the human dimensions central in matters of practical affairs. And it kept rhetoric unique as an art of disputation, as suggested earlier. From ancient times, rhetoric and dialectic—or "logic," in the Renaissance—were regarded as "counterparts" (so Aristotle called them) in offering instruction in *controversia*. The difference between the two was that dialectic exclusively prized the mind in debate, while rhetoric prized the body as well. Dialectical thought was abstract; rhetorical thought was experiential.

Wrongly viewed, the rhetorical process can degenerate into what we now call sophistry, and even into demagoguery. Indeed, once humanism disintegrated, its residual rhetoric was thought of as leading simply to aggrandizement and manipulation—as the plays of Marlowe reveal.[36] Rightly viewed, rhetoric is not simply an access to power but, like dialectic, an avenue to certain at least provisional truths, an epistemology. The latter is the view toward which humanism directed its—ultimately doomed—efforts. For, as epistemology, rhetoric by its nature encourages a certain freedom, beyond the usual philosophical limits. This is not license, for the bounds are marked by the three forms of appeal, or proof: logos, the discourse; ethos, the speaker's character; and pathos, the audience's emotions.

One might imagine Folly's response here. Those three elements are illusory. The rhetorician concerns himself with appearances— with what will *appear* to be logic or morals to a certain audience. What constitutes reasoning—to use some modern examples that Folly might appreciate—might not be quite the same at a school board meeting in a small town as at a faculty meeting of a philosophy department. Indeed, illusions are more than merely acceptable in rhetoric; they are, as Folly has already declared and shown us, its very stock in trade. Rhetoric can thrive in a world of flux and change, in which meaning, quality, and truth itself are variable and relative. Virtually everything can be related to situations—to people in this time or that place. Even holy writ, as Erasmus showed, can—and should—be interpreted according to speakers and audiences.

But is the *control* on that freedom, even that hermeneutical freedom, also illusory? The question is a crucial one, for its answer undergirds any potential strength of rhetoric as a philosophy. There were two approaches to the problem—the faces of Janus, again. This time they are at the core of humanist rhetoric.

One approach was to regard rhetoric merely as an ethically neutral instrument, a "double-edged sword," as it was occasionally called in the Renaissance, as useful to cut in one direction (*pro*) as in another (*contra*) and also as useful to work for *good* as for *evil*. Rhetoric belonged to that stoical, out-of-the-self class of "things indifferent." This, as we have seen, is an alternative most attractive to philosophers in our own age, who do not wish to attribute any philosophical substance whatsoever to rhetoric. But once rhetoric was in fact placed in the category of neutral instrumentality, both rhetoric and humanism began to disintegrate, as we shall see. We shall see, too, that ethical neutrality is carried deep within Ciceronianism.

A second approach was to regard rhetoric as being attached to an ethical perspective, and there were two ways of doing that—again, two faces. The first was St. Augustine's solution, which we shall explore next in this study. He believed that one should Christianize rhetoric, make it useful to the Christian orator—that is, attach it to the Christian views of nature and totally dismantle *controversia*. The second was to place the control in the speaker himself and insist that the speaker must be a man of good moral character. A good person would not engage in demagoguery. This insistence, which is implicit in Plato and Aristotle, became explicit in Cato and Quintilian, who define an orator as "a good man skilled in speaking." But Isocrates was the actual preceptor here, the first to insist that moral consciousness grows out of the process of rhetorical composition, as he argues in *Antidosis*[37]:

> I do hold that *people can become better and worthier if they conceive an ambition to speak well,* if they become possessed of the desire to be able to persuade their hearers, and, finally, if they set their hearts on seizing their *advantage* . . . in the true meaning of the term.[38]

For, in the first place, when anyone elects to speak or write discourses which are worthy of praise and honour, it is not conceivable that he will support courses which are unjust or petty or devoted to private quarrels, and not rather those which are great and honourable, devoted to the welfare of man and our common good; for if he fails to find causes of this character, he will accomplish nothing to the purpose. In the second place, he will select from all the actions of men which bear upon his subject those examples which are the most illustrious and the most edifying; and, habituating himself to contemplate and appraise such examples, he will feel their influence not only in the preparation of a given discourse but in all the actions of his life. . . .

Furthermore . . . who does not know that words carry greater conviction when spoken by men of good repute than when spoken by men who live under a cloud, and that *the argument which is made by a man's life is of more weight than that which is furnished by words?* Therefore, the stronger a man's desire to persuade his hearers, the more zealously will he strive to be honourable and to have the esteem of his fellow-citizens.

Admittedly, the view is optimistic, but it is infused with the kind of optimism concerning human nature that held the humanists entranced—and is no less naïve, it seems to me, than Aristotle's or Plato's view of rhetoric, which assumed that the orator's first allegiance must be not to "advantage" but to "truth." Aristotle, Plato, and St. Augustine belong in the category of those who hold one philosophical view of rhetoric. Isocrates, Protagoras, Gorgias, the sophists generally, and Cicero belong in the category of those who hold a quite different but equally philosophical view of rhetoric, a view that is skeptical of truth, however positive it is about human nature and the morally instructive process of rhetoric. Nor does this second view fall exactly into the stoical solution, whereby the *self* is the center of all ethical control—the center, for that matter, of everything that matters—and all outside that self are "indifferent." On the contrary, this second view holds that rhetoric is not indifferent but a moral instrument, a means whereby virtue can be inculcated in the self. It was Cicero who conveyed the Isocratean lesson to Renaissance humanists, though Augustine *seemed* to show them how it worked in practice and Quintilian *seemed* to show them how it might be taught to the young.

The period that we call the Renaissance was itself a nexus of contraries, as we noted briefly in the first chapter of this book. In this essay, I have tried to arrange some of these contraries into certain Janus-faces in order to explore the deep affinities between humanism and rhetoric. Early humanism presented twin faces, of stoicism and Augustinianism. Rhetoric has *always* presented twin faces, ethical neutrality and ethical instrumentality. The phenomenon both were centered on, man, was himself a composite of dual natures: mind (with reason and will) and body (with imagination and passions). But the humanists, in offering an ancient theory of composition as their alternative to traditional philosophy, did little to change the order of things—even when, and perhaps mostly when, the formal nature of that order could only be expressed as a controversy. Consequently, their thought, intellectual method, and writing reveal a complexity that, to the reformers of the age, presented only a single face—one of disorder.

Augustine

Augustine's eloquence is a source of his long-lasting appeal. In turn, a source of this eloquence (Augustine would insist that its only source is God) seems to lie in his remarkable personalism, that quality rhetoricians call ethos.

St. Augustine (354–430) was a man steeped in pagan literary culture who, through doubt and spiritual restlessness, forged an intensely personal relation with God. Sensuous pleasures—lust and wantonness—and *affectus*, our feeling and emotion, were obstacles to as well as instruments of that personal relation: in Peter Brown's words, "the life of the senses, he insisted, was not in itself evil, only the tension that arose when the will, directed by reason, clashed with the appetites."[39] The stage for this drama of salvation was within the penitent's own character and what he knew to be true of his own inner motives and desires. The result was a philosophy that is, as one writer puts it, "Augustinocentric."[40] Thus, even today, readers read Augustine not simply for his Latinity, style, or "mere eloquence," a quality that upon his conversion from the error of his ways (including the teaching of rhetoric) he most forcefully rejected,[41] but also for the drama of ethos in his prose, the contest between reason and the senses for control of the will, and amidst all these dualisms, a conscious effort to escape dualisms.

Three documents of Augustinianism had great effects on Renaissance humanism, though they were not particularly important in the preceding ages: *The City of God, The Confessions,* and *On Christian Doctrine.* These works represent, respectively, the most complete expression of Augustinian thought, the clearest evidence of Augustinian rhetoric at work, and the fullest articulation of Augustinian rhetorical theory. Obviously, the last of these deserves most of our attention, but brief comment on the first two may help us understand Augustine's role as a rhetorician warring on rhetoric, the role that is the theme of this discussion.

The City of God was Augustine's masterpiece. Written late in his career and inspired by Alaric's sacking of Rome in 410, the work imagines two cities as an oppositional dualism. The first is the city of this world, Babylon. The second is the city of God, Jerusalem. But if Rome is the "real" example of the former, destroyed by God for its worship of false gods in its literary culture, it is also in a certain way a hazy glimpse of the latter, which exists not simply as an ideal but also as a possibility that could be realized were man only to turn from the motives of Roman imperialism and toward Christian love, *caritas*. The thought appears "controversialized," a lingering sign of Augustine's first profession. The aim of his argument is not to encourage asceticism or other-worldliness but to show men how to become other-worldly while living in the world.[42]

In *The Confessions,* a somewhat richer work for our purposes, we are brought close to the public heart of a rhetorician skilled in the uses of *apostrophe*—a tactic in which the orator ostensibly turns from his audience to address another. Augustine's confessions are apparently addressed to God but in fact are offered publicly, a strategy he makes explicit several times (e.g., *Conf.* II.iii, X.i). Within this rhetorical situation Augustine insisted that only one principle could be persuasive: *caritas,* love (or "charity" in Donne's English). It is important to note the prominence and prevalence of precisely that word in Augustine's writings. He thought he could be believed only by those readers whose ears had been opened by "charity" (X.iii.3), as his own had been. Therein lies the rhetorical premise of Augustine's eloquent personalism.

To elaborate, not only was *caritas* the supreme Christian virtue for Augustine, it was also the ultimate principle requiring that Ciceronian rhetoric be abandoned. That rhetoric *had* to be abandoned is made evident throughout *The Confessions* by its characterization as a pagan, materialistic, deceptive art—so characterized, moreover, by one who himself had been a successful rhetorician:

> During those years I was a teacher of the art of public speaking [*artem rhetoricam*]. Love of money had gained the better of me and for it I sold to others the means of coming off the better in debate. [*Conf.* IV.ii.2]

Although in this translation[43] Augustine's *artem rhetoricam* is rendered "art of public speaking," elsewhere, in this translation and others, it is variously translated, as it has to be for the modern reader, "rhetoric," "public speaking," and "literature." These variations indicate not, as with *caritas,* any conceptual difficulty so much as the debasement of the term *rhetoric* in English through its loss of its associations within pagan culture. For Augustine, rhetoric is on the one hand a commodity, something to be bought and sold. On the other it is evil itself, parodying the actions of God, and substituting lies and insane battles for the truth and peace God alone can give (*Conf.* IV.ii.2). Augustine knew that rhetoric belonged deeply to the very culture he as a Christian sought to transform. Nowhere was this belonging more evident, perhaps, than in Julian the Apostate's opposite efforts: in the second year of his reign, Julian issued an edict prohibiting Christians from teaching rhetoric (cf. *Conf.* VIII.v.10). In this way, Julian would preserve pagan studies, including both "literature and oratory," from contamination.

In his war on this pagan rhetoric, Augustine pursues essentially three strategies. First, he argues that truth is not a function of words. This, Augustine claims in *The Confessions,* he learned at the age of 29: one must distinguish between merely charming eloquence (*suaviloquentia*) and truth, reality, the actual nature of things (V.iii.3). A rhetorician might pose, as Cicero does, a collapsible distinction between *eloquence* and *wisdom,* but *truth* does not enter the picture, not quite in the way Augustine brings it in. Indeed, for Augustine, real truth, the truth that matters, is not even a function of scientific talk: a Christian may be forgiven for his erroneous statements about the material world so long as he holds no beliefs unworthy of God, the creator of the material world (V.v.9). There is only one truth that matters, and it proceeds from the source of all truth—*Deus ipsa Veritas* (XII.xxv.35): the voice of that "inner teacher" he describes in *De magistro,* the Christ within us. Nonetheless, eloquence can help truth, as shown in Augustine's response to Ambrose's speech (*Conf.* V.xiii–xiv), when Augustine finds that although he has been consciously attending mainly to Ambrose's charming manner, the bishop's words have made their way into his soul. *Eloquence* is not to be abandoned, but the illusion that Ciceronian rhetoric offers, that eloquence produces truth, *is.*

The second strategy is more complex. To describe it, let us consider first Augustine's description of a certain Janiform hermeneutic:

> Suppose that I am going to recite a psalm that I know. Before I begin, my faculty of expectation is engaged by the whole of it. But once I have begun, as much of the psalm as I have removed

from the province of expectation and relegated to the past now engages my memory, and the scope of the action which I am performing is divided between the two faculties of memory and expectation, the one looking back to the part which I have already recited, the other looking forward to the part which I have still to recite. But my faculty of attention is present all the while, and through it passes what was the future in the process of becoming the past. As the process continues, the province of memory is extended in proportion as that of expectation is reduced, until the whole of my expectation is absorbed. This happens when I have finished my recitation and it has all passed into the province of memory.   [*Conf.* XI.xxviii.38]

It happens. Nor do we understand how or why it happens, an admission that plays into Augustine's hands as he goes on to relate the phenomenon to man's life and to the whole (Christian) history of mankind. In *The City of God* (VII.vii), Augustine argues that all purposeful activity looks backward and forward at once—and he complains that the Romans failed to grasp the emblematic richness of their own god Janus in this matter. These two passages are the source of the Janus-faced temporal effect I described at the end of Chapter One. Janus, I suggested, looks backward and forward much as we do when we read a literary work in anticipating its coherence and completion, and much as we do (and as the humanists did) in interpreting the past while remaining mindful of the present and the future (Milton's "contemporary of time"). But we miss Augustine's point unless we remember that Augustine's Janus is moving toward God, primarily facing the future while confidently remembering what is most needful from the past. This view of history is Christianized, a view that looks for the resurrection of the dead and the life of the world to come.

In Augustine and in other Christian thinkers, a principle of spiritual hierarchies has been introduced that gives time a direction. More than that, just as the first strategy makes debating irrelevant to truth, the second shatters controversial thinking, for there could no longer be any genuine doubleness of arguing, any true *pro* and *contra,* whether the question in dispute concerns eschatological or quotidian matters, in the face of such hierarchies. Herein Augustine found a most effective means of controverting pagan rhetoric. Once there is an *a priori* principle whereby truth may be determined, rhetoric can no longer be a

103

means of thought, only a means of expressing or ornamenting thought. That *a priori* principle was, for Augustine, based on ostensible dualisms: pagan and Christian, or not-charity (*cupiditas*) and charity, which are both hierarchical, the former temporally, the latter morally. Paganism is an unfulfilled, at times debased form of the true wisdom of Christianity; not-charity is simply evil. Any arguing can, thus, no longer be temporally or ethically horizontal. Controversial thinking always pertains to debating both sides of a question, but the nature and conditions of an intellectual debate radically shift when the conclusion is foregone—as when, for example, one debater is identified as the "devil's advocate" or when, in the contest of will in Donne's "Goodfriday," half of one's mind faces in a direction that he and his audience know is spiritually obligatory. By this means, rhetoric, like Augustine himself, was brought to a "turning," a conversion.[44]

The third strategy in this war on rhetoric was *theoretical,* Augustine's disintegration of Ciceronianism, in *De doctrina christiana, On Christian Doctrine.* By way of introduction, it may be useful to recall that this work bridges some of the intellectual distance between Erasmus and Cicero. Erasmus not only published an edition of the work but also summarized Book II, in *The Antibarbarians*—or, rather, his persona Batt summarized it and said that Augustine's argument, however prolix, was nonetheless useful in showing that pagan literature was not harmful, or useless, or suspect, at least to the "charitable" Christian. Augustine set a pattern that later humanists found difficult to resist or to gainsay. The pattern we are now concerned with is the one whereby he Christianized pagan rhetoric by shattering its theoretical integrity.

De doctrina has many echoes of Cicero's *De oratore*—as we might expect, for the latter was Cicero's major effort to philosophize rhetoric—or, better, to rhetoricize philosophy. Renaissance humanists considered *De doctrina* and *De oratore* vital to their efforts to expand thought, a consideration reflected partly in the printing history of each work. The fourth book of *De doctrina* was the first work by Augustine to be printed, in 1465 at Strasbourg. Soon thereafter the treatise as a whole was published, and within less than a century it was blazoned to the humanist world through the great Erasmian edition. Cicero's *De oratore* was the very first book printed in Italy, also in 1465, at Subiaco. Of course, both documents had been distributed for centuries in manuscript. But if, as recent studies have shown, what we call the Renaissance could not have occurred without the use of the newly invented printing press,[45] an equally compelling relation exists between the Renaissance and the priority it gave rhetorical documents. When we reach back into these documents—in particular, these two primary ones by Augustine and Cicero—we are entering the core of that humanism that gave the Renaissance its character, and we are approaching, for that matter, those controversies that were finally to undo humanism itself. It is apparent that the last, the fourth, book of *De doctrina* stirred humanist interest because it seemed historically the first book specifically devoted to a Christian rhetoric. That it did not totally supersede Cicero's pagan rhetoric in the humanist canon says something about both humanist scholarship and the humanist commitment to expansion.

Moreover, the initial separate printing of the fourth book as if it contained the whole of Augustine's Christian rhetoric points toward a certain short-sightedness, one that some humanists, but not Erasmus, were guilty of. Erasmus (or Batt) knew that Augustine's project was to Christianize pagan learning and that the only way to succeed was, literally, to *transform* it, and so change its intentions, to replace its pagan soul with Christ. Erasmus/Batt's attention to Book II of *De doctrina* is an attention to that transformation of paganism, of which rhetoric is a most significant part.

Augustine's specific way of achieving the transformation of rhetorical theory was to deprive the discipline of its major element, its system of thought. *Controversia* is at the center of rhetoric's system of thought, which, as we noted briefly in the preceding section, is *pro* and *contra* analysis comprising three modes of proving: ethos, pathos, and logos. These are distributed by Cicero into five parts: *inventio, dispositio, elocutio, memoria,* and *pronuntiatio.* The integrity of rhetoric's system of thought depends upon keeping the three modes of proving and the five parts of composition in an indissoluble mixture. That integrity can be shattered by isolating any one of those ingredients, insisting, say, that logos be considered apart from the speaker's character or the nature of the audience, or making the five parts steps to be taken discretely in sequence. If one "invents" abstractly or initially— that is, first, before arranging material, attaching style, and so on— then rhetoric is not a system of thought; it merely uses thought whose nature has been determined elsewhere. Such a shattering of rhetoric's theoretical integrity became Augustine's final strategy, one that has proved to be both effective and long-lasting. The rhetorical theory ostensibly relegated to *De doctrina's* fourth book—which itself, as Augustine tells us in his *Retractions,* was completed long after the first three—actually depends for its life blood on the first three books. Those who assume that rhetoric no longer has life blood are unable to see that dependency. That is, those who find Augustine's rhetorical theory only in the fourth book have applied to the extreme a lesson Augustine most eagerly teaches in the first three—that for the Christian there is no rhetorical mode of thought.

Augustine's lesson took—and it still takes. There are modern students of this document who cannot see the theoretical relation of the fourth book to the first three, a situation well reviewed by Gerald A. Press.[46] As Press argues, "the whole work is a rhetoric, but a rhetoric that devotes three fourths of its length to just one of the traditional five parts," invention. In support of that view, Press has offered a careful examination of the work's form.[47] For Augustine, life itself has become a kind of text to be read and understood—in a Christian way, of course.[48] And the Christian rhetor's thought, analysis, or invention has become an hermeneutical act of will, or more specifically, willed *caritas.* The point is structurally emphatic, occupying three of the four books of Augustine's Christianized rhetoric.

Inventio (modus inueniendi) is the first requisite for communication, Augustine begins, and the second (to be set forth in Book IV) is "publication" (*modus proferendi*). For Cicero, *inventio* meant analysis through which the orator—by considering the subject, audience, occasion, and his own character, intention, and task—discovers controversially the means of achieving argumentative advantage. For Augustine, *inventio* is primarily a means of testing one's understanding of something against the rule of charity. The word is *caritas,* the same word we have encountered in the previous Augustinian documents. In *De doctrina,* Augustine attempts to make this word a technical term. So important is the term that anyone who thinks he has understood Scripture but who offers an interpretation that does not build up a twofold love of God and one's neighbor (*caritas*) does not in fact understand the Scripture. On the other hand, anyone who offers an interpretation of Scripture that is useful to *caritas,* even though he has failed to grasp the precise meaning of a passage, has not made a pernicious error, nor is he guilty of deception (I.xxxvi.40). In sum, anyone who knows that the end of God's teaching is *caritas*, and who "out of a pure heart, and of a good conscience, and of faith unfeigned" makes his understanding of Scripture bear upon these three graces, can approach his interpretive task with an easy mind (I.xl.44). In dealing with any difficult, particularly figurative passages, the rule may be simply expressed: "to carefully turn over in our minds and meditate upon what we read until an interpretation be found that tends to establish the reign" of *caritas* (III.xv.23).[49]

Caritas is the rule, *regula* (the same rule, *regula lignea*, on which Monica stood in her famous dream; see *Conf.* III.xi.19), and the means of interpretation. It is at the heart of Augustine's Christian hermeneutics, the process of interpreting Scripture, reality, life—a process that has swallowed up the whole of rhetorical *inventio*. Paul wrote, as reported in Jerome's Vulgate, that *caritas* is the greatest of the three Christian virtues (1. Cor. 13:13): "manent fides, spes, caritas; tria haec: maior autem horum caritas." For Augustine, God's own will seems evident mainly in *caritas*. Therefore, the Christian orator must bend *his* will to that evidence. It is, in fact, the supreme evidence he is to "invent." In this way, *a priori* truth makes its blinding appearance. However perplexing its form might be to those of us not blessed with Augustinian vision, the rule itself, like taste, is not for disputing.

Every good Christian must recognize that wherever he may discover truth ("ubicumque inuenerit ueritatem," II.xviii.28) it belongs to the Lord. Reason, for example, has invented a means of testing the truth of propositions, valid inference. But this means, Augustine insists—astoundingly—was not instituted by men; rather, it was discovered, like the gold God placed in the earth, and was not to be enjoyed for itself but to be used under the rule of *caritas*.

So far as the propositions themselves are concerned, as opposed to the forms of reasoning to which they are subjected, their truthfulness is to be determined by reference to the Scriptures (II.xxxi.49). And, however great the use to which the science of disputation may be put, disputatiousness itself is to be avoided (II.xxxi.48). The point would seem simple enough. To make it more so, Augustine gives ludicrous examples of mere disputatiousness (using the rhetorical strategy *reductio ad absurdum*). But the point, however simple and however demonstrably absurd, only further reflects the pernicious habits of rhetoric that Augustine sought to cure. That somehow truth—a truth—could be found in the pursuit of something for its own sake, such as rhetorical display, disputatiousness, controversial thinking, or the creation of art, is profoundly alien to Augustine's program. Truth is the end of his cured rhetoric, and the beginning, and altogether outside its methods.

That is, directionality is operative in this theoretical work: the "aim" of *inventio* is *caritas* and pre-existent truth. Operative too is Augustine's *first* strategy in his war on rhetoric. Thought and speech are divorced; the lesson is repeated in *De doctrina:*

> Just as when we speak, in order that what we have in our minds may enter through the ear into the mind of the hearer, the word which we have in our hearts becomes an outward sound and is called speech; and yet our thought does not lose itself in the sound, but remains complete in itself, and takes the form of speech without being modified in its own nature by the change.
> [I.xiii.12, trans. Shaw, p. 14]

This profoundly antirhetorical doctrine is based on Christian revelation: God's word (which for Augustine is always *verbum,* never *sermo*) was made flesh that our senses may apprehend it, but its essential nature was not changed. Therefore, we too have thought, which precedes speech, and the speech that fleshes out this thought does not change its essential nature.

That is the first and greatest dualism, and all the others are dependent upon it. The first three books of *De doctrina* set forth a *modus inueniendi* that is silent, meditational, willed—and it *precedes* the speaking allowed in the fourth book. In this way, truth becomes divorced from words in Augustine's philosophy, as it is in most neo-Platonic systems of thought, a divorce marked by a term that has always seemed curiously ironic, *realism.* Specific words no longer matter; they are shadowy representations of abstract truths that do not depend on words or on any corporeal manifestation for their existence. With a stroke, Augustine dispatches from further consideration the relation of thing and word, *res* and *verba,* and further dismisses rhetoric from any serious standing among the humane arts.

That rhetoric could possibly be an end in itself is, of course, out of the question. Quintilian had said, flatly, that the end of rhetoric is rhetoric—not persuasion but speaking well ("non persuadendi sed bene dicendi," *Institutio oratoria,* XI.i.11)—and a host of theories, extending from Cicero through the age of Milton, actually *define* rhetoric as the art of speaking well. But for Augustine, as we have seen, rhetoric is in the service of a truth that depends neither on words nor on the forms of argument. The end of rhetoric is always to persuade to truth—and the words Augustine uses for persuasion are important: the end of all eloquence is persuasion ("dicere apte ad persuasionem," IV.xxv.55), but persuasion in turn is linked to a certain quality, or power, of style that allows the orator to be heard not simply with intelligence or with pleasure but with obedience ("ut intellegenter, ut libenter, ut oboedienter audiatur," IV.xv.32, xxvi.56). This is not the shaping of an attitude, perhaps momentary and perhaps even idle, but the bending of wills.

So far as the structure of Book IV is concerned, it is largely dualistic. In the main, there are two classical precepts of rhetoric, mostly drawn from *De oratore:* the intentional (to teach, to please, and to move—best achieved when one's doctrine is intelligible, attractive, and attended to obediently), and the stylistic (low or plain, moderate, and grand; the three styles are best mixed, and, at any rate, the three intentions are to be achieved in any one). Another key dualism, with which Augustine begins and ends, is that between "wisdom" and "eloquence." This is a dualism Cicero concerns himself with, as we shall see; indeed, it was Cicero who raised the issue of this dualism in such a persuasively eloquent manner that it caught the attention of almost all succeeding rhetoricians. It is important to note here that Augustine equates Cicero's wisdom (*sapientia*) with one quality alone: a man speaks with more or less wisdom as he is the more or less versed in Holy Scripture ("sapienter autem dicit homo tanto magis uel minus, quanto in scripturis sanctis magis minusue profecit," IV.v.7). If one thoroughly acquires this wisdom, eloquence virtually takes care of itself; it is the inseparable handmaid of such eloquence and will follow even when uninvited (IV.vi.9). As for the rules of eloquence, they are best acquired rapidly, by the young, and by example (IV.iii); dependence on God through prayer is the primary requisite to speech preparation and rhetorical principles are at best a secondary help (IV.xv–xvi). Ultimately, the chief source of persuasiveness is not in the orator's words but in his character and life: no matter how great his eloquence, the life of the speaker has even greater force in making him attended to obediently ("Habet autem ut oboedienter audiatur, quantacumque granditate dictionis maius pondus uita dicentis," IV.xxvii.59). Again, as we shall see, this final matter is an incorporation of a Ciceronian doctrine into a context that utterly transforms it.

Augustine's fears reveal much about rhetoric and the pernicious habits it carries into Augustinian Christianity. In Augustine, recall, that is evil which is praised or undertaken without reference to God. His famous theft of the pears in his adolescence reflected just this kind of perversity (see *Conf.* II.iv–vi); it was undertaken *gratis malum*, for the sake of itself, and therefore for the sake of evil, containing a kind of malicious parody of undertaking something for the sake of God. By this reasoning, rhetoric too is evil. Its parameters are people and situations; its aim is efficaciousness or advantage; its subject is humane—that is to say, uncertain—knowledge; and its intellectual method is controversy. What rhetoric *does* is center those people and that situation *in a work of art*. Its effects may not be long-lasting, but the impermanence of any humane object is a cause of concern more to philosophers than to rhetoricians.

Augustine's antirhetorical crusade was waged in a host of other documents not indicated, to mention only two: his battle with the skeptics early in his life and with the Pelagians late in his life. The practiced uncertainty of the skeptics could not be sanctioned, nor could the Pelagian doctrine that man is not innately or by inheritance "fallen." For in Augustine's view, to allow doubt or to make irrelevant man's depravity opens the doors to rhetorical reasoning. Anyway, man is persuaded not by argument, Augustine believed, but as he himself had been, by a "turning" and a willful holding on. To practice doubt is no way to find Christian truth. That man turns from truth when he faces it is evidence of his depravity.

The force of Augustine's own efforts to escape from depravity reverberated for centuries. Here was a man who knew his rhetoric, both what it was and how it was to be practiced. Here was a man, too, who knew how to create on paper that ideal image of himself,[50] full of tension, drawn by the very things he believed he must reject, beset not simply by temptations but by devils, uncomfortable in this world yet almost overwhelmed by its beauty, intellectually restless to the end. Little wonder that the Augustinian face looks humanistic. The triumph Augustine achieves lies within the grasp of any man. It is a triumph of the will. Because the will has to be charmed, Augustine does not shun rhetoric as a practical instrument, though he avoids it as a way to spiritual truth. When faced with worldliness, his assertion gives way to meekness, argument becomes prayer, and by force of will the traps and inconsistencies of the material world are laid at the feet of God. Such is the nature of the "obedience" he would have the Christian preacher seek. Such, too, is the nature of the obedience he earned. "Forgive me, Augustine," wrote a humanist in the Quattrocento when again the necessity and the lures of rhetoric were capturing men's minds. "Forgive me, Augustine, father of highest reverence, whom I fear to oppose even for the sake of the truth."[51]

Cicero

Anyone who attempts to deal with Ciceronian rhetoric—particularly the rhetorical *theory* of the great master (106–43 B.C.) of Latinity, oratory, and law—must come to terms with two central concepts, wisdom and eloquence. Quintilian (A.D. ca.35–ca.95) endeavored to systematize these twin concepts into an educational scheme. Then, Augustine tried to transform wisdom, *sapientia,* so that it meant simply "versed in Scripture," and to relegate what was left of *eloquentia* to Book IV of *De doctrina christiana.* But Cicero actually fared better in Augustine's hands than in Quintilian's. In Augustine's hands he was at least taken seriously by a philosopher, as he himself would have desired; in Quintilian's hands his writings suffered admiration by an idealistic but shallow-thinking educational theorist. Of course, in neither case did he fare well. The destructive treatment Augustine gave Cicero had a long-lasting effect, even among Neo-Ciceronians, such as the Renaissance humanists. And among those humanists, Quintilian's theories were more admired than followed—ironically, similar to the treatment the theorist gave his master.

Always, even when his own writings touched on pedagogy, Cicero sought a place among philosophers. This he believed he deserved through his efforts to forge a union, which he insisted was older than Socrates, between rhetoric and philosophy, statesmanship and learning, eloquence and wisdom. But those efforts were doomed, first by the fall of republican Rome—this he seemed to acknowledge—and then by what he could not foresee, the rise of Christianity and its replacement of pagan epistemology with the myth of fallen man. To that latter cause we might add a further one, the absorption by Christian philosophers of what appeared to them best in paganism. But the single feature of Ciceronianism that most Christian philosophers would not stomach was the alliance he forged—that "specious" alliance, Folly calls it, in her pointed half-ironical way—between rhetoric and philosophy. However, that alliance is the *sine qua non* of Ciceronianism and, as noted earlier, an important characteristic of humanism. To pursue it in the writings of Cicero, we must keep in mind not only *sapientia* and *eloquentia* but two other terms pertaining

112

to a certain Ciceronian—that is to say, not necessarily Christian—
view of man, *honestum* and *utile*.

Pinning down the latter set of words is not easy—nor, surely, did
Cicero, with his rhetorician's delight in capturing truth with an
echoic and associative language, intend them to be easily defined. For
the most part, *honestum* seems to mean moral goodness or rightness;
it also means virtue and beauty, and it can mean worthy of honor or
distinguished. Good men often undertake a thing not for material
reward but simply because it is proper, moral, and right.[52] Thus, morality and character—moral goodness as defined not abstractly but
by a person's, especially a statesman's, virtuous behavior—are compact in the term. The English word we have derived from the term,
honest, lacks some of the public nature of Cicero's meaning, perhaps
because, for us, it has been filtered through Romantic sensibility and
tends to mean something less public, such as inconsequential sincerity or being true to one's own private feelings. *Honestum* includes the
meaning of *virtus* and, as the stoics claimed, was, like virtue, its own
reward. Like virtue, too, *honestum* is part of man's own nature (the
word *virtus,* Cicero points out, was derived from *vir,* man).[53] But
whereas "manly excellence" would seem to be a sufficient translation
of *virtus,* something like "acting in the public good" or "statesmanship" seems more a part of Cicero's meaning of *honestum,* resonant as
it is of *honestas, honos,* and *honor*—all of which lack the intensely private dimensions the stoics attached to *virtus* (or the Romantics to *integrity*).

Utile (echoing *utilitas* and *utor*) means, of course, useful, but not
simply in a Benthamite way. Its meaning is more Isocratean: advanta-
geous, but in no quantitative sense of, say, the greatest good for the
largest number of people. English humanists, such as Roger Ascham
and Thomas Wilson, translated *utile* in the sixteenth century as
"profit." In our age, the word is most frequently translated as "expediency"—mere expediency, we often say, as if *utile* operates, because
it has to, with little thought for *honestum.* Cicero's master stroke was
to equate *utile* with *honestum* and so to bring the statesman's process of
making decisions into alignment with his public, moral character.
The equation is Cicero's version of finding rhetorical "advantage" in
the Isocratean sense: argumentative efficaciousness becomes the
skillful means of advancing causes in the public good.

Cicero achieved this equation best in a work of his mature years,

De officiis. He wrote it in the form of a letter to his son, Marcus, to offer him instruction, not in statesmanship exactly or in manners, though the work is a precursor of Renaissance books on behavior, courtly and otherwise. Nor is it a work about *noblesse oblige,* though it does recognize a class distinction. Rather, the work is on the duties or obligations of the honorable man, trying to show how it is possible to act morally in a world that seems to operate mostly by mere expediency. Cicero considered the work his masterpiece—a regard in which it was held by the humanists, some of whom, like Petrarch, found in the work an adumbration of Christian principles. (But Petrarch's interpretation may say less about the work than about a certain, perhaps only incipient, broadening that had begun to occur in Christianity by his time.) *De officiis* appeared in print for the first time in 1465, the same year that saw the printing of *De oratore* and Book IV of *De doctrina.* A brief review of the work will help us approach *De oratore,* and help us understand Ciceronianism generally, by clarifying those principles and methods of thought without which rhetoric to Cicero was merely an ethically neutral instrument or worse. For Ciceronianism offers a practical and conceptual means of joining *sapientia* to *eloquentia,* and *honestum* to *utile;* throughout this review, throughout this essay, we shall concentrate on those means, for they were in turn important principles of humanism.

De officiis (On Duty) is divided into three books. Book I discusses *honestum,* Book II *utile,* and Book III resolves the apparent conflict between the two. Structurally, the work would seem to have the movement of Hegelian dialectic—thesis, antithesis, synthesis—but in this the thesis and antithesis were set up by a lawyer, Cicero, who is offering moral instruction to a young man, his son. Or perhaps we should say *ostensibly* offering instruction to his son, for Cicero is just as obviously advocating a case before all whose eyes may light upon his words. The purposes of the apostrophist are usually unconcealable, just as the lawyerly habits of mind are usually unfailing in their quest for "advantage." It is *controversia,* not dialectic, that structures this work: Cicero discovered (invented) his materials on duty by considering two ostensibly polar opposites, *honestum* and *utile,* by letting each "speak" in his imagination, and by stepping in—seen particularly in Book III—as the judge to offer a resolution of the apparent differences. Ultimately, however, the entire work—all three books—

is more like a judicial opinion, delivered after all the speaking is over and all the "facts" are in.

The work shows that Ciceronian *sapientia* (including *prudentia*) lies in the perception and development of truth. This wisdom (plus prudence) is one of the components of *honestum*. But all virtue is active; therefore *sapientia* is active. Ciceronian *sapientia* is an activity that, from the outset and inherently, resembles the orator's *inventio*. *Sapientia*, that is, and *eloquentia* are joined at the center. For the truth that the Ciceronian discovers (invents) is probability. And we Academicians, Cicero says (II.ii.7), are always misunderstood on this score. We seem to have given up on truth, for we claim nothing can be known, and yet we offer our opinions on a number of matters. But therein lies the crux: Academicians offer opinions, not assertions (I am not a wise man, *sapiens*, Cicero says in the *Academica*, but an *opinator*; II.xx.66). Our claim is that nothing can be known with certainty, everything must be argued for. This claim does not prevent us from having opinions about the probable, but you cannot have an opinion about the probable until you put the facts in contention, argue all sides of any matter, and make a final judgment, which is like a comparative estimate (II.ii.8). Here, in epitome, is the method of rhetorical-philosophical thought, *controversia;* it involves playing the judge as well as the advocates in a forensic battle. And it is always the duty, or office, of the judge, my dear Marcus, to search for the truth, just as it is sometimes the role of an advocate to argue as forcefully as he can for a plausibility (*veri simile*), however less than the truth it may actually be (II.xiv.51).

All in all, the statesman formed by *De officiis* (to bring my review of this document to an end) is a man who walks warily—not from fear of public fickleness but from the very human condition posited by the Academics. The stance may redeem Cicero's own philosophical writings from appearing a little too pat, facile, or shallow. Given the difficulty of knowing even *probabile,* man's noblest—and, one must assume, safest and most serviceable—action is in suspending his judgment on all matters, by practicing doubt. Suspension of judgment is the starting point and rationale of *controversia*. In this way, too, Cicero's union of rhetoric and philosophy—or, for that matter, his effort to give rhetoric intellectual value—depends on the skeptic's stance toward truth.

Cicero's skepticism, that is, promotes controversy. As Richard McKeon puts it, Cicero's philosophy is

> . . . an unusually persistent, if not always subtle, effort to avoid dogmatic assumptions. It is centered not on a conception of the nature of things or of the biological constitution of man or of the psychological forms of his thought or of the social circumstances of his associations but on the doctrines that men have developed.[54]

Cicero's examination of the nature of the gods (in *De natura deorum*) is, for example, actually an examination of doctrines men dogmatically assert: it is a controversy first between an Epicurean and an Academic and then between a stoic and an Academic—all framed by Cicero, whose stance in questioning the dogmatic assumptions of anti-dogmatism becomes, ironically, more Academic than the Academic spokesman in the dialogue. Though Cicero saw Carneades as the true conservator of the Academy, his own philosophic method owes much to Socrates as well. But it is a *multiplex ratio disputandi.* It is not simply dialogic or two-voiced but sometimes many-voiced, usually antithetical, and always disputatious. The method begets and proceeds by *controversia:* statement, refutation, restatement, further refutation, judgment. "In *controversia,*" Buckley says,

> there is a merger of the uses of philosophic discourse and of oratorical training: the method is the same and its product is either the conclusions of philosophy or the command of a polished oration.[55]

We have seen something of this procedure in our hasty review of *De officiis.* At least two voices, one speaking for *honestum* and one for *utile,* inhere in the inventive process, and having situated the two in a debate, Cicero tested each for its probability and then placed the results in the form of advocacy, that "polished oration" that is *De officiis.* Such is the method of sapience, its many voices essentially the Janiform two of controversy—or, as Titian's *Allegory* later represented it, the three of prudence (see Figure 3, page 61).

Many Ciceronian philosophical works are actually in the form of conversations, in which men are heard advancing contrary or antithetical positions: *De natura deorum* is one, we have noted; so is *De oratore.* Augustine also found the dialogic method useful, if not for *inventio* then certainly for the final form of a work, its publication. Most significantly, Augustine's *Contra academicos* (Against the Academicians), one of the first works he produced upon his conversion, is in the form of a dialogue. We shall return briefly to this document at the conclusion of this essay. But let us here anticipate that return: skepticism, even a Christian skepticism, is not possible in Augustine's epistemology, and because it is not, Ciceronian rhetoric is also not possible. As we have seen, Augustine carefully dismantled that rhetoric in *De doctrina,* severing its parts, particularly the part of thinking from the part of speaking, and dispersing them. For Augustine, rhetoric could have no part of philosophy: *caritas* changes doubt to certainty just as surely as it transforms *honestum* into *beneficentia* (*De doctrina,* III.x.16).

Any revival of Ciceronian rhetoric that also attempts to restore the thinking part, if only under the attitudinal rubric of antidogmatism, must necessarily combine its efforts with the restoration of Ciceronian skepticism. Such is the position in which Renaissance humanists found themselves. Even those humanists who sought to revive Cicero for the sake of his Latinity were unavoidably bringing one "pernicious habit" (in Augustine's terms) into the classroom. Those students who became familiar with Ciceronian *inventio*—whether in *De inventione,* or *De oratore,* or even in the *Rhetorica ad Herennium,* all of which we shall shortly examine—were at least vaguely aware of an attitude that could not tolerate either unexamined assertions or metaphysical speculation having no bearing on the world of practical affairs. Other humanists, of course, inside the classroom as well as out, were quite conscious of all the ramifications of this skeptical *inventio* and its place in the humanist scheme of learning. But whether in the hands of the humanist schoolteacher or in the hands of the humanist philosopher, the *efficaciousness* of Ciceronian skepticism ultimately depends less on text than on context, less on the nature of the document before one than on the ambience in which it is interpreted. As studies have shown, *De inventione* was one of the most influential and widely read works in the Middle Ages—an era not known for its skepticism, or for its susceptibility to the pernicious habit of challenging dogmatism.

The humanist context is a profoundly skeptical one, as Charles Schmitt has shown in his excellent history of Cicero Skepticus in the Renaissance.[56] Schmitt concentrates in particular on the rise and fall in popularity of the *Academica*. Indeed, the history of the rise and fall of that work is almost exactly the history of the rise and fall of Ciceronian rhetoric in the Renaissance—or, for that matter, the rise and fall of humanism itself—a point Schmitt does not make. Nor does he, regrettably, carefully distinguish the unique nature of Ciceronian skepticism or recognize the close connection between it and Cicero's entire rhetoric-centered philosophy.[57] Nonetheless, that skeptical teaching reemerged in the Renaissance is a strong and very useful thesis of Schmitt's work. Popkin and Hallie, too, have vividly presented historical case studies of skepticism's various strands,[58] many of which pervaded the Renaissance and became associated with scientific or pseudo-scientific thought, where suspension of judgment is essential to progress. But Ciceronian skepticism, with which my own study is directly concerned, is peculiar to a "literary culture," the educational program of humanism, and to its philosophical cohort, rhetoric. Of course, all strands of skepticism in the Renaissance tended to converge in attacking a mutual enemy, scholastic dogmatism. For dogmatic truth, skepticism—all skepticism—substitutes *probabilism*. But Cicero, through his Latinity and his learning, seemed to speak most directly to the man of literary culture: that is, to the man who, informed by the *studia humanitatis,* moves warily, acting on the basis of practiced doubt in a world in which there is no really disinterested pursuit of knowledge, nor is science divorced from eloquence, or "truth" from poetry.

Let us now examine three documents that directly pertain to the rhetoric in Renaissance humanism: *De inventione, Rhetorica ad Herennium,* and *De oratore.* The first was a work of Cicero's youth, the last a work of his maturity. The second was not by Cicero at all, yet it continued to be included among Ciceronian documents and was a constituent of Ciceronianism even for those humanists who, like Valla and Erasmus, knew that Cicero had not composed it. All three works were greatly influential in the Renaissance. In examining them we shall concentrate in particular on skepticism and *controversia,* the twin components of Cicero's rhetoricized philosophy, and on *honestum* and *utile,* the almost unavoidably twin faces of Ciceronian rhetorical theory.

When Cicero viewed *De inventione* from the vantage of *De oratore,* he virtually turned his back on the earlier work, speaking of it as something incomplete and hardly worthy of his mature thought (*De orat.* I.ii.5). This did not amount to a renunciation exactly, and the work retained a kind of popularity far in excess of that accorded Cicero's other works, not only during the Middle Ages but during the Renaissance as well. Perhaps the popularity of the book depended more on its usefulness as a manual—a how-to-do-it book by Rome's Demosthenes (or, to a reader with more sophisticated historicity, by a young man who was to become Rome's Demosthenes)—than on either its eloquence or its philosophical import. Like many such manuals, even in our own time, *De inventione* offers clear and simple classifications. Two of these are particularly important so far as the structure of the work is concerned. The first divides all oratory into three kinds—the epideictic, the deliberative, and the judicial (I. v. 7)—and of these the judicial, or forensic—that is, pleading a case in a court of law—gets the lion's share of the theorizing, as we might expect. The art of rhetoric is divided into five parts (I. vii. 9)—*inventio, dispositio, elocutio, memoria,* and *pronuntiatio*. After defining these, Cicero calls *inventio* the most important of all the parts and proceeds to devote the entire work to that one part, concluding (II. lix. 178) with a promise to provide later books on the other parts, a promise which—so far as we know—was never fulfilled, though some readers mistakenly assumed it had been, in the *Rhetorica ad Herennium*.

In *De inventione* the definition of *inventio* reveals, it seems to me, the heart of Ciceronianism: "Inventio est excogitatio rerum verarum aut veri similium quae causam probabilem reddant" (I. vii. 9). That is, *inventio* is the discovery or devising of true or seemingly true arguments for the sake of making one's case appear probable. This sounds like chicanery, until we realize that it is we, not Cicero, who are most likely guilty of too facile a distinction between the true and the false, the real and the apparent, the certain and the uncertain. The theme of Ciceronianism is *probabilitas,* not *veritas:* most truth can never be known with certainty. Moreover, truth is not even the measure of effective argumentation. All argumentation, he points out (I. xxix. 44), aims at either the *necessary* or the *probable:* the necessary is that which has formal validity, like a valid inference from consequence or from posing a dilemma; the probable rests on received opinions or expectations of the outcome of events—or on arguments resembling such opinions and expectations. By contrast, *self-evident* arguments are not matters for *controversia,* though certainly they may be used by the orator to establish the probability of his case; for example, there can be no dispute that Orestes killed his mother. The word Cicero uses for the self-evident

119

argument—that is, argument removed from *controversia*—is *perspi-cuum*, literally translated as "transparent" or "seen through." Thus, unless rhetoric rests on an epistemological belief that few things in this life are truly perspicuous and on a moral code stating that man's highest, most honorable and "honest" actions lie in establishing the probable or the verisimilar in a life devoted to practical affairs, especially political action (in I.v.6, Cicero actually classifies oratorical ability as a part of political science), it could hardly partake of serious, let alone meaningful, intellectual endeavors.

Classification, not *controversia*, is the method of *De inventione*. Not only does Cicero classify his inventive principles, but he also indicates that the orator, too, invents partly at least by classifying, using the topics, places, or *loci* that are either (1) unique to the particular case or kind of oration or (2) universal to all controversy. In the latter case they are known as commonplaces (II.xv.48).[59]

It is significant that the discussion of *loci* is combined with a discussion of the parts of an oration: how to find what to say for an introduction in any one case, or an exordium, *divisio*, narrative, and so on. For that matter, it is significant that the parts of an oration are treated extensively in a work on *inventio*. They would seem to belong to the next promised work, on *dispositio*. Yet it becomes evident—in this work and throughout traditional rhetorical theory—that the so-called parts of the rhetorical process are not discrete or even totally sequential steps. One does not invent, exactly, and *then* arrange, and *then* add style, and so on—though even in Cicero's mature writings the words used for describing the process indicate that the steps are apparently discrete and sequential (see, for example, *De orat.* II.xix.79). If in the creative process one does take the steps in this order, one must nonetheless at various times consider all the parts at once. *Inventio*, for example, is talked about as a systematic means of composing discourse not only by analyzing *pro* and *contra* the question in dispute,[60] but also by considering the nature of the finished product. One must, of course, keep one eye on the audience while one invents, but one keeps the other eye on form. At the heart of *controversia*, analysis is the central mental activity of *inventio*, but considerations of audience and form are tangential activities. They become central, in turn, in *dispositio*, where a further refinement of audience considerations and form is to be made. But *dispositio* is itself not discrete from *inventio*—at least, not in Ciceronian rhetoric. Severance of the two from each other and from the other parts of rhetoric was to become a project of antihumanist theorists in the Renaissance. All five parts—however discrete and sequential they appear—were integral: as such, they were analytical means of systematizing *at once* the creative process and its final, finished, artistic product. That integrity, as noted many times in this study, is essential to rhetoric, and to its unique mode of thought.

Too, one might justifiably call *De inventione* a manual for achieving *advantage,* particularly in judicial or forensic oratory. One might justify that interpretation by pointing to Cicero's elementary advice on how to argue a case from the standpoint of prosecutor or defense attorney (Book II, passim)—as if skillful tactics were all. Yet *advantage* in this sense is virtually the same as *establishing a case with a high degree of probability,* and prosecution and defense are but two necessary sides in a process of controversial thinking. When one further realizes that for Cicero—particularly the mature Cicero—probability is truth and *controversia* is philosophic method, one's charges about advantage or manual of tactics might seem beside the point. As always, advantage, or *utile,* rightly considered, is both a part of *honestum* (II.lv) and the method of sapience.

Nonetheless, outside the Ciceronian system there must have remained an elementary need for a manual of tactics, a how-to book on achieving merely argumentative advantage, regardless of the freeing of the matters from ethical or moral considerations. For *Rhetorica ad Herennium* fills just that need. That Cicero was for a long time, albeit erroneously, considered its author only increased its popularity. The work was apparently written at about the same time as *De inventione,* and in the late Middle Ages was referred to as Cicero's *Rhetorica secunda,* to distinguish it from *De inventione,* his *Rhetorica nova.* It was first printed in Venice in 1470, in the very century in which, amidst a new interest in Cicero and a refinement in methods of historical scholarship, Valla became the first of the humanists to question its Ciceronian authorship. And it is still available in print, among the Loeb Library's twenty-eight volumes devoted to the writings of Cicero.[61] In that work, the translator, Professor Harry Caplan, provides useful footnotes inviting comparisons with *De inventione* and *De oratore,* and the Loeb Library is careful to bracket Cicero's name, in the places where the author's name usually appears. The work is, however unjustly, attached to Ciceronianism—and no amount of historical criticism will disrupt that attachment. For our purposes, it is useful in clarifying a component of the Ciceronianism that Renaissance humanists revived inadvertently and unavoidably.

If the *ad Herennium* is a pale reflection of philosophical impulses at the heart of Ciceronianism, it also makes patent certain correlative impulses, which are mechanical, at times merely clever, and above all, nonphilosophical.[62] If *De inventione* is emphatically on the side of *honestum*, the *ad Herennium* is almost as emphatically on the side of *utile*. Indeed, the *auctor*, whoever he might have been, at one point regards *honestas* as a division of *utilitas* (III.ii.3)—a subsumption directly contrary to Cicero's doctrine. However, an even greater cause for almost anyone's despair is the easy way in which the *auctor* reveals the propensity of rhetoric—even Ciceronian rhetoric—to abandon its philosophical attachments: rhetoric's *sapientia* can be facile or simple-minded and its *eloquentia* merely a matter of scoring. The impulses are present in Quintilian—at times crassly so, as in Book IV, where he advises lying as useful to the orator—but the impulses are also present in an even more complex way in *De oratore*, as we shall see.

Earlier, in my analysis of Milton's speech, I called Ciceronian the advice that arguments should be arranged according to their degree of possible impact: stronger, strong, strongest. The advice appears in the *ad Herennium* (III.x.18), where, in Professor Caplan's translation, it is part of a discussion that ends in a revealing metaphor: "This arrangement of topics in speaking, like the arraying of soldiers in battle, can readily bring victory" (p.189).

When read after Cicero's *De inventione*, the *ad Herennium* seems like an outline, a listing of strategies for creating illusions—for example, how to create the illusion that we have only the best intentions in speaking even when our cause is discreditable (I.vi.9), or the illusion that we have not prepared too much (I.vi.11). Only a shallow or cursory treatment is given to theoretical matters, and the work therefore has a striking and most significant inconsistency: at the beginning of Book II *inventio* is called the most important, or primary, and the most difficult of the tasks (*officiis*) of rhetoric, but later the writer denies that any one of the five can be called most important, though *pronuntiatio*, delivery, does appear to be of the greatest *utile* (III.xi.19).

There are many points of similarity between *De inventione* and the *ad Herennium*, so many that the imputation of the latter to Cicero becomes easy to understand. But despite these similarities, there are vast and important contextual differences. Both works, for example, define *inventio* in exactly the same terms.[63] However, to conceive of *inventio* as the contriving of true or seemingly true matters that will make the lawyer's case seem probable has special force when placed in a context that pays only lip service to ethics and morals. On the whole, for the *auctor* rhetoric is a neutral art, an instrument, centered in *controversia*. But here, much more than in *De inventione*, controversial thinking is divorced from ethics. "It is a fault to disparage an art or science or any occupation because of the faults of those engaged in it," says the *auctor*, "as in the case of those who blame rhetoric because of the blameworthy life of some orator" (p. 137). There is the ethical control of neither Cicero's *honestum* nor Quintilian's "good man." Indeed, says the *auctor*, the point is to make our Invention "keen and prompt, our Arrangement clear and orderly, our Delivery impressive and graceful, our Memory sure and lasting, our Style brilliant and charming." And then he adds, "In the art of rhetoric, then, there is no more" (p. 411).

Cicero's most experienced and thoughtful views on rhetoric are in *De oratore*, which was influential in his own time and later. Augustine's *De doctrina* is sprinkled with allusions to the work. Roger Ascham's *Scholemaster* (1570) called it "the best book that ever Tully wrote." But, however much it represents Cicero's maturity as a rhetorician, *De oratore* shows that the basic system or art of rhetoric has remained the same, from *De inventione* to its own time, that it is still possible to abstract the art from moral considerations, and that the latter are made necessary to the former largely through an act of will.

These twin faces—rhetoric as a neutral instrument, and therefore no humane art but a collection of procedures drawn from successful experience, and rhetoric as an instrument of morality—are given voice in *De oratore* by two *honesti*, two highly learned and gifted men who had been successful advocates and statesmen. Obviously, the work itself is yet another example of *controversia*. And it is also an example of advocacy, like *De officiis*. Again, the frame of the work is a letter, written by Cicero to his brother, Quintus. This book, too, was composed in Cicero's forced retirement. Just as the dialogue is less Socratic in nature and more like a debating contest, the letter that frames it is also a piece of advocacy, written by no impartial judge of the contest but by a distinguished orator who favors *a priori* the second position mentioned above. But as the author of the dialogue, he clearly holds dogmatically only one position: that the only question to which there are not two sides is whether there are two sides to every question.

De oratore consists of three lengthy books. My purpose in reviewing the work is not to track all the interweavings of conversation, in which a total of seven men participate, but to review the arguments of two central figures, Antonius and Crassus, who represent the twin faces of Ciceronian rhetoric. Antonius was the grandfather of Marc Antony, and Crassus was the most distinguished Roman orator before Cicero. We shall also, of course, keep one eye on Cicero, the writer of the framing letter, who was no more than 15 at the time of this dialogue and whose *excogitatio* is based on the report given him by one of the minor participants.

Crassus speaks for Ciceronian philosophy in the debate, and his initial arguments are set forth in Book I. All of Crassus's ideas on rhetoric center in his conception of the "perfect," or "complete," orator (I.viii.34)—one who is never at a loss and who can speak copiously and with variety, charm, knowledge, method, and dignity on any matter whatsoever (I.xiii.59 and xv.64). The perfect orator must encompass all learning but is a specialist in that division of philosophy which is devoted to knowledge of "life and mores" (I.xv). He must be a man of culture and breeding (I.xvi). So far as his training in rhetoric is concerned, Crassus epitomizes the rhetorical theory we have seen expounded at length in the earlier documents (I.xxxi–xxxiv).

Like a counterpoint, Antonius offers his position—respectfully and briefly, for the book belongs to Crassus. Nonetheless, Antonius makes clear the position that will emerge more fully later: Crassus's ideal is unpractical and unattainable (I.xviii); his ideal orator needs the acumen of a dialectician, the wisdom of a philosopher, the diction of a poet, the memory of a lawyer, the voice of a tragedian, and the bearing almost of the consummate actor (I.xxviii.128).[64] Neither wisdom nor statesmanship is to be found in the petty treatises produced by rhetoricians (I.xix). The real orator does not need philosophy, with its abstract discourses on the *summum bonum;* he needs, rather, to know men's souls, feelings, and thoughts (I.li). Indeed, philosophy can even get in the way of effective pleading (I.liii–liv). In sum, *practice* is the important thing in training the consummate orator, who is "the man who can speak in a way calculated to convince" (I.lxi.260). For that, who needs philosophy? Who needs to dissipate his energies over a wide field of learning?

Book II is again framed by Cicero speaking to Quintus, and he virtually rips off the masks worn by Crassus and Antonius. The two were in fact very deeply and broadly learned men. Crassus's successful career depended in part upon his giving the impression that he placed Latin learning above Greek and consequently he earned the reputation that he had a little but not much learning. Antonius, on the other hand, believed that he would achieve most success with Latin audiences if it appeared that he had never engaged in study at all.[65] Obviously, Cicero goes on, no one has ever achieved real excellence in oratory—such as that achieved by these two men—without taking all knowledge for his province. The two men are a case in point, in spite of their reputations—and in spite, one must assume, of their tactics in the debate. Cicero's position, here as always, is manifest if not unambiguous.

Book II belongs almost solely to Antonius. Oratory, he claims, is not the highest form of art. The best rules—some clever ones, for playing upon men's emotions and will—can be drawn from experience (II. viii). Some men have attained proficiency in oratorical skills even without regular training (II.ix.38). Again, practice is the best teacher. His own practice, like that of all Ciceronians, invents by means of controversial thinking:

> It is my own practice to take care that every client personally instructs me on his affairs, and that no one else shall be present, so that he may speak the more freely; and to argue his opponent's case to him, so that he may argue his own and openly declare whatever he has thought of his position. Then, when he has departed, in my own person and with perfect impartiality I play three characters, myself, my opponent and the arbitrator. Whatever consideration is likely to prove more helpful than embarrassing I decide to discuss; wherever I find more harm than good I entirely reject and discard the topic concerned.[66]

This is one of the most succinct theoretical versions of *controversia* in Cicero: a thinker faces a question in dispute and analyzes it by looking for what Isocrates would call "advantage." Technically, Antonius is trying to find the *status* or *constitutio* of a case, the very heart of the matter beyond self-evident facts, where only the probable can be known. There, in that heart, are the true *locus* of *controversia* and the true *habitus* of any lawyerly minded philosopher. Note, moreover, that the search has not simply two voices but three: one voice is that of the "arbitrator," the *iudex,* who must judge the worthiness of the probability offered, not just its logical rigor but its human significance (the role Cicero plays in *De oratore*).

Isocratean "advantage" always tries to determine what it means—to people—to give the unknown something of the character of the known, beyond reasonable doubt. Of course, it may only mean winning a case at law, as Antonius seems to suggest. But Antonius is, we are never allowed to forget, one of Cicero's own voices: for purposes of this debate, this *multiplex ratio disputandi,* he is meant to be practical and nonphilosophical. That is, he is meant to remove *controversia* from Cicero's preferred context, but *that* does not diminish the accuracy of what Antonius says about basic controversial procedure or make his character and reasoning less attractive.

In the course of Antonius's conversation, again virtually the entire theory of rhetoric is covered, for which Crassus compliments him and calls him, with some pointed irony, a master of theory (II.lxxxvi.350). But Antonius is careful to put theory in perspective: the entire efficacy of rhetorical theory is that it simply brings to consciousness the naturally gifted orator's development. It cannot give the orator something with which he is not already endowed or teach him something that is not better taught by practice, through exercise and observing models. Rhetoric is, thus, only a pseudoscience (II.lxxxvii.356).

As the book ends, Crassus's final tactic is to argue that Antonius has actually furthered his, Crassus's, own case. Antonius, we all thought, was merely going to expound the orator's techniques, drawn largely from his own practice, and leave the discrimination of those techniques as well as their embellishment to Crassus. But, Crassus notes, he has actually done all of these things, and so laid the groundwork for his own case. On that note, of rhetorical suspense, the book ends.

But before Crassus speaks in Book III, Cicero, again addressing Quintus, notes that Crassus died soon after this discussion. The observation allows Cicero to embark on a long panegyric to Crassus, during the course of which the death of the other characters, Antonius included, or their banishment is also noted. Their fate (most of the deaths were suicide) as great statesmen and patricians was sealed by the civil war, a fate Crassus escaped only by his earlier death. In sum, the book opens by recalling a great age of Roman republicanism and by investing Crassus with the aura of the ideal.

When the dialogue resumes, Crassus's task is to reunite rhetoric and philosophy. He does this by arguing that Antonius separated matters that cannot really stand apart—just as style and ideas are not really separable but are dependent upon each other. The orator needs the philosopher's wisdom and knowledge, and the philosopher to be effective needs the orator's skill. Otherwise these disciplines are as empty as style divorced from matter. Moreover, in the realm of the ideal—and here Crassus's peculiar brand of Platonism becomes evident—all humane disciplines and forms of knowledge are united. Rhetoric, conceived of in terms of the ideal, is practiced philosophy, the art of living (*vivendi ratione*, III.xxxi.123). In sum, it is by keeping one's eyes on the ideal (*summus*) orator that the rules of rhetoric may be admitted to status as an art.

However unconvincing the entire argument of *De oratore* may appear, its method is patently that at work in rhetorical *inventio*, controversial thinking. Two opposing views are given voice, like two advocates. They are held in a friendly but tenuous relationship by a third voice, an adjudicator, who has already—recall that the entire work is a piece of advocacy for Crassus's position—heard the arguments and pronounced judgment. The *dispositio* of the entire work moves Crassus into the most favored positions: first and last.[67] Crassus's ethos, moreover, invests, or is meant to invest, his arguments with a persuasive power they might lack in logos. Nor is pathos lacking in his appeal, as for example the awe with which he regards the power of rhetoric, used as an argument for the *necessity* of combining rhetoric and philosophy (III.xiv.54–56). The weapon should be placed only in the hands of the ideal orator, the true subject of this entire work, who is to be trained in the old way—that is, the way of the pre-Socratic sophists. It was Socrates, Crassus argues, who shattered the ideal educational scheme, with the result that we now go to one professor to learn how to speak and to another to learn how to think (III.xvi.61). We need to return to a sophistic wholeness in education, a point that in no way moderates, in spite of its criticism of Socrates, Crassus's overriding Platonism but serves it by insisting on ideal educational unities.

Now that we have glimpsed Ciceronian rhetoric, let us return to the earlier point that its theory seems to incorporate twin impulses, *utile* and *honestum:* the combination of an ethically neutral, purely instrumental collection of strategies for making a case seem probable with the moral character of a culturally well-bred statesman. Producing that character is the entire purpose of Cicero's ideal educational scheme, in which rhetoric is conflated with philosophy in order to give wisdom to one and efficaciousness to the other. For the inherent morality of the ideal orator is meant to provide a safeguard against the misuse of rhetoric's power over the public. Cicero's preferred rhetoric, in sum, is ethos-centered. But this *honestum,* or moral character, on which Cicero's ideal rhetoric rests is not the same as the doctrine of self in Augustinocentrism. *Honestum* is a product of culture and art. A man can be "honest" and at the same time eclectic, speaking like a stoic at one point, like an Academic at another—an apparent inconsistency that drew St. Thomas's notice.[68] By contrast, Augustinocentrism poses a central, progressively stable, God-given, and ultimately divine self. This self, with God's help, develops in time toward the truth. It is a self to which a man could be true. The Ciceronian self, or any rhetorical ethos for that matter, is fully aware of its cultural heritage and of its own artificial nature and instrumentality, for it can be fashioned by the needs and possibilities of the speaking situation: the operative questions in fashioning this self are what role must I play for this argument? and what does my audience know about me already?

Another way of putting this final matter concerning the *artificium* of the self is that Ciceronianism did not have the Fall. Depraved, fallen man is not at the center of its epistemology. Fallen man has access to truth, whether through God's once and ongoing revelation or through sparks of divine reason within himself. A deepening sense of man's sinfulness through the centuries following Cicero and an increasing respect for formal logic are more than merely historical correlatives.[69] But fallen man, with his divine reason, will always be at war with himself, a struggle between the urging of his appetites on the one hand and the wisdom of his reason on the other. Ciceronian man recognizes the battleground but is less convinced that "truth" lies within or is to be found by exclusively contemplative means. On the contrary, he substitutes for the anguished and intense interiority of Christianity the public quest for probability. There is therefore a strong connection between rhetoric and secularism—a hazard for all humanists and would-be humanists, from Erasmus to Milton and back to Augustine.

Augustine's first—and, one must wonder, perhaps his greatest—theoretical enemy was Ciceronian skepticism. His *Contra academicos* disparages even the Academic *probable*. He calls it a fiction created by the Academics to allow them to act on *something*. They must create this fiction, Augustine contends, if for no other reason than to perform their duties, for they who would not assent to anything could not accomplish anything either (II.v.11–12). But his longest lasting attack on Ciceronian skepticism came later, when the *De doctrina* dismantled Ciceronian rhetoric by depriving it of *controversia*, its Academic *inventio*, thereby removing the center wherein its twin impulses were joined and man's "honesty" confronted.

A History of English
Humanist Rhetorical Theory

Humanism was rhetorical, and the rhetoric at its center was fundamentally Ciceronian; therefore one could identify humanist rhetoric—theory and practice—by looking for the Academic *controversia*
within it. Such is the enthymeme proposed by the preceding sections
of this chapter. In England just before the age of Donne and Milton
some striking theoretical developments further illuminated the
ground we have covered. Again, our search must be *ad fontes*—though
we are taken part way by modern historians of rhetoric.[70]

The period of humanism in English rhetorical theory was brief
indeed, little more than a quarter century. Between 1553 and 1588, the
first comprehensive English version of Ciceronianism appeared, as
did the first books marking the true disintegration of humanist
rhetoric. It seems appropriate, therefore, to proceed as before by
case study.

The English humanist rhetorician par excellence was Thomas Wilson (ca. 1525–1581), whose *Arte of Rhetorique* (1553) underwent eight
editions in the sixteenth century, an indication of its large readership
and influence. In an important sense, this was the first complete English rhetoric, for it was the first to treat in English all five Ciceronian
arts, from *inventio* to *memoria*. But what makes the work an example
of typically English humanism is not merely its full treatment of
those arts but its complex and utterly doomed efforts to make Ciceronianism at home in sixteenth-century England. Therein the book reveals a nexus of contraries that are characteristic at once of controversial thinking and, in their unresolved state, of English humanism.
That very nexus left humanist rhetoric vulnerable to attack by educational reformers in the name of order, formal simplicity, and coherence. Too much was thrown into the scale—Cicero and the Christian
myth of the Fall, in particular—and the patent imbalance greatly
served the cause of humanism's enemies.

Large sections of Wilson's work are simply translations of Cicero.[71]
His discussion of deliberative oratory, for example, or of virtue, in-

cluding the cardinal virtues, follows *De inventione* closely. He refers directly to *De oratore,* which he calls Cicero's book on a "perfect Oratoure" (fols. 88, 94ᵛ, and 118ᵛ), and follows at least two long sections of it with some precision. Wilson also—and, recalling our earlier discussion of Cicero, this is quite important—casually includes references to the *Rhetorica ad Herennium.* As a learned humanist, Wilson must have known that Cicero was not the *auctor* of *ad Herennium.* But, also as a humanist, he must have known that the *ad Herennium* was useful, and sanctified by a long association with Cicero. Nor, as a humanist, could he, or would he want to, escape the overtly *utilitarian* nature of the *ad Herennium.* Utilitarianism was *in* Ciceronianism. Turn it loose, though, and it could dismantle Ciceronianism, or reveal that its philosophical connections were only an overlay.

Of course, Wilson had philosophy enough. He had not only Ciceronian "honesty" but also Christianity, and he would do what he could to make them lie down in the same bed. For example, when Wilson discusses Ciceronian status theory, he adds "Gods lawe" to the "legal" issue (fol. 52ᵛ). And throughout his work, he continually has his eye on the needs of the Christian preacher—even at times showing how the rules for forensic oratory, pleading a case at law, pertain to sermonizing (fol. 59ᵛ). The differences in these—between Ciceronian *honestum* and Christian virtue, and between legal oratory and preaching—as Wilson presents them, seem less significant than their similarities. Perhaps *that* only reflects Wilson's inability to think very deeply, but perhaps, too, it reflects something that is essential about English humanist rhetoric—its eclecticism at the expense of consistency and depth.

But there is another disparity that no blithe eclecticism could numb or dispel, which is seen best in Wilson's attempt to revive Ciceronian *epistemology* within orthodox Christianity, even though the orthodoxy of that Christianity was beginning to show some cracks and crevices. Christian man is fallen man. The immortal part of his soul lies in his reason; there the divine sparks of God are at work and often at war with his animal nature, his body. The dominance of this myth of the fallen man, with its emphasis on the divinity of reason, helps us understand why *logic* was preeminent in the centuries before the humanist revival of ancient learning. The supreme discipline could only be one that fosters man's God-like faculty. Throughout the humanist revival, there

131

were reverberations of medieval logic, which as a mode of thought was far more extreme than Augustinianism. It was, in effect, a segregated, bodyless, and closed system of reasoning. As I understand it, medieval logic tended to be of two sorts. One was nonverbal and symbolic, the kind we associate with mathematical and quantitative reasoning, which underwent a resurgence with the rise of science in the sixteenth century. The other was dialectic, a highly verbal and hair-splitting *controversia*. Both were sanctified, but the second was dominant in education. And from this mode of logic Ciceronianism had to reclaim the right to teach disputation and the forms of thought.

Thus, like all Renaissance humanists, Wilson comes to rhetoric from logic. But in his case the progression was literal. Two years before he published *The Arte of Rhetorique,* Wilson published *The Rule of Reason, conteinyng the Arte of Logique.* The work was another innovation, the first English logic.[72] The logic of which Wilson speaks is the second kind mentioned above, a means of argumentation, in which one person denies a proposition while another defends it. Called both logic and dialectic, this form is obviously a kind of *controversia.* Wilson in *The Rule of Reason* outlines the duties of the "aunswerer" (the denier) and the "apposer" (the defender). The argument, or disputation, proceeds until one person caves in or until the audience or judges are ready to deliver a verdict. The public involved in this proceeding, including the "aunswerer" and "apposer," are all experts, all men of learning—unlike the usual public in rhetoric. Moreover, Wilson shows that for him the true difference between logic and rhetoric lies not in the forms of thought but in the audience. Rhetoric, he says in *The Rule of Reason,* using an ancient comparison, is an "open" hand (p. 11); that is, it addresses a heterogeneous audience—that "beast of many heads," as Horace once described it. Rhetoric therefore could not be so tight-fisted as logic, the "closed" hand—it could not be so tight-fisted or so reasonable or so divine.

As Wilson says in the *Rhetorique,* the logician's specialty is "plaine teachyng," whereas the rhetorician employs "large amplification and beautifying" of his subject (fol. 13). Logic, that is, gives us reason alone. Rhetoric adds something to it. In the *Rhetorique,* Wilson places at the first of his discussion the three ends that Cicero made prominent at the close of his career: teaching, pleasing, and moving. Cicero spelled out those ends in the *Orator,* his last work on rhetoric, which was an attempt to redefine the discipline in the face of criticism from the "Attici," who tried to argue that significant communication has only one end, to teach, and only one style, the plain. On the contrary, Cicero claims, rhetoric has three ends, each correlated with its own style. Wilson's move is similar to Cicero's: to justify rhetoric by arguing for its expansive nature. But Cicero's argument makes rhetoric complex; Wilson's makes it a weak sister.

Logic, tight-fisted as it was, had only two parts to rhetoric's five; but logic's two parts, judgment and invention, were close in nature to rhetoric's first two, though in reverse order. Ominously, in the *Rhetorique* Wilson calls logic "that arte, whiche by reason findeth out the truthe" (fol. 61). And in neither work does he build any skeptical foundation, as Cicero does, on the probable. In *The Rule of Reason,* his first definition of logic epitomizes *controversia:* "Logique is an Arte to reason probably, on bothe partes, of al matiers that be putte foorth, so ferre as the nature of euery thing can beare" (p. 8). His second definition—again, from *The Rule of Reason*—is even more to the point, and more ominous for rhetoric: "Logique, otherwise called Dialect (for thei are bothe one) is an Art to try the corne from the chaffe, the trueth from euery falshod, by definyng the nature of any thing, by diuidyng the same, and also by knittyng together true argumentes and untwinyng all knottie subtleties, that are bothe false and wrongfully framed together" (pp. 10–11). The preeminent art for thinking, even for controversial thinking, for this first humanist English rhetorician, would appear to be unskeptical *logic,* wherein truth is firm and knowable. Thus, he attends generously to "amplification" in rhetoric: how to take an invented matter and amplify it, through style, examples, and fables, to move an audience. That is, in the *Rhetorique* he gives amplification and style the prominence they had in the *ad Herennium* and in Quintilian.

Wilson would not be a Ciceronian if he did not build into his *Rhetorique* controversial thinking. It's there, obscured at times, and always with a nod toward logic. Even though Wilson discusses the demonstrative oration first—there isn't much in Cicero on demonstrative, or epideictic, oratory—he frames all his theoretical matters with judicial-oratorical considerations. That is, like Cicero, Wilson makes clear that all the principles of rhetoric can be learned through studying judicial oratory—for it is in learning *that* form of oratory that we learn the all-important process of controversial thinking, thinking like a lawyer pleading a case.

Moreover, like Cicero, Wilson makes it plain in the *Rhetorique* that all five tasks—invention, disposition, style, memory, and delivery—are involved in each other. Even though he separates each for a discussion, he moves back and forth from one to the other, as Cicero does, indicating that the rhetorical creative process is a field of activity in which one thinks, organizes, ornaments, speaks, remembers all more or less at once. Indeed, the all-at-onceness of rhetoric is important in a way that Wilson himself does not seem to recognize, overtly at least. The rational and irrational, the mind and the body, the private and the public self all work together in the rhetorical creative process, and an implicit acknowledgment of their union is essential in any work that, like Wilson's, purports to be—and is purported to be—Ciceronian.

In sum, thinking like a lawyer is at the heart of *both* of Wilson's books; and thus controversial thinking was something one was to learn both in logic and in rhetoric. But logic, as I have tried to show, has prior claim on truth and on the means whereby truth is discovered. Rhetoric, by contrast, adds the body to an intellectual enterprise—and in the English Renaissance the body was still regarded as less divine than reason, in spite of the efforts of the earlier Italian humanists to insist upon the body's goodness. In this way, the presence of Wilson's work on logic clarifies the tensions in his rhetoric. That rhetoric alone carried into the Age of Elizabeth all the skeptical premises and earthly morality of Ciceronianism coupled with the utilitarian vice of the *Rhetorica ad Herennium,* and then set the whole system within the Christian myth of fallen man, and spoke to a reader who was used to thinking of logic as the discipline whereby we learn to think and of rhetoric as the discipline whereby we learn style, usually Latin style. *That,* in short, was English humanist rhetoric. Like most northern humanist efforts, it was aimed at increasing human possibilities for thought and action without, somehow, disrupting the myth of fallen man and his access to certain truth. Such were the theoretical boundaries of Academic *controversia* in Renaissance England.

Wilson's theories would thus seem to be useful and interesting largely as materials in intellectual history. In theory he tried to integrate the utterly unintegratable, and his efforts reveal the intellectual currents of his time. Catching the inconsistencies would be tantamount to catching glimpses of the mind, or *geist,* of the period. But Wilson is also worth reading partly because he is still readable. And he

134

is still readable because he learned—perhaps because of his rhetorical theory, perhaps in spite of it—how to put his *voice* on the page; particularly is this true of the *Rhetorique*. Note the following passage. For the sake of making Wilson's voice as audible as possible to our ears, I have modernized the spelling and punctuation:

> Wherefore is the law profitable? Undoubtedly because no man could hold his own, if there were not an order to stay us and a law to restrain us. And I pray you who getteth the money? The lawyers no doubt. And were not land sometimes cheaper bought, than got by the trial of a law? Do not men commonly for trifles fall out? Some for lopping of a tree spend all that ever they have. Another for a goose that grazeth upon his ground tries the law so hard that he proves himself a gander. Now when men be so mad, is it not easy to get money among them? Undoubtedly the lawyer never dieth a beggar. And no marvel. For a lawyer begs for him and makes away all that they have, to get that of him the which the oftener he bestoweth the more still *he* getteth. So that he gaineth always, as well by increase of learning as by storing his purse with money, whereas the other get a warm sun oftentimes and a slap with a short tail for all that ever they have spent. And why would they? Tush, if it were to do again, they would do it; therefore the lawyer can never want a living, till the earth want men and all be void.   [fols. 20ᵛ–21]

Wilson sounds like a man speaking, a result, I believe, of rhetorical *controversia*. Look back through those passages again and note within them the sense of a respondent present in the speaker's own thoughts. His putative audience is a young man who is considering becoming a lawyer, and for this person the speaker is analyzing (inventing) his subject by means of Ciceronian "circumstance" (to whom? when? where? wherefore?). But question-answer, give-take—that is the general movement of the speaker's mind. He interjects, exclaims, maybe even chuckles. He moves proleptically, with an ear to objections. He uses irony. The presence of controversy is, perhaps, best sensed in Wilson's perilous way of barely stopping short of delivering a broadside against the legal profession: all debaters know that affirmation presupposes refutation. Above all, Wilson has a sense of himself speaking and a sense of his audience. And his audience, actual as well as putative, would seem to be the rhetorician's, not the logician's—not learned, not expert, but probably, by its very nature, exclusive of the serious-minded.

By contrast, *The Rule of Reason* is somewhat hollow and toneless. In that book, though Wilson writes about controversial thinking and gives examples, his writing shows that "logical" *controversia* does not produce voice quite in the way rhetorical *controversia* does—for example (again, I have modernized the spelling and punctuation):

> When the shape or form is made, the effect or thing done may follow. Take away the shape and the use also is taken away. A cup is made, ergo a man may drink in it. Break the cup, and how shall you drink of the same cup? The element goeth compass wise, because it is round. Reason is called the shape of man. Therefore I may say, such a one lacketh the gift of reason, ergo he is a fool. [p. 112]

If *The Rule of Reason* is an example of teaching in the "plain style," one would have to say that its "voice" is that of desiccated pedagogy. I cannot imagine someone today sitting down and reading that book with pleasure, though I can imagine someone today enjoying Wilson's *Rhetorique*. In *The Rule of Reason* there seems to be no audience, respondent or otherwise, present to provoke Wilson's mind to move this way and that and to force a clear definition of his own persona—both characteristics of the truly humanist voice.

We come away from the *Rhetorique* with a strong sense of Wilson's own character, or at least the one he created for purposes of teaching Ciceronian rhetoric. Indeed, ethos would seem to be a more significant formal cause of the work than any orderly distribution of the principles of rhetoric (an orderly distribution of those principles is not quite possible in Ciceronianism anyway). However, not once does Wilson mention ethos. He addresses logos, of course, in both books. And he devotes much time in the *Rhetorique* to talking about pathos, moving the audience's emotions. But if he doesn't *discuss* ethos, he certainly *demonstrates* its effects, possibilities, and efficacy in amplification.

I think that in this matter of voice, or ethos, we see the very best of humanist rhetoric at work: the self—how to create it artificially and how to get it down on paper—is a desideratum of humanism,[73] and is one of the reasons the humanists loved not only Cicero's writings but also Augustine's *Confessions*. The *theoretical* foundation of that self—

Augustine would never admit this, of course—is *controversia,* in a rhetorical setting, the *pro* and *contra* movement of the mind in the presence of a nonexpert, perhaps even nonserious respondent, whether inside or outside the work. The key here is a self thinking controversially *in order* to produce an effect on an audience—thinking, that is, *with* the body and *of* the audience's body, comprising sense, imagination, and emotions. Reason addresses only reason in "logical" *controversia.* The forms of reasoning are always less important in rhetoric than the effect those forms, or any form, have on a moveable audience—as shown even in the forms of Wilson's theorizing. In view of what we have seen of humanism on the theoretical level, where vivid presentations all but mask a notable lack of coherence, we might think of the confusion as at least a productive one. For if English humanists never managed to produce a coherent rhetorical theory, and they didn't,[74] at least through their mishmash of Ciceronianism and Christianity they showed people what *voice* is and how to use it. In humanism, *voice, character, self,* and *ethos* all have the same meaning, for rhetorically they all come down to one quality: a sense of a person speaking to other people—to Antonius, say, or to God, or to a young man who would be a lawyer, or to a putative respondent as fictive as the speaker's own self.

That voice was totally silenced in Ramism, the chief antihumanist movement which set in toward the close of the sixteenth century in western Europe. Ironically, and significantly, it was the sort of movement that could be born only of humanism. Its founder, the Frenchman Pierre de la Ramée (1515–1572), or Peter Ramus, early proclaimed his intention of restoring a pure Aristotelianism by correcting and wiping away its overlay of scholasticism. Ramus proposed a new logic as the *scientia scientiarum,* regardless of the task of the composer, be he orator, poet, dialectician, or philosopher. This logic had only two parts: invention and disposition. For invention, Ramus merely offered an abridgment of the old system of "places." For disposition, he offered some instruction on how to compose axioms and syllogisms and a discursive arrangement his followers exalted, called "method." The latter was the simple doctrine that any writer or speaker should begin with his most general proposition, then divide it up by means of dichotomies, and proceed to the most specific, or least known, elements. Moreover, although he called this logic "dialectic," he actually did not think of it as a disputatious art.

The art was to become that of "teaching"—that is, simply *revealing* the truth to others—and this teaching was to be offered in the style in which Cicero said it should be offered, the plain style.

Ramist rhetoric, which also consisted of only two parts, style and delivery, further reveals that a totally non-Ciceronian epistemology seems to be at work, as if people need only to be shown the truth for it to work on them. If it may be argued that this is the reappearance of that stoical face of humanism, it must also be argued that it returned with a vengeance, shoving aside even those vestiges of Ciceronianism, such as emotion and memory, that the softer Augustinian face would allow. Ramus did not himself write a rhetoric, however. That task was left to his colleague Omar Talon. Still, Ramus's stand on the matter was unmistakable, as shown in his preface to Talon's rhetoric, in 1567: only the discipline of logic was to offer instruction in thinking. And, as is apparent from Ramist logic, even the orator's thinking was not to be controversial thinking. Truth itself was not to be "invented" by means of *controversia*. Rather, truth was something to be *intuited*.

"Natural reason" was a phrase very much bandied about in the Ramist books on logic, as it was in humanist books as well; it referred to those sparks of divine reason implanted in every man by God. But the Ramist application of the doctrine of "natural reason" was far stricter than the humanists', and even went well beyond Augustine's *magister:* the mind, their system presupposes, can spontaneously see the connections between things in the universe. Our sparks of divine reason might be fanned somewhat by the systematizing offered in Ramist logic—but even that tutoring was not absolutely essential. Truth was something that was *there.* Even its communication seemed no longer to depend on discourse. Thus, the Ramist system is profoundly antihumanist because it is also profoundly not just anti- but nonrhetorical.

Two books by the English poet and lawyer Abraham Fraunce (ca. 1558–1633) exemplify these trends. The first is called, ironically, *Lawiers Logike* (1588). The title is ironical because it would seem to offer the very essence of Ciceronianism. But there is little disputation in this book, and there are neither the means nor the manner of Ciceronian *controversia.* It seems unlikely that a lawyer using *this* mode of logic would be very successful:

> The Art of logike . . . layeth downe the right vse of naturall
> reason: and this that wee call shewing or declaring how to rea-

son, is no giuing of reason to him that had it not, but an applying or directing of the minde to the view and contemplation of
that, which of it selfe it might perceaue if it were turned and
framed therevnto. [fol. 4ᵛ]

Fraunce's book, written in English, Latin, and the "Hotchpot French"
(sig. ¶3ʳ) of England's early works on law, may be aimed at lawyers. But
he makes it very plain that his principles of logic were for all people,
anyone who wished to be "reasonable" and who wished to find out how
to be so in a systematic way. The system, its adherents claimed, was
only a patina on divine processes in man's nature itself.

And if that were true, then man's nature had no voice. The Ramist
books were among the dullest of the time. I doubt that we would still
be reading them, had we not been shown, by Ong and Howell, that
they had tremendous effect on later developments in logic and rhetoric.[75] Through their emphasis on a quality we have later come to call
"objectivity," these books obviously connected with developments
that produced what we think of as the scientific method. Simultaneously, they obviously looked backward to the symbolic and quan-
tified logic of the Middle Ages, which received something of a resurgence in their simplified dialectic. And, so far as looking backward
goes, they thought they were looking backward to a purer Aristotelianism, freed of the obfuscating later commentaries on Aristotle's
work, now revived and recharged for the sake of keeping the arts as
discrete as possible. But such views, where they revealed the epitomizing the Ramists themselves believed, proudly, was the hallmark of
their reform, only showed the epitomizing for what it truly was, a
crude abridgement—accomplished, moreover, unlike the perhaps
equally crude synthesis of humanism, at the expense of voice. Review
that statement from Fraunce quoted earlier; note that he says the mind
"views" truth and "contemplates" it—silently, we must suppose. Or
listen to his voiceless voice in *The Lawiers Logike* (again I have modernized the spelling and punctuation):

There be two parts of logic: exposition of the nature of arguments and disposition of the same. Exposition is the first part of
logic which expoundeth the divers kinds of arguments by their
several affections and mutual relations one to another, which
for that it helpeth to invent arguments is called invention. An
argument is any several concept apt to argue that whereunto in
reason it is referred. [fol. 4ᵛ]

That is how a Ramist discourse unfolds. A general statement is broken into two parts, which are likewise broken into two parts and so on, like a cell dividing. There is not much talk there.

Fraunce's "General Table of the Whole Book"—his table of contents—looks like a diagram for a modern athletic tournament, though printed in reverse, as if the winning teams were on the left, the pairings on the right. On the left, we have "logic," and bracketing away from it are "invention" and "disposition," and each of these has two brackets, and so on, until we reach all the bracketed items on the right margin. Most of the writing merely reaffirms the dichotomizing. Rhetoric and logic are discrete; so are invention and disposition, and so are their various parts—in this way, composition is no longer that (confusing to the Ramists) field of activity it is in Wilson. Note the definition of *argument* that Fraunce gives us above: it depends upon a prior sense that everything in the universe coheres and is related to everything else; reason is a means whereby those intuited relations are severely insulated from each other and held in meaningful order, for ready reference. The form of Fraunce's "General Table" reveals the reason at work in his book:

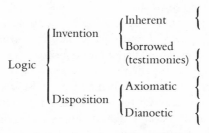

One can imagine the brackets continuing until one reaches the indivisible. If we leave Wilson's book on rhetoric with a sense of the man's character and his book on logic with an abstract sense of logical procedures, we leave Fraunce's two books with a strongly visual sense of diagrams. As always, form—a book's organization, or arrangement—largely demonstrates the writer's intention.

Fraunce's rhetoric appeared the same year as his logic. Predictably, the work divides rhetoric into two parts—style and delivery—and proceeds by dichotomies to list the various figures and tropes, each defined and exemplified, and to list the elements of voice and gesture. Again, his title was surely meant to have audience appeal: *The Arca-*

dian Rhetorike (1588) capitalizes on the popularity of Sir Philip Sidney's *Arcadia*. In both cases, of course, Fraunce's titles were more than simply advertising. *Lawiers Logike* had Agricolan as well as Ciceronian precedents, actual in the first instance, ironical in the second. And, as a literary person and protégé of Sidney, he surely intended the title of his rhetoric book as a tribute; then, too, the title may indicate that Fraunce saw something in Sidney's *Arcadia* that was radically Ramistic.[76] Of course, devoted Ramists, like Fraunce, tended to see Ramism everywhere in the great writings, which, they supposed, were only following nature. Examples of style in Fraunce's rhetoric book are drawn from the *Arcadia,* from *Astrophel and Stella,* and from the *Iliad,* the *Aeneid,* Cicero, Tasso, Horace, Erasmus, Scaliger, and Ovid, among others—all set within a theoretical discussion whose dryness makes the prose in Wilson's logic seem florid.

The point here is that the Ramists totally shattered Ciceronian rhetoric—and in non-Augustinian ways. They placed the major burden of the creative process on *invention,* but placed *invention* about as close as one can come in theory to the process whereby ideas are merely intuited. Even as a "place" logic the system is scant. *Controversia,* whether dialectical or rhetorical, has been removed from the inventive process—literally, by Fraunce, who places it not in *invention* but in *disposition,* as a form whereby invented arguments may be arranged:

> In every syllogistical conflict and controversy, there is a defendant and an opponent. The first is to urge, prove, conclude; the other to repel, avoid, and drive back. The disputation being once begun, it is an unorderly confusion for the same man sometimes to answer, sometimes to reply, and never constantly to play out his own part. . . . I have therefore in a word or two, laid down some general instructions and directions for orderly disputations. [*Lawiers Logike,* fol. 101 (modernized)]

The passage seems to look directly at Wilson: what had been diverse now appeared chaotic. Thus, in the name of order, Ramists not only separated "wisdom" from "eloquence"—drastically—but totally revised Ciceronian "wisdom" to give it little dependence upon complex, give-and-take speaking, *multiplex ratio disputandi, controversia.* In this way, the Ramists gave great impetus to the initial and lasting disintegration of humanist rhetoric.

However, the disintegration of humanist rhetoric was perhaps inevitable. It had been an unstable mixture to begin with. But what may have finally done it in was the manifest need of the age for a "new rhetoric." The printing press was capturing the popular imagination. And humanist rhetoric seemed a relict, a throwback to an ancient age of speaking in forums and public assemblies. Such was not actually the case—it only seemed to be, because of rhetoric's heavy reliance on Cicero. Humanist rhetoric, Wilson's for example, explicitly encompassed written discourse—including the whole *ars dictaminis,* the art of letter-writing, from the Middle Ages. Apparently, however, it could not, on the theoretical level, claim or show that controversial thinking was also a means for achieving voice in writing. Instead, humanist rhetoric stood idly by, with a jumble of confusing and contradictory doctrines in its hands, while reformers of logic claimed that *they* had access to the real, the natural truth—and that the access was largely silent, as were the forms of truth themselves. Though Ramists made no mention of the affinity of their communicative theories with the printing press, the two shared certain qualities, such as rapid assimilation, a memory based on visual structures, and the transformation of words into uniform objects.[77]

Following the Ramists, three options open to rhetorical theory exemplify my general point, that by marking the initial disintegration of humanist rhetoric these reformers also mark the initial disintegration of humanism itself. The seventeenth century became increasingly obsessed with the scientific method, which itself tended to be of two sorts, each presenting an option to humanist rhetoric. The first was radically, even rabidly antirhetorical. The members of the Royal Society, for example, were to use mathematics as their model in communication; words were to be used sparingly, always in the effort to become as transparent as possible—there is that "perspicuousness" again. Truth in this case, unlike Cicero's *perspicuum,* was not simply self-evident but certain, something to be seen in spite of language, which generally tended only to interfere with it.[78]

The other sort of scientific method was Baconian, which at first seems much more sympathetically rhetorical. Francis Bacon, as Ong has noted, was "inextricably tangled in the rhetorical tradition."[79] However, Bacon, like some skeptics but unlike most Ciceronians, accepted a certain dualism comprising things that belong to faith and things that do not, with those not belonging to faith requiring testing. The position is rationalist, finally, and it was turned on rhetoric, where the faculty of reason was to put a check on the faculty of imagination: it is both the "duty" and the "office" of rhetoric, Bacon argued in a passage that directly controverts our earlier characterization of Erasmianism, "*to apply Reason to Imagination* for the better moving of the will."[80] A similar rationalism was turned on the materials of rhetoric: Bacon's "idols" are the first serious critique of language and its uses. But perhaps Bacon's deep entanglement in the rhetorical tradition is best shown in his own scientific procedure, which was itself patterned after controversial thinking—with a notable difference. Neal Gilbert has pointed out that Bacon actually transformed debating procedures into a method of scientific inquiry, "in which Nature replaced the respondent and the challenger became the scientist."[81] Nature, of course, says nothing back, and the mode of examination would seem to be more like an inquisition than a disputation.

Of these two options the century opened to any continued (beyond humanism) developments in rhetorical theory, then, the first was totally destructive, the second transformative through rationalism. But at least one other avenue existed. Intuitiveness like that at the heart of Ramism flowered, I think, in the meditative tradition.[82] Now meditation was itself a highly complex mode of communication. Its interweavings with rhetoric and Ramism need further examination—certainly more than I can give them here—but I wish to offer the following brief consideration. Any communicative mode that is at heart intuitive is at heart nonsystematic; its surface procedures are incantatory, or ritualistic, using words in the service of a nonverbal reality. Here is the greatest paradox of the Ramist system: it is outwardly systematic and verbal, inwardly unsystematic and nonverbal. Meditation has the same kind of paradox. But in humanist rhetoric, the paradox is partly reversed. Outwardly unsystematic (beyond its indiscrete division of activities into five parts), it was inwardly systematized: predicated on the idea that truth is probable, Ciceronian rhetoric is implicitly systematized epistemologically in its further insistence that probable truth is a function of public interaction, of verbal exchanges between people, of the construction of public form, and the search for advantage in persuasion. And only in rhetoric are both the outer and inner appearances verbal.

Thus, all the major options open to rhetorical theory shared at least one key characteristic of Ramism: all denied rhetoric its inner system, for all denied that rhetoric even had a unique or important mode of thought. Too, all were embarked on a quest for a greater certainty than rhetoric could possibly afford. And all believed they were prepared to face certain mysteries that Ciceronian rhetoric was inherently unequipped to face.

When Ciceronian rhetorical theory began to return in the seventeenth century and try to recoup some of its losses after the incursions of Ramism, Baconianism, and meditation, it too offered an *inventio* in which truth was discoverable with something like certainty, through intuition.[83] Then, for centuries, truth exceeded the grasp of rhetoric altogether. Humanist, or Ciceronian, *inventio* was dead. Nor could it return until we became ready, once more, to respect *controversia* as a mode of thought—and that meant becoming ready, once more, for Ciceronianism's particular brand of skepticism.[84]

Donne's Rhetoric

"No, my lord, words don't matter."

"What are you talking about?" I said. "Are you crazy? The entire Bible is the word of God, isn't it? God Himself is the Word, isn't He? If you don't care about these things, you neglect them. If you neglect them, you're the heretic, not Erasmus. For he deals in nothing but words."

[Richard Pace, *De fructu,* 1517]

Pilate therefore said unto him, Art thou a king then? Jesus answered, Thou sayest that I am a king. To this end was I born, and for this cause came I into the world, that I should bear witness unto the truth. Every one that is of the truth heareth my voice.

Pilate saith unto him, What is truth?

[St. John 18:37–38]

As what is true can never contradict what is true, we determine that every proposition which is contrary to the truth of the revealed faith is entirely false.

[The Lateran Council, 1512]

Doubt is the heightened awareness of insistent variety.

[Philip Hallie, *The Scar of Montaigne,* 1966]

Donne's final union is achieved, not through the denial, but through the affirmation of those things which would present insurmountable obstacles had not the Word been made flesh: his selfhood and his sins.

[M. M. Mahood, *Poetry and Humanism,* 1950]

145

Inconstancy Begets a Constant Habit

The following poem is an epitome of rhetorical *controversia,* the true Ciceronian, and humanist, *inventio:*

Womans constancy

Now thou hast lov'd me one whole day,
To morrow when thou leav'st, what wilt thou say?
Wilt thou then Antedate some new made vow?
    Or say that now
We are not just those persons, which we were?   5
Or, that oathes made in reverentiall feare
Of Love, and his wrath, any may forsweare?
Or, as true deaths, true maryages untie,
So lovers contracts, images of those,
Binde but till sleep, deaths image, them unloose?   10
    Or, your owne end to Justifie,
For having purpos'd change, and falsehood; you
Can have no way but falsehood to be true?
Vaine lunatique, against these scapes I could
    Dipute, and conquer, if I would,   15
    Which I abstaine to doe,
For by to morrow, I may thinke so too.

The process of thought in this poem recalls the one Antonius uses to discover the disputed issues in a case at law (*De orat.* II.xxiv. 102– 103). It recalls, too, Cicero's imaginary defense of Orestes in *De inventione* (I.xiii. 18–19). It is an advocate's *pro* and *contra* analysis, aimed at defining a case, in order to marshal arguments toward a central point. In this instance, the advocate's analysis is practiced by a lover who, the lover himself assumes, is about to be jilted.

The speaker—let us momentarily refer to him in the masculine gender—imagines several possible defenses, none of which places *her* in a favorable light. To begin with, *that* she will leave, will jilt him, is casually assumed. Then five ostensibly random defensive arguments are imagined. The tone of the arguments, including the abrupt way in which jilting is casually assumed by the prospectively injured party, would seem to follow Antonius's advice to conduct the controversial *inventio* "with perfect impartiality." Yet one assumption *we* are always safe in making about Donne's argumentation is that it is never impartial, even when it is disguised as analysis. The randomness, that is, is only ostensible. What we have before us is not analysis but the results of analysis, and they have been suffused with intentionality.

The first two defensive arguments center, respectively, in the vow and in the persons. She will make a new vow, then antedate it, or she will claim—appealing, one might suppose, to some Heraclitean concept of nature—that the lovers themselves are changed from one day to the next. The next two arguments also center, respectively, in the vow and in the persons. Oaths made under duress are not binding, or else the change wrought by sleep parts the lovers and unties the contract, as death ends the marriage vows. The fifth, and final, imagined defense moves onto another level. The first four—two pairs—considered *both* lovers, their vows and persons. The fifth considers only the jilting one: perhaps she can remain true to her own personal vow of fickleness only by being false. Too, this fifth imagined defense prepares us for a similar shift at the end of the poem, to the jilted lover, who makes only one claim, that his skills in prosecution could shatter her defense, and offers only one personal argument, that he may be ready for change by tomorrow himself.

The arrangement of the poem, then, is from imagined arguments that center in the lovers' vows and persons to a final argumentative coupling, the jilting lover's personal vow and the jilted lover's vaunt. The vaunt both contemptuously dismisses her possible "scapes" ("escapes" we would call them, like loopholes in a contract) and admits his own possible culpability. That is, through the first four arguments the two lovers, their vows and persons, are on the stand. In the last two—the fifth defense and the jilted lover's response—the two face each other directly.

But the entire poem is a rhetorical fantasy, an imaginary forensic contest occurring before the fact, and projected by a lover who is at present in a condition apparently quite the opposite of the one he imagines. One might suppose the speaker is a cynic or a self-tormentor, who can neither enjoy the present nor indulge in only momentary joy. But is the poem about the speaker? Let us examine Donne's intention as revealed not simply by the controversial nature of the poem but also by its resulting form.

The fantasy is constructed on the assumed, unargued, and unproven claim that she will be false. To an extent, the vigor with which the speaker pursues his analysis itself substantiates the initial assumption. This has happened before, it will happen again, and furthermore I'm just as responsible as she is. There is no sense of crisis in this poem, no attempt to get her to stay or to prevent her from being false, to use the upcoming fickleness to intensify the present moment or, for that matter, even to encourage her faithfulness. The final emotion is one of cancelling out, of diffidence, the skeptic's emotion. But it is not the lover's skepticism that makes the poem a clear example of controversial thinking.

Nor is it the lover's use of legalistic terms. Finding such terms in Donne's writing requires no effort, by the way—even outside the elegies and sermons he composed at Lincoln's Inn. "Father, part of his double interest / Unto thy kingdome thy Sonne gives to mee, / His joynture in the knottie Trinitie, / Hee keeps . . ." begins one of his Holy Sonnets. Donne never escaped sounding like a lawyer or—more to the point of my thesis in this book—thinking like one.

What makes this poem a clear example of *controversia* is its division between two argumentative positions: hers and his, defense and prosecution, *pro* and *contra*. Every debater tries to outguess his opponent and deflate the force of his opponent's argument through "prevention"—that is, through getting there *first*. This anticipatory refutation has historically been known in rhetoric as *prolepsis*, a somewhat risky tactic, for it can often prompt arguments that might not otherwise be considered—the jilting lover, for example, might not think of antedating a new-made vow. But no risk is involved if the debater is ready to meet the argument, as in this poem the jilted lover claims he is. The result of the entire process is an utterance that is full of turnings, in the Ciceronian, not the Augustinian, sense. Recall the example cited earlier from Thomas Wilson's *Rhetorique:* in Wilson's endeavors to persuade a young man to enter the study of law, the presence of controversy is evident in part from the overt use Wilson makes of prolepsis. Indeed, his arguments in favor of the legal profession as a career at times sound very much like an attack on the profession itself: the arguments come close to turning on themselves. The skillful use of the tactic lies in the speaker's control, in how he manages to take the wind out of the opposition's arguments by offering them first himself; the closer the arguments come to turning on themselves the more the speaker's control, or lack of it, becomes evident.

How can we assess the speaker's skill in this poem? Note the manner in which each imagined defense is proleptic: each has been set up in a way that, if it does not collapse through its own absurdity, makes us anticipate its demolition by the speaker. We have noted that each one of the imputed arguments places the jilting lover in an unfavorable light. Her fickleness is initially assumed; her deviousness and falsity are imputed through the arguments the speaker "invents" for her. The refutation, the overall rebuke of the woman's moral character, is patent. Is that, then, the point, to present her in an unfavorable light? Consider, once more, that *form is the best gauge of intention.* We have seen that Donne has arranged the arguments in such a way that all six of them are paired. We are led to the final, direct confrontation of the two opponents only to discover *no* confrontation. The patent sophistry of the imagined defense is now claimed by the speaker, as something he himself might employ tomorrow. The controversy dissolves into thin air, even the initial controversy between the speaker's present state and its opposite, a controversy that had merely been created out of thin air in the first place. Truly, in his beginning was his end, and vice versa.

Most critics assume the speaker of this poem is male. At least one has suggested that the speaker is female.[1] I shall propose that the speaker may be either, and that *that* is the very point of the poem. If the speaker is male, the ultimate turning in the poem is the final one, in which all of his chauvinistic assumptions about female fickleness, so ironically expressed in his title, are "true" of his own character as well. If the speaker is female, again the ultimate turning is the final one (and the title is no less ironic): in that final turning her satire on the trappings and posturings of male logic is dismissed with her confidence in her own abilities at the game. Constancy, on either lover's part, is no constancy. And the reverse is just as true: no constancy can become a constancy. The poem is, finally, a poem on love, less cynical than skeptical in its confrontation of the possibilities of change in human relationships; it acknowledges that even the resistance to, let alone fear of, change may change.

Thus, the poem is not simply an example of controversial thinking, but it is also a forensic tour de force. Controversy exists here on all levels, from the disparity between the speaker's present state and the initial, projected fantasy, to the ultimate disparity, in which the possibility of controversy faces the possibility of noncontroversy and each cancels the other out. Cynicism may remain in the one unchallenged assumption, that a jilting will occur. But the cynicism is moderated by two unanswered questions: Is it really a jilting if the jilted party doesn't mind? and Should I fear jilting when, after all, I may initiate the action myself? Male and female are alike implicated in the vagaries of love, and are equally guiltless. The guilty party—if guilt must be assigned—in human relationships is the intricate structure of blameworthy self-justification. But this structure is only a linguistic filigree that ultimately assigns no blame, for the filigree can be pulled apart with one tug: "I may think so too."

A failure to understand what Donne is up to with his controversial thinking has resulted in the misreading of his poetic intentions, to cite two examples—modern but a quarter of a century apart. Clay Hunt calls Donne's formal turnings "reversals," notes that they are quite characteristic of Donne's manner, and offers such obvious examples as "The Indifferent," "Goe and Catch a Falling Star," "Loves Deitie," "The Dampe," "The Blossome," "The Good-Morrow," and "The Canonization." Indeed, so characteristic of Donne's manner are these proleptic turnings that a host of other examples come easily to mind—for example, "The Prohibition" shows an arrangement of paired arguments quite similar to "Womans constancy," though quite different in intention.[2] For Hunt, the effect of the "reversals" is tour de force in the worst sense:

> his basic drive in these works seems to be the desire to dramatize the fact that John Donne is more complicated than most people think they are. . . . just as soon as the reader is sure that he knows what Donne is saying, or what the tone of a poem is, and has begun to settle comfortably into understanding where this poem is headed, Donne jerks him around and heads off in the opposite direction. This was not what he meant at all, it seems, and he really means just the opposite, and you mustn't think that conventional people like yourself can understand John Donne so easily.[3]

Nor does John Carey take seriously the formal effect of controversy in his work on Donne. For "reversal" Carey prefers the term "peculiar vacillation," which is, he says, "quite natural to Donne."[4] Its purpose would appear to be no more than vacillation, irresolution. To counter these positions, I would offer both my own analysis and the insistence that even display has its argumentative purposes. No skillful debater vacillates without assessing carefully its effect and meaning.

Another poem by Donne will help clarify these formal turnings as the results of controversial thinking. In "Aire and Angels" the turnings seem less like anticipatory refutation and more like corrections, or efforts at reconciliation. But the action retains basically the same motive and is profoundly characteristic of Donne: he is always arguing, even when, as in this poem, too, he speaks through a thin mask.

> Twice or thrice had I loved thee,
> Before I knew thy face or name;
> So in a voice, so in a shapeless flame,
> *Angells* affect us oft, and worship'd bee,
>   Still when, to where thou wert, I came   5
> Some lovely glorious nothing I did see.
>   But since my soule, whose child love is,
> Takes limmes of flesh, and else could nothing doe,
>   More subtile then the parent is,
> Love must not be, but take a body too,   10
>   And therefore what thou wert, and who,
>   I bid Love aske, and now
> That it assume thy body, I allow,
> And fixe it selfe in thy lip, eye, and brow.
>
> Whilst thus to ballast love, I thought,   15
> And so more steddily to have gone,
> With wares which would sinke admiration,
> I saw, I had loves pinnace overfraught,
>   Ev'ry thy haire for love to work upon
> Is much too much, some fitter must be sought;   20
>   For, nor in nothing, nor in things
> Extreme, and scatt'ring bright, can love inhere;
>   Then as an Angell, face, and wings
> Of aire, not pure as it, yet pure doth weare,

> So thy love may be my loves spheare;   25
>   Just such disparitie
> As is twixt Aire and Angells puritie,
> 'Twixt womens love, and mens will ever bee.

"Donne's best poems," observes Arthur Marotti, "are linear, rather than iconic."[5] Yet it is difficult to imagine which of Donne's poems are truly iconic. One would have to be the most narrowly objectivist critic, or think of poems solely in terms of images, or conceive of form as largely visual or stationary, not to be overwhelmed by Donne's progressive mode of argumentation. *Change* is the assumption Donne makes about life (as well as about "musike, joy . . . and eternity"), and it is also his aim in discourse: the speaker or audience (or reader) can or will or should change. Argument is the agent, reflection, or justification of change. Those later Donne poems that do less arguing than presenting also presuppose change and are therefore progressive and linear, as we shall see. Admittedly, the view is enforced by my own critical approach: in rhetoric, form is always a mover and doer. But that concept is, in turn, confirmed by what such works as "Aire and Angels" say about form, that it moves and does. (Later in this chapter I shall review a related matter: to humanist rhetoricians, form is also associated with emotion.)

I have suggested that the change involved in the action of this poem might be described as a process of correction, or reconciliation. The speaker sought, literally, a realization of his love and, to achieve it, was progressively forced to correct the actions of his disembodied inspiration. A certain vagueness of the inspiration is suggested in the opening words—"Twice or thrice"—then capped in the phrase "lovely glorious nothing." Love must have a body to be *seen* and to "doe." The opening analogy equates bodiless ideas with angels who "affect us" in a voice or in a mysterious light and whose appearance provokes our worship. The specific idea, I shall propose later, is that of beauty— associated with her, or with what she represents to the soul. Love is the child of the soul—begotten, we may assume, in the Platonic way (as suggested in the *Phaedrus*), by the idea of beauty on his soul. And as the child of the soul, love must seek a body by its nature (just as its parent soul seeks "limmes of flesh") and in an urgency foreign to angels (who *can* "be," without a body). And because she, or what she represents, is the other parent, it is her body that his love assumes.

But in this assumption it fixed, or attached, itself, not to the entire body, but to those parts that excite admiration and praise in conventional love poetry, her "lip, eye, and brow."

Such "fixing" becomes the base for the next reconciling movement of the poem, in the second stanza, which echoes the first. Love is not fulfilled in admiration, the earthy counterpart of "worship" in the first stanza. Therefore, admiration must be "sunk." Love "inheres" finally—and this is his ultimate invention—not exactly in her body but in her love. A difference between her body and her love as the container of his love is expressed as a difference between a "pinnace" (a small ship, conventionally thought of as female) and a "spheare," the translucent orbit of moveable stars, whose principle of action is an angel or an intelligence (as we noted in our discussion of "Goodfriday"). Within this final invention is a comparison that seems to engulf, and perhaps encapsulate, the preceding corrections: her love is the "air" worn by an angel, his love; though her love is pure, his is yet purer, and will always be, given the nature of men and women.

In what sense does this final invention conclude the poem? I shall suggest that it is the reader, and "she," who conclude the poem with an unstated argument—that, in a sense, the final utterance of the speaker is like the minor premise in a syllogism whose major premise has been provided by the recounted action. Before proceeding, however, let us first consider an opposing view.

A. J. Smith, in an essay on this poem, offers a kind of argumentative analysis that merely uses formalism as its foil without taking advantage of a uniquely argumentative, that is to say rhetorical, view of form. The poem, in his view, is indeed not iconic; rather, it works through a series of arguments to a final resting point, a conclusion, that *seems* to be offered as a discovery. But the discovery, Smith notes, is actually a commonplace: women's love is inferior to men's, and a quotation from Sperone Speroni offers evidence of the widely held notion among Platonists. Smith continues:

the angel wears the air, takes it up, and moulds it to his purpose, whereas the air is just passive, waiting to be used, though perfectly responsive to the user when he comes. Here, presumably, in this mere passivity or initial neutrality, lies woman's inferiority as a minion of love. . . . Love's office is 'indulgently to fit Actives to passives,' and though both sorts have their worth, the actives, working spontaneously, are the purer devotees.[6]

The passage Smith quotes in his final sentence is from "Loves Deitie," and it is no support for his argument. In that poem, Donne is addressing a topic quite the contrary of the one Smith has described: *not* a man initially awakening love in a woman; rather, a man who does not even experience love until it has simultaneously touched two hearts with an even flame. When cases at law are used as judicial opinions, one should be wary of the plasticity of language: *active* and *passive* hardly apply with equal force in both instances. But it is Smith's unequivocal and formalistic reading of the conclusion of "Aire and Angels" that is at issue here, for it allows him to assume that Donne's intention is merely to display his witty use of a commonplace on women's inferiority.

The conjecture I shall offer is based on a different, more rhetorical view of a poem's form as its principle of movement. The reader—and she, too—discover the final truth in the way all truths in the poem are discovered, or invented—by means of correction, or reconciliation. The poem emerges as one of the most anti-idealist in Donne's canon. It is less Platonic than Thomist, and less scholastic than humanist. What good is the ideal without the real? Love must *inhere*— and until it does it is either worship or admiration, neither of which satisfies the lover. Like the humanist, Donne argues that all we truly have is what we can use, possibility. The poem may conclude in a commonplace but it provokes the reader, and her, to correct its apparent overtones. To the extent the final lines conclude the argument, they also raise other questions: how desirable is purity? how praiseworthy is men's love after all? With these questions we begin to see more of the implied controversy. Let us pursue these matters through examining certain emblems.

The faces of Janus have served as a useful (if incongruous, because they are static) emblem for characterizing the action of controversial thinking. These dual faces express a pairing of opposites; when used as an emblem for rhetorical *controversia*, in my argument, a further implication is that the burden of reconciliation is on the observer. But other Renaissance emblems make the reconciliation of opposites explicit, as in the tricephalous Prudence (see Figure 3, p. 61). When viewed as a modification of the Janiform in which a third face has been added at the center facing forward, the emblem embodies *both* controversy *and* reconciliation, or argument *and* judgment. Later in this chapter I shall argue that this modification of the Janiform can serve as an especially useful conceptual model for the voice of Donne's sacred compositions. At present, our approach to "Aire and Angels" is facilitated by a particular emblematic reconciliation beloved of Renaissance Platonists: the three graces, expressing Pulchritudo—Amor—Voluptas.[7] The emblem is usually in the form of three beautiful women, Pulchritudo facing left, Voluptas facing right, with Amor in the center, sometimes facing us, sometimes with her back to us. Amor is always in the position of reconciliation: love joins the idea of pure beauty with sensuous pleasure.

In Donne's poem we find the two ostensibly reconciled, only to have "disparitie" reiterated and "puritie" set before us once more. The reconciliation of pulchritude and voluptuousness through love would appear to be no reconciliation unless, possibly, we have been brought to a vantage from which the disparity and the purity are seen for what they are. And if *that* is the case, then the vaunted superiority of men's love over women's seems idle indeed.

The man's pursuit of pure beauty verges on foolishness from the outset: the "angelic" Idea of Beauty—at best, a vague apprehension somehow associated with her—incites his worship. Worshipping angels is, moreover, something the Bible explicitly forbids (Colossians 2:18). The man, however, is a captive of his emotions, and his first move to *do* something about his emotions beyond worship involves the first controversion of extreme Platonic doctrine. For Ficino, Pico, and Bruno supreme love is *blind*—or as Helena muses in *Midsummer Night's Dream* (I.1.248–249):

> Love lookes not with the eyes, but with the minde,
> And therefore is wing'd *Cupid* painted blinde.

But the speaker wishes to *see,* and in pursuit of pulchritude all he saw was "nothing," though "lovely" and "glorious." The love of beauty, born of the soul, a thoroughly Platonic doctrine, is subjected to Thomist analysis: the soul needs a body; love must, too. The results are applied humanistically, through searching for consequences, and, again, foolishness results. He goes to the other extreme, voluptuousness. The speaker's final discovery is that love can *inhere* in neither extreme, neither in ethereal beauty, which is "nothing" (the word is heard three times in the poem), nor in the fragmented pleasures of sensuousness (her lip, eye, brow, her every hair, things "Extreme, and scatt'ring bright"). Both extremes are in a sense no thing: the former like the angel's voice, the latter like the shapeless flame, both lovely, glorious nothings. Man's love may be like the angel, but the angel's *purity* is itself conceptually ineffectual in this life, beyond merely inciting (forbidden) worship or (pointless) admiration. That is the ultimate discovery, and it occurs as a correction to the conclusion's partiality.

Further, a curious reversal in this poem, which has rarely been noted in published criticism,[8] is in the angel's significance. At first the angel seems to be associated with *her.* Beauty is a formless idea to be pursued, he senses, by pursuing *her* (so "to where thou wert, I came"). By the end of the poem, it is associated with *him,* with men's love. At first, she affected him in the bodiless way angels affect us. At the end of the poem the impossibility of pure love, which is what the angel comes to signify, is associated with the man. To St. Thomas Aquinas,[9] angels assume bodies of air but are not composites: the angel is not even the form of this matter, this air-body, but its mover; the body is only the representation of motion. Such "inherence" that preserves the bodiless purity of the angel, or ideal love, is exactly the position both stanzas reject. Further, though the speaker plays the "active" male role, there is nothing in the poem to indicate she did *not* initially love him or feel love until he awakened it in her (impressions that are essential to Smith's interpretation). The sexless angel hovers over both, to become ultimately the means of disparaging the man's misdirected activeness.

Angels serve only as guardians and harbingers. To allow them to provoke admiration is theologically unsound. To allow them to become a simile for male-female love is unwise in the extreme. The movement of the poem is, throughout, one of teetering on the brink between satire and seriousness—characteristic of much of Donne's irony, paradox, and prolepses—with an ultimately comic effect.

The "inferiority" of women's love is quite beside the point. Though iterated in the final comparison, it is denied by the action of the poem. What we are left with is Donne's lawyerly *via media* between the ideal and the real, as a rhetorical revisitation of the tripartite Platonic Amor. It is the reader who must piece the ideal and the real together in a final correction to arrive at the anti-idealist doctrine of the poem, balanced as it is against a slightly less forcefully argued anti-materialism, both surveyed by a conclusion that offers a disparity between what it seems to say and what has preceded it. If the woman makes the correction, the poem becomes the speaker's tribute to her love, a tribute that shares a peril with all Donne's proleptic movements, of becoming its contrary.

Thus, the "turnings" of controversy can involve not simply prolepsis but corrections and reconciliations. Many of Donne's poems reveal similar movements, to cite only a few: "The broken heart," "A Lecture upon the Shadow," "A Valediction: forbidding mourning," "The triple Foole," "Sweetest love, I do not goe," and among the divine poems, "A Hymne to God, my God in my sicknesse."

Finally, it seems unwise in dealing with a demonstrably skeptical poet to assume he uses conventions at no more than their face value. In the poem just examined, the speaker seems to play the conventional male role: aggressive, creative, active. In a sense, though, the woman too has performed a male function, through an "angel" parenting love upon the man's soul. Woman is conventionally passive, but she can become the aggressor in love—as in "Breake of Day" and, perhaps, in "Womans constancy." Man can be the passive recipient of love's effects, as shown initially in "Aire and Angels," and as shown to a comic extent in "The triple Foole." The crossing of sexual roles is carried to an extreme in *The second Anniversary,* where Donne invites the young, dead virgin, Elizabeth Drury, to be a "Father" unto his Muse, since her (the Muse's) "chaste Ambition" is to bring forth a child, such as that poem, every year (ll. 33–36).

Donne's diffidence can extend to certain theological conventions as well, which in the following poem are both enhanced and complicated by another convention, the controversial turning between octave and sestet:

Holy Sonnet VII

At the round earths imagin'd corners, blow
Your trumpets, Angells, and arise, arise
From death, you numberlesse infinities
Of soules, and to your scattred bodies goe,
All whom the flood did, and fire shall o'erthrow,   5
All whom warre, dearth, age, agues, tyrannies,
Despaire, law, chance, hath slaine, and you whose eyes,
Shall behold God, and never tast deaths woe.
But let them sleepe, Lord, and mee mourne a space,
For, if above all these, my sinnes abound,   10

> 'Tis late to ask abundance of thy grace,
> When wee are there; here on this lowly ground,
> Teach mee how to repent; for that's as good
> As if thou'hadst seal'd my pardon, with thy blood.

A poem Donne wrote perhaps a decade after this sonnet has a similar beginning, "Vpon the translation of the Psalmes by Sir Philip Sydney, and the Countesse of Pembroke his Sister":

> Eternall God, (for whom who ever dare
> Seeke new expressions, doe the Circle square,
> And thrust into strait corners of poore wit
> Thee, who art cornerlesse and infinite)

Both poems begin with the impossibility of either squaring a circle or circling a square. The utterance is like a rhetorical *correctio:* possibility is denied, only to remain as another kind of possibility, one that is beyond our reach, including the reach of our linguistic conventions. In this way, the conventions themselves are not exactly rejected but are used, for all they're worth.

At the opening of Donne's Holy Sonnet VII, the earth's roundness is a given; its corners are imputed. Yet at those corners the angels are asked to sound the Day of Judgment. Then the Day of Judgment *emotionally* overwhelms both the given reality and the imputed construction (not unlike the process of self-justification that overwhelms both the present state and the imputed jilting in "Womans constancy"), so much so that it seems to belong to another order of things altogether, beyond the reality of the earth's roundness or the imputation of its corners. Again, this is a typical controversion, built on prolepsis and reconciliation: when two matters are in controversy, one gives way to another or they both give way to a third—either in the poem or in the mind of the audience. In many of the holy sonnets generally less arguing and more petition or presentation occur, effects we shall note later, but the habits of controversial thinking remain.

My present purpose in examining this holy sonnet is to note the effects of controversial thinking on conventions. I have already noted an initial one: *dies irae* has a transcendent reality, beyond geographical conventions and, for that matter, beyond all other forms of knowledge. And so does the human drive to repent, which Donne at the end of the poem seems perilously to balance against another convention, Christ's suffering for the sins of the world. To the literalist, there is no "as if." God, through Christ, *has* sealed our pardon with his blood. For Donne, the drive to repent, the presence of his own sins, the immanence of Judgment—these have a force beyond conventional interpretations of the meaning and purpose of Christ's suffering. And to the extent these interpretations are true (to the extent there is no "as if"), they only confirm his case: but You have sealed my pardon; therefore my repentance *is* as good as that action. But the conditional moderates, and prevents, any easy comfort in learning "how to repent." Further, even to the slight (for Donne's period) extent that the "as if" leaves the door open for the reader who is no literalist, even that reader must nonetheless reconcile the controversy on the level of personal belief, or fail to reconcile it. Thus, the controversy is between personalism and convention. The two are joined at the conclusion by a (to us almost maddening) conditional, which, however much it continues the controversializing, ultimately shifts the burden of proof (and experience and emotion) back to the intensely personal without exactly letting go of conventions either.

The sonnet recalls "Goodfriday 1613" and a host of other poems that use conventions but strain if not challenge their literal nature, their casual assumption of certitude, and their impersonality—for example, "The Relique," "The Dissolution," "Negative love," "The Paradox," "Farewell to love," "A nocturnall upon S. Lucies day"—and, above all, "The Extasie." Because the last-named poem is such a clear example of formal effects we have reviewed in Donne, let us examine a certain crux in critical studies of that poem.

The major turning in this seventy-six-line poem occurs in line 49. More than half of the poem is devoted to a description of an "ecstatic" state: the two lovers sit, then recline, on a river bank, holding hands (their only physical union), quiet and speechless as statues while "Love" mixes, then remixes their souls. Each soul becomes so "interinanimated" that it becomes in effect a new soul, combining the two in every atom. If some man stood by and if he were an initiate into love's mysteries and had grown "all minde," he could hear the speech of both souls speaking as one. Then, as if to confirm our suspicion that the tone of this poem is comic, Donne moves *us* into that man's position and allows us to hear a speech by the newly constituted soul analyzing itself:

> This Extasie doth unperplex
> (We said) and tell us what we love,   30

> Wee see by this, it was not sexe,
>   Wee see, we saw not what did move:
> But as all severall soules containe
>   Mixture of things, they know not what,
> Love, these mixt soules, doth mixe againe,   35
>   And makes both one, each this and that.

Any listener (the man, or us) Donne had earlier promised would upon hearing this speech "part farre purer then he came"—provided we were "all minde," of course. Once more, as in "Aire and Angels," incorporeal love is "refin'd" and pure and more than a little ridiculous. As Donne was to write in one of his final poems, "From thinking us all soule . . . Lord deliver us" ("The Litanie," ll. 143–144).

Then comes the turning (l. 49): the soul descends to the two bodies, like "intelligences" entering "spheares," and proclaims,

> We owe them thankes, because they thus,
>   Did us, to us, at first convay,
> Yeelded their forces, sense, to us,   55
>   Nor are drosse to us, but allay.

The poem in its turning is pervaded not only by correction (as in the last-quoted line) but also by anticipatory refutations. All the reasons for contempt of the body are treated proleptically—in a passage that for us echoes "Aire and Angels":

> On man heavens influence workes not so,
>   But that it first imprints the ayre,
> Soe soule into the soule may flow,
>   Though it to body first repaire.   60
> As our blood labours to beget
>   Spirits, as like soules as it can,
> Because such fingers need to knit
>   That subtile knot, which makes us man:
> So must pure lovers soules descend   65
>   T'affections, and to faculties,
> Which sense may reach and apprehend,
>   Else a great Prince in prison lies.

A crux centers on the nature and identification of this "great Prince." Helen Gardner claims, to begin with, that the poem is *either* a poem of seduction *or* a philosophical poem. She chooses the latter and

161

bases her reading on Leone Ebreo, in an unwise attempt, made by too many critics, to ascribe to Donne this or that set of dogmatic beliefs. The poem, for Gardner, is Platonism believed; the subject is literally ecstasy. The presence of the hypothetical listener (who appears first in ll. 21–26) turns the poem into a narrative (and so allows the speaker to view the ecstatic experience through the past tense), and he helps to underscore the "mission" of the perfect lovers (particularly when he is mentioned again at the end of the poem, ll. 71–79). Their "mission" is to show others this new soul—which, if it is not revealed to others, is like a great Prince in prison. Ecstasy, then, makes missionaries of the newly converted, the transported lovers—and in her tonally flat reading of the poem Gardner goes on to fault it for not rendering the ecstatic experience directly, and for offering instead something that appears to be more like an *argument* about ecstasy.[10]

Earl Miner chooses the other alternative—reading the poem as one of seduction. "The Extasie," he claims, is a "serious parody" of a seductive poem. The listener is there to render the narrative more dramatic (and thus his presence bolsters Miner's case about the nature of Metaphysical poetry—that it is more dramatic than narrative). The "great Prince" is the rational soul, which must use senses and faculties to procreate, to produce another rational soul.[11]

For Arthur Marotti,[12] the listener is there to contrast with the lovers and to reflect the reader as well, and some of the ways in which the poem is using him. For Marotti, obviously, the poem is rhetorical. But he insists that, so far as the poem's nature or intention is concerned, it is "a rhetorically sophisticated defense of conjugal love," an hypothesis that is perhaps not necessary to the establishment of his more significant and still accessible point: that the poem is ironic, using the vocabulary of Platonism to disprove Platonism. The "great Prince" is the lovers' newly combined soul—for that matter (as in "Aire and Angels"), *any* soul[13]—which is a prisoner in itself if it refuses to join with the body, to become the body's "allay."

Man, the speaker says, consists of a "subtile knot," spirit and body, mind and senses, reason and emotion.[14] Untie that knot and our manhood is lost. This is the true—and we should note, truly humanist—nature of man; "subtile" would therefore seem to mean precisely what it means in "Aire and Angels." "The Extasie" ends:

> To' our bodies turne wee then, that so
> Weake men on love reveal'd may looke;   70

> Loves mysteries in soules do grow,
>> But yet the body is his booke.
> And if some lover, such as wee,
>> Have heard this dialogue of one,
> Let him still marke us, he shall see   75
>> Small change, when we'are to bodies gone.

There would seem to be *three* kinds of hypothetical listeners: the man grown all mind, who observed the ecstasy and parted more pure than he came; weak men, who can only derive lessons from love revealed in the body, who are in short the opposite of the first man; and finally, the lover, like those in the poem, who is both mind and sense and who can remark in the bodies' sexual union their spiritual union as well. It is disunion on all levels that the poem rejects. Thus Donne uses ecstasy as Erasmus's "Folly" does, to controvert conventions—in this case, the conventions of ecstasy itself. The third listener is the moderator or judge, the poet's surrogate and ours. But overall intentionality is measured by form, as refutation or dismissal is measured by controversy, which impugns ecstasy in this poem only to the extent that "inherence" is impugned in "Aire and Angels."

This, of course, is not to say that man does *not* have a soul or that lovers' souls do *not* intermix, or that the ideal does *not* "inhere" in the real. It is, rather, in a special, controversial way to affirm these very things. A passage from one of Donne's sermons makes the point, and in a controversial way, when he asks us

> piously and civilly to consider, that Man is not a soule alone, but a body too; That man is not placed in this world only for specu-lation; He is not sent into this world to live out of it, but to live in it; *Adam* was not put into Paradise, onely in that Paradise to contemplate the future Paradise, but to dresse and to keep the present; God did not breathe a soule towards him, but into him; Not in an obsession, but a possession; Not to travaile for knowl-edge abroad, but to direct him by counsell at home; Not for extasies, but for an inherence.   [*Sermons* VII, p.104]

As always, it is the extremes we must avoid. Through the ways of controversy, Donne goes to those extremes in order not simply to reach the "means" but to place us there, too—for example, from an-other sermon (IX, p.63), *"Man liveth not by bread onely,* says Christ;

but yet he liveth by bread too." This habit of thought and movement of mind extended throughout Donne's career as poet and priest.

Inconstancy begets a constant habit: prolepsis, correction, and skepticism produce controversy, and vice versa. Only one truth appears unchallengeable: man as a God-created mixture of intellectual restlessness and the body's appetites. All other truths—with a few exceptions, which became increasingly prominent—are open for debate. On that rhetorical foundation, Donne fashioned a clear voice, using a discernible speaker, an identifiable audience, and, for the most part, an advocatory intention. These are the constituents of humanist rhetoric, and the tradition extends from Cicero through Erasmus to Donne. For all three, a lawyerly *via media* had its correlative rhetorical goal, to place the reader in an undogmatic middle position by means of *controversia* with *its* correlative *via diversa*. This strategy is risky, particularly when, as in "Aire and Angels," the poet himself does not serve as moderator, for it then presupposes that the reader will assume the burden of reconciliation—and, along with it, at least momentarily a certain attitude toward language. Arthur Kinney has expressed precisely the strategy at work in Erasmus, in a way that, for me, looks back to Cicero and forward to Donne:

> *Moriae Encomium* asks us, finally, not to endorse the double perspective of inside-outside, defendant-respondent, but the third view of a judge. And this third view—like the many roles we play in a single life—depends on the judge, the occasion, and the context: meaning is potentially multifold.[15]

The process, the Academics insisted, is itself productive of a certain attitude, the humanist dubiousness that any language but the fluid, paradoxical and ironic, language of the imagination, uniting as it does reason with emotion, can capture multiform truth. Such was the attitude Donne maintained throughout his career as poet and priest, in which now the reader, now Donne himself plays the role of moderator, *iudex,* judge.

I continue our examination of Donne's rhetoric next from a point of view contrary to the one this section has proposed. Then, in the final section of this chapter, I shall salvage the point of view developed in this first section, modifying it as necessary to examine Donne's later career.

John Donne's Augustinian Formalism:
A Trial

Cannot an equally plausible case be made for Donne's formalism as for his rhetoric? And is formalism after all so contrary to rhetoric that the presence of the latter excludes considerations of the former? I would answer both questions with a qualified yes. Let us consider them in reverse order.

Although formalism varies, as does rhetoric, my attempts to characterize the two throughout this study have posited a simple but I think necessary difference: literary form is a static object of contemplation in formalism but a principle of motion in rhetoric. An audience is thus ancillary to formalists' view of what a poem is and "how it means," but an audience is central to rhetoricians' view. As this statement suggests, the difference between the two becomes most crucial in the study of poetry: indeed, formalists with their reifications of literary genres often claim the whole of poetry and relegate all nonpoetic discourse (sermons, for example) to rhetoricians; rhetoricians, however, view genres as they view all literary forms, not as immutable signs of identity but as strategies in communication, and therefore poems, like sermons, fall easily within the rhetorical purview.

A case for Donne's formalism should, I think, proceed as did my case for his rhetoric, by trying to delineate the particular kind of formalism most applicable. What follows is only an outline of a possible formalist case, a prospectus. But why attempt, here, to build it at all? Mainly to illuminate the nature of Donne's rhetoric. To further, as it were, the affirmative case by letting the negative speak, though I cannot pretend that my momentary switch to the other side will have the "perfect impartiality" of Antonius. Milton in the *Areopagitica* asserts "that which purifies us is triall, and triall is by what is contrary," a humanist-sounding principle. Let us think of what follows, then, as a contrary, formalist claim on Donne, based largely on the patent influence of Augustine: any Augustinian will at some point turn away from humanist rhetoric; any Augustinian who is also a poet may turn toward something like formalism.

■   ■   ■

165

That Donne was directly influenced by Augustine in his religious thought has been noted by many scholars. For example, there is the remarkable fact that Augustine is *not* mentioned in only five of Donne's surviving 160 sermons.[16] Indeed, so striking is the similarity between the English poet and the early Church father that Louis Bredvold, in one of the first thorough studies of Donne's Augustinianism, argued that "the final study of Donne must be biographical."[17] For Donne's life, like Augustine's, was intricately twined with his spiritual as well as his artistic development. But what would seem to be called for is a biographical study not of the sort offered by Gosse[18] or Bald,[19] but of the critical, particularly formalist, sort suggested in this essay. We need a study not of the actual man but of his artistic self, a self that is at once the locus and measure of "truth" in both Augustine and Donne. Because that locus and measure remained the same for Donne in both his secular and his sacred poems, Augustinian formalism gives us a significant means of moving toward the center of his life as a poet.

Augustine saw the world as "incomplete, transient, overshadowed by Eternity."[20] In this cosmology, truth is "out there"—tangible and certain to prevail—and it is "in here" as well. Looking for it in one place is as profitable as looking for it in the other. The introspective man who sees himself neither as a unique and lonely individual, nor as a "microcosm" exactly (nor, as I shall try to make clear in the final chapter of this book, as a "prophet"), but as involved in all of God's creation—such a man can, with effort, find truth within. Thus, the intense absorption with self in Augustine is always an intense absorption with God. *The Confessions* are a realization of that self. To call it a "creation" of a self, as a rhetorician might, would be in Augustine's terms blasphemy. For the self is made real by being shown in what to Augustine is its most urgent and most realistic action, the search through its outer as well as its inner life for signs of God. As Peter Brown has noted, what is distinctive about Augustine's religious attitude is "a sharp note of unrelieved anxiety about himself and a dependence on his God."[21] The two are absorbed in Augustine's hermeneutical rule of *charity*: the inconsistencies, contraries, vagaries, the lack of fit between sign and meaning, can all be overcome by a willed remembrance that all reality is designed to promote love of one's neighbor and that God, as Donne puts it in one of his sermons, *is* "Charity."[22] "Out there" and "in here" are meant to coincide, and truth is largely a product of will and character. Augustine's artistic self is a reflection on paper of this epistemology.

Donne lived in a time not unlike Augustine's, when the search for truth was complicated by warring schools of philosophy. The Ciceronian *probable,* for example, in addition to its reappearance in secular forensic argumentation, had been all but submerged in the Jesuits' *probabilism* and the Calvinists' *probabiliorism*[23]—and the word *probable* itself through the sixteenth and seventeenth centuries, as the OED reports, popularly meant "specious." Donne, referring to his poems, wrote that "I did best when I had least truth for my subjects,"[24] a statement that might delight those formalists who wish to see a poem as itself unique and lonely, a closed-off little universe with its own truth; but Donne is just as likely here referring to the efficacy of his own, Augustinelike, participatory imagination. In another passage, written twenty years earlier in his life, Donne speaks of truth first in a lawyerly way, then ends with an observation that seems to refer the search to Augustinian charity (here "peace"):

> Contemplative and bookish men, must of necessitie be more quarrelsome than others, because they contend not about matter of fact, nor can they determine their controversies by any certaine witnesses, nor judges. But as long as they goe towards peace, that is Truth, it is no matter which way.[25]

"Truth," he said in a famous passage in his "Satyre III," stands on a huge hill, difficult of access but attainable, particularly if we seek the help of tradition ("Ask thy father . . ."). Studies are not to be ignored but the major battles—in Augustine as in Donne—are to be fought within:

> The Scriptures will be out of thy reach, and out of thy use, if thou cast and scatter them upon reason, upon philosophy, upon morality, to try how the Scriptures will fit them, and believe them but so far they agree with thy reason; but draw the Scripture to thine own heart, and to thine own actions, and thou shalt find it made for that.   [*Sermons* II, p.308]

The locus of truth is in personalism, in the inner relationship of a person to a truth—not ethos or *honestum,* but the kind of personal centering Augustine found and treasured. John Carey has argued that "Renaissance scepticism was a poetic advantage to Donne . . . because it made all fact infinitely flexible."[26] But it was through an Augustinian interiority that the flexibility of fact was controlled and immutable truth itself was discovered and realized. Not reason alone but each person's heart and actions try the truth and—for the poet, especially—reflect it.

The controlling principle of this Augustinian epistemology is like *probability* in dramatic criticism, the congruence between character, action, and utterance. However, the dramatic critic might seek *only* congruence (is it likely, or probable, that *this* character would say and do this?). Something more is sought by the Augustinian. To dramatic critics, character is known as persona; to rhetorical critics, ethos. Both are masks, indicating type or nature—persona being additionally useful for measuring congruence, ethos for effect on an audience. But *character* as used in this essay is more general, a stable and extensive though personal locus of truth.

Of course, the *variety* of speakers in Donne must be accounted for in any study, under whatever approach; for example, he speaks as a woman in "Breake of day," as a divorced man in "To Mr. B. B.," as a retiring scholar in the satires, as an effeminate fop in "Elegie IV," as his outer and inner selves in "A Feaver." These personae would seem to be good rhetorical practice, like schoolboy exercises in ethos. Certain rhetoricians approaching Donne's poems find in this variety evidence of Donne's "wit,"[27] all converging to produce an overall sense of the character of the poet himself (his ethos) as the "monarch of wit."[28]

But to Donne these various personae came to mean something more than display or wit or idleness. They were, partly, "seeds of better Arts," a phrase he uses in his verse letter to Mr. Rowland Woodward, and continues:

> Seeke wee then our selves in our selves; for as
> Men force the Sunne with much more force to passe,   20
> By gathering his beames with a christall glasse;
>
> So wee, If wee into our selves will turne,
> Blowing our sparkes of vertue, may outburne
> The straw, which doth about our hearts sojourne.

The plural "selves" is significant. So, too, is their possible equation with the "sparkes of vertue," which earlier in the poem (l. 16) he defined as "Religion." Virtuous selves are religious selves. In another letter to Rowland Woodward, he concludes:

If men be worlds, there is in every one
    Some thing to answere in some proportion   30
All the worlds riches: And in good men, this,
    Vertue, our formes forme and our soules soule, is.

The various worlds or selves of Donne are all parts of his involved worlds and religious selves; in the latter they center. The virtuous selves are *in imitationem Christi*—they draw all, as Erasmus would put it, unto themselves, take all the world's folly on themselves, as Christ did, as Augustine did, and lay it at the feet of God. This performing role—of drawing all unto himself and of serving God's purpose in humility—is consistent in parts of Donne's poetic career, early and late, early in the satires and late in the divine poems. The selves of the middle years, of the *Songs and Sonets,* are the straw about the heart.

Change was indeed an assumption Donne made about life. But its value needs critical reexamination. For change was more like Donne's bête noire and inevitable companion: change—variety, mutability— plagued him as it plagued Spenser and other poets of the age, and urged accommodation to its requirements. However, because this essay proposes a project not in intellectual history but in literary criticism, it is aimed at uncovering whatever *literary formula* will be useful in the individual reading of any one of his discourses—prose or poetry, but particularly the latter. It is, accordingly, constructed on this hypothesis: Donne found in Augustinianism a means of confronting change, and the reader will find in formalism the means of confronting Donne's discourse. The two converge. Donne's Augustinianism is of the formalistic kind: he found the means of making intense personalism into art. And the reader's formalism must be Augustinian in emphasis: each discourse is iconic, a static object of contemplation, behind and through which is the sense of a person, that "naked thinking heart" the communication of which is the poem's objective, its "formes forme and soules soule."

To begin with, one could note that Donne uses the term *form* in his poems in a variety of ways.[29] But what is more to the point is something that has rarely been remarked: Donne's use of *form* in a purely aesthetic sense. One of the few poems Donne ever wrote on the nature of poetry, and the only extended discussion he gave the subject, is "Vpon the translation of the Psalmes by Sir Philip Sydney, and the Countesse of Pembroke his Sister," which begins,

169

Eternall God, (for whom who ever dare
Seeke new expressions, doe the Circle square,
And thrust into strait corners of poore wit
Thee, who art cornerlesse and infinite)
I would but blesse thy Name, not name thee now;   5
(And thy gifts are as infinite as thou:)
Fixe we our prayses therefore on this one,
That, as thy blessed Spirit fell upon
These Psalmes first Author in a cloven tongue;
(For 'twas a double power by which he sung   10
The highest matter in the noblest forme;)
So thou hast cleft that spirit, to performe
That worke againe, and shed it, here, upon
Two, by their bloods, and by thy Spirit one;
A Brother and a Sister, made by thee   15
The Organ, where thou art the Harmony.

The opening echoes Donne's skepticism and complaints about language ("Language, thou art too narrow, and too weake," as "Elegy on Death" begins). Merely human language cannot perfectly match either our emotions or our noblest conceptions. But of more import is the relation these lines pose among "spirit," "matter," and "forme." The Holy Spirit was David's muse, who allowed that poet to match high matter with noble form—as if each of which, matter and form, had its own language ("a cloven tongue"). Once again the Spirit speaks, this time through a brother and a sister, to "performe" the same matter. Once again the Spirit is "cleft," a language of matter and a language of form. In effect, the Sidneys become the latter, themselves "formes," united into one, paradoxically, by this "cleft" (cloven but also musical) Spirit through whom God has accomplished once more the "work," the musical work, of the Psalms. A further passage makes clearer this double action of cleaving and uniting matter and form:

The Organist is hee
Who hath tun'd God and Man, the Organ we: 30
The songs are these, which heavens high holy Muse
Whisper'd to *David*, *David* to the Iewes:
And *Davids* Successors, in holy zeale,
In formes of joy and art doe re-reveale

170

To us so sweetly and sincerely too,   35
That I must not rejoyce as I would doe
When I behold that these Psalmes are become
So well attyr'd abroad, so ill at home,
So well in Chambers, in thy Church so ill,
As I can scarce call that reform'd until   40
This be reform'd;

Form is separable from content, "matter." (The idea controverts a
central aesthetic credo of *modern* formalism, but recall that our search
is for the kind of formalism most applicable to Donne.) Form is the
instrument of "matter," he writes in this poem. Prosody, music, even
language are all forms; and matter can be "translated," carried across,
from one instrument to another.

Further, there are in a sense theological or religious implications
even to this aesthetic dimension of form, as seen both in the usage of
Donne's time and in references in the poem: the church itself may be
"re-formed" without loss of its essence, or infusing spirit. But aesthetic
form is always personalist. Note that Donne subtly shifts his appella-
tion for the poet: at first, the Sidneys are the "Organ"; later, they become the "Organist" and "the Organ we." In both senses the Sidneys
are forms, first through whom the work is performed by the Holy
Spirit, and second by whom the work is reperformed through us.
Thus, aesthetic form is suffused with a certain personalism: in shaping
matter into "Harmony," form carries the imprint of the poet's spiritual
presence (in this poem the humility of Donne's presence is explicit in
the opening lines, as he dwells on the limits of his/our own shaping
powers). Personalism is there, but in service of a higher power.

In that sort of personalism Augustinian concepts of form also center. At times Augustine uses *form* to mean "soul," as in Aristotle, or
disembodied Idea, as in Plato.[30] At those times, he means by *form*
what Donne means by *matter*. In *The Confessions* (XII.xxix.40),
Augustine uses *form* (*formatum*) in a way similar to Donne's use of
aesthetic form; here Augustine speaks of the difference between *sound
(sonus)* and *song (cantus)*: *sound* is like unformed matter; *song* is matter
and form, and it is through the latter, form, that the will of the creator
is known. For Augustine, matter precedes the thing made; the thing
made is matter and form; knowledge of form, which must be the goal
of our efforts, is attainable on a level of abstraction, in contemplation

171

of the thing made. This is attained, as he says in *The City of God* (XI.xxix.30), by referring the work to the praise of the creator. Thus, all uses of the term *form* converge in one hermeneutical task: we must contemplate form—that is, the thing made—in order to gain knowledge of its creator. So, prospectively, Donne's poems should be contemplated for evidence of *their* creator, not necessarily the "real" Donne or the various Donnes but the intense, Augustinian personalism that is his poems' major principle and theme.

In Augustinianism, once matter has received the impress of form, once sound has become song, the work can be re-formed without loss of its truth. Augustine shows this in *The Confessions* (XII.xxx.41), when he proposes that seemingly incompatible interpretations of Moses (Genesis) may all be ways of encompassing a single truth. There *is* a single truth through all the varieties and contraries of forms—the truth of the creator. Where "divers senses arise," Donne says in a sermon (IX, p. 95), interpreting this same passage in Augustine, all can be true when none oppose truth—that is, God. "And what is God? Charity." The point is remade in a way that gives the literary critic an access, when in another sermon Donne speaks of the difference between what can be known through reason and what most moves us, what most persuades us:

> for the Resurrection is not a conclusion out of naturall Reason, but it is an article of supernaturall Faith; and though you assent to me now, speaking of the Resurrection, yet that is not out of my Logick, nor out of my Rhetorique, but out of the Character, and Ordinance which God hath imprinted in me, in the power and efficacy whereof, I speak unto you, as often as I speak out of this place. [VII, p. 95]

Donne's own Augustinianism seems abundantly clear. To follow the hermeneutic that influence calls for, one should approach the poems contemplatively, allow the separation of poet from poem, and locate communicative efficacy of the poem not at the level of the text but at a metatextual level, one's sense of the creator. The poem, that is, is a metonymy for the poet.

As suggested earlier, in all these respects but particularly in its separation of poet from poem, this Augustinian formalism diverges from the work of modern formalists, who might excuse Donne's primitive, rhetorical-seeming, or unrefined separation of *form* from *matter* in his poem on the Sidneys but who would be unforgiving of any formalism that tried to read a poem mainly for the poet it reveals. Consider T. S. Eliot's work on Donne. Eliot's pronouncements—that Donne was the poet who taught us how to think in the lyric, to "feel" our "thought"[31]—resemble the dogma of the New Critics in their insistence that poetry is a fusion of form and content, emotion and thought.[32] In the heyday of New Critical formalism, the worth of any one approach—that is, its formalist value—was often proved by its special ability to shed light on the fusion of only nominally separable qualities in a poem by Donne. If form is emotion, content is thought, and "feeling the thought" was but another way of expressing the credo of these critics. They no longer call themselves New Critics but use *formalists* to display their overriding concern for the formal beauty, or formed integrity, of the individual work of art, though the name itself seems curiously dissonant with their own credo. Formal beauty is all-important—far more so than a work's ideas or arguments, and much more so than the character of the poet, real or implied, or even his surrogate persona. Donne, for them, was only the poet who gave us this beauty, in which thought is felt. In what must surely be a formalist's vaunt, Cleanth Brooks has exclaimed, "Our age rejoices in having recovered Donne; but in doing so we have recovered not just Donne's poetry, but poetry."[33] Then, in what must just as surely be a formalist's *tour de force,* Brooks in that same article argues that we may find in Milton, too, those qualities we celebrate in Donne and call poetic: functional metaphor, dramatic tension, the fusion of thought and emotion. Form and content are so tightly meshed they exclude all considerations of that other *form,* the Augustinian one, the creator. Poetry, for most formalists, is such an integral whole that it stands apart from its creator—a little universe whose God has left it, or stands aside from it, as Stephen Dedalus said, silently paring his nails.

Not one of these formalists has taken into account Donne's own aesthetic concepts, as found in his poem about the Sidneys. Nor have they considered a possible Augustinian influence on Donne's aesthetic thought. For to do so would force a revision of their own doctrine. It is where these angels fear to tread that this prospective study rushes in—its foolishness moderated, perhaps, by its effort partly to maintain one crucial feature of formalist doctrine. On the level of the text, form and content can be separated, as both Donne and Augustine suggest. But, as Augustine indicates and Donne implies, they come together on another level, in the character of the poet, the creator. The formalist goal of maintaining a doctrinal fusion of form and content is to preserve the poem's integrity, as a centering of attention and as an offering of conceptual completeness, or perfection—all we know and all we need to know. But that completeness lies, finally, not at the level of the utterance but at the level of the speaker, Donne's artistic self—form in the Augustinian sense but form in the formalist sense, too, for in that self all elements of the poem fuse. Such a view would not only shift the locus of integrity but also, in so doing, treat two matters that are often slighted in formalist criticism: Donne's concept of truth and his use of personae. Both of these, as was suggested at the beginning of this essay, are Augustinian in nature. We are now ready to restate and attempt to apply a working hypothesis: Augustinianism is the major principle of Donne's poetry, most explicitly revealed in the early satires and in the later divine poems but at least implicit in those variations on Augustinianism, the *Songs and Sonets.*

This brief essay can do no more than suggest how a study might proceed. One might examine Donne's poems in chronological order from the perspective of the foregoing hypothetical position, by assuming that Augustinianism is the "soul" of Donne's poetry and that the poems themselves might offer evidence of the growth and identity of that soul. Further evidence could be sought through scholarship on the canon of Donne's poems, on Renaissance humanism, and on the development of Augustinianism and Anglicanism. Excursions might be made into Donne's prose, particularly into the sermons, where his Augustinianism seems fully articulated. The value of any such work must lie, as noted earlier, in its ability to shed light on Donne's poetic career—on such esoteric matters as his kinship with Quevedo[34] (Augustinianism may be the single base on which all such poetic kinships can be measured) and on such exoteric matters as structural effects in poems directly in the English-humanist (e.g., the satires) and Anglican (e.g., the holy sonnets) traditions. Examples of these exoteric matters may provide an appropriate conclusion to this brief essay, since they span Donne's career.

Two of the satires (II and IV) draw to conclusions whose *probability* has been overlooked. The closure of each poem should follow either logically, from arguments advanced earlier, or dramatically, as utterances congruent to the speaker's character. Moreover, "Satyre II" lampoons lawyers, particularly poet-lawyers, and examining it is therefore particularly useful in establishing the antirhetorical nature of Donne's poetical career. The poem begins with a rather mild disparagement of poetry writing generally (among other things, writing poetry brings "dearths, and Spaniards in"). But the greatest "hate" is reserved for "Coscus," the "scarse Poët" turned lawyer:

> jollier of this state,
> Then are new benefic'd ministers, he throwes   45
> Like nets, or lime-twigs, wheresoever he goes,
> His title of Barrister, on every wench,
> And wooes in language of the Pleas, and Bench:

The theme leads into a rich characterization of the foolish poet-lawyer's speech, then into strong words about the deviousness, materialism, and selfishness of lawyers generally. Finally, the poem draws to a curious conclusion, which in one sense follows logically but which in another sense seems no conclusion at all:

> In great hals   105
> Carthusian fasts, and fulsome Bachanalls
> Equally I hate; meanes blesse; in rich mens homes
> I bid kill some beasts, but no Hecatombs,
> None starve, none surfet so; But (Oh) we allow,
> Good workes as good, but out of fashion now,   110
> Like old rich wardrops; but my word none drawes
> Within the vast reach of th'huge statute lawes.

The speaker argues that the true source of blessedness, the impulse to observe "meanes" (and avoid extremes), is within, not without, enforced by laws. Indeed "Good workes" are now out of fashion, in our observance of externally imposed laws—the very laws, we assume, that are in fashion (like legalistic poetry) and that produce such vapid pettifoggers as Coscus. So much would seem to follow logically from the earlier structure of the poem and would seem, too, to be iterations of Augustinian virtue. But from what source comes the final complaint, concerning the speaker's "word"? The speaker himself would disdain the title of "lawyer," but he cannot so easily disclaim the title of poet. What sort of poet? The proposed answer is Augustinian. For insofar as writing the poem was not merely an act of futility, the speaker seems finally to rest his case on a recognized and shareable

175

interiority—readers, at least, *are* drawn to his word, to his interiority through their own, both beyond the reach of external laws. Like Augustine's case in *The Confessions,* Donne's in the satires is self-confirming, in both senses of the term: the writer's strategy makes the reader's interiority, like his own, patent.

"Satyre IV" lampoons courtiers. As in II, where an interiorized virtuousness is used as a foil for external, man-made laws (a similar foiling is used throughout III), the opening of IV contrasts the court with the church and religion:

> Well; I may now receive, and die; My sinne
> Indeed is great, but I have beene in
> A Purgatorie, such as fear'd hell is
> A recreation to, and scarse map of this.

The "Purgatorie" is the court, where the speaker encounters a man who epitomizes all its vices: vain, toadying, proud. The man is particularly proud of his linguistic abilities, but here he is outdone by the speaker himself, who capitalizes on all the fellow's ambiguities and does not merely parry each thrust but also thrusts home:

> He, like to a high stretcht lute string squeakt, O Sir,
> 'Tis sweet to talke of Kings. At Westminster,
> Said I, The man that keepes the Abbey tombes,   75
> And for his price doth with who ever comes,
> Of all our Harries, and our Edwards talke,
> From King to King and all their kin can walke:
> Your eares shall heare nought, but Kings; your eyes meet
> Kings only; The way to it, is Kingstreet.   80

Later the man begs a "crowne" from the speaker and departs. Rapidly the speaker returns home "in wholesome solitarinesse," where he indulges the musings of his "precious soule." The soul sends him a dream in which other vices of the court appear—varied, but none (for a dream) more fantastic than their embodiment in the earlier proud linguist. The dream vanishes and the poem concludes:

>   Preachers which are
> Seas of Wit and Arts, you can, then dare,
> Drowne the sinnes of this place, for, for mee
> Which am but a scarce brooke, it enough shall bee   240

> To wash the staines away; Although I yet
> With *Macchabees* modestie, the knowne merit
> Of my worke lessen: yet some wise man shall,
> I hope, esteeme my writs Canonicall.

In II, the foils were, first, poets and lawyers, then poet-lawyers and the speaker, who would seem to be a poet of a certain kind. In IV the foils are religion and the court ("Truth" and "Religion" seem to be the same mistress, as argued in III), then preachers and the speaker, who, again, seems to be a religious of a certain kind. His "writs Canonicall" contrast with the fine "suits" of the courtiers, both as something worn or displayed and as something petitioned. The "wise man" can esteem this religious vestment, the poem, and can also value the writing as being "Canonicall," comfortable to religious thought. Who is this "wise man"? Surely it is someone who, like Donne in the satires or Augustine in *The Confessions,* can be in the world but not of the world, can practice a peculiarly worldly other-worldliness, and can in the midst of vanity and sensuousness yet preserve the sanctity of an interiority where, as each believes, he is joined by what is best in the interiority of other (wise) men. This interiority is the true norm against which in the satires the debasements and assaults of the exterior world are measured.[35]

Such a view of the satires complements the one offered by Andreasen,[36] who sees them as a sequence spoken by the same persona. The view, too, places into perspective the satires' classical models: Donne's Christianity is more prominent than his reliance on Horace, Juvenal, or Persius.[37] The various personae of the satires are, obviously, not totally distinct from the speaker, even in their vices. They become part of his own Christian burden—as Donne confesses in one of his sermons:

> We make *Satyrs;* and we looke that the world shall call that *wit;*
> when God knowes, that that is in a great part, self-guiltinesse,
> and we doe but reprehend those things, which we our selves
> have done, we cry out upon the illnesse of the times, and we
> make the times ill: so the calumniator whispers those things,
> which are true, no where, but in himselfe.   [VII, p. 408]

To the extent that Donne points toward his own earlier, unredeemed wit, he encourages us to track the growth and development of his artistic persona—the character of the implied poet—from the satires through its variations in the *Songs and Sonets* to its maturity in the divine poems.

Reconsider Holy Sonnet VII ("At the round earths imagin'd corners") as examined in the preceding essay. Significantly, the rhetorical approach is able to offer little more than a view of the poem as the working out of a stance toward external religious verities. Donne's speaker would seem to be skeptical of all truths but those he can immediately experience. Some say the world is round, others speak of its corners. Religion describes the Day of Judgment and teaches us that Christ made the perfect sacrifice and oblation for the sins of the whole world. Balanced against these verities—which are, almost blasphemously, placed in the same, indifferent category—are the realities of the speaker's emotions. That he will be judged is certain, as is the urgency of his desire to learn repentance. Suppose we ask, boorishly, of the rhetorical critic, So what? What does the poem come to, in your view, beyond a structural balancing of ostensibly controversial elements and an expression of the speaker's "intense personalism"? We will surely be offered no more than the kind of didacticism the rhetorical critic invariably finds. The poem, that is, would appear to be aimed at awakening in others the desire to repent. Judgment *is* a reality, beyond the at times foolish nature of our conventions. We must repent, learn how to repent, now, if we would partake of Christ's sacrifice.

By contrast, the view proposed in the present essay shifts the emphasis in a search for intentionality away from a form aimed at an external audience and onto an *interiorized speaker and audience,* which are the informing components of Donne's poetic Augustinianism. External events, like an external audience, are interiorized, questioned, and transformed into truth. Donne reveals in this poem as in his satires a personalism that outflanks skepticism, whether the subject be virtue or religion (the two are one). It outflanks but does not "prevent," arrive before or avoid. Skepticism—which in the satires is expressed as a caustic attitude, usually of rejection—is first on the scene, as in this holy sonnet. Throughout his career, Donne preserved a skeptical attitude toward rational philosophy while persistently relying on faith experienced personally. Several decades ago, Bredvold expressed the point precisely, though in specifically biographical terms:

178

But all his experience, his youthful interest in the relativist thought typified by Montaigne, his search for the true church, his wrestling with scholastic divinity, his gradually deepening religious insight, had all directed him towards the conclusion of Pascal, that philosophical dogmatism is a danger to the religious life, that the heart has its reasons of which the reason knows nothing. Pascal's thought is a fusion of the scepticism of Montaigne and the Augustinianism of the Jansenists. Donne had studied the same scepticism, in Sextus Empiricus and probably in Montaigne, and cultivated Augustine as his favorite religious teacher.[38]

The heart has its reasons. Donne dramatized the lesson in both a secular and a sacred way. But as he looked back across his career, he found the little secular dramas peopled with selves that were only "straw about the heart." Donne found his true center within, as Augustine did—not in any Romantic self or in any solipsistic stance, but in a realizable, shareable interiority. It is *that* we must grasp in this holy sonnet or in any of Donne's poems—an interiority that is Donne's highest artistic achievement, self-fashioned but ultimately in imitation of Christ who, as Erasmus stated, drew all things unto himself.

An apt title for the proposed work, naming the value Donne found, strayed from, and then refound, might be "Constancy Regained."

Rhetoric as a Habit of Thought
and Movement of Mind

First, *the day of Iudgement* is subject to *scorne,* some laugh at it;
And then (in a second consideration,) it induces *horror;* The best
man, that is but man, trembles at it; But *wee,* (which is a third
branch) those that have laid hold upon *God,* And (in a fourth
place) have laid hold upon *God,* by the right *handle, According to
his promises,* Wee (which will constitute a fift point,) *Wee expect;*
We blesse *God* for our *Possession,* but *We looke for* a greater *Reversion;* which *Reversion* (in the next roome) is, *new Heavens,* and
new Earth; And (lastly) such *Heavens,* and such *Earth,* as may be
an everlasting *Dwelling* for *Righteousnesse.* And through all these
particulars, we shall passe, with as much *cleerenesse,* and *short-
nesse,* as the *weight,* and *number* thereof will admit.

[Sermons VIII, pp. 64–65]

So says Donne in the *divisio* of his sermon on the death of Lady
Danvers, his old friend and patron Magdalen Herbert. The sermon
resembles the one I discussed in the first chapter of this book, Donne's
oration at the funeral of Alderman Cockayne. Again, there are two
texts, a biblical passage (2 Peter 3:13: "Nevertheless, we, according
to his promises, looke for new heavens, and new earth, wherein dwel-
leth righteousnesse") and a departed "sister," whose living "family"
are present in the audience. Again, Donne is faced with a problem of
praise: Magdalen Herbert scandalized society by taking as her second
husband a man half her age. Donne's efforts to soften these facts lead
him into some of the most outrageous juggling in all his sermons.[39]
The juggling is more than overwhelmed, however, by a moving account of Lady Danvers's charity, hospitality, and devotional life, and
by a final adjuration against any *"halfe calumnies . . . any whisperings."*
Again, the interpretation of the first text echoes through the interpretation of the second: we are moved beyond *"scorne"* in both.

Donne's method of interpreting the first text, seen in miniature in
the quoted *divisio,* is a useful introduction to this final essay in which I
must attempt to refute the preceding essay on Donne's supposed Augustinianism and to reaffirm a rhetorical approach to all of Donne's

180

poetry and prose, and thereby justify my interpretation of him as a humanist.

The passage is a useful introduction because, to begin with, it recalls Donne's Holy Sonnet VII ("At the round earths imagin'd corners . . .") in its reference to and attitude toward the Day of Judgment. In both passage and sonnet, there is an *anchoring:* in the passage, in the promises made by God to man through the Scriptures; in the sonnet, in the memory of Christ. This anchoring, I shall argue, caused Donne's controversial thinking to shift, even to become somewhat displaced from the nature and prominence it had in the *Songs and Sonets.* But the opening passage also shows that, nevertheless, *controversia* continued as a certain habit of Donne's thought. Partly, the habit is expressed by the legalese Donne always uses in interpreting Scripture: "possession" and "reversion" echo cases at law; in this particular case, "we blesse God" for this life and anticipate coming into an even greater estate, as shown by his "will," in the scriptural text. Of course, the legalese Donne used throughout his secular as well as sacred writings only reflects his early training as an aspiring lawyer. But to manifest a habit of mind (a thoroughly non-Augustinian habit of mind), rhetorical *controversia* should be remarkable not so much at the level of diction or style *(elocutio)* as at the levels of *inventio* and *dispositio.* Here, the continual corrections and reconciliations in this passage ("scorne" and "horror," "man" and "wee," "possession" and "reversion") more fully reveal that habit. Controversial thinking pervades especially the part of the sermon in tribute to Lady Danvers, who emerges as a kind of figure of the *via media et serena,* the Anglican church.[40] As always, the ultimate resting point of controversial thinking was, for Donne at least, the middle point, "mediocrity" or the "meanes" which (he avers in "Satyre II") bless.

Further, the opening passage reflects Donne's characteristic, and continuing, skeptical attitude toward linguistic form. In reviewing the sermon on Alderman Cockayne, we examined Donne's attitude toward language and his diffidence about the extent to which any perceptible form contains immutable truth. Indeed, we have examined the point several times in this book as we reviewed Donne's arguments concerning body and soul, air and angels, spheres and intelligences. What "form" seems to be suggested in the passage quoted at the first of this essay? It is impossible to put together the various terms Donne uses and arrive at a stable, let alone static, notion of the very form of his sermon: "consideration," "branch," "place," "point," "room," "lastly," "weight," and "number." Is the discourse a deliberation, a plant, a location, a geometrical figure, a building, an event, a body? It is surely all of these things and none of these things, since Donne has made an overt effort to switch the terms each time. One possibility remains, however: a passing through "particulars." Passing is, of course, the great theme of the sermon itself—passing through the particulars of this life (*"scorne"* and *"horror"*) to our reversion in the next, a passing that offers the only possibility whereon (here the legalese becomes prominent) anything like certainty can be construed. But passing is also, most importantly, the nature of *rhetorical* form. We move through most discourse by Donne not simply by means of *accumulatio*—addition of information and expansion of understanding—but controversially, by means of correction and reconciliation; something happens to our understanding en route. An Augustinian contemplation of form, as proposed in the preceding section, seems utterly contrary—here as elsewhere—to Donne's artistic intentions.

We shall traverse three points, then, on our way to a conclusion: that Donne's controversial thinking realigned itself in his career as Doctor of Divinity; that it remained nonetheless a habit of thought, with its characteristic move toward the *via media;* and that its continuing skepticism of form involves the reader in action at the level of the text, rather than at some hypothesized metatextual level like that proposed in the preceding attempt at an Augustinian view of Donne. I have made little effort to keep these three rigorously distinct in the sections that follow. Nor have I arranged them in exactly a Ciceronian pattern, though the last is, if not the strongest, then the most important.

OF CONVERSION AND CONTROVERSY.   *Turning* is a key to Augustine. His life as a rhetorician was radically altered when he turned toward God, for then conversion replaced all controversy. Indeed, conversion became for Augustine the very answer to hermeneutical problems: trying all things by willfully turning toward God and applying the rule of charity could even dispel inconsistencies in Scripture.

Outward similarities in the lives of Augustine and Donne have been noted by many students—including Donne himself. Both were profligate youths, both had a sensuousness that seemed always to prevent arid rationality, and both demonstrated life-long devotion to their mothers. Still, these similarities are ultimately superficial; they break down in the crucial question of conversion. Donne's abandonment of Roman Catholicism for a long period of doubt followed by an acceptance of Anglicanism is not even remotely similar to Augustine's abandonment of Manichaeism for orthodox Christianity. Nonetheless, it would appear that *something* tantamount to conversion happened to Donne early in the second decade of the seventeenth century.

Having begun what looked like a brilliant career in the employ of Sir Thomas Egerton, Donne himself abruptly halted the progress of that career in 1601 by secretly marrying Anne More, Egerton's niece and ward. From the viewpoint of Anne's family, the marriage looked disastrous: she had married one of the fashionable young men, a known womanizer, with a ruined fortune. Insofar as that view of Donne is accurate, his marriage must have been his reformation, for he remained devoted to Anne for the almost seventeen years of their marriage. With preferment at court now impossible, and with Donne's health failing and his family responsibilities increasing (a child was born almost every year of their marriage), all sorts of crises were inevitable; yet the marriage endured. Donne received some largess from his wife's cousin, worked with the Bishop of Durham, produced "controversial" and satirical prose. Then, with the composition of the two Anniversary poems in 1611 and 1612, he was given patronage and employment by Sir Robert Drury. He served as a member of Parliament, and finally took Anglican orders in 1615. Two years later Anne died. He never remarried. Seven children survived her, the eldest of whom was fourteen upon Anne's death. Four years later, in 1621, Donne was appointed dean of St. Paul's, and for the decade that remained of his life he became one of the leading spokesmen— preacher, poet, essayist—of the Anglican church. Did this development represent a change of heart? conversion? career decision?

For Hiram Haydn, a change of heart, a "turning point" in Donne's career, came with the composition of the Anniversary poems: Donne abandoned reason and adopted a fideism, which alone "could answer the profound questions which troubled him."[41] The idea that Donne had experienced a "conversion" following Anne's death was introduced by his Victorian biographer, Edmund Gosse.[42] Recently, R. C. Bald has argued that in the period following his wife's death Donne experienced not a conversion exactly but a "deepened sense of Christian truth."[43] Nonetheless, it *can* appear that, with one career avenue blocked, Donne sought advancement by another: Izaak Walton, his first biographer (1640), states that King James induced Donne to take orders by countering all his petitions for secular employment with an expressed desire that Donne enter the priesthood.

But from a rhetorical point of view, Bald's interpretation seems most meaningful: a firmer sense of *a priori* truth enters Donne's process of argumentation, as seen particularly in his writings from "Goodfriday 1613" on. When read biographically, that poem suggests that Donne had always been turned toward Christ, even when he was willfully turned away. Christ was always present in his "memory," an Augustinian might insist, pointing out that Donne himself says in a later sermon that memory *is* salvation, as it would be to a Christianized Platonist. But Donne's writings equally show that he was never comfortable with that view. And it is his writings and their strategies, not his biography, that are more at issue here. Regardless of what we call Donne's spiritual experience, his writings show that the Christ who embodies *a priori* truth was himself—partly at least—rhetorical, or controversial, in nature, more like Erasmus's Christ than (as we shall see) Milton's. Donne's own rhetoric shifted, consequently, with the admission in evidence of *a priori* truth, but underwent no dramatic alteration in nature.[44]

Donne himself perpetuated certain fictions about his life. Mostly he saw it as Janus-faced with one of the faces turned at last in a true direction. In 1619, when he sent *Biathanatos,* his book on suicide—or, rather, on justifiable self-homicide—which he had written just ten years earlier, to Sir Robert Ker, he said, "let any that your discretion admits to the sight of it know that it is a book written by Jack Donne, not by Dr. Donne." But he did not totally repudiate Jack. The remainder of his instruction to Ker is revealing for what it refuses to say: "Reserve it for me if I live, and if I die I only forbid it the press and the fire; publish it not, but yet burn it not, and between those do what you will with it."[45] He called his own sonnets, those written by Dr. Donne, "holy," yet throughout their lines the voice of Jack Donne is clearly audible—perhaps nowhere more clearly than in one in which, seeking comfort from Christ's face at the imagined Day of Judgment, he recalls an argument that he used seducing his "profane mistresses." Further, in a letter in 1623, he refers to poetry as "the mistress of my youth," and to divinity as "the wife of mine age."[46] But any distinction between the two that might indicate a change of mind or direction is obliterated by similarities in "poetic" and "divine" rhetorical strategies—similarities Dr. Donne might find Solomonic. He mentions Solomon's artistry in a sermon delivered just four months following Anne's death:

> *Solomon,* whose disposition was amorous, and excessive in the love of women, when he turn'd to God, he departed not utterly from his old phrase and language, but having put a new, and a spiritual tincture, and form and habit into all his thoughts, and words, he conveyes all his loving approaches and applications to God, and all Gods gracious answers to his amorous soul, into songs, and Epithalamions, and meditations upon contracts, and marriages between God and his Church, and between God and his soul. . . .   [I, p. 237]

The elegies on Donne that appeared in the 1633 edition of his complete poems—particularly those by Thomas Carew, who calls Donne *"Apollo's first, and last, the true Gods Priest,"* and by Sir Thomas Browne, who finds the late poems embodying *"Goodnesse,"* the early ones *"Crimes"*—seem, like later biographies, to force a distinction.

Throughout Donne's writing at least one value remains constant: the middle ground, the *via media,* the avoidance of extremes. That value spans his career; he praises the "meanes" that "blesse" in "Satyre II" and in 1627 commemorates Magdalen Herbert's "mediocrity." The Anglican church, too, was a *via media,* defining Donne's choice—not between Christianity and atheism but between Roman Catholicism and the radically reformed churches. Any *via media* is always a middle ground in *controversia,* which is of course the only way to locate a *via media.* I shall pursue this mode of argumentation in the second section of this essay; my subject now is Donne's ostensible conversion and its impact on his rhetoric.

From "Goodfriday 1613" on, Donne increasingly anchored his lawyerly habits of mind in Christ, the God-Man. I allude to an image that Donne himself adopted: his seal, in 1615, became a "cross" grown into an "anchor."[47] But if Christ was an anchor, he was also the embodiment of a *via media* (a "moderator," as in Erasmus) and Janus, too (though Donne mentions Janus only once, and *that* in Janus's Christianized version as Noah).[48] The *a priori* truth that is now admitted as evidence in Donne's courtroom comes as Christ, who is, outside the

185

argument, a cross grown into an anchor; however, inside the argument Christ becomes both Janus and the *via media*. I have jumbled the images, to make them echo my own case. Better, clearer, and less confusing comparisons are available from Donne's writings, comparisons that equally serve my point, that Donne's truth always remained partly controversial.

Late in his career, Donne articulated with approval two kinds of persuasion: one is closely akin to rhetoric, the other to prophecy. Both are in evidence throughout his career. But a growing desire to "conform" to truth caused both to shift: *controversia* became more ritualized; prophecy, secondary early in his career, became more prominent.

I shall let Donne, from the perspective of his late career, describe the difference between these two kinds of persuasion. On December 19, 1619, he preached a sermon at The Hague on Matthew 4:18, 19, and 20:

> And Jesus walking by the Sea of Galile saw two brethren, Simon called Peter, and Andrew his brother, casting a net into the sea, (for they were fishers,) and he saith unto them, follow me, and I will make you fishers of men; and they straightway left their nets, and followed him.

Eleven years later, in 1630, as he lay ill in Essex, Donne revised his "short notes" on the sermon and "digested" them into two sermons. Both sermons, besides giving evidence of much deliberation, offer the most definitive statements Donne has made on the act—or acts— of persuasion. His position is summarized in this paragraph:

> And therefore how easie soever *Iulian* the Apostate might make it, for Christ to work upon so weake men, as these were, yet to work upon any men by so weake means, onely by one *Sequere me, Follow me,* and no more, cannot be thought easie. The way of Rhetorique in working upon weake men, is first to trouble the understanding, to displace, and to discompose, and disorder the judgement, to smother and bury in it, or to empty it of former apprehensions and opinions, and to shake that beliefe, with which it had possessed it selfe before, and then when it is thus melted, to powre it into new molds, when it is thus mollified, to stamp and imprint new formes, new images, new

opinions in it. But here in our case, there was none of this fire, none of this practise, none of this battery of eloquence, none of this verball violence, onely a bare *Sequere me, Follow me,* and *they followed.* No eloquence enclined them, no terrors declined them.   [II, pp. 282–283]

Let us consider each of these acts of persuasion.

Rhetoric, as Donne indicates, is a process of in-forming. But rhetoric itself is involved in a total action of *advocacy,* whereby old forms and old materials (of understanding and judgment) are displaced, then replaced. The learned method of advocacy, as we have discovered from the materials in this book, is Ciceronian *controversia,* and we find its formal realization in the ironies of Erasmus and in the ironies, paradoxes, prolepses, and reconciliations of Donne. One looks in both directions in order to get his audience to look in one.

The other kind of persuasion is "conformity" to God Incarnate, following Christ "doctrinally": "To persevere to the end in the whole Gospel, this is to follow Christ in Doctrinall things." Again, the process is an active one. It is a *doing,* as Donne vividly describes in developing the command *tollat crucem:*

> ... when my crosses have carried mee up to my Saviours Crosse, I put my hands into his hands, and hang upon his nailes, I put mine eyes upon his, and wash off all my former unchast looks, and receive a soveraigne tincture, and a lively verdure, and a new life into my dead teares, from his teares. I put my mouth upon his mouth, and it is I that say, *My God, my God, why hast thou forsaken me?* and it is I that recover againe, and say, *Into thy hands, O Lord, I commend my spirit.* Thus my afflictions are truly a crosse, when those afflictions doe truely crucifie me, and souple me, and mellow me, and knead me, and roll me out, to a conformity with Christ. It must be this *Crosse,* and then it must be *my crosse* that I must take up, *Tollat suam.*   [II, p. 300)]

Christ's way is renovation, not innovation (II, p. 305): just as God gave a star to the astrologers, the Magi, so Christ makes "fishers of men" out of simple fishermen. The "net" by which we are caught, Donne argues, is Christ: not "Eloquence," not "Tradition," "onely the Gospel" (II, p. 307). Once we recognize its truth, it becomes our truth.

Advocacy is the clearest and best name for the way of rhetoric. The second way is more difficult to name. "Prophetic" was implied earlier, but the term is best reserved for Milton's radically different ethos. We could call it "sermonic," perhaps, if we meant by that title *sermo,* as Erasmus translated the *logos* of John 1:1, to contrast with the static *verbum* of the Augustinians. But a better name may be one drawn from the Mass itself, in which Christ is called both "mediator" and "advocate."[49] Or in Donne's own words:

> Therefore the Angel gave him that name *Iesus, For he shall save his people from their sins.* So, because to this purpose Christ consists of two natures, God and man, he is called our Mediator, *There is one Mediator between God and man, the man Christ Iesus.* Because he presents those merits which are his, as ours, and in our behalfe, he is called an Advocate, *If any man sin, we have an Advocate with the Father, Iesus Christ the righteous.*　　[VI, p. 313]

Mediator gives the role an active function, as reconciler, or peace maker: the "blest Hermaphrodite" which Donne calls Mr. Tillman "after he had taken orders" (in the poem by that title, l. 54), a role which is, like Christ's, dualistic but thereby intermediary. Donne attempts to play the role of mediator, as we have seen in his satires, one who draws all the various follies unto himself and with whom on the most interior level the reader can identify. In *The second Anniversary* he concludes by assuming the role of mediator, in this case, one who is in an intermediate position between man and God, a position that causes him to use a singular (for Donne in his middle years) comparative:

> Since his will is, that to posteritie,
> Thou should'st for life, and death, a patterne bee,
> And that the world should notice have of this,　　525
> The purpose, and th'authoritie is his;
> Thou art the Proclamation; and I am
> The Trumpet, at whose voyce the people came.

The dead young woman is addressed; she becomes the "Proclamation," formally authorized by God; only the proclaimer's office is Donne's. It was this role, as mediator, that underwent the greatest deepening in Donne's career—specifying may be the better word. Christ became his pattern, ranging from Donne's identification with common humanity in his congregation, to his assuming the role of Christ in his holy sonnets, to his hanging upon the feet of Christ crucified in his final sermon. Christ actually embodied the value of "meanes" and "mediocrity" as well as "medium," like the "Trumpet" in *The second Anniversary* or the "Organ" *and* "Organist" in Donne's poem on the Sidneys. The two functions, advocate and mediator, are shown in brief in another passage from Donne's sermons:

> The Preacher doth so infuse the feare of God into his Auditory, that first, they shall feare nothing but God, and then they shall feare God, but so, as he is God; and God is Mercy; God is Love; and his Minister shall so spread his wings over his people, as to defend them from all inordinate feare, from all suspition and jealousie, from all diffidence and distrust in the mercie of God. [VIII, p. 44]

These, then, are twin roles, one adversarial, the other loving; one threatening, the other comforting; one predicated on otherness, the other on familiarity.

The role of advocate underwent not so much a specifying as a shift in Donne's career—just as truth underwent a shift, from compromise to something like certainty. Rhetoric became no longer a means of "inventing" truth but a means of reasoning about it and arguing for it—*rhetoric* here in the sense used by Donne in the passage above or, as defined in another sermon, as the process of making "absent and remote things present" (IV, p. 87). The method of rhetoric, *controversia*, remained the same, but its ends were different, and so was its starting point. Donne's "Goodfriday 1613," with its peculiar Janus faces, is the drama of a struggle not to find truth but to admit its presence; the poem sets a pattern for Donne's later career. Once *a priori* truth was admitted, the rules of his rhetorical thinking changed: *controversia* became prestructured as a mode of thought, and thus for the most part reduced to strategic ritual.

I now turn to a further consideration of *controversia* in Donne's later career. But let me here recall my thesis: controversial thinking and the imitation or semblance of controversial thinking, or Ciceronian rhetoric even when set amidst elements profoundly antagonistic to it— these are the qualities that identify the humanism in Donne.

OF JANUS AND THE *VIA MEDIA*.   In those prose writings known as his "controversial" works, composed before "Goodfriday 1613" and during the period of his deepest Christian skepticism—*Biathanatos* and

Pseudo-Martyr—Donne speaks in a lawyerly way, as a lay advocate. These works are truly "controversial," in a technical sense: *controversia* is at once their method and their point. Again, the faces of Janus provide a clear conceptual model for the total movement of Donne's mind. One position is counterbalanced against its opposite. Dogmatism is continually undercut. So characteristic is this movement that modern readers approaching these works can find them jumbled and perplexing; one perceptive reader records her response to *Biathanatos* in this manner:

> the constant blurring of distinctions and the repeated attacks on the certainty of judgment have the further effect of suggesting the impossibility of clear perception or sure judgment by the individual conscience. Donne seems to be trying to establish some degree of probability for the lawfulness of suicide within the body of theological opinion rather than striving to provide the means for full assent by the individual conscience. In this context, his attack on the externality of probabilistic casuistry weakens his argument; satire becomes self-parody, and the case of conscience becomes paradox.[50]

Donne wrote both books more as a lawyer than as a casuist. His Christianity had not yet anchored itself. Atheism seemed no meaningful alternative, but within the tenets of the Christian faith *omnia probate,* all things were to be examined. This is the position of Christian skepticism, itself something of a paradox. But, again, we find *controversia* flourishing on its native grounds, however paradoxical, or partial, the skepticism.

In 1610, Donne published *Pseudo-Martyr,* whose full title indicates its thesis and context: *Wherein ovt of Certaine Propositions and Gradations, This Conclusion is euicted, That Those Which are of the Romane Religion in this Kingdome, May and ovght to take the Oath of Allegeance.* The first address in the book is to King James—who was, apparently, so impressed with the work that he determined that Donne should have a career in the Anglican ministry. The second address, "An Advertisement," is to the general reader, in which Donne establishes his own ethos:

> as I am a Christian, I haue been euer kept awake in a meditation of Martyrdome, by being deriued from such a stocke and race,

> as, I beleeue, no family . . . hath endured and suffered more in
> their persons and fortunes, for obeying the Teachers of Romane
> Doctrine, then it hath done.   [sig. ¶1]

The facts *were* well known: his mother's family, the Heywoods, were
all but ruined for their Catholic convictions; more recently, his
brother had died while imprisoned for harboring a Catholic priest. To
argue for the oath of allegiance, in effect to acknowledge that a subject's loyalty to the king supersedes his loyalty to the pope, if only in
some matters, would have been extraordinary for a member of this
family.[51]

The third address is "A Preface to the Priests, and Iesuits, and to
their Disciples in this Kingdome." It is in this address that Donne virtually outlines the controversial thinking that undergirds his argument:

> They who haue descended so lowe, as to take knowledge of me,
> and to admit me into their consideration, know well that I vsed
> no inordinate hast, nor precipitation in binding my conscience
> to any locall Religion. I had a longer worke to do then many
> other men; for I was first to blot out, certaine impressions of the
> Romane religion, and to wrastle both against the examples and
> against the reasons, by which some hold was taken; and some
> anticipations early layde vpon my conscience, both by Persons
> who by nature had a power and superiority ouer my will, and
> others who by their learning and good life, seem'd to me iustly
> to claime an interest for the guiding, and rectifying of mine
> understanding in these matters. And although I apprehended
> well enough, that this irresolution not onely retarded my for-
> tune, but also bred some scandall, and endangered my spirituall
> reputation, by laying me open to many mis-interpretations; yet
> all these respects did not transport me to any violent and sudden
> determination, till I had, to the measure of my poore wit and
> iudgement, suruayed and digested the whole body of Diuinity,
> controuerted betweene ours and the Romane Church. In which
> search and disquisition, that God, which awakened me then,
> and hath neuer forsaken me in that industry, as he is the
> Authour of that purpose, so is he a witnes of this protestation;
> that I behaued my selfe, and proceeded therin with humility,
> and diffidence in my selfe; and by that, which by his grace, I

tooke to be the ordinary meanes, which is frequent praier, and
equall and indifferent affections.   [sig. B2ᵛ–B3]

Let us admit that the passage itself may be a rhetorical move, an appeal
to the Catholic reader to keep an open mind as Donne claims he has
done. Nonetheless, the similarities between this passage and the procedures of humanist rhetorical invention—even the specific procedures Antonius recommends in *De oratore*—are striking. Add to
these similarities the one between Donne's description of the "longer
worke" he had to do and his definitions of rhetoric discussed earlier,
and we begin to see the truly re-creative and in-forming nature of a
Donnesque enterprise in persuasion, including self-persuasion. Finally, add to these similarities the patently controversial movement of
much of Donne's prose and poetry, and one has a concrete description
of a habit of mind that was usually operative in Donne's approach to
composition, whether secular or sacred, before or beyond the period
of his deepest religious skepticism.

Two contrary positions are reviewed. Each is allowed to speak,
while the examiner tries—with "impartiality," Antonius says; with
"equall and indifferent affections," Donne says—to judge. Once
judgment is reached, then advocacy may proceed. But the process of
advocacy itself reflects this initial *inventio*. The writing tends to fuse
contraries, often proleptically, with corrections and reconciliations
sometimes left up to the reader. But, invariably, two positions—*pro*
and *contra*—are discernible. Following this path, or method, Donne
appears to justify in the one book suicide, in the other the oath of
allegiance. But it is a mistake to see either work as philosophically
serious. On the contrary, both are rhetorical structurings of emotionally charged matters. Donne "controversializes" these matters to
such an extent that the ultimate effect of these two works is a remarkable diffidence in the face of zeal.[52]

However, doubt, even Christian skepticism, was not a position
Donne could be comfortable with. It "was not to him, as it had been to
Montaigne, a soft pillow on which to rest his head, but pain and restlessness, search and endless labor."[53] We are brought very close to that
torment in "Goodfriday 1613." In a letter written that same year,
Donne says, speaking first of what we would call "scientific demonstrations,"

192

Except demonstrations (and perchance there are very few of them) I find nothing without perplexities. I am grown more sensible of it by busying myself a little in the search of the Eastern tongues, where a perpetual perplexity in the words cannot choose but cast a perplexity upon the things.[54]

Again, in that same year, Donne's poem on the death of Prince Henry begins with a comparison that totally restructures the controversial faces of Janus:

> Looke to mee faith, and looke to my faith, God;
> For both my centers feele this period.
> Of waight one center, one of greatnesse is;
> And Reason is that center, Faith is this;

The looking outward of Janus is too anarchic. But something of the habit continued, even when Donne found, or admitted, an anchor in both his centers: one anchor—Christ—for both Reason and Faith.

A value that spanned Donne's career, as noted in the preceding section, and that seems a correlative of *controversia* is the middle position, "meanes" or "mediocrity." The Anglican (or "established") church could itself become a *via media*, as Donne recognized, and his restless, controversial thought seemed to bring him there as a compromise, one that he would pursue as a pragmatic solution to a long, intensely personal but legalistic battle. The church never made the appeal to his "heart and imagination it did to George Herbert," as Grierson has noted.[55] Rather, the Anglican church was a *via media* for Donne in a way that it never was for Herbert; any *via media*, after all, can only be realized or identified *as such* when the alternatives are fully operative—with Rome on the one hand, Calvin or Knox on the other. "Superfluities" must be excised in favor of a mean, which can only be measured by extremes: the poor man who puts himself to superfluous expense in his diet and apparel and the miserly rich man who hoards all while denying himself the "conveniences" he can afford are alike condemned in one of Donne's sermons (VI, p. 197). Presumably, the poor man continues poor, the rich man rich, each adopting a mode of life that is more decorous, more appropriate to his "meanes." Thus, as we have noted, *via media* is a measure of secular as well as sacred matters, the means that bless. Faith does not replace reason, nor does reason, for Donne, proceed noncontroversially even about matters of faith, such as Scripture and church traditions. But as Christ became more firmly the anchor in both his "centers," making them both one center, so Christ began also to embody the goal of reason, the *via media* itself, and became at once Advocate and Mediator. That is, the faces of Janus began to take on their tricephalous Prudential aspect: *controversia* is usually discernible, but as a background for the voice from the center. Let us pursue our earlier terms, advocate and mediator. Advocacy, the Christian advocacy practiced by Donne, continually allows extremes to speak, though their center has been predetermined. Mediation is the voice from the center, and in that center, Donne came increasingly to believe, all distinctions, including even those between sacred and secular reasoning, collapse.

Once he had reached that position, he was ready to write his *De officiis*. It was, as we would expect, in the form of a sermon. On February 20, 1628 /9, Donne preached a lenten sermon at Whitehall, on James 2:12: "So speake ye, and so do, as they that shall be judged by the law of liberty." His audience were the *honesti* of his time—the statesmen, advisers, and courtiers close to the king:

> the Holy Ghost, in proposing these duties in his general *Ye,* does principally intend, ye that live in Court, ye whom God brings so neer to the sight of himself, and the pourtraiture of his Court in your eyes: for a Religious King is the Image of God, and a Religious Court is a Copy of the Communion of Saints.
>
> [VIII, p. 336]

The *divisio* immediately follows this passage, and it is one in which Donne clearly articulates his own understanding of rhetorical form:

> Our Text hath two parts . . . first, in the obligation that is laid upon us, upon us all, *Sic loquimini, sic facite:* And then in the Reason of this Holy diligence, and religious cautelousness, *Quia judicandi,* Because you are to be judged, *by, etc.* which two general parts, the Obligation, and the Reason, flowing into many sub-divided branches, I shall, I think, do better service, both to your understandings, and to your memory, and to your Affections, and Consciences, to present them as they shall arise anon, in their order, then to pour them out, all at once now.   [p. 337]

The assumption that the major function of rhetorical form is to aid the understanding and memory—one the Ramists held in Donne's day—is proved limited and partial by this and other passages in Donne. Indeed, as Donne asserts, and as I shall argue later, the truly functional association is between rhetorical form and emotion (*emotion* is our term; *affections* and *consciences* are Donne's).

The first part has two subparts: speaking and acting. Each is divided into three sub-subparts: for example, speaking to God in prayer, which is itself a *doing* (thus we call the liturgy *service,* and so once more Donne dissolves distinctions); speaking to God's representatives (which leads Donne back into his initial similarity, between heaven and the court); and speaking to the images of God, to men "of Condition inferior to your selves." Acting, *facite,* has a similar tripartite division. In all these, the single value he continually asserts is *via media,* the middle way between extremes—the extremes, say, of a king's adviser who makes himself too easily accessible and one who is inaccessible. As always, the *via media* is not a levelling (only death is that), but a middle way in a given order.

The second part concerns judgment *per legem,* the law of liberty. The question of a law leads naturally into questions of controversy. About the law itself, God's law, which Donne calls "the Mystery of Godlinesse," there can be no "controversie": "and godliness is, to believe that God hath given us a Law, and to live according to that Law" (p. 345). But, having acknowledged that anchor, one does not *forsake* controversy. Since God operates legalistically, we only have a firmer ground for disputation:

> When I have pleaded Christ, and Christ, and Christ; Baptism, and Blood, and Teares; will God condemn me an oblique way, when he cannot by a direct way; by a secret purpose, when he hath no law to condemn me by? Sad and disconsolate, distorted and distracted soul! if it be well said in the School, *Absurdum est disputare, ex manuscriptis,* it is an unjust thing in Controversies and Disputations, to press arguments out of Manuscripts, that cannot be seen by every man; it were ill said in thy conscience, that God will proceed against thee *ex manuscriptis,* or condemn thee upon any thing which thou never saw'st, any unrevealed purpose of his. [p. 348]

195

The law of liberty is "the Gospel," and "it gives us a better meanes of prevention before, and of restitution after, then the natural man, or the Jew had." The law of liberty is, moreover, a law of constraint: just as the Jew is under heavier condemnation than the natural man, so the Christian is under the heaviest of all, for "he shall be judged by the law of Liberty." Christ is the lawmaker and the law. God, having sent that law (a law of liberty, which places us under condemnation), does not proceed

> meerly and onely by commandment, but by perswasion too; And, though he be not bound to do so, yet he does give a reason. The reason is, because we must give account of both; both of Actions, and of Words; of both we shall be judged, but judged by a Law; a Law which excludes on Gods part, any secret ill purpose upon us, if we keep his Law; a Law which excludes, on our part, all pretence of Ignorance; for no man can plead ignorance of a Law. And then, a law of Liberty; of liberty to God: for God was not bound to save a man, because he made him; but of his own goodness, he vouchsafed him a Law, by which he may be saved, a law of Liberty to us: so that there is no Epicurism, to doe what we list; no such liberty as makes us Libertines; for then there were no Law; nor Stoicism, nor fatality, that constraines us to doe that we would not do, for then there were no Liberty. But the Gospel is such a law of Liberty, as delivers us, upon whom it works, from the necessity of falling into the bondage of sin before, and from the impossibility of recovering after, if we be falne into that bondage. And this is liberty enough.
>
> [p. 354]

Law, whether humanly or divinely instituted, is still a law. It places constraints on lawgiver and "citizen" alike. This law, as a divine law, is an act of God's "liberty," and defines "liberty" for man. Reasoning about the law like a lawyer—that is, controversially—so that liberty becomes constraint, moves Donne into the center, between Epicurianism and Stoicism. All distinctions, when they collapse, collapse toward the center, and in Donne's Christian *controversia* the center is Christ.

To call the procedure self-consuming, as Stanley Fish has done, is somewhat misleading. In Donne's final sermon, "Deaths Duell" (on Ps. 68:20, *in fine:* "And unto God the Lord belong the issues of

Death"), Fish has perceptively noted Donne's use of two kinds of memory: the rhetorical, which depends upon arrangement, *dispositio,* or discursive form; and the Augustinian, or Platonic, wherein we remember Christ. Donne spends the first half of that sermon, according to Fish, in an effort to reason about the text; the procedures, however, become not "a chain of inferences leading to a triumphant conclusion, but . . . a succession of graves." Rational inquiry is shown to be irrelevant, so we turn at last to "the motion of the heart," acceptance of and conformity to Christ. Thus, in Fish's view, the movement of the sermon is self-consuming, for it begins using modes of reasoning that it later shows are fruitless, as if to entrap the auditors while rejecting rhetoric.[56] But Donne's method is rarely one of surprise. From the outset he shows that his distinctions are collapsible: each *exitus* is also an *introitus* and a *liberatio;* each issue, as from the womb, is also an entrance into life and into death, and is also a step toward deliverance. Donne's skepticism about linguistic form, a well-known (to his usual audience) characteristic of his controversial thinking, is evident throughout the sermon, as is his willingness to use, not abandon, form. The sermon, I should argue, is a concrete example of two speaking roles, advocate and mediator, both necessary and unavoidable, each with its own mode of persuasion; the former ultimately and inexorably collapses into the latter. After all, God's own persuasion is twofold, by reason or rhetoric and by commandment or Christ. When we are in "conformitie" to Christ our very soul has been reshaped. Controversy takes us part of the way, but rhetoric is never— as it has to be in Fish's philosophy—abandoned, for *its* form is aimed not simply at our understanding and memory, but also, and more importantly, at our emotions, to the humanist the most efficacious and instrumental features of our soul. For reasoning on any matter Donne found controversial modes of thought a natural procedure. Then, when controversy produced extremes that eventually collapsed in an *a priori* truth, it remained the function of rhetorical form to place the action in our imagination, and heart.

One of Donne's final poems offers more evidence of this habit of thought and motion of mind:

Holy Sonnet VIII

If faithfull soules be alike glorifi'd
As Angels, then my fathers soule doth see,

And adds this even to full felicitie,
That valiantly I hels wide mouth o'rstride:
But if our mindes to these soules be descry'd   5
By circumstances, and by signes that be
Apparent in us, not immediately,
How shall my mindes white truth by them be try'd?
They see idolatrous lovers weepe and mourne,
And vile blasphemous Conjurers to call   10
On Jesus name, and Pharisaicall
Dissemblers feigne devotion. Then turne
O pensive soule, to God, for he knowes best
Thy true griefe, for he put it in my breast.

Legalistic aspects of religion seemed always to occupy Donne's mind, even after that mind had acquired a "deepened sense of Christian truth." This poem, unlike so many of his poems on judgment, begins confidently. Then, as the speaker entertains a second, and contrary, and apparently equally plausible conjecture, his initial confidence vanishes. Finding himself with a case that is impossible to pursue, the lawyer-defendant has no alternative but to throw himself on the mercy of the court. Therefore, the poem would seem to be a drama of emotion, one that shows the futility of rhetorical reasoning in facing this most urgent uncertainty and so shows, too, the consequent abandonment of advocacy. The present emotion is the only true emotion; it is "griefe," which displaces the initial confidence, as thoughts of God replace the initial thoughts of the dead father. Thus, self-consuming, perhaps, the poem *seems* progressively antihumanist, particularly in its final sorrowing dependence on the Creator of that dependence.

However, recalling what we know of rhetorical *controversia,* let us reconsider the poem and note the ways in which it might follow a typically Donnesque, typically controversial pattern: two alternatives are counterpoised; both are rejected in favor of a third, which is actually a *via media.* If the poem is read as a reflection of controversial thinking, then "griefe" must be a middle position, between the "mindes white truth" and its opposite.[57] What the "mindes white truth," which the speaker seems eager to have "try'd," might be is suggested in the opening quatrain: it would seem to be a resolve, a resistance to temptation, the undissembling appearance—which would produce "felicitie" in any father—of the son's virtuousness.

198

The truth is "white" because it is, apparently, not the whole truth, as the next lines (wherein the phrase appears) suggest. The "white truth" is only the sort of truth perceptible to angels, a truth wherein action and resolve are matched, a kind of purity angels may see and approve. But angels—this point will be discussed in the next chapter, as we read Donne's "The Dreame"—cannot know man's thoughts, and the speaker of this is obviously deeply aware of the full range of his own thoughts, his pensiveness. The second alternative that the speaker entertains—that the father's soul may perceive not like angels but like humans—presents another truth, the *opposite* of the "white truth": the circumstances and signs of the son's behavior show him to be at times an idolator, a blasphemer, a Pharisee. Turning to God is a turning not to a middle position but to a different level of perception altogether, for God *can* read thoughts. God, moreover, is the cause of yet another truth, which is the only truth of consequence because it is (for us as for the speaker) "immediate," the *true* "griefe"—the grief of knowing that the "white truth" is not the whole truth, and that idolatry, blasphemy, and dissembling are also parts of his truth. This "true griefe" *is* in a middle position, a mediator, and into that position the other distinctions collapse.

The force of this controversial argument, or disposition, lies not simply in its progress through alternatives but in its progress through the speaker's emotions, represented here by various selves arraigned at a "trial." The first self is confident of a trial by angels, and not a little proud. However, his mask is all but ripped away with the charge of "white truth" and the revelation of at least three other selves who, before other judges, would have veracity as witnesses equal to that of the confident self. The confidence is replaced by fear. The final emotion is a compound of both, as we are returned to an emotional center and all masks save one are dropped. The "pensive soule" is the final self, and it, too, is "immediate," for its truth is the poem: pensiveness attests to pensiveness. But, as always in Donne, even that pensiveness inheres mainly in advocacy and the advocate's habit of thought, *controversia*. The soul's trial is not simply a submerged but a controlling metaphor. How shall my soul be tried, and by whom? is the question posed—and, though answered controversially, there can be only one answer, God, who is in turn the source of the question and the motive of conscience, or the soul's pensiveness. Though God is not in a middle position, grief is, for it compounds confidence with fear.

199

Thus, even when the answer preexists or causes the question, controversy is not exactly overthrown, not in Donne. Though *controversia* as a means of *inventio* in the Ciceronian sense depends upon a certain skepticism about truth, for Dr. Donne it remained a form of reasoning whereby Christian truths were not simply reconfirmed but were approached through the distance between them and the individual soul. Donne's Christianity seemed to place all certainty in God, but it placed otherness in God, too, and left the individual mind confronting uncertainty day by day. That man will be judged seemed certain, and by whom, but which self is the "true" one, the one to be judged? And how does one bridge the otherness between all my selves and God? On the Day of Judgment, Donne said in one of his last sermons, "*Veniet dies, quae me mihi revelabit,* comes that day that shall show me to my selfe; here I never saw my selfe, but in disguises: There, Then, I shall see my selfe, and see God too" (IX, p. 129). Uncertainty and otherness are at least the spiritual equivalents of intellectual diffidence and skepticism, and they maintained *controversia* in Donne's thought throughout his career.

The second essay in this chapter, which attempted an "Augustinian formalist" approach to Donne, is partial at best. Donne's rhetoric never quite became Augustine's. Though formalists might find in Donne the same efficacy of ethos as in *The Confessions,* willed truth does not have the preeminence in Donne's work it has in *De doctrina,* controversy is never replaced there by the tactics of comparison and contrast as in *The City of God,* and the vagaries of personality are not continually subjected to the measurement of certain and divine rule. Perhaps Augustine was looking for a superhuman certitude he knew was there but not given—and Donne was trying to find ways to stand toward the superhuman as a given but without surrendering the humanist means required, because these were constantly needed as a brace and reminder.

The point is, Donne never abandons *controversia.* Nor does he bring it forward—as we shall find Milton doing—only to show its limitation. To do so, for Donne, would be to forsake the real for the ideal, to abandon our limited means for admittedly limited certainty—or, worse, to deny the point of the poem we have just read and admit that what is "immediate" for us, whether in modes of thought or present emotion, has *no* part of the truth.

Such is the rhetoric, and the humanism, in Donne.

DISPOSITION: FORMAL, EMOTIONAL, AND FINAL. After "Goodfriday 1613," Donne's deepest religious skepticism seemed to moderate, but skepticism itself never totally left him. Donne remained skeptical throughout his life about many matters, most enduringly about human instruments of knowledge. Yet he never stopped practicing his art—and, except for the subtle shifts just noted, he never much changed its characteristics either.

For Donne, man lives in and with uncertainty. What certainty we can achieve, he seems to say, is attainable through means that we cannot use with confidence. How imperfect is all our knowledge! he intones again and again in the first sermon we examined in this study. Our understanding, because it is a discursive, not an intuitive, understanding, must rely on forms—a situation that is cause neither for despair nor for confidence, but for that middle attitude, diffidence. Was his art, then, not an instrument of knowledge? Was Donne diffident about artistic form?

Form itself is detachable, such as form from content in discourse, soul from body in man. To note *that* is to note that Donne was a *dualist,* like most men in his day. Later, radical Protestants, such as the "mortalists" and Milton, introduced a certain *monism* into theological and artistic thought—and, significantly, their monism was allied with a new intellectual temper, which found certainty more accessible than Donne seemed to find it. Yet how could Donne continue the practice of his art—whether in sermons, poems, or essays—with *no* confidence in the *efficacy* of its forms?

This final section will offer this answer: Donne was confident (or less skeptical) of the efficaciousness of form as an instrument of *emotion.* For Donne, the forms of knowledge and understanding may have been dubious, but emotion and its forms were not. Those forms of knowledge and understanding were least dubious, therefore, that encompassed the forms of emotion—an epistemology firmly grounded in rhetoric, as Chapter Two attempted to show.

Let us pursue this consideration. We shall take *form* here to mean primarily discursive form—verbal shapes we can recognize, such as figures of speech, syntax and syllogisms, discursive organization and structure. We could summarize Donne's diffidence concerning form as an instrument of knowledge and understanding—a diffidence noted several times in this study—by pointing to his continual exploitation of *ambiguity.* In his sermons, for example, we find him wringing every ambiguity—lexical as well as syntactical—out of a text. He approaches the Bible like a lawyer approaching the law: "issues" means "entrances" as well as "deliverances," and "of death" can mean "of, in and through death." In the same way, he had earlier approached the questions of suicide and martyrdom, and even earlier the experiences of love and society, courtship and Courtship. To wring ambiguity from a text—any text—was his effort as interpreter and as artist, a function not simply of his legal training but also of his diffidence toward form as an instrument of the intellect.

By contrast, Donne reveals a confidence in form as an instrument of emotion. This is a confidence, moreover, that keeps him well within the humanist mainstream, and well outside the currents of Ramism. Ramists, the most outspoken antihumanists of Donne's youth, did not even consider form in its emotion-arousing function; for them, emotion only interfered with the operation of reason, which had its own pure form. Donne's confidence belongs well within traditional humanism because it is a confidence in the peculiarly *rhetorical* nature of form. As he shows us in the *divisio* cited at the first of this essay, form is useful as a means of engaging the audience's affections: all-at-onceness does not engage affections; only a progressive unfolding does. The most efficacious art is, therefore, not emblematic or iconic but linear or temporal in its arousing of emotion. That artistic function is itself preserved in the ambiguity of a word Donne's time used for rhetorical form: *disposition*. As a rhetorical term it collapses the distinctions, noted earlier, between "outer" and "inner" form; it is linear, intentional, and emotional.

Disposition means arrangement, of course, as with placing the parts of an oration, with sequencing arguments to make the strongest come last, or (the primary meaning the Ramists would allow in their reformed use of the term) with creating a perceptible and reasonable order:

> So, if one knowledge were made of all those,
> Who knew his minutes well, hee might dispose
> His vertues into names, and ranks . . .
> ["Obsequies to the Lord Harrington," ll. 57–59]

And *disposition* also means a tendency or bent of mind—for example, to be favorably or unfavorably disposed, as we still say:

202

What time in years and judgement we repos'd,
Shall not so easily be to change dispos'd
["Elegie XVII," ll. 78–79]

Or it means a native hue and cast of mind:

Soft dispositions which ductile bee,
Elixarlike, she makes not cleane, but new
["To the Countesse of Huntington," ll. 27–28]

For the rhetorician, one meaning of *disposition* implies the other. Note again Donne's definition of *rhetoric* as a process whereby one form in a person (attitude or opinion or knowledge) is displaced or destroyed and another is substituted. A prior disposition, in all meanings of the term, is replaced by one the rhetorician fashions. The process is both mind- and mood-altering. Thus, Wilson, in *The Arte of Rhetorique,* moves naturally from the subject of arrangement to the subject of emotions, from a discussion on ordering the parts of an oration to how the orator may influence the emotions of an audience (Book II). The two subjects belong together, as they had in his Ciceronian sources. Disposition—the order of a discourse and the manifestation of a speaker's intention—is ultimately the form the audience's emotions are to take. Always, the point of humanist rhetoric is not simply to shape a discourse but *to form an audience,* one that will hear and judge—and, more, become the discourse.

As audience, one might pause to admire a well-constructed *divisio,* a ringing alliteration or an ingenious *gradatio,* a beautifully executed gesture, or a powerful comparison. But if the *dispositio* is skillfully constructed, the pause is only temporary in a progressive building of emotions. In this way, "feeling the thought" becomes a function not of texture but of structure. The humanist lesson seems clear: *art disposes.*

For our final disposition of Donne's speaking role as humanist, let us approach yet another poem on the Day of Judgment. It is also another poem in which controversial thinking is not apparent or foregrounded. If it fits into any of our earlier distinctions, it shows us a speaker who is struggling to become not the advocate but the mediator. But it is a clear example of Donne's use, as artist *and* interpreter, of rhetorical form: in this poem, he both shapes an event and argues for the meaning of its form.

Holy Sonnet XIII

What if this present were the worlds last night?
Marke in my heart, O Soule, where thou dost dwell,
The picture of Christ crucified, and tell
Whether that countenance can thee affright,
Teares in his eyes quench the amasing light,   5
Blood fills his frownes, which from his pierc'd head fell.
And can that tongue adjudge thee unto hell,
Which pray'd forgivenesse for his foes fierce spight?
No, no; but as in my idolatrie
I said to all my profane mistresses,   10
Beauty, of pitty, foulnesse onely is
A signe of rigour: so I say to thee,
To wicked spirits are horrid shapes assign'd,
This beauteous forme assures a pitious minde.

To look first at the poem's shape, we might note that Donne employs a fusion of Petrarchan and Shakespearean conventions. The poem is divided into an octave and a sestet, in rhyme scheme as well as in argument. And it also divides into three quatrains and a couplet. The latter form, imposed on the former, allows the speaker to use the smooth rhythms of the couplet to match his, and guide the audience's, emotions, while, again, allowing us to be somewhat diffident toward forms drawn from conventions.

The *lover's* soul dwells in the heart, which, in the conventions of Donne's day, was the seat of emotions. It is the lover, too, who keeps the picture of his beloved in the heart. Donne, whose diffidence toward conventions seems limited only by their rhetorical efficacy, could locate the picture of Christ in his memory (as we have seen in "Goodfriday 1613") or in the will (see *Sermons* IX, p. 84). But here his argument is served by placing Christ in the most volatile part of man's being, a location warranted by man's role as lover, a role the speaker plays throughout the poem. The picture of the beloved is horrifying, the head of Christ tortured and dying, but it is later to be called beautiful in a sense which *we* must reconcile.

Where is the beauty that brings the speaker out of the horror of his meditation? Certainly it is in Christ's selfless action of dying upon the cross for our sins and of praying forgiveness for his foes. This is the true "forme" of the beloved, in appearance and action, unlike the "horrid shapes" given wicked spirits whose inward and outward forms require no depth of judgment. The lover's judgment of his beloved's "forme" is beyond "idolatrie," though idolatry may be a pattern for it: true beauty *is* outward but not *simply* outward. The picture of Christ crucified is, therefore, not simply idolized, as the "profane mistresses" were, but subtly interpreted.

However, the form of the beloved is not the only beauty in the poem. Its other beauty, moreover, also risks and flaunts idolatry. It is the beauty of the argument itself. Ostensibly the speaker is addressing his soul, awakening horror in it first, matching that horror with the anguish of Christ's final moment, and then consoling the soul by finding the true beauty of "forme." The consolation comes about as a remembrance—not simply of Christ, a remembrance that initially increases the horror, but of the speaker's own life as a love poet ("a great visiter of ladies," one contemporary called Jack Donne). The urgency of the present is resolved in a form useful for resolving an urgency in the past: beauty is a sign of pity, ugliness is a sign of cruelty; therefore, my beloved's true nature shows forth, though appearances seem contrary, and that true nature only increases my hope. As always, the controversial habit of thought provokes corrections and reconciliations. *Her* beauty was only outward, Christ's is not; her actions were cruel, Christ's were not. The "profane" argument was used for flattery and seduction; its sacred version is used to seduce the soul into consolation. The argument becomes idolatry controversialized—as does the poem itself. But the diffidence that results from this controversializing is an initial stage in the discovery of comfort. The speaker's comforting realization (lines 11–12) is placed in the form of argument that rhetoricians call the *zeugma:* a parallel syntactical construction in which one element (in this case "A signe") is meant to be used in both parts of the construction. The figure is itself a "signe" of the speaker's conscious control of his formerly terrified emotions and thought (a *zeugma* must be planned), and it imposes that control, that disposition, on the audience.

Is the audience only the speaker's soul? We cannot avoid, it seems to me, the impression that *we* are being directly addressed in the sestet: "so I say to thee." We are hearing as well as overhearing, with the soul's probable response serving as a pattern for our own. Nor does the ambiguity stop there. "This beauteous forme" is Christ, *and the zeugma, and* the disposition of the poem itself, rightly understood.

"Pitious" means both full of pity, or compassionate (in which case the "minde" is Christ's), and pitiful, or moving to compassion (in which case the "minde" is the speaker's, and ours). Thus, "assures a pitious minde" can mean at least three things: that the picture of Christ crucified gives clear evidence of divine compassion, that the evidence assures or gives comfort to the speaker's own pitiful mind, and that the source of the comfort—for the speaker partly but above all for us as we join with the speaker and seek assurance for our own piteous minds—is "forme" in the sense of emotion, rhetoric, poem.

Donne's response to the experience imagined in the poem is the poem. Christ gave us one form, Donne another. As mediator Donne sought "conformity" with Christ, to speak with Christ's voice; as artist he gives us for conformity a form imitating Christ's passion—from *My God, my God, why hast thou forsaken me?* to *Into thy hands, O Lord, I commend my spirit.* The *zeugma* marks a stage in this gradual conformity. Then the *zeugma* is itself transformed into the harmony of the final couplet, with its confidently regular rhythms, echoing sounds and balanced concepts (wicked spirits, horrid shapes / beauteous forme, pitious minde), and perfect rhymes. This progressive emotion is, like all Donne's artistry, offered to dispose *our* minds as it disposes and reveals Donne's: "forme" and "minde" are, indeed, balanced concepts, for each signifies intentionality and purposiveness. The outward "shape" of Donne's art may be an address to someone or something else, but its true "forme," when we know how to interpret it (and Donne himself shows us how), is designed emotionally to place us within the text and the text within us. The subtle disproportion between "shape" and "forme"—between sonnet conventions and poetic truths, between idolatry and true religion, between *zeugma* and actual argument—may be a source of Donne's skepticism. If so, it is best seen, and in our age of formalist criticism best clarified, by approaches drawn from the humanist union of poetry and rhetoric.

To Augustinians, Donne's definition of poetry might seem blasphemous: it is "a counterfait Creation, and makes things that are not, as though they were" (*Sermons* IV, p. 87). To rhetoricians, Donne's definition, like his practice, is as revealing as it is inclusive. This process of making, this parodying of God, is unquestionably meant to include creating the reader by *in*forming him with the text—any text, poem or sermon, spoken or written. Such would be the "poetry" in all utterance. And thus I end where I began with Donne in Chapter One.

"I know what dead carkasses things written are, in respect of things spoken," Donne states in a dedicatory letter to the Countess of Montgomery prefacing a copy of one of his sermons. Then he continues in a way that at first seems distinctly Augustinian:

> But in things of this kinde, that soule that inanimates them, receives debts from them: The Spirit of God that dictates them in the speaker or writer, and is present in his tongue or hand, meets himself again (as we meet our selves in a glass) in the eies and eares and hearts of the hearers and readers: and that Spirit, which is ever the same to an equall devotion, makes a writing and a speaking equall means to edification. [*Sermons* II, p. 179]

The idea that the Spirit seeks his own reflection (cf. "Goodfriday 1613," "Restore thine Image, so much, by thy grace, / That thou may'st know mee") is a disarmingly simple Augustinianism. So, too, is the notion of the truly operative principle in human instruments (cf. Donne's poem on the Sidneys: God is the true Creator). But in this quoted passage, Donne has fused these arguments with another signifying intentionality and purposiveness: the function of writing and speaking is to create an emotional, participatory form of self-knowledge. The human artistry involved is not mentioned, but my study has attempted to specify it as the rhetorical—that is, humanist, essentially controversial— means whereby, through our eyes and ears and hearts, Donne's texts progressively fulfill their designs upon our selves.

Miltonic Form

Man is but a creature whose severall parts and members are endowed with proper natures or Faculties, each subservient to other, to make him a living Rationall Creature . . . it doth not follow, that those Faculties together are a Being of themselves immortall: For as the members cannot be perfect members without them, so they cannot be faculties without their members; and separation cannot be without destruction of both . . . The *Forme* is so in the *Matter,* and the *Matter* so in the *Forme;* as thereby, and not else, is an *Existence,* or *Humane Entity.*

[Richard Overton, *Mans Mortalitie,*1644]

Of the *probable* and the *marvellous,* two parts of a vulgar epick poem, which immerse the critick in deep consideration, the *Paradise Lost* requires little to be said. It contains the history of a miracle, of Creation and Redemption; it displays the power and the mercy of the Supreme Being; the probable therefore is marvellous, and the marvellous is probable. The substance of the narrative is truth; and as truth allows no choice, it is, like necessity, superior to rule.

. [Samuel Johnson, "Milton," 1783]

The Disintegration of Humanist Rhetoric

We shall begin with a single summarizing observation and pursue it through the remainder of this essay: discourse as *an embodiment of truth* rather than as *an action,* as *a form to be contemplated* rather than as a *dispositio,* marks a significant difference between Milton and Donne and also—to reiterate the thesis of this book—signifies a correlative development in the history of rhetoric. English humanist rhetorical theory had largely disappeared by the age of Milton. And discourse generally was losing its most distinctively humanist feature, controversial thinking. *Controversia* had been all but displaced by a confidence in the availability of truth and in one's access to truth through *forms,* including certain discursive forms, as instruments of knowledge and understanding. If humanist rhetoric offers an illuminating approach to much of Donne, some other approach to Milton must be sought.

That other approach, I shall suggest, lies in formalism, not of the Augustinian sort (which is too intensely personalist for Milton), but a formalism nonetheless contrary to rhetorical criticism. Milton's intentions are patently and demonstrably nonrhetorical. They are in the service of a "stronger impulse" beyond personalism, and beyond voice, too. To understand the special, nonrhetorical nature of Milton's "stronger impulse," Donne will be our base and point of comparison. Though Donne is not the humanist rhetorician *par excellence* (Erasmus and Thomas Wilson are closer to that ideal), enough *controversia* and its attendant *dispositio* have been seen in his work to qualify it as humanist rhetoric in practice.

Poems have been, and shall remain, our major examples because they are sources of never-ending fascination in the works of both men. Too, our search has centered on form in *any* genre as a signifier of intention and principle of purposiveness, the outer and inner shape of thought and action. Form itself shows us what we are meant to do with it, as it reveals too the extent of the artist's trust in form. Donne's use of form in all genres reflects his skepticism; Milton's, his faith, and consequent desire for *re*form. Further, I think the center of my search, discursive form, gives me sufficient warrant to pass over certain other

211

differences between the two poets that in another study, particularly another historical study, could be crucial: for example, Donne chose to be an Anglican, wrote no dramas, and failed to complete his epic *(Metempsychosis)*—characteristics that are themselves the results, I believe, of certain attitudes toward form and its nearness to truth and strength against the assaults of irony.

Milton's opening of *Paradise Lost,* because it is so characteristic of all we have come to think of as Miltonic, is a good place to begin.

> Of Man's First Disobedience, and the Fruit
> Of that Forbidden Tree, whose mortal tast
> Brought Death into the World, and all our woe,
> With loss of *Eden,* till one greater Man
> Restore us, and regain the blissful Seat,   5
> Sing Heav'nly Muse, that on the secret top
> Of *Oreb,* or of *Sinai,* didst inspire
> That Shepherd, who first taught the chosen Seed,
> In the Beginning how the Heav'ns and Earth
> Rose out of *Chaos:* Or if *Sion* Hill   10
> Delight thee more, and *Siloa's* Brook that flow'd
> Fast by the Oracle of God; I thence
> Invoke thy aid to my adventrous Song,
> That with no middle flight intends to soar
> Above th' *Aonian* Mount, while it pursues   15
> Things unattempted yet in Prose or Rime.
> And chiefly Thou O Spirit, that dost prefer
> Before all Temples th' upright heart and pure,
> Instruct me, for Thou know'st; Thou from the first
> Wast present, and with mighty wings outspread   20
> Dove-like satst brooding on the vast Abyss
> And mad'st it pregnant: What in me is dark
> Illumin, what is low raise and support;
> That to the highth of this great Argument
> I may assert Eternal Providence,   25
> And justifie the wayes of God to men.

There is controversy in these lines, but only in the sense of looking backward and forward—back to Adam and forward to Christ, back to the Hebrew traditions and forward to the Christian, back to the classical songs and forward to the present.[1] There is no *via media,* "no middle flight," as the past is brought into the present and absorbed within it in the great overriding intention expressed in the final lines. There are, thus, not two alternatives but only one possibility. The relevance of our Janiform conceptual model, even in its prudential aspect, recedes. Otherness is no longer a rhetorical principle. Even a possible distinction between the singer and the muse he invokes has been largely overcome before the first word is uttered. The appeal to the spirit is formal in a limited sense—*pro forma,* literally, for it is an epic convention[2]—and not urgent; the very joy and confidence of the singer, as expressed in his extraordinary control ("this beauteous forme," as Donne would call it) show that the appeal has been answered. *Veni spiritus creator,* Donne might cry in the words of the Church's great hymn, and so create a poem argumentatively trying to bridge the gap between himself and the creative spirit (and place us in a vantage point that keeps both shores visible). But in Milton's beginning, that gap has already been bridged, and the effect transforms the terms of controversy ("Argument," "assert," "justifie").

Donne states in one of his sermons (VI, p. 6) that it is the *conclusion* of a poem that gives it "currency," like the imprint of the king's face on a gold coin. The doctrine does not perfectly fit his own practice. For in some of his poems the final lines do not exactly achieve closure, do not "shut up" the activity the poem begins, but rely on the reader to do that. A certain principle remains, however, expressed by the doctrine even when it does not fit and thus evident in all of Donne's practice: discourse for him was linear. Most of the poems and sermons by Donne that we have examined are combative, their outcomes initially obscure where they are not uncertain and almost always provisional. But in the opening lines of *Paradise Lost,* the reader is told the outcome in advance, an effect that does not make unnecessary the reading of the subsequent twelve books but that does shift the emphasis away from the *what* and *why* and onto the *how.* More than that, the opening lines show us how to read the entire poem—from the perspective of the poet, the creator. When we do, we grasp an "Argument" that is above narrative linearity and less forensic than conceptual. Indeed, one might even say that Milton's poetry is iconic, at the risk of provoking the ire of his iconoclastic and anti-idolatrous spirit. The point is that Milton, as opposed to Donne, is operating inside a rather different, nonrhetorical concept of poetic form. Miltonic form is action at a distance—a race whose outcome is known in advance, and whose contours are those of truth itself. The end is in the beginning, but Donne's beginnings have different "ends."

Much happens to the reader of a Milton poem.[3] The reader may change, though the poem's speaker may not ("on the morrow" the speaker may not think any differently than he does at the present moment). Obviously, this speaker had to be exceptional: Milton's central poetic role had to be unmasked, public and open, a kind of voice we seem to hear throughout his lyrics and in the "narrative" parts of his epics. The conventional view of this role or voice in Milton is that it is *prophetic*. In the words of Marvell, concerning *Paradise Lost:*

> Just Heav'n thee like *Tiresias* to requite
> Rewards with Prophecy thy loss of sight.

But this is a role Milton had felt comfortable with for many years, even before the onset of his blindness. For example, twenty years earlier he argued that divine inspiration had revealed to him the true Christian doctrine of divorce, and in the *Second Defense of the English People* he claimed that "I and my interests are . . . under the protection of God."[4] *Prophetic* may give us the sense of a certain preferred role, or ethos (as in "The Nativity Ode"), one that is clearly not *personalist* in a Donnean or Augustinian sense of painful, often sinful and limited individuality. Ethos, perhaps, then, but what about voice? *Voice* as a critical term seems to require the individuating that *prophet* denies: for the rhetorical critic, at least, "prophetic voice" is an oxymoron. Perhaps the important question may finally be, How useful is *voice* as a critical term in approaching Milton's art? As we continue, we shall find that what seems truly Miltonic has less to do with any voice than with a certain idea of form as a mode of thought: as Marvell suggests, *prophecy* has more to do with vision or *in*sight than with voice.[5]

To begin with, recall that statement from Milton that provides the conceptual model of my own argument: "The Temple of Janus, with his two *controversal* faces, might now not unsignificantly be set open." Earlier I noted that Milton tends to be humanist in his statements while Donne is humanist in his practice, that Milton eloquently articulates the humanist enterprise while Donne shows us that enterprise in action, and that the controversial faces of Janus more nearly express Donne's mode of discursive thought and action than Milton's. Let us now look at the form of Milton's sentence. Its own rhetorical figure is *litotes*, a figure that expresses a middle ground ("not unsignificantly") while looking in two directions at once (significantly and unsignificantly)—that is, it affirms by negating. The figure can be deeply expressive of an entire structural principle—as suggested earlier concerning More's *Utopia* (see the conclusion of my essay on Erasmus, Chapter Two). *Litotes* can also be absorbed into larger mental postures, such as paradox and irony, which tend to be the characteristic outcomes of Erasmus's and Donne's profoundly controversial *inventios*. Or the figure can be, as it is in Milton, a local effect, here imitative of the principle it articulates—but on a small scale, its paradoxical nature attenuated by the limits of the possibilities it offers and by the conditional auxiliary verb "might be." For that matter, the effect is even further enhanced by the sentences that follow this passage: Milton's battle cry is offered with the assurance that truth *is* in the field and will prevail. For Donne, controversy is a function of language and man's knowledge, his grasping for a truth that may not be there; controversy is therefore a necessary constituent of man's voice whether in public or from his "naked thinking heart." But for the nature of Milton's art we must search somewhere other than in controversy, regardless of how brilliantly—in *Areopagitica*—he conceptualizes controversy for us.

Developments in rhetorical theory—our mirror and lamp on differences between Donne and Milton—again reveal a possible avenue for search. The disappearance of *controversia* in rhetorical theory was marked by innovations in *dispositio*—indeed, by an almost frantic and nonhumanist urgency to *organize clearly*. In accord with that new doctrine, we shall dichotomize the remainder of our discussion into, first, another overview of developments in rhetorical theory after Thomas Wilson and, second, certain examples of post-humanist rhetoric in Milton's practice.

The rhetorical avant-garde, as noted, were the Ramists. Their three "laws"—truth, justice, and wisdom—were used for reorganizing and reforming the arts, the sciences, and the content of discourse. Much has been made of the Ramists, ranging from Tuve's finding that the Ramist reorganization of the discipline of composition gave new impetus to the Elizabethan love of style, to Ong's view that the Ramists were descendants of medieval quantifiers of thought who marked the change in the Renaissance from conceiving of discourse as something heard to conceiving of it as something seen.[6] There have also been those who have warned us against making too much of the Ramists.[7] I have charged the Ramists with being antihumanist, a charge that can be substantiated mainly on a comparative basis—as I attempted to do earlier, with Wilson as the model humanist. Without attributing great influence to the Ramists, I shall rest my case on a point that should emerge in the succeeding discussion, again to be advanced comparatively, that the Ramists at least *reflected* a philosophically more complex antihumanism. That their reform was applied directly to rhetoric has made them uniquely apropos of my study. In this regard, Milton's own Ramism, however much it has been slighted in recent years, deserves a second look.

For the humanist Wilson, rhetoric is a field of activity, encompassing invention, disposition, style, memory, and delivery. These activities are not discrete. When Wilson discusses one, he invariably talks about one or more of the others. You cannot invent, Wilson seems to say, without considering arrangement, or arrange without considering style and decorum. At the very heart of Wilson's theory, as I tried to show, is controversial thinking: to think rhetorically means, in effect, to think like a lawyer, inventing a discourse by means of charge and countercharge and arguing proleptically, always with one eye on the audience. Lawyerly modes of thought are at the center of an integrated system, encompassing all activities of composition and delivery.[8]

But the Ramists with their three laws shattered the system, segregated its parts, and insisted that all characteristics of one activity uniquely so define it that they cannot belong to another. Invention became a discrete activity. So did disposition. These two activities became parts of "logic" and so could not be parts of "rhetoric"; the only two parts of rhetoric were style and delivery—which were, themselves, largely unnecessary to *thought*. Style meant ornament, delivery meant oral performance—neither overlapped the other. At the pinnacle of the Ramist system was the contemplative intellect, not man speaking. There was no controversial thinking: one invented simply by means of "analysis," taking any subject—silently—through an abbreviated version of the "places" with no sense either of opposition or of audience. One's only audience in the process was another contemplative intellect, or the supposedly vast, ocular body of "natural reason." The Ramists disintegrated humanist rhetoric but, paradoxically, reintegrated discursive form with discursive content, for a different, nonhumanist epistemology was at work. Any art, science, or discourse was to be judged on only one basis: its formal fitness for expressing truth—not for capturing truth's multiform appearance or moving an audience or scoring points in a contest of wits and wills.

Humanist rhetoric never quite recovered—if not from the onslaughts of the Ramists, then from what the Ramists reflected: the rise of confidence in the contemplative intellect, in the availability of truth, and in the forms of certainty. This confidence is, of course, shown in other ways, most notably through Puritanism, with its belief that natural reason with guidance from the Scriptures is enough for salvation, that any man with a Bible under his arm is equal to the pope. Such confidence is also shown in the new science of the seventeenth century, in which the word *experiment* began to take on its modern meaning, changing from merely *experiencing* through the senses to *finding a form* by which sense experience could be controlled and judged. My concern, however, is with the impact of this confidence on the once central discipline of composition and interpretation—that is, on rhetoric. That impact is best viewed through the major conduit of communicative confidence, the Ramists—who, because their theories embodied this confidence, were profoundly antihumanist.

For the Ramists, the rise of confidence propelled a separation of the processes of thinking from other rhetorical instruments. After the Ramists, the continuing rise of confidence propelled a merger between rhetorical invention and intuition, including systematic (at least, silent and solitary) meditation,[9] and later, in the forthcoming "Age of Reason," between *inventio* and psychology.[10] The central lesson from Ramism that extends through these developments can be expressed simply: man is best taught by offering him a form of thought that is most like the operation of natural reason. True logic, *scientia scientiarum,* is the superior and most general of all humane disciplines: it alone teaches us how to think rightly. Thus, true—that is, Ramist—logic now contains the most important activities of rhetoric, *inventio* and *dispositio*. Each of these consists of two parts, each of those parts consists of two further parts, and so on.

Any Ramist textbook is itself a demonstration of this "true" form of natural reason. The Ramist book begins with a general statement—for example, logic is an art of thinking—and immediately proceeds to dichotomize, in a form of organization known as "natural method." The form reveals the distance between Ramist and humanist *dispositio*. Methodical arrangement (*dispositio* "methodized"), the

217

Ramists believed, is the ideal form for teaching, for it presents truth in a manner that the audience's mind itself can perceive unaided—with no distraction by or even assistance from pathos or ethos. Truth in its proper form is intuitive, impersonal, clear of emotion, and ultimately nonverbal. The system conceptualizes a kind of natural order, with first things first; those first things were either general or antecedent.

Thinking, the Ramists insist over and over again, may be done without speaking, but the reverse is not true; therefore, "by the method," thinking comes first, is superior, general, *and* antecedent. Logic comes before rhetoric; logic is about thinking (invention and disposition) and rhetoric is about presenting (style and delivery). But consider, too, the kind of silent thinking Ramist logic presupposes. In this regard, recall Fraunce's diagram (noted on p. 140, and reflecting the pattern of Fraunce's own table of contents); it is itself the very "natural method" that both *charts* thought, in this case the thought of his book, and *embodies it*. Natural method was more to be seen than to be heard, for the patterns were largely conceptual, not verbal. There is a dualism here, but not of the body-soul or material-spirit variety. Even the ostensible dualism between thinking and presenting or speaking disappears when the latter is properly, Ramistically, regarded as secondary to thought. For the dualized—or, rather, dichotomized—branches of spoken thought can proceed in the opposite direction, back toward the conception away from which they branch and whose truth they analyze. And that conception has everything to do with thinking, nothing necessarily to do with presenting. Speech and words only reveal thought; they are never thought itself. The position elevates the contemplative intellect without dematerializing it, for material form—if only a geometrical diagram— remains its habitus and mode of operation.

Emotion—an essential, for Donne as for all humanists, of rhetorical *dispositio*—was irrelevant to Ramist thought. Irrelevant, too, was discrete attention to rhetoric's office of memory. The well-organized discourse appeals to forms inherent in the mind itself; its most significant patterning, its structure, requires only contemplation for assimilation, persuasion, and memorability. In sum, the Ramist reform and what it represents in the development of rhetorical theory leave no room for skepticism, the *sine qua non* of rhetorical *controversia*. Nor do they leave much room for dialectical *controversia* or for any form of thought other than "natural method." *Dispositio,* the Ramists said, has two parts: axiomatic (statements) and dianoetic (the arrangement of statements into discourse). The latter is of two sorts: syllogism and method. And method is of two sorts: natural and "hidden or concealed"; the terms are purposefully loaded. Natural method, Fraunce says, "onely, and none other is to bee obserued, so often as wee teach any art or science, or take vpon vs to intreate perfectly of any generall matter."[11] Milton agreed.

True, Milton was no precise Ramist.[12] But there is Ramism *in* Milton, and it's deeply expressive of the kind of confidence that runs counter to humanism. Perhaps the attraction Ramism held for him was that of a radical and revolutionary alternative to the institutionalized humanism of his schooling. For even by the time Milton entered St. Paul's school, humanism—that is, training in rhetorical *controversia,* usually in Latin—was no longer revolutionary, but rather had become established, conventional, and undoubtedly not a little vapid. As William Riley Parker has noted, in the disputations that capped the Cambridge training for the bachelor's degree, "conviction was irrelevant; one must be prepared to debate either side of a question," which would of course be true of any exercise in *controversia.* But "reason and common sense were also irrelevant, for, in practice, success in argument depended upon one's effective use of the established techniques."[13] The times demanded conviction, beyond the merely provisional. Rising to that demand, the Ramists offered the means of truth itself. Milton was bound to be attracted. But his mind was too complex, and too expansive, to be confined to the Ramists' stunning but ultimately shallow gridwork. In formulating a conservative alternative to humanist skepticism, the Ramists were not even at home with lexical ambiguity—a simpler, and more local, version of the skeptical attitude. Ambiguity, as Milton's own poetical and exegetical practice shows, is unavoidable in words; but the *patterning* of those words, he believed—and here he does join with the Ramists—should allow no room for skepticism.

Let us pursue this matter through two documents, one composed—probably—in Milton's Cambridge days, the other a work of his maturity.

In 1672, two years before Milton's death, there was published *Artis Logicae Plenior Institutio*—that is, *A Fuller Institution of the Art of Logic, Arranged After the Method of Peter Ramus, by John Milton, an Englishman.*[14] This Latin work, it is often conjectured, had been completed many years earlier. Nonetheless, it was offered to the public with no disclaimer by its famous author or any indication that he no longer adhered to its tenets. Many students have ignored this work because it does not seem to square with Milton's most famous practice: its bare, naked, methodical approach to truth seems so unlike the sensuous grandeur of the great poems and prose. Yet the work is essential to understanding an epistemology that underlies all of Milton's practice. Its usefulness in this regard is only enhanced by the probable composition of the work in Milton's youth and its publication in his maturity.

To begin with, the *Logic* could further clarify a sense in which Milton's art is "prophetic." All Ramist logic assumes that the mind naturally assents to truth, that truth has only to be presented, not argued for or explained. Earlier it was suggested that this epistemology is stoic. If it is *also* a prophetic epistemology, it does not quite fit the nature of *Miltonic* prophecy—as I shall note further below. Nonetheless, however unlike the Ramists and stoics Milton seems on some scores, he does share with them an epistemological belief that knowledge is *impersonal* and that the persuasive force of its truthfulness lies in its proper framing, configuration, or *form*. True knowledge is independent of voice—man's as well as God's, as Milton says in discussing the "place" in *inventio* called "testimony":

> Yet I commonly attribute to testimony very little power for proof in investigations of the deepest truth and nature of things; this would seem to apply to divine as well as human testimony, and I do not see why it should offend any one, for testimony whether human or divine equally gets all its force from the author, and has none in itself. And divine testimony affirms or denies that a thing is so and brings about that I believe; it does not prove, it does not teach, it does not cause me to know or understand why things are so, unless it also brings forward reasons.   [p. 283]

Knowledge depends upon a quality or force *per se*. Applied to Milton's discourse, the doctrine means that the knowledge imparted is not a function of the individual voice we hear (in its elevation of impersonality, the passage offers striking comparisons with Donne's remarks on man's role in divine rhetoric; see p. 172 above). True knowledge, even when mediated by voice, "brings forward reasons"—not necessarily causal relations but a juxtaposition of things within that

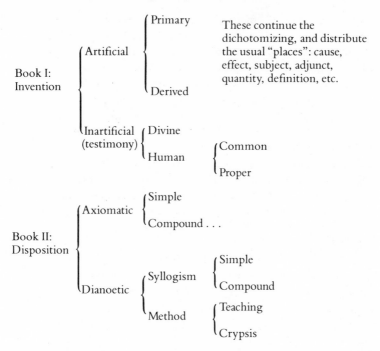

Book I:
Invention
- Artificial
  - Primary — These continue the dichotomizing, and distribute the usual "places": cause, effect, subject, adjunct, quantity, definition, etc.
  - Derived
- Inartificial (testimony)
  - Divine
  - Human
    - Common
    - Proper

Book II:
Disposition
- Axiomatic
  - Simple
  - Compound . . .
- Dianoetic
  - Syllogism
    - Simple
    - Compound
  - Method
    - Teaching
    - Crypsis

greater form that, in his case, is the configuration of the poet-prophet's vision.

Let us continue our examination of this remarkable work. The accompanying diagram is a partial representation of its configuration, form, or "method." The diagram is a table of contents. And it offers, as in Fraunce, an outline of the book's progression of thought, the veritable pattern of the writer's reasoning.

Like all Ramists, Milton assumes that there is a "natural reason" with its "natural logic." The latter is the means whereby the former is trained. Like all Ramists, he upholds the "three laws" used to distinguish the various arts—in fact, to insulate them from each other. Like all Ramists, he upholds the use of "method" to teach the principles of any art. And, as in all Ramist books, his use of "method" in the *Logic* has profound implications: it is the true pattern of "natural reason." Therefore, anyone teaching any art would, if he were a Ramist, use this method—as Fraunce, Fenner, and Butler do when they write their arts of rhetoric, and as Milton himself acknowledges when he mentions the use of "method" in teaching physics and ethics (pp. 479–481). But *logic* offers the very form of knowledge itself. For Milton, knowledge must be "methodized" to be taught—as if what Donne might call the "imperfections" of our knowledge were corrigible through perfecting the forms whereby we know.

Several differences set Milton aside from mainstream Ramism, but none of these diminish his demonstrable confidence in a truthful form—a confidence that is all the more remarkable when compared with Donne's "formal" skepticism.

One immediately striking difference between Milton and other Ramists is that the work is a *plenior institutio*—a fuller development, explanation of, or introduction to Ramist principles. This is itself something of a contradiction of Ramist epistemology. Truth, to the Ramists, does not require "full development." It needs only a stark presentation. Their books are, consequently, brief, pithy, sententious. Indeed, nowhere, not even in their "art of rhetoric," do they allow for the ancient Ciceronian principles of *amplification*. Milton actually *discusses* the various principles. Knowledge requires it, as he notes in the passage on testimony, though the only copiousness he mentions is "copiousness of clarity" (p. 3).

Another difference, which seems to follow from the first, is that Milton provides a much longer discussion of the syllogism than does any other Ramist before him. His reason is simple—and to a Ramist surely antagonistic: syllogisms are required by "the weakness of the human intellect, which because it is not able by the first intuition to see the truth and falsity of things in the axiom, turns to the syllogism in order to judge of their consequence and lack of consequence by its means" (p. 367). Ramists leaned much more heavily on man's intuition, and consequently relied much more on axiomatic presentation—that almost skeletal coldness whereby words are framed into true statements, and then arranged methodically.

Third, Milton's conclusion would thwart most Ramists. He says that "orators and poets" have their *own* "doctrine of method," which can be learned from those "who teach oratory and poetics." Method, essential arrangement or natural *dispositio,* was, for Ramists, no longer a part of either art, or if it was, it was only a debased version of method in logic. The "three laws" mentioned earlier were designed to prevent any serious conceptual overlapping. What thwarts strict Ramism in Milton is not so much his distributing the doctrine of

method among logic, rhetoric, and poetry as his acknowledgement
that these other arts could have complex, praiseworthy ends: "When
the auditor is to be allured *with pleasure or some stronger impulse* [italics
mine] by an orator or a poet—for they commonly make that their
chief concern," then these other methods may be employed. Most
Ramists measured other methods by the true and natural one in logic;
a century earlier Roland MacIlmaine was fierce about the subject:
there is only one method for teaching, he claimed, and any composer
could have one of only two purposes, either to teach or to deceive.[15]
But few Ramists had Milton's understanding of oratory and poetry.
Most of them had contempt for oratory and regarded poetry as nothing more than metered prose. That there could be in these other arts
"some stronger impulse" than "pleasure," an impulse that was somehow not only different from but perhaps even on a plane with teaching, would have seemed extraordinary. However, Milton is *far* from
the Erasmian *via diversa,* with its multiple roads to and protean shapes
of truth, and closer to the *via una* of the Ramists in their belief that
truth *has* a form, as we shall continue to find.

Finally, at one point in Milton's *Logic* there is a much stricter adherence to "method" than there is in the master's *Dialectique.* This
difference, particularly when viewed in light of the third difference
just noted, does not make Milton a more ardent Ramist but it does
underscore his Ramistic confidence in form. Interestingly enough,
Milton's stricter adherence to method comes in a discussion of the
four causes—efficient, material, formal, and final. Let us pause for a
moment and review some of our considerations of the formal cause.

In Chapter One of this book, I noted that to the rhetorician "form"
is always a separable quality. It is, primarily, the means whereby a composer strategically arranges his content to produce an emotional effect
on an audience. All four causes are accounted for in that view—
composer is the efficient cause, content is the material; strategic arrangement, formal; and intention, final. In rhetorical criticism, as in
rhetorical creation, form is separably viewed largely in order to assess
its operational intentionality; that is, form can be thought of as a "doing" quite apart from stated intentions. Moreover, humanist *dispositio*
conflates "inner" and "outer" form and measures intention largely in
terms of emotional effect; therefore, it has further conflated "cause"
with "effect" and centered both in "form." If this form is the "soul" of
a discourse, as the "formal cause" is philosophically the "soul" of a

man, that soul is pure strategy. Material cause, or content, would seem to be lowest on a scale of *operational* significance. To the philosopher, this rhetorical view is rank heresy and utterly confusing, because the philosopher wishes to consider the formal and material causes—in fact, all *causae*—as "causation," not "cases"; that is, he wishes to consider them apart from such rhetorically existential forces as ethos and audience.

Oddly enough, Ramus himself, though driven by a desire to insulate all constituents of any art from each other, made no grouping of the causes.[16] But Milton methodizes the causes, placing them into two dichotomies. In the first are the efficient and the material, for these precede the creation of the thing. In the second are the formal and final, which appear upon creation. The grouping follows the order of precedence, and "therefore . . . method." Ramus's "cautiousness" in leaving the genera of causes nameless is acknowledged but not obeyed. True, the final cause may indeed precede the others, in moving the creator to create—but when the final cause "is merely in the mind of the efficient and is not yet obtained, it does not yet truly exist; and how can it be a cause when it does not yet exist?" (p. 65). In some ways, Milton outdoes the Ramists in insisting on the irrelevance of an immaterial idea. But the insistence, as we shall see when we come to the second work, is not quite the same as Donne's anti-idealism or the humanist rejection of the inconsequential.

Form, Milton says, following doctrines we have encountered earlier, individuates, makes a thing what it is. When considered apart from its effect (something a rhetorician does not do), form must therefore be appropriate to its content, and indeed it is the only means whereby the content, or matter, is perceived. Moreover, since form individuates and since it is a product of matter (essence as well as substance), it cannot be shared by more than one person or thing. I have paraphrased Milton's discussion, but I wish to quote directly his exclamation when he reaches this point in his discussion: *"Here let the theologians awake"* (p. 59). The significance of individuating form, as a product of matter, is that it lays the basis, in the second work we shall consider, for demonstrating a "logical" impossibility in orthodox views of the Trinity and in attempts to distinguish body from soul in man. In that work, as in this one, the subject is knowledge and its most reasonable form.

Perhaps I have shown enough of this work to posit a distinction that will guide us through the remainder of my study: whereas for Donne discursive form—all form—is suppositional, protean, and flexible, for Milton discursive form is in service of yet higher forms of knowledge which are themselves firm, conceptual, and non-verbal. As noted at the outset, *The Art of Logic* stands as a vivid example of Milton's epistemological confidence. The book is about the primary art, reasoning. Milton begins with, and accepts, the Ramist difference between reasoning and speaking: rhetoric and grammar are the language arts; but logic is general and antecedent, because there can be reason without speech, but no speech without reason (p. 17). If nothing else, the book offers testimony of Milton's acknowledgement of the silent intellect as the seat of reason. But the book does more than that. Like all Ramist texts, it shows how and why reason descends to speech, to attain or convey to others certainty by using the forms of discourse—more syllogisms than the Ramists prefer and even more methods—but all to establish the conceptual patterns of *intuition*.

If Milton had never used Ramist method again, *The Art of Logic* might be regarded as a parody—in the seventeeth-century sense—of Ramism. But he did use it again, in his Latin *Grammar* (1669) and in his theological treatise. In these works he uses method somewhat more loosely than in the *Logic,* but the word *method* itself means exactly the same in all three. His use of Ramist method in the theological treatise—again, to teach, to convey certainty—is most important for our purposes, for in this work Milton is quite explicit as to what he means by *form.* The implications are *radically* revolutionary, as I indicated earlier, which may be the reason why he, or others, suppressed the work for so long.

De Doctrina Christiana is a lengthy systematization, written in Latin, of Milton's Christian beliefs. He wrote much of it in the 1650s, perhaps in the years following the death of his first wife Mary Powell and his infant and only son John, and at a time when he had become totally blind. The juxtaposition of this biographical information is useful only in pointing up the emotionless, almost bloodless, quality of the style of writing and the total absence of any sense that a personal crisis underlies Milton's doctrinal thought. Another juxtaposition, of Milton's *Doctrina* with Augustine's, points up the same qualities; in that juxtaposition, the comparative impersonality of Milton's style becomes all the more evident. Ironically, this impersonal document is about "personal belief," for God, as Milton says in the preface, has "opened the way of eternal salvation" to "individual faith" only. Each man must find his own way, and this work represents Milton's way: individual reason in union with the Scriptures. The work is at a far remove not only from Augustine's personalism but also from that father's dualist epistemology: "The understanding flies on ahead," Augustine wrote on the Psalms, "and there follows, oh, so slowly, and sometimes not at all our weakened human capacity for feeling."[17]

Milton presents himself as a Protestant and a student of the Bible, and above all as a reasonable man doing what he believes a reasonable man would do: he would set forth a "methodical tractate of Christian doctrine," a phrase in which "methodical" has peculiar force. He wrote, he claimed, in order to "establish" his own faith and assist his own memory. Publication is not his aim—not his stated aim—but neither is concealment. Should the work be published, he would have it known that "it is to the learned that I address myself. . . . I should at least wish to submit my opinions to men of a mature and manly understanding, possessing a thorough knowledge of the doctrines of the gospel." The work was not published until 1825. All of my quotations are from this first edition.[18]

That a work lies fallow for 150 years does not diminish its capacity to illuminate its writer's characteristic modes of thought, whether the searcher for those modes is a rhetorician or a critic of some other school. The rhetorician would still study form in a characteristic way, as an embodiment of strategies for—potentially, at least—reaching (teaching, pleasing, and moving) an audience. He would find Milton's preface suffused with *praeteritio:* Milton's claim that he writes largely for himself is, in the rhetorician's eyes, an effort to create an intimate relationship with his audience, as is his claim that, if the work should be published, he sends it out to find men like himself. Milton, the rhetorical critic would insist, merely follows Ramist method in another attempt to reach and shape his audience: this disposition, separately considered, only signals an attempt to "teach" in isolation from the other rhetorical functions of pleasing and moving, to (ostensibly) "rightly" frame an argument that unadorned will appeal to other men's rational instincts, their contemplative intellects. If the preface is a ploy, the form of the work only confirms the audience strategy, however impersonal and dispassionate.

But, as suggested in my review of *The Art of Logic,* there is another way to view form, a nonrhetorical way, one that could involve allowing more Ramism into our readings of Milton than we are accustomed to. For the present, we need only entertain the idea that Milton may have genuinely believed that form is most significantly understood in its fusion with matter, or content—that it is, literally, a product of the material cause. Let us at least begin with that belief and consider abandoning the rhetorician's obsession with words. Whereas rhetorical form as a complex of verbal strategies may be separable from content, conceptual form may not be.

Reason, as Milton argues in *The Art of Logic,* may operate without speaking. The arts of speech, grammar and rhetoric, are inferior because they depend upon reason, without which they are nothing. We have already drawn several implications from that doctrine. We may draw another here, as we examine his *Doctrina:* speaking necessarily affects reason, makes it something it is not, sullies pure thought, even that almost purely rational "speaking," or formalizing, that is "method."

Doctrina is, of course, in two books. (This entire "methodical tractate" proceeds by dichotomies and can be cast—down to the most minute details—in the form of a Ramist bracketed diagram.) "Christian doctrine is comprehended under two divisions,—*Faith,* or *the knowledge of God,*—and *Love,* or *the worship of God*" (I, p. 14). Book One discusses faith, Book Two worship. Then Milton makes a statement that, I believe, has great significance: "These two divisions, though they are distinct in their own nature, and put asunder for the convenience of teaching, cannot be separated in practice. . . . Besides, obedience and love [i.e., practice] are always the best guides to knowledge, and often lead the way from small beginnings, to a greater and more flourishing degree of proficiency" (I, pp. 14–15). Teaching is itself second best. Practice, faith plus worship, is the greater way. The active intellect, however, seeking to train itself, posits a distinction between faith and worship, and the act of teaching puts them asunder (in Book One, and Book Two). Nonetheless, the intellect recognizes that the two are profoundly indivisible.

The same formal, methodical hierarchy is also true of the Trinity. That the "son" is "begotten of God" is only a "figure of speech" (I, p.

227

108). God cannot in truth be both the Father *and* the Son (and, Milton argues later, the Holy Spirit). The idea offers "violence to reason" (I, p. 114). Here I would add that it offers *no* violence to that reason that is skeptical of form and views it, as Donne does, as but further examples of our "imperfect knowledge" in this world. Of course, Milton continues, "two things may be called one in more than one way," as when "they speak and act with unanimity," or are "in love, in communion, in agreement, in charity, in spirit, in glory" (I, p. 123). This ambiguity is allowable on a local level, and must be recognized for what it is. But the Father and the Son differ in number and therefore in essence, though not in substance: the Son, that is—and here again the "method" of "natural reason" assigns everything to its proper place, due order, and precedence—came after the Father and is second to him; but by the same token, if the two are of the same substance, the Father would seem to be material, to have a body, as Jesus had a body. Two may share a common substance—but that two would share a common essence is formally, logically, absurd. How, then, could they be two? "[H]ow can reason establish (as it must in the present case) a position contrary to reason? Undoubtedly the product of reason must be consistent with reason, not a notion as absurd as it is removed from all human comprehension" (I, p. 126).

In this review, I should point out that I am tracking Milton's progress of his own reason. He himself, however, turns for evidence of his thought to the Scriptures; indeed, his work is largely a pastiche of Scripture interlaced with his own statements—a "tractate" of the Scriptures, like Augustine's *De doctrina,* but "methodical," almost coldly so. In addition to acknowledging the primacy of reason and the inviolability of the Scriptures, he turns briefly for further evidence of faith to the Apostle's Creed, which he calls "the most ancient and universally received compendium of belief in the possession of the Church" (I, p. 200)—and which, we should note, unlike the later Nicene Creed or dogmatically Trinitarian Athanasian Creed, leaves room for considerable doubt that the personae of the Trinity are one or even coequal.

The Holy Spirit, Milton argues, is "inferior to both Father and Son" (I, p. 212). The Son calls on the Father, as indeed does the Spirit itself. How then can we believe that the three are one? In reading these arguments, one is likely to recall Tertullian's famous resolution *credo quia absurdum.* But Milton's rhetorical technique in dealing with the

Trinity, particularly in discussing the Holy Spirit, is *reductio ad absurdum*. How can three persons be in one form, or vice versa? The idea of the formal equality of each member of the Trinity offends reason and, he insists, is unwarranted by Scripture.[19] Milton seeks certainty, above all *formal* certainty even beyond the divisions momentarily allowable to autodidactic reason.

Milton's most shocking, and for us most useful, argument appears in Chapter VII, "Of the Creation." Just as he has argued the absolute indistinguishability of God into three persons, so here he argues the absolute indistinguishability of matter and form—that is, soul and body. God did not make Creation out of nothing, but out of himself—out of his own substance. And that includes man, who too is one substance with the Father, though differing in essence. Man's nature is itself indivisible—and here Milton's arguments have most bearing upon our thinking about his prose and poetry:

> man is a living being, intrinsically and properly one and individual, not compound or separable, not, according to the common opinion, made up and framed of two distinct and different natures, as of soul and body,—but . . . the whole man is soul, and the soul man, that is to say, a body, or substance individual, animated, sensitive and rational.   [I, pp. 250–251]

This is a monist, "organic" view of man. Form is in matter and matter is in form, as the Puritan and mortalist Overton puts it; by conversion of terms, the view means that the soul is in the body and the body is in the soul. The soul is equally diffused throughout the entire body, Milton goes on to argue, and, further,

> every *form*, to which class the human soul must be considered as belonging, is produced by the power of matter.   [I, p. 257]

The statement correlates perfectly with Milton's earlier statement in *The Art of Logic* whereby he grouped the four causes according to their precedence. Moreover, his argument concerning the Trinity correlates with his arguments on form (it individuates and is a product of matter, both essence and substance) in the earlier work—marked in the *Logic* by a warning to "theologians." Thus, there are doctrinal similarities in the two works. These similarities point to the locus of Milton's confidence; more particularly, both works show that he places most confidence *in the forms, not necessarily verbal forms, which are apprehensible to*

natural reason: reason recognizes verbal form as a conceptual convenience, to be dissolved in that form's union with matter and in reason's
apprehension of the truth both embody—the ultimately informing
truth, like that "practice" that is faith plus worship.

Indeed, when his doctrine of form is applied to his own work, one
is led away from rhetorical criticism into formalism. In speaking of
form in *Doctrina,* Milton, as we have seen, argues positions that we
associate with modern formalism: that form and matter are inseparable, that form pervades every part of the whole, and that the whole is
greater than the sum of its parts. The ontology, or being, of a poem
would thus seem if not iconic, then more objectlike than argumentative. At any rate, only formalism, not rhetoric, has the conceptual
monism to match Milton's. But this is a subject we shall pursue later.
Let us here consider further the locus of Milton's confidence.

The point we have reached in our review of these two documents
would seem to disparage speaking as a mode of apprehending truth.
Intuition is the primary mode, all Ramists believed. Milton has
Raphael affirm the divinity of that mode in commenting to Adam on
the dissimilarities /similarities of heaven and earth: the ontology of
the mind is in reason, Raphael states, which is

> Discursive, or Intuitive; discourse
> Is oftest yours, the latter most is ours,
> Differing but in degree, of kind the same.
> [*PL,* V, ll. 488–490]

Intuitive in Milton's lexicon had within it the Latin *intueor*—to gaze at,
to contemplate. It was obviously nondiscursive, as Raphael's usage
shows. In Ramist logic it served to define the means and end whereby
natural reason is trained—"an applying or directing of the minde,"
Fraunce states, "to the view and contemplation of that, which of it
selfe it might perceaue, if it were turned and framed therevnto" (fol.
4ᵛ). In Adam's descendants, natural reason, mostly discursive but
partly intuitive, is fallen (that is, a gap has widened between the two in
"degree" and 'kind") and is therefore in need of training—more
training, Milton believed, than the Ramists offered, because reason
can rely more on the discursive than the Ramists wished to admit.
Though not precisely Ramist, Milton's epistemology nonetheless diverges sharply from Donne's, for the intuitive remains hierarchically
above the discursive. Optimistic, and not exactly stoic, the epistemol-

230

ogy is nonskeptical and, however much it differs in certain particulars, it *is* ultimately more Ramist than humanist. Miltonic angels do not perceive merely the "white truth," as in Donne, with the whole truth somewhere between angelic and mortal perception. Rather, man, Milton never lets us forget, though fallen has yet the divine within him, and he may be trained to share its view.

We cannot escape discourse in this world, nor should we try, but our reason abandons its intuitive function altogether if it stops with the merely discursive. We must concentrate not simply on *matter*, which is thought in words, but also on *form*, which is arrangement or structure and which is a product of the thought in those words. In one place Milton sounds strikingly like a rhetorician: "the passages quoted in the New Testament from the Old will have still less weight, if they be produced to prove anything more than what the writer who quoted them intended" (*Doctrina*, I, p. 57). However, considering his teaching on the nature of reason and on the formal cause, it would seem that he means something other than rhetorical analysis. He means that it is not enough to analyze a part of a discourse; we must view that total soul, or form, that part implies or represents. That total form, when we arrive at it, may not finally look like a Ramist diagram, but it will not be distinguishable from thought in words, its matter. And it will be something apprehensible only to the silent intellect—operating on a plane of sensibility like the one Milton proposes at the outset of *Paradise Lost*.

It is in this elevation of the silent intellect, in this disparagement of speaking as a mode of knowledge, and in this confidence in the forms of truth that we see most clearly those forces that produced the disintegration of humanist rhetoric. With Milton we have entered an intellectual *mise-en-scène*, in which thought no longer thrives on skepticism and provisional truths. We are worlds away from the Erasmian *via diversa:* Jesus proclaimed *himself* "the way" but for Erasmus Jesus could be compared to Proteus, and for Milton, as we shall see later (in *Paradise Regained*), Jesus is comparable to a "solid rock." We are worlds away from "Augustinocentric" Christianity as well: to methodize Christian doctrine is to impersonalize it, or to address oneself to reason alone, beyond individuality, beyond, even, will and "human feeling." Obviously, we are also worlds away from Ciceronianism. But that distance we shall try to assess in the next two essays.

Milton's Rhetoric: A Prolusion

"Natural logic," whether purely Ramist or Miltonic, does not give primacy to the discursive functions of "natural reason." Primacy— the locus of the general and antecedent—is reserved for intuition. "*Right* reason" would seem to be trained natural reason, but it, too, is not necessarily verbal; it is a "feeling," Milton states in *Doctrina* (Chap. II), calling it also our "conscience," like urges springing from deep within our natures that confirm the existence of God. Training reason to be aware of "right reason" is to put a gloss, a commentary, on nature. Teaching requires the use of words (even when natural reason teaches itself). But it is not the words that teach reason, one must suppose, so much as their conceptual (their "axiomatic" and "dianoetic") form.

In the *Logic*, Milton states that each basic art can be divided into two, and only two, discrete and unique parts. The parts of logic are "invention and disposition"; of grammar, "etymology and syntax"; of rhetoric, "elocution and action" (p. 233). His *Logic,* as we have seen, follows that teaching perfectly. His Latin *Grammar* also follows that teaching, with its principles distributed into "etymology" and "syntax." He never wrote a rhetoric, but one can assume that if he had its principles would have been distributed into "elocution," which involves adding style to logic's truth and grammar's correctness, and "action," which involves presenting a discourse orally.

At one point in the *Logic* (p. 323), he claims that thinking is not a part of rhetoric. Neither is disposition or memory. For including *inventio, dispositio,* and *memoria* in rhetoric offends against the Ramist "law of justice," which requires the members of any art to be only those essential to it. Milton's teaching on "equipollence" is revealing:

> Equipollence is defined *as agreement in fact and sense of propositions discrepant in word;* thus *Some man is learned* and *Not every man is learned* are of the same value, and so are similar statements. . . . So equipollence when it resides in words only, not in things, should be turned over to grammar or rhetoric and copious supply of words. [pp. 335–337]

Logic is for "things"; rhetoric for words. The ancient *res-verba* distinction is used to keep logic and rhetoric in their places, with logic well ahead in the work of grappling with truth. What is essential to rhetoric, it seems, is only the verbal varying of truth—something added to truth after reason has done the real work.

Throughout his writing, Milton never conceives of rhetoric as a mode of thought. References to rhetoric invariably link it to merely verbal considerations. In his 1642 *Apology,* for example, he justifies his use of *style* by reference to "the rules of best rhetoricians, and the famousest examples of the Greek and Roman Orations."[20] True eloquence, moreover, he insists in the same work, transcends style and depends upon a "serious and hearty love of truth" (p. 361), a truth, one can only surmise, that itself depends if not on intuition then on *logical* invention. Many other examples might be cited. I am thinking of the observation that hell in *Paradise Lost* is a "tissue of words"[21] or of the famous disparagement of classical learning in *Paradise Regained*—and of most references to *rhetoric, rhetorical,* and *rhetorician* sprinkled throughout Milton's prose writings.[22] What is important, however, is that Milton *bought* the Ramist division between thinking and speaking, along with the Ramist doctrine that the avenues to truth lie in the former, not in the latter. I do not find those attitudes shifting in Milton's career, but, as I have repeatedly insisted, I would not characterize him as a thoroughgoing or extreme Ramist. In one crucial matter, as we noted earlier, he breaks with Ramists: he is softer in his attitudes toward other methods. As he says in the 1642 *Apology*—a work that has been prized for centuries as central to understanding Milton's attitudes toward poetry—"in the teaching of men diversely temper'd different ways are to be try'd" (p. 312). For extreme Ramists there was only one way, or method.

Nonetheless, there would seem to be a stable and thoroughly Ramist hierarchy in Milton's ideas: the intuitive, followed by the discursive. This hierarchy may be analyzed in the following manner: *truth* (the "right reason," which is independent of speaking) is on top, followed by *form,* and then *words.* Rhetoric centers on words but verges on form. Logic centers on form but verges on truth and words. Thus, in Milton's epistemology, there could be *no* rhetorical thinking; for rhetoric is merely a process of selecting styles or *conventional* verbal forms for truth (and then orally delivering that truth). But truth itself has been arrived at by other means.

There are, of course, times when the humanistically trained Milton sounds Ciceronian.[23] In the 1642 *Apology,* for example, he says that the "truly eloquent" man is a "good man," and that the poet ought himself "to be a true poem, that is, a composition, and patterne of the best and honourablest things" (p. 303). This sounds very much like the Ciceronian conception of the orator as the *vir bonus,* the finest product of humanist education, whose character is imprinted on his discourse. One might argue, accordingly, that the ultimate "formal cause" of Milton's discourse lies in the poet's ethical or moral sense.[24] But for Milton that moral sense springs from the poet's intuition, conscience, or "right reason." There would be no need for practice in *controversia* as a source of ethos. That source has obviously been supplanted in Milton: *contra* Isocrates, debating could not itself make one a better person. One might also argue that there is little or no controversial thinking in Milton because truth is the source of all eloquence, and truth, for him, was immutable, firm, and apprehensible by nonverbal means. But I shall postpone that argument awhile and take here another tack.

The following is somewhat adversarial in its critical temper. Another incongruous perspective, like those employed throughout this study, it offers a view, from the standpoint of rhetoric, of Milton juxtaposed with Donne. Admittedly incongruous from the outset, it is an exercise, like a critical prolusion on "whether or no there be rhetoric in Milton's poetry." Because the nature of the question weights the analysis in favor of Donne, the exercise should further my case on the limits of humanist rhetoric as a just approach to Milton's art.

■　■　■

There is little discernible controversial thinking in Milton because in much of his discourse the opposition vanishes early or is barely present throughout. There is little discernible sense of *otherness*— even, for that matter, little conscious sense of man's estrangement from knowledge, truth, or Christ, senses vivid in Donne. What opposition is there is seldom a principle of thought or structure. Opposition, division, otherness, an urgent sense that one is separated or apart from someone or something else—this is crucial to *controversia.* There must be two sides, each with its own valid or justifiable claims. *Controversia* sees both and is as capable of arguing for one as for the other. Discourse produced by this mode of thought is often full of such rhetorical contrariness as paradox and irony, or it proceeds proleptically or by means of reconciliation; in either case, the other side—the one not argued for—is still there, observable as the alternative, the *contra,* to the position taken.

Any sense of opposition in Milton has been absorbed in or preempted by his conceptions of form and ethos. These two conceptions are, ultimately, not distinct, though they will be separated in the following discussion "for purposes of teaching." Most of our attention will center on *form.*

Early examples of Milton's efforts *formally* to define, limit, and absorb opposition are his ostensibly controversial poems "L'Allegro" and "Il Penseroso." Upon first encountering these poems, one might—by taking their titles and tones literally—read the former as a poem about mirth, the latter as a poem about melancholy, as Dr. Johnson did. But, Dr. Johnson notwithstanding and in spite of their titles, the poems are not disquisitions on opposing themes. Indeed, to readers of Burton's *Anatomy of Melancholy* (1621), both poems would appear to be on the same subject, melancholy: "L'Allegro" is an attempt to dispel less noble, black melancholy, depression; and "Il Penseroso" is an attempt to indulge in the more noble, white melancholy, pensiveness.[25] Further, when the poems are paired, any perceptible opposition between them is finally submerged in our realization that each is simply the mirror image of the other.[26] Each follows the same formal procedure, the same organization of material: dismissal, invocation, listing of companions, catalog of pleasures.[27] And each ends conditionally with the speaker yet in his initial state: *if* you (mirth or melancholy) can give me these pleasures, then with you I mean to live. The poems offer no impulse toward resolution—toward, say, an "Il Moderato"[28]—because there is truly no debate. *Controversia* has been muted, apparently for the sake of formal harmonies.

To have *controversia* one must not simply acknowledge opposition but maintain it and keep it constantly before one throughout the debate. Another way of putting all this is to say that *controversia* is an adversarial mode of thought—and in the poems we just touched on, neither "mirth" nor "melancholy" is presented as an adversary of its speaker or of the other. Let us continue this examination of Milton's nonrhetorical thinking by contrasting Donne's confrontation of death with Milton's confrontation of time.

235

Holy Sonnet X, by John Donne

Death be not proud, though some have called thee
Mighty and dreadfull, for, thou art not soe,
For, those, whom thou think'st, thou dost overthrow,
Die not, poore death, nor yet canst thou kill mee.
From rest and sleepe, which but thy pictures bee,   5
Much pleasure, then from thee, much more must flow,
And soonest our best men with thee doe goe,
Rest of their bones, and soules deliverie.
Thou art slave to Fate, Chance, kings, and desperate men,
And dost with poyson, warre, and sicknesse dwell,   10
And poppie, or charmes can make us sleepe as well,
And better then thy stroake; why swell'st thou then?
One short sleepe past, wee wake eternally,
And death shall be no more, death, thou shalt die.

On Time, by John Milton

Fly envious Time, till thou run out thy race,
Call on the lazy leaden-stepping howrs,
Whose speed is but the heavy plummets pace;
And glut thy self with what thy womb devours,
Which is no more then what is false and vain,   5
And meerly mortal dross;
So little is our loss,
So little is thy gain.
For when as each thing bad thou hast entomb'd,
And last of all thy greedy self consum'd,   10
Then long Eternity shall greet our bliss
With an individual kiss;
And Joy shall overtake us as a flood,
When every thing that is sincerely good
And perfectly divine,   15
With Truth, and Peace, and Love shall ever shine
About the supreme Throne
Of him t'whose happy-making sight alone,
When once our heav'nly-guided soul shall clime,
Then all this Earthy grosnes quit,   20
Attir'd with Stars, we shall for ever sit,
    Triumphing over Death, and Chance, and thee O Time.

In Donne's poem, the oppositional otherness of death is prominent throughout. Death is personified, but, paradoxically, in less than human terms—which is, of course, the entire point of the poem, sealed by that final reversal: it is death who is truly mortal, not we. Throughout the poem, the personhood of death is never lost sight of: he is proud, called mighty and dreadful, overthrows, can be pictured, is a slave, dwells, strikes, swells, and, finally, dies. Death, our foe, is like us, but he is truly perishable whereas we are only apparently so. The speaker's control is also manifest throughout, but less in the careful way in which he has distributed his materials into a Shakespearean sonnet form than in the confident manner in which he confronts his adversary, in the evenness of his tone, and in such local effects as the denigrating address to "poore death" and the *zeugma* of lines 5 and 6. Indeed, the couplet sounds more like the conclusion of a challenge hurled in the adversary's face than a formally anticipated closure.

In Milton's poem, time's opposition is acknowledged, but the speaker's eyes are on eternity, and thus there is little real adversarial relation in the poem, which moves from a glance at the wretchedness of time to the exaltation of heavenly triumph. Time seems less a person than a monster: it lacks the magnificent if false attributes of death and is hardly a worthy opponent. There is, consequently, no real confrontation in this poem, though time is our acknowledged enemy. Rather, in typically Miltonic fashion, the otherness of time is absorbed into the grandeur of the poem's form.

By confrontation, I am thinking of the effect, which is ever prominent in Donne, of a spoken case, like a case at law in which one's opponent is called to judgment. And just as Milton's poem seems less confrontational, so it seems less argumentative. Milton had apparently intended the poem to be "set on a clock case," and if it were, time would be conceptually reduced even further, to a timepiece. As it is, the physical appearance of a timepiece is mentioned in the "plummets" of line 3, and its movement is represented by the sounds of lines 7 and 8. The clock becomes one icon, the poem another. Between the two, there is no contest.

Rather than a contest, confrontation, or argument, the poem offers a narrative, which in one respect ends on line 12, when time has devoured itself and eternity has greeted us each individually and indivisibly.[29] A vision of heavenly bliss amplifies the conclusion: the *anaphora* (the "when . . . then . . ." construction) of the conclusion is not only expanded but "reformed." Note that the "when" clause of line 9 speaks of the consuming of time and the "then" clause of line 11 speaks of the bliss of eternity. The two are reversed in the "when" clauses that begin in lines 14 and 19, which describe "Joy," and the "then" clause of line 20, which mentions "Earthy grosnes." The reversal further signifies the end of time: its movement has ceased, its linearity cancelled, and we "for ever sit, /Triumphing." Death is named in the last line, as is chance, though both are implicit in the poem and are parts of the "Earthy grosnes" of time.[30] The final, direct address to time is from a position of total supremacy. We had forgotten about time until that final address and *that,* I believe, is the point of the final structure, the final ten lines, where we are—in our perspective as well as in our emotions—above and beyond time. The poem is iconic, not linear, in that it takes us beyond a segmental view and beyond emotions, to offer a formally integrative concept.

Conceptual form is Milton's primary mode of poetic communication, and its use preempts argumentation. The speaker practices—as always in Milton—not controversy but the virtues of endurance and greater vision; those virtues were acquired outside the poem, or before it begins. They seem to take a form that shows few battle scars and is, rather, self-assured—neither proleptic nor self-corrective.

Donne, by contrast, in another poem (Holy Sonnet XIII, "What if this present were the worlds last night?") also resolves a problem through form, one that is less self-assured than self-assuring. A troubled self is present, and in need of assurance. Donne poses the problem adversarially: the speaker confronts his own fears of Judgment Day. The poem is the result of two speaking selves who, in anguish, progressively become one voice. The "beauteous forme"—Christ, the poem (the elements we enumerated in our earlier discussion of this poem)—is arrived at painfully. The speaker wins out by posing a "forme," a largely verbal form, but only after a hard-fought and narrowly victorious battle, and we see and hear the entire process. There is simply less striving in Milton— in "On Time," for example. Victorious and conclusive form is present from the start, and somewhere above the verbal level.

The final two poems I wish to compare are about estrangement, a subject close to the heart of rhetoric and well suited to its intellectual method. The comparison of these two poems may be irreverent, but is, I hope, illuminating.

The Dreame, by John Donne

Deare love, for nothing lesse then thee
Would I have broke this happy dreame,
  It was a theame
For reason, much too strong for phantasie,
Therefore thou wakd'st me wisely; yet   5
My Dreame thou brok'st not, but continued'st it,
Thou art so truth, that thoughts of thee suffice,
To make dreames truths; and fables histories;
Enter these armes, for since thou thoughtst it best,
Not to dreame all my dreame, let's act the rest.   10

As lightning, or a Tapers light,
Thine eyes, and not thy noise wak'd mee;
  Yet I thought thee
(For thou lovest truth) an Angell, at first sight,
But when I saw thou sawest my heart,   15
And knew'st my thoughts, beyond an Angels art,
When thou knew'st what I dreamt, when thou knew'st when
Excesse of joy would wake me, and cam'st then,
I must confesse, it could not chuse but bee
Prophane, to thinke thee any thing but thee.   20

Comming and staying show'd thee, thee,
But rising makes me doubt, that now,
  Thou art not thou.
That love is weake, where feare's as strong as hee;
'Tis not all spirit, pure, and brave,   25
If mixture it of *Feare, Shame, Honor,* have.
Perchance as torches which must ready bee,
Men light and put out, so thou deal'st with mee,
Thou cam'st to kindle, goest to come; Then I
Will dreame that hope againe, but else would die.   30

Sonnet 23, by John Milton

Mee thought I saw my late espoused saint
 Brought to mee like *Alcestis* from the grave
 Whom *Joves* great son to her glad husband gave
 Rescu'd from death by force though pale and faint.

239

Mine as whom washt from spot of child-bed taint   5
   Purification in th' old law did save,
   And such, as yet once more I trust to have
   Full sight of her in heav'n without restraint,
Came vested all in white, pure as her mind:
   Her face was vail'd, yet to my fancied sight   10
   Love, sweetness, goodness in her person shin'd
So clear, as in no face with more delight.
   But O as to imbrace me she enclin'd,
   I wak'd, she fled, and day brought back my night.

In Donne's poem, two contraries—dream and truth—are in controversy, which is resolved only when one is superimposed on the other. The superimposition is made only to show that *this* opposition is evanescent; it is difficult to determine which is dream, which is truth. Uncharacteristically for Donne, *controversia* in this poem does not resolve itself into some "middle way." And that irresolution is itself a strategy: it forms an appeal to the *real* opposition, which is between him and the sought-after woman. The woman is the speaker's true adversary; her otherness and his are the true controversy.

The speaker's erotic dream was interrupted at its near climax by the woman dreamed of—at least, he claims she is the woman he dreamed of and, at least, his audience appears to be the woman herself, not a dream. But he can't be sure. Moreover, even his initial conjecture, as to why she "wisely" awakened him, disappears into the poem's action and is later replaced by another conjecture. But first he supposes that she awakened him because his dream was too strong for dreaming, for fantasy; it, the dream, should be reasoned about, consciously—which he proceeds to do. "Yet" her present reality only has the effect of appearing to continue his dream. For she is truth itself—that is, God, God-like[31]—"so truth" that "thoughts" of her (whether in "reason" or in "phantasie") dissolve the line between "dream" and "truth": such "truth" is always and everywhere truth, whether thought of, dreamt about, or—one must suppose—encountered. Here she is. Does he dream or wake? Never matter. Her appearance has continued his momentarily interrupted dream, so "let's act the rest." "Rest" here anticipates the conclusion of the poem—with "die," when one sees God, unmistakable truth, as well, of course, as the Elizabethan comic reference to orgasm.

He continues to "reason" in the second stanza, but it is a reasoning that at first is only fantasy: at first he thought she was an angel. But she could see his thoughts, whereas an angel could not.[32] Therefore it is "prophane" to think her "lesse" than God, who alone can see our thoughts. The irony is unmistakable: reading a dreaming man's erotic thoughts at the physical stage in which the woman finds him requires no God-like omniscience. Considering the unmistakableness of the irony and the ludicrous hyperbole of calling her God for her ostensible omniscience, the further irony of thinking "thee any thing but thee" is also clear: such *interruptus* is apparently characteristic of the woman addressed.

The levels of irony continue, as does the dream. The first three lines of the final stanza point in two directions at once. First, that you have not faded away like a dream shows that you are present, are real, but my rising from my bed and finding you still here makes me doubt your presence (are *you* truly here, by of all places my bed?). Second, your coming to my room but "staying"—not entering my arms, as I had begged—shows me that you are indeed *you,* but my "rising" (my sexual arousal and continuing hope) makes me wonder if perhaps the you I see is only the dream you. The second meaning is especially poignant to the Petrarchan, who seeks in dream what is denied in reality, a willing mistress. Because "feare" in line 24 echoes "doubt" in line 22, one might suppose the observation in the next lines refers to *his* "love"—but that supposition mixes the two elements (he and she), which in this poem cannot mix, except in dreams. The lines, we see, actually follow through on the second meaning just noted, of the preceding lines. Just as *he* is mixed (so he says) of reason and fantasy, dream and truth, so is "*that* love," which must be *her* love: not only fear but shame and honor are mixed in her love and keep her from his bed, though near it. So he dreams on: perhaps you came to kindle me, to have me ready when you return for the "act," if ever you do. The conjecture reverses his initial one, in the first stanza. But which is "truth"? There is none, only "hope." I will hope that you come back for the "act," I will "dreame" that you come back for the "act"; without that hope I would die (and so see God and truth), and—flatly—I *would* rather "die," would rather have sex than the dream.

A theme for reason? If so, the comedy of the poem lies in its compounding the structures of reason with the structures of fantasy. Conscious control, however, is apparent throughout, in the contest between these obscuring linguistic structures and the speaker's unconcealable state—or, what amounts to the same thing, the contest between the real or imagined woman and the speaker's unrest. The overused sexual joke in the final word of the poem is like the end of a rope on which are tied all the hyperboles, all the references to hope, spirit, "prophaneness," angels, rest, and God: this is where they all end, in the stark reality of a sexually aroused man, who may or may not see before him the woman, whose only stark reality is a compound of desirability and timidity. The reader has not been misled from the first, nor, most likely, has the man either. The hyperbolic identification of the woman as "truth" in the first stanza all but evaporates in the man's urgent plea at the end of that stanza. We know what he's up to. If we forget, the sexual overtones of "act," "joy," "came," "comming," "rising," and finally "die" remind us. But linguistic structures, reason, fantasy, dream, truth, hope, and fear are also parts of living—as are the woman's timidity and the man's all but overwhelming urgency—and the starkness of their reality is restored in the final line, whose balance between "dreame that hope" and "die" does not simply recapitulate the poem but virtually starts it over again. Such, it seems to me, is the characteristic operation of Donne's skepticism (which, I fear, I can only pursue further at the risk of turning this comic poem into a heavily philosophical one).

A dream founders on present physical reality in the Milton poem as well, but the hope that the dream represents in this case becomes the greater, more significant truth. There is no irony. And the comparisons, though seemingly hyperbolic, become largely—through the strength of the word "trust"—typological.

Like Donne's poem, Milton takes us into the intimate life of a man. But the sense of *a* man, *a* woman—a sense that heightens the inescapably present physical realities in Donne's poem—gives way to an even greater sense, of man's place in history. A sense of man's place in history, in turn, is the source of consolation in this formally significant poem: it makes the "night" as momentary as the "day." Truth is not at question in the Milton poem; the speaker does not "hope," but rather "trusts." The poem, moreover, does not develop like Donne's, in linear fashion. If it did, it might end with two emotions yet in opposition: hope of eternity and anguish of the present. But the potential disharmony of the final line is drowned in the echoing harmony of the entire poem: however real the anguish, it is enveloped within the dominant structure of trust, hope *with* faith.

The three vehicles of the dream are arranged in chronological order: the Greek myth of "death-bullying Heracles" (as Richard Wilbur calls him) signifies a primitive or unredeemed concept of immortality; this is succeeded by the Jewish "law," the covenants of God, which in turn are implicitly contrasted with the new "law," Christ's mercy and the promise of "individual" (cf. "On Time") life after death. The emphasis on the individual actually frames mention of the Greek myth and Jewish law: "Me . . . I . . . my," the poem begins, and "mine" begins the sentence in the second quatrain—as if the Christian, individual salvation is not merely the climax but the embodiment and fulfillment of man's earlier hopes.[33] She is a "saint," and her saintliness is proved by the visible "love, sweetness, goodness" of the dream. The speaker's confidence frames and controls the subject of "fantasy": sight of her was "fancied," nor was it "full" or "without restraint," for "her face was vail'd." That the beloved apparition was only an apparition is acknowledged—in a way it never is in the Donne poem. But that the apparition was an apparition, an expression if not of his "hope" then of his "trust," is less the point of the poem than the final weighing of the ultimate and inevitable outcome against the momentariness of the present. The former overbalances the latter and defeats the transitoriness of the dream. That greater form—reason's method—is never close to shattering, however real the speaker's plight, for even after the conceptual, and dramatic, pivoting of the poem on line 13, we are never allowed to forget that the difference between the two parts is that which makes our day a night, our vision a blindness.

Much effort has been expended by critics in attempting to establish the biographical "facts" of this poem.[34] Some believe the "saint" must be Mary Powell, Milton's first wife, others that she is Katherine Woodcock, Milton's second wife. The poem's probable dates of composition have been introduced as proof, as have the references to "purification" rites and such facts as that Mary died in childbirth, Katherine soon after childbirth, each having given birth to a female child, which in the "old law" (Lev. 12:5) requires a longer period of "purifying" than delivering a son. Yet all these efforts seem to me very wide of the mark. Nor does the final "night" refer only to Milton's blindness. The "facts" are that *a* man dreamed he saw his dead wife, a dream dispelled by the "day," which is itself a kind of night because it ended, temporarily, his desired "sight." Temporarily is the point, for day and night will pass into eternity, and eternity will restore his sight, forever, and with more purity. To reduce the poem to biographical facts controverts the significance of its form.

I can now treat briefly the second point I wish to raise, concerning the speaker's ethos in Milton's poetry. I have already approached the matter in noting that attempts to specify the speaker in Milton's Sonnet 23 are beside the point. Indeed, the very point of all Milton's writing would seem to be that the individual, however important he may be and however acknowledgeable is his individuality within Christian doctrine, is less important ultimately than his place in history. Of course, there are poems that openly display their topicality—such as most of the sonnets Milton wrote—and seem restricted in meaning. But I am speaking of errors in reading those *other* poems, whose formal intentions deny topicality and restricted meaning. Among those other poems I would list Sonnet 23.

This point, concerning the importance Milton gave man's place in history, seems a curious one, I realize, given the widespread impression Milton has left, and that we take, of his egotism. In the autobiographical references throughout the 1642 *Apology, The Reason of Church Government, A Readie and Easie Way,* "Ad Patrem," "Mansus," he seems to speak pridefully of his divine calling as a poet. Milton's interest in the Interregnum may have been primarily to shape a government safe for poetry—the kind of poetry *he* planned to write.[35] Milton said that a poet must be the true poem, and often we, understandably, take that saying literally and encounter Milton when we should be encountering his poems.

But properly approached, the form of some of Milton's poetry draws our attention away from the voice we hear and places it on the total conception of the work. Some of Milton's poetry is truly an "escape from personality"—Eliot's desideratum and the Christian virtue, too, of submerging one's self into something greater. Perhaps we should take literally Milton's statement that the poet must be the poem—and no more than the poem. Then studies of Milton's use of typology would be applicable to the poet, causing him too to melt into history. Studies of the "prophetic strain" in Milton's poetry might be seen as simply another way of assigning function to what-

244

ever voice we hear, giving it due proportion within the patterning of the work and giving due proportion, too, to overtly biographical references, such as those in the invocation of Book III in *Paradise Lost.* My own approach has been to argue that Milton absorbed within the form of some of his work both his own voice and its opposition; that is, both are functional to the extent that they establish form, within which they both disappear.

Without a firm and continuing sense of the opposition there can be no debate, no controversy. My previous chapter has argued that *Donne* frequently creates distinctions in order to make them collapse, usually toward the center. Certainly Milton will allow for distinctions—between time and eternity, vision and "night"—but the distinctions do not collapse by force of argument. They collapse, rather, by the unrolling of Christian time—the advent of eternity, of immortality. We see this unrolling best when we grasp total form: just as all lines meet in infinity, so all divisiveness disappears at the level of total conceptual form, the vision merely verbal forms can serve through their reasonable coherence.

Among modern philosophers, Kenneth Burke has offered perhaps the most comprehensive view of rhetoric—of traditional rhetoric, that is, argumentation, not style.[36] But even in Burke's view, there can be no rhetoric unless there is some recognizable division, some perceptible separateness between people or ideas, some sense of estrangement that a person does not merely acknowledge but strives against. Rhetoric is, in Burke's view, the process whereby the otherness is dissolved and an "identification" or "consubstantiality" is created. In Milton, estrangement is submerged in coherent form, the poet's greater vision. Whatever rhetoric is at work would seem to be formalistic, verbal tactics and strategies that make us contemplate form and so acquire that larger perspective that "justifies" the oppositions within it. Or, to use seventeenth-century terms, we might say that the only rhetoric in Milton is in fact no more than style: it is that stylistic management that makes form conspicuous, such as the repeated *anaphora* in "On Time" or the convoluted syntax in Sonnet 23. Conceptual form, once made conspicuous, is so important that it submerges the poet's voice and ethos—or, better, all three are consubstantial: Miltonic form, greater vision, and the poet's moral character.

There are exceptions. I have earlier acknowledged that some works are narrowly autobiographical and that my observations seem to apply mostly to those works that are not. Nonetheless, I would argue for the general applicability of my conclusion—and reinforce it with the observations Stavely makes about Milton's prose:

> Milton does not adapt his rhetoric to the real world, even provisionally. He never does that. Instead, he makes the real world adapt itself to his rhetoric and to his explicitly literary universe. He absorbs these two or three events into a patterned eloquence, seeking to embody that still time beyond chiding which is his goal for all political reform.[37]

Stavely has described here precisely those effects I have tried to examine in Milton's poetry. Milton's obliqueness, indirection, eyes on the spatially and temporally distant, prominence of syntax and verbal arrangement—necessarily assume that the real world will adapt itself to his mode of communication. Calling that mode "rhetoric," as Stavely does, begs for qualification—formalist rhetoric at most, stylistic rhetoric at least. For the difference between *humanist* rhetoric and "patterned eloquence" is something of the difference between urgency and endurance.

Finally, there would seem to be little sense of estrangement even in Milton's view of God—at least, not that anxiety and urgency Donne experienced when he imagined a frightful otherness in Christ. It may not be too far-fetched to consider theology and poetry together. Both are involved with creation. In the English Renaissance, humanists delighted in referring to God as a poet who created by speaking.[38] Putting theology and poetry together will allow me to conclude my remarks on the rhetoric in Milton and offer a final comparison with Donne.

God created the world not out of nothing but out of his own *subtance,* Milton argues in his *De Doctrina Christiana.* Thus, there would seem to be a precedent and, ultimately, antecedent "consubstantiality" that negates otherness and makes rhetoric, even in the Burkean sense, woefully short-sighted. In fact, there may be no real otherness between the world and heaven—as Raphael remarks, in explaining matters that might seem to be beyond Adam's (and our) understanding:

>   . . . what surmounts the reach
> Of human sense, I shall delineate so,
> By lik'ning spiritual to corporal forms,

As may express them best, though what if Earth
Be but the shaddow of Heav'n, and things therein
Each t' other like, more then on earth is thought?
[PL, V, ll. 571–576]

There are differences, of course, as the poem itself shows: the earth is
at best a foreshadowing of heaven. But in one matter heaven is remarkably like earth: angels have sex. And, although Raphael blushes
to talk about it, angelic sex is—appropriately enough—far better
than ours. Adam asks,

Love not the heav'nly Spirits, and how thir Love
Express they, by looks onely, or do they mix
Irradiance, virtual or immediate touch?
　To whom the Angel with a smile that glow'd
Celestial rosie red, Loves proper hue,
Answer'd. Let it suffice thee that thou know'st
Us happie, and without Love no happiness.
Whatever pure thou in the body enjoy'st
(And pure thou wert created) we enjoy
In eminence, and obstacle find none
Of membrane, joynt, or limb, exclusive barrs:
Easier then Air with Air, if Spirits embrace,
Total they mix, Union of Pure with Pure
Desiring; nor restrain'd conveyance need
As Flesh to mix with Flesh, or Soul with Soul.
[PL, VIII, ll.615–629]

Donne might find *that* heaven enow, a consummation devoutly to
be desired. The speakers of his love poems do indeed desire it, and
whenever they achieve something like it (as in "The Extasie") flaunt it
for all its strangeness in this life. As for the next life, Donne seemed to
lack if not Milton's theology, certainly Milton's confidence in such
knowledge that what we have here, and desire, is a type of what we are
coming to, and will achieve, in the hereafter. In Donne's "The Relique,"
for example, the speaker and his lover loved each other so thoroughly,
spiritually, and physically, that in their strangeness they became
"adored" upon their death, like saints:

. . . we lov'd well and faithfully,
Yet knew not what wee lov'd, nor why,

247

Difference of sex no more wee knew,   25
Then our Guardian Angells doe;

Such love makes one extraordinary in this life, Donne believed, setting the lovers apart, and angels appear to have no sex whatsoever, not
even sexual differentiation. Donne's theology, whether of love or of
heavenly matters, is one in which "consubstantiality" is the exception, and the rule is otherness. The reverse of that theology awaits the
reader of Milton, whose art it informs.

Here, however, we have reached a potential error and an actual imbalance, urged upon us by our mode of investigation. I seem close to
suggesting that there is no typology in Donne—a patent error, but its
correction would take us well beyond the bounds of my study and, I
think, only leave my comparative remarks intact (typology, I shall
suggest in the following section, is more Miltonic for some of the
very reasons the comparisons have so far uncovered). In this section,
my mode of investigation was to search for the conditions of rhetoric,
the constant and functional oppositions that, I have argued, are more
present in Donne than in Milton. Donne thought controversially.
Milton, apparently, did not—and in that negative observation humanist rhetoric as an approach to Milton ends. However, I have yet to
balance Donne's *controversia* with a conjecture on Milton's mode of
thought.

Thinking Mythologically:
"Some Stronger Impulse"

Rhetoric, with its unique mode of thinking, *controversia*—which makes it a humanist rhetoric and, for that matter, humanism itself—has been exemplified in this study by some of the writings of John Donne. It can also be exemplified by the character of Milton's Satan. I am not suggesting that Donne is connected with Satan in Milton's mind. But I do suggest that Donne must have represented everything in humanism that Milton abhorred: its revelling in ambiguity and skepticism, its approach to moral issues as if they were fit subjects for cases at law, its union of words and reason, and its disunion of God and man and Satan. Donne's art, which is predicated on opposition and which proceeds by means of controversial thinking, is an art that Milton totally rejected. The terms of his rejection are made explicit in and through the character of Satan.

But if the ways of humanist rhetoric are the ways of error, it would be sinful to employ them even in rejecting Satan. That is, Milton, and we, must neither admit nor act on Satan's otherness. Consequently, Satan's presence in Milton's work must be a presence-without-otherness, and our dealing with that presence must be noncontroversial. In our reading of the *Areopagitica,* we encountered a traditional doctrine that Milton upheld at the risk of becoming alienated from other Puritans, that good and evil are mixed in fallen man's reason. Accordingly, though Satan embodied as a character in *Paradise Lost* may be evil unmixed, he must also be both in the fallen poet who speaks the poem and in us. Milton's key strategy in dramatizing Satan's presence-without-otherness is to show us that Satan operates through certain modes of persuasion, particularly through the use of words to overthrow "right reason." He inheres not so much in doctrines as in what Milton calls, contemptuously (as we shall see), "rhetoric." In the temptation scene in *Paradise Lost,* for example, Satan employs doctrines that seem drawn directly from the *Areopagitica,*[39] but he uses them evilly. And effectively, for throughout *Paradise Lost* there are times when Satan's apparent goodness misleads us, when we are "surprised by sin."[40] Thus, Satan's presence, even when embodied, is not always external, but is, to an important extent, in us—in our easy acquiescence to his apparently reasonable doctrines and, fatally, in our attraction to his modes of persuasion. Learning how to reject Satan becomes a Miltonic lesson in learning how to deal with the errors of humanist rhetoric. For it is Satan, not the poet or his heroes, who consciously employs and is virtually dramatized in those ways of error.

Paradise Lost and, to an even greater extent, *Paradise Regained* show us how to reject Satan. Like the former poem, the latter dramatizes him to make his presence recognizable and, if surprising, seen for what it is, as not totally other to man. Both poems, but especially the latter, show that the successful confrontation of Satan's presence does not proceed by means of controversy, not in the humanist sense. For controversy in the humanist sense depends not simply upon opposi- tions but also upon a skeptical attitude, an uncertainty that truth can ever be perfectly sorted out from error. Mixed they may be, in Milton, like good and evil, but the sorting out of truth and error is one of the most elevated acts of "right reason," as is the confrontation of error or evil once sorted out. And, Satan's *recognized* presence—whether dramatized or not—is surely meant to challenge both the limits and the morality of humanist skepticism and *controversia*. Throughout both poems, the narrator refers to Satan as our "adversary," and at one point in the latter poem (IV, l.527) Satan calls Jesus *his* "adversary." But a feature of both poems is that there is no adversarial reciproca- tion, whether on the part of Jesus or on the part of the narrator. In *Paradise Regained,* where confrontation is most direct and most ver- bal, the adversariness is all one-sided, Satan's, as he tries unsuccess- fully to turn the action into a debate. But Jesus refuses to debate. *His* mode of thought and the narrator's are an escape from and an alterna- tive to controversy, and thereby a pattern for our behavior toward Satan within or without.

The purpose of this final essay is to examine that other mode of thought, which I shall call "mythological." So important is this alter- native, I believe, that it can be identified with that "stronger impulse" Milton attributed to the orator or poet, beyond "pleasure," which un- Ramistically allows these other arts their own "methods" or forms. As the preceding essay attempted to argue, Miltonic form absorbs or preempts opposition. Let us continue examining this point by turn- ing to *Paradise Regained* to search for the noncontroversial means whereby Jesus and the narrator transform their confrontations with Satan from *controversia* into *mythos.*

In *Paradise Regained,* Satan's rhetoric is predicated on otherness, and at a most significant point in the work, the moment of apparent *anagnorisis,* or recognition, he uses controversial thinking. Satan's speech at that point is, in fact, one of the most concrete examples I have discovered of controversial thinking in Milton's writing: rhetorical thought thus becomes the devil's logic, a corruption and conflation of two arts—logic and rhetoric—that for "reason's" sake should be kept distinct. Our examination (I shall treat only a few parts directly) will center largely on that moment, in Book IV. I must, however, first put in a disclaimer: I shall slight many serious and complicated interpretive questions here,[41] not because I consider them unimportant but because I consider them approachable from the critical perspective I am trying to define. Questions as to the meaning of this poem, for example, or as to the extent of Jesus' uncertainty about himself and his destiny, can be approached through a critical perspective on what we know of Milton's rejection of rhetoric as a mode of thought. Book IV of *Paradise Regained,* unique among Milton's work, virtually centers on rhetoric—and on its correlative, humanism—though the subject itself is apparent throughout, in Satan's tactics.

The alternative I have suggested to humanist rhetoric in Milton, mythological thinking, may also be apparent from the outset, as we consider the biblical story on which the poem is based and the choices the poet faced and made. This is the story, as told by St. Matthew (4:4–11). After his baptism, Jesus was led by the Spirit into the wilderness, to be tempted of the devil. When Jesus had fasted forty days and nights, Satan appeared and said to him (appealing to his hunger if not his self-doubts), "If thou be the Son of God, command that these stones be made bread."

> But he answered and said, It is written, Man shall not live by bread alone, but by every word that proceedeth out of the mouth of God.
> Then the devil taketh him up into the holy city, and setteth him on a pinnacle of the temple,
> And saith unto him, If thou be the Son of God, cast thyself down: for it is written, He shall give his angels charge concerning thee: and in *their* hands they shall bear thee up, lest at any time thou dash thy foot against a stone.

251

Jesus said unto him, It is written again, Thou shalt not tempt the Lord thy God.

Again, the devil taketh him up into an exceeding high mountain, and sheweth him all the kingdoms of the world, and the glory of them;

And saith unto him, All these things will I give thee, if thou wilt fall down and worship me.

Then saith Jesus unto him, Get thee hence, Satan: for it is written, Thou shalt worship the Lord thy God, and him only shalt thou serve.

Then the devil leaveth him, and, behold, angels came and ministered unto him.

The identical story is told by St. Luke (4:1–13) with one notable exception: the mountain episode is placed second, the pinnacle episode is placed last. It was *Luke's* arrangement, not Matthew's, that Milton chose—for two reasons, I believe, each mythological in nature.

The first is the operation of typology, an essential component of Milton's mythological thought. By placing the pinnacle episode last, the entire dramatic action can end with a "fall," which Milton adds: it is Satan, not Jesus, who literally falls from the pinnacle, in effect recalling the fall of Adam. Thus, Adam's fall prefigures Satan's, as the temptation of Eve prefigures the temptation of Jesus; the former are types of the latter and therefore reveal providence and its operation in time, God's presence in the *mythos* of human history. In this manner, in his use of prefiguring, or foreshadowing, typology, the poet asserts the validity of our history.[42] The process extends, of course, to pagan myths. These too are valid as history to the extent that they find fulfillment in the Christian myth. And, I would suggest as a consequence of this mode of thought, the reverse is true and a sign of Milton's reformational spirit: those structural features of Christian myth, where some doubt as to arrangement arises, can themselves be solved by reference to typology. Typology reveals that *falling* is the "theme" of Jesus' temptations, and as theme it is further substantiated by two myths, each of which is referred to at the moment of Satan's fall in *Paradise Regained* (IV, ll. 563–575): first, the myth of Hercules, whom humanists generally took as a prefigure of Christ (cf. "Nativity Ode," ll. 227–228), and the giant Antaeus, son of the earth, who, because he drew continual strength from his mother each time Hercules threw him to the ground, had to be destroyed in—had to fall from—the air; and, second, the myth of the Sphinx, who "fell" as a power when her riddle was solved. The answer to the Sphinx's riddle was "man"— and that answer echoes throughout the entire poem, from first to last, not only as the solution to the riddle, the dilemma, that Satan poses at the moment of climax (to be noted below), but also as an answer to the question the poem itself poses. Milton's mythological thinking, suffused and motivated by typology and firmly based on a Christian view of time, is, I believe, at the center of the *dispositio* of the poem itself—and, for that matter, at the center of his thinking about Christ as Man. One might call this a reformed humanism; nonetheless, it is very remote from rhetoric.

The revelation of Christ's particular manly virtue may be a second reason that Milton chose St. Luke's version. The first episode concerns turning stones into bread and the only "person" named is God ("the mouth of God"). The second episode—in Luke; the third episode in Matthew—takes place on a mountain, and in this episode Jesus names the tempter Satan ("Get thee behind me, Satan"). In Luke's and Milton's final episode, Jesus *on one level of meaning* identifies himself with and as God ("Thou shalt not tempt the Lord thy God"): it is God whom Satan tempts. This process of recognition is, of course, dramatic and epic, and warrantable on those formal grounds. But it is surely also significant that it is warrantable on mythological grounds. The final identification of Jesus with God— which I read as Jesus' deepened realization of his manhood as well as of his Godhead—is itself the result of the character's own mythological thinking: the identification is realized actionally, by Jesus' acceptance of his role in God's providence, an acceptance shown not so much through words as through a conscious bending of will. This bending is more complicated than it sounds, for it is an act of the manly virtue of "magnanimity," which Milton defines in *Doctrina* as something that motivates us "when in seeking or avoiding riches, advantages, or honors, we are actuated by our own dignity, rightly understood."[43] To rightly understand his dignity is the purpose of Jesus' wanderings in the wilderness; to test that understanding is the function of Satan at the conclusion of the forty days and nights. But it is an understanding that is more apprehensible through *form* than through *words*. Though Jesus refers to the law and the prophets—"it is written"—what they all come to, finally, is what he *is,* as revealed not through arguing or debating or speaking so much as through acting and so "uncloistering" and trying his understanding of his own dignity. This Jesus realizes (recognizes and makes real) at the climactic moment of the poem. When Christ came into the world, "The Nativity Ode" shows, he banished darkness and error and false gods not through speaking but simply, as an infant, through his presence. It was his being that radically altered the universe. In *Paradise Regained,* Christ-like being becomes a kind of manliness, which, *for the epic poet,* is the typological fulfillment of the heroic and manly virtues of all myth, and hubris in this case is prevented by a conscious submission to a greater will.

Obedience is, thus, the conclusion of thought in this poem, and because the obedience is conscious it is of the very nature of manliness. If Adam fell by attempting to be more godlike, Jesus "rose" by realizing the true nature of his manhood—whereby he set a mythological pattern for other men, including the poet. The Miltonic lesson about oppositions is thereby made apparent. No longer would the choice be the agonizing one that faced St. Jerome, between Cicero and the Gospel, so long as Cicero is rightly understood as a writer on moral virtue later embodied and fulfilled in the character of Jesus. The dignity of pagan literature can be somewhat reasserted; at least, typology would seem the only basis on which its dignity could be salvaged after Jesus' apparent attack on it in this epic. To rightly understand the dignity of pagan literature was, as we have noted, a humanist enterprise. But whatever humanism we find in Milton must be carefully distinguished as absolutely nonrhetorical. Insofar as humanism is to be identified with Ciceronian rhetoric, just so far is Milton's humanism diminished. For to Milton, rhetoric could offer instruction in style and delivery, but rhetorical *thinking* was diabolic—the logic practiced by sons of the earth, in disobedience to the example offered by the Son of God.

Paradise Regained begins:

> I who e're while the happy Garden sung,
> By one mans disobedience lost, now sing
> Recover'd Paradise to all mankind,
> By one mans firm obedience fully tri'd
> Through all temptation, and the Tempter foil'd   5
> In all his wiles, defeated and repuls't,
> And *Eden* rais'd in the wast Wilderness.

> Thou Spirit who ledst this glorious Eremite
> Into the Desert, his Victorious Field
> Against the Spiritual Foe, and broughtst him thence   10
> By proof th' undoubted Son of God, inspire,
> As thou art wont, my prompted Song else mute,
> And bear through highth or depth of natures bounds
> With prosperous wing full summ'd to tell of deeds
> Above Heroic, though in secret done,   15
> And unrecorded left through many an Age,
> Worthy t' have not remain'd so long unsung.

As in the opening of *Paradise Lost,* the general theme is set forth. Too, just as the earlier song pursued "Things unattempted yet in Prose or Rime," this one will record things "unrecorded left" (the recording justified, as noted earlier, by mythological thinking). The line of the dramatic action is also indicated: we shall see the Spirit bring Jesus from the "desert" (meaning also the wilderness of his own thought) after testing his knowledge that he is the "undoubted Son of God." Again, the Holy Ghost is the poet's muse, inspiring the poet as he led the Son. Donne had used a similar idea, of two people (Sir Philip Sidney and his sister) united by the Spirit, but in Milton's poem a spiritual union through the pattern of truth is far more thematically significant, as I shall attempt to argue later. Note here, however, that *Paradise Regained* actually *begins* with a direct reference to the poet himself, not merely, I believe, in order to recall the earlier poem but also to make visible his own action as a poet—first a conscious submission to a greater will (his own obedience), then a gradual absorption into myth. That theme, I shall argue, is at least coequal with the first one mentioned.

As the poem proceeds, Jesus' baptism is retold. When the Spirit descends in the form of a dove and God's voice pronounces Jesus his "beloved Son," Satan—whom the poet speaking as narrator calls initially "the Adversary"—sees and hears. Immediately Satan convenes a council of his dark powers to tell them the "ill news," that a man "is late of woman born" who (as was foretold) is destined to crush them. He retells the baptism but is baffled by its *mythos*—in particular, its symbolism, the dove and the proclaiming voice. And though he knows God's "first-begot" (in jealousy of whom the war in heaven began; see *Paradise Lost,* V, ll.659–665), he sees only "glimpses" of the Father in the man Jesus. Urged on by his perplexed sense of Jesus'

255

otherness, he proposes to learn who this man is and resolves to "oppose" him, as he had so successfully ruined Adam. The powers greatly approve. Later, as Jesus enters the wilderness, we enter the wilderness of his thoughts:

> O what a multitude of thoughts at once
> Awak'n'd in me swarm, while I consider
> What from within I feel my self, and hear
> What from without comes often to my ears,
> Ill sorting with my present state compar'd. 200

In his youth, as he read the "Law of God," listened to the teachers in the temple, and responded to his own spirit, Jesus began to aspire to heroic deeds, rescuing "Israel from the *Roman* yoke" and then establishing "truth" by force, even "proud Tyrannick pow'r" over the earth. But he put aside this aspiration in favor of another way:

> Yet held it more humane, more heav'nly first
> By winning words to conquer willing hearts,
> And make perswasion do the work of fear;

Thus Jesus *had* arrived at the belief that his messiahship was to be more rhetorical than military—but this belief, it is partly the function of this entire poem to reveal, was based on incomplete knowledge, *before* he had learned "Humiliation and strong Sufferance." It is, in fact, *Satan* who uses "winning words," not Jesus; indeed, as we shall see, Satan uses his own knowledge of Jesus' earlier belief to try to trap him.

After forty days and nights, Satan appears disguised as "an aged man in Rural weeds" who had seen the baptism and, recognizing Jesus' hunger, he offers the first temptation, to change stones into bread. Jesus' reply ends with contempt, charging that each knows who the other is—but the recognition is curiously though significantly muted, in that neither actually *names* the other. Satan, dropping his disguise, and admitting that he is indeed "that Spirit unfortunate," claims he has not lost his capacity "to love" goodness and virtue, which is his motivation in approaching the person he has heard declared "the Son of God." He hopes his motive "to love" will make all the more pitiable his statement that he knows *man* will be restored but *he* will not. Jesus is not taken in, and he replies "sternly" (the only time he speaks so in the poem): you have *deserved* your fate and, as for your alleged "love," you are but an instrument of God, "serviceable to Heav'ns King," as in challenging Job's faith, though you now pretend that you are motivated by "obedience" rather than, as you actually are, by "fear" and "pleasure to do ill." There is more to the speech, of course, but in our brief paraphrase we note Jesus' growth in realizing the nature of "perswasion": the true alternative to "fear" is not "perswasion" but "obedience," which Satan has mis-named "love." Satan begs to be allowed into his presence, since "thy Father" (he uses the phrase; Jesus uses *aloud* "our Father," "God," "Heav'ns King") suffers even hypocrites and atheistic priests into his presence. Jesus' response is obedient to God's will: do as you find permission from above, he replies. Satan disappears, night falls, the first book ends.

Book II begins by making us aware of modes of thought, the rea-soning we use when faced with doubt or uncertainty. Andrew and Simon, who had been present at the baptism, wonder why Jesus is no longer in their midst, and they call to their aid typology—an incipi-ent or partial typology, based on imperfect understanding. Did Jesus disappear as Moses did for a time "in the mount" or was he translated like Elijah into heaven? For contrast, Mary's thoughts are revealed to us: she finds comfort in a simpler and more Christ-centered typol-ogy, recalling the time when Jesus as a youth was missing, only to be discovered in the temple, going about "His Father's business"; thus "some great intent / Conceals him" and she—a divine model of en-durance in contemplating imperfectly understood portents of great events—"meekly compos'd" her mind and "awaited the fulfilling." Satan next speaks, in council, as he tries to reason about the nature of the man he has encountered: if Jesus is "Man by his Mothers side," he is inferior far to Adam, but apparently adorned with "more then hu-man gifts." During the council scene, Satan's reasoning and Belial's are by means of analogies, examples, comparisons, contrasts—not, in sum, by typology. The consultation ends in the resolve to "try" Jesus' apparent otherness on the "manlier" level, his hunger for food or for "honor, glory, and popular praise."

When next we hear Jesus speaking to himself, it is, indeed, hunger he expresses. But the body's hunger, he realizes, once satisfied recurs in kind and is only a type of the soul's hunger, which when fed "with better thought" hungers "more to do my Fathers will." The line re-calls the discovery of the child Jesus in the temple and is the second time in the poem Jesus has called God "my Father," but again, silently, in his thoughts. The next morning—after Jesus has dreamt of food, the feasts of Elijah and Daniel—Satan appears, urges him (mock-typologically) to think of how God had fed such servants as Elijah, and sets before him an enormous feast—so lavish the poet /narrator comments on the by comparison "crude apple that diverted *Eve*," and Satan, too, taunts Christ by pointing out that *these* are not forbidden fruits. But Jesus "temperately" rejects the feasts and concludes his speech with a play on words that itself mocks Satan's style: I "count thy specious gifts no gifts but guiles."

Satan makes the banquet disappear and offers riches, suggesting for comparison the riches that made "*Juda's* Throne" accessible to Antipater and his son Herod. Jesus "patiently" rejects the tempta-tion—and the reasoning, outmatching Satan's comparison with ty-pology: it was a poor "Shepherd lad" whose offspring sat on Juda's throne for many years and will again "reign in Israel without end." The meaning of "Israel" has, of course, shifted for Jesus, the narrator, and the reader—but not for Satan. (Dramatic irony is the poem's fun-damental rhetorical technique, but it is in service of a greater manage-ment of thought well beyond rhetoric.) True power, Jesus states, comes from reigning over the anarchy of spirits within, and true magnanimity can lie in refusing a crown. Riches are therefore "need-less," either for themselves or for the reason Satan has offered. This is the closest Jesus has come to debating Satan on his own ground—but he does it by absorbing Satan's grounds within his own greater vision.

The book, having opened on forms of reasoning, ends sounding like a debate. Still, the reader realizes, the terms of the debate are not fully understood by "the Adversary," Satan. Thus, carefully, the poet /narrator makes us adopt his and Jesus' greater vision, which dissolves controversy. Jesus, of course, is an actor in that vision, as the poet is an actor in the form whereby we understand the vision—and as the Spirit is the true giver of both vision and form to the two heroes in this action.

Book III is more forensic—that is, ostensibly adversarial—than any other in the poem. As if Satan had realized some success in getting the Savior to debate, here he presses his apparent advantage. He stands a while confounded, however, by Jesus' last answer, but then resumes with flattery:

> I see thou know'st what is of use to know,
> What best to say canst say, to do canst do;

258

> Thy actions to thy words accord, thy words
> To thy large heart give utterance due, thy heart   10
> Conteins of good, wise, just, the perfect shape.

The implicit rhetorical doctrine, that the moral character of the speaker (or poet) should *inform* the speech, is Milton's conversion of a Ciceronian doctrine—as I noted earlier and shall note again later, when I consider the poet's un-Ciceronian role in this poem. Here the doctrine is misapplied as flattery, for Satan does not truly know or recognize that "heart." He tries comparing Jesus with Alexander the Great, Pompey, Julius Caesar—all conquerors of the world. Jesus responds "calmly" and refers to the heavenly fame and trial of Job, echoing a reference he, and God, had used in Book I: Satan's temptations of Job prefigure the temptations in the wilderness, as Job's patience prefigures Christ's own—and as Socrates' suffering does also. The mention of Job several times throughout the poem may recall, for some readers, Milton's own reference to the Book of Job as a "brief model" of an epic.[44] But the mention of Socrates in this book in a typological way is extraordinary and, as we shall see, part of the poem's overall design.

Satan replies that even "thy great Father" seeks glory, from all men. To this Jesus "fervently" responds: God seeks not simply glory but glory with "reason," consciously and knowingly given. "Reason" is ironically and pointedly thrown into the face of the great arguer. Satan shifts his ground and begins speaking of "thy Father *David's* Throne," which Jesus is meant to inherit. So I will, Jesus responds, in time, in God's good time, but why are you so concerned, since "my rising is thy fall?" Satan "inly rackt" dissembles his true feelings and says that now his only "hope" is that Jesus will stand between him and "thy Fathers ire":

> If I then to the worst that can be hast,
> Why move thy feet so slow to what is best,
> Happiest both to thy self and all the world,   225
> That thou who worthiest art should'st be thir King?

Satan's mind is, as ever, "analytic."[45] This, however, is the first move he has made toward controversial thinking—but it is brief, merely anticipating the more sustained use he makes later.

Satan offers then to teach this rustic young man, who knows little about the world outside Galilee. So he proceeds to the second temptation, wherein the "Monarchies of th' Earth" are viewed from the mountain top. Some of vast, ancient history passes before them, and twice Satan mentions "thy Father *David*." Jesus will need military power to secure David's throne. But the Savior is "unmov'd"—answering that, as he had told him before, "my time . . . is not yet come." Satan again is confounded, having tried first appealing to Jesus' patrimony as the Son of God, then to his patrimony as the descendant of David. But Jesus does not seek the glory of the world, its kingdoms, or its power—nor, as he shows in his final reply to Satan, does he seek to "save" people through great deeds. "So spoke *Israel's* true King," the *poet* says, voiding all Satan's wiles—"so fares it when with truth falshood contends." In contention, truth has a stability, a rocklike quality, the very opposite of Proteus, that does not itself contend but cancels contention. Thus, part of the Erasmian lesson is controverted. The book ends.

Debate has been tried and it is, to all intents and purposes, over as Book IV begins. Now we shall slow our hasty review and concentrate more on the details of speaking in this final book. Satan, if beyond hope, is not beyond trying. Book IV opens with reference to Satan's chief instrument, rhetoric—a rare appearance of this word in Milton's poetry,[46] and its prominence here offers a clear signal of a major subject:

> Perplex'd and troubl'd at his bad success
> The Tempter stood, nor had what to reply,
> Discover'd in his fraud, thrown from his hope,
> So oft, and the perswasive Rhetoric
> That sleek't his tongue, and won so much on *Eve*,   5
> So little here, nay lost; but *Eve* was *Eve*,
> This far his over-match, who self deceiv'd
> And rash, before-hand had no better weigh'd
> The strength he was to cope with, or his own:

Yet he will try, urged on by an otherness in Jesus that he had not found in Eve. The poet/narrator shapes four similes, each expressing attempts that are unavailing but unstoppable—to name only one, waves surging "against a solid rock"—an amplification of a simple idea, dramatically effective in recalling by the nature of the waves Satan's obduracy (the converse of endurance) in assailing a rock, the greater and unassailable perseverance that is Jesus'.

Rome is the next temptation offered from the mountain, powerful Rome, to whom all nations pay "obedience" (Satan's use of the word shows how little he understands Jesus' meaning). His argument ends on one point: why not aim for the highest? Sitting on David's throne cannot be for long, given Rome's power. Therefore, accept Rome from me, replace the corrupt Tiberius, and free his people "from servile yoke." Jesus' answer is, partly, that the Roman people, "victor once, now vile and base," do not deserve freedom. Jesus ends his speech, drawing a distinction between "inward" and "outward" freedom and referring, once more, to the fulfillment of God's will in time.

It is at this point that Satan attempts to continue the debate by moving it onto a different plane though yet predicated on Jesus' perplexing but (he assumes) estranging otherness. Earlier he had attempted to reach Jesus in general terms, as the Son of God and as the Son of David. Now he attempts to reach him on a personal level, as only the Jesus revealed thus far in the poem. The attempt is through controversial thinking—here applied in a manner encountered frequently in Donne, as persuasion wearing the formal mask of analysis. Two sides are reviewed; each is acknowledged to have its own claims to validity, and on that acknowledgment some resolution is attempted. The mode of this thought, as noted throughout this study, is skeptical; no reference is made to or implied of *a priori* truth or an overriding hierarchy of values. The Tempter reasons:

> I see all offers made by me how slight   155
> Thou valu'st, because offer'd, and reject'st:
> Nothing will please the difficult and nice,
> Or nothing more then still to contradict:
> On th' other side know also thou, that I
> On what I offer set as high esteem,   160
> Nor what I part with mean to give for naught;
> All these which in a moment thou behold'st,
> The Kingdoms of the world to thee I give;
> For giv'n to me, I give to whom I please,
> No trifle; yet with this reserve, not else,   165
> On this condition, if thou wilt fall down,
> And worship me as thy superior Lord,
> Easily done, and hold them all of me;
> For what can less so great a gift deserve?

You do not value my offers, yet I value them highly. Therefore in return for my gift I shall require from you only something that matches your estimation of it, something that is "Easily done." The conclusion is paradoxical: "For what can less so great a gift deserve?" This passage moves to the heart of what is truly Donnesque, thinking by means of controversy. As we have seen, Donne will often use the mode to trap a desired "opponent." Consider, however incongruous the perspective at this point, Donne's "The Flea," in which the speaker describes the insect as a "mariage bed, and mariage temple," since, having bitten both him and his too coy mistress, the flea contains their blood within it; she, finding his reasoning absurd, kills the flea and proclaims herself as well as himself none the less for her having done so; the speaker accepts her reasoning to advance his case:

> Just so much honor, when thou yeeld'st to mee,
> Will wast, as this flea's death tooke life from thee.

In *Paradise Regained* this mode of thinking becomes the devil's logic— resorted to out of desperation and out of a further misapprehension of Jesus' nature: he is resisting, Satan assumes, because he is "difficult and nice," hard to please not simply with gifts themselves but with the reasons for giving, or pleased only by "contradicting" the gifts and their reasons. But Jesus is not being coy, nor has he exactly *contradicted* Satan's reasons—as we, from the poet's perspective, realize. Satan's *controversia,* the lawyerly and skeptical way of finding truth amidst otherness and beyond reasonable doubt, is doomed, based as it is on faulty assumptions about the "opponent." Truth, Milton himself seems always to be saying (and here he says it pictorially), is closer to us than *controversia* admits, and it is apprehensible by other means.

The passage marks a turning in the poem, the moment of full recognition, but in this poem the epic or dramatic *anagnorisis* is special. Jesus now fully characterizes his opposer and calls him for the first time by name, as if in that moment of requiring Jesus' fealty— presented in a form of reasoning that reveals the shallowness of Satan's perception—the last vestiges of disguise had fallen away. The "recognition" marks a furthering of that "proof" mentioned in the opening lines of Book I, whereby Jesus' own resolve as to what he must *do* is tested. The proof is outside rhetoric, and the recognition beyond Satan. For the Savior apparently sees his opposer in a way that Satan cannot as yet see Jesus, though Jesus now for the first time calls himself aloud "the Son of God." Jesus replies disdainfully to the "abominable terms" of Satan's offer, an "attempt bolder then that on Eve," and he ends

> Get thee behind me; plain thou now appear'st
> That Evil one, Satan for ever damn'd.

Satan, however, believes that he has not yet totally failed, that perhaps he is succeeding in moving the debate onto a more personal level. He admits he does not know what "Son of God" means, since both "Angels are and Men." Now that Jesus has rejected earthly kingdoms, he offers him wisdom as the means of fame, and here he moves onto the *intensely personal* level: wisdom will be useful to you, he says, since you intend to rule "by perswasion." Thus, he shows he was privy to Jesus' most personal thoughts, for Jesus' resolution to let "perswasion do the work of fear" was *silently* meditated when he first entered the wilderness. For Satan, of course, "perswasion" can mean only one thing, rhetoric. And since, in best humanist thought, true eloquence is linked to wisdom, he offers Jesus Athens, classical learning. Satan would give Jesus a classical education, by means of great poetry, great oratory, and great philosophy.[47]

Jesus' answer does not exactly dismiss classical learning, though he blames the classical figures for arrogating glory to themselves and giving God none, and claims that learning is beside the point unless the learner has within himself "a spirit and judgment equal or superior." Here, as throughout Milton, there is a firm belief, seldom encountered in Donne, of a "right reason" that is beyond the discursive.

Jesus calls Socrates the "wisest" of classical philosophers. This is the second time in the poem Socrates has received the Savior's praise: first, for his patient suffering unto death for the sake of truth; second, for his wisdom in knowing only that he knew nothing. Consider this praise, however, twice encountered in a poem that is largely a dialogue between two unequal "opponents." Might it not invite a comparison between this poem and the Platonic dialogues? In their dramatizations, in their balancing of true wisdom against the specious, and in their continual stance against the purely verbal trickery of rhetoric (taught by sophists but transformed by Plato's charges into what we now call sophistry), the Platonic dialogues and *Paradise Regained* share certain characteristics. But these resemblances only heighten the differences, which are greater by far. Satan may be prefigured by Protagoras and

Gorgias, but Jesus is prefigured—as the poem itself tells us—more by Job than by Socrates. And the poem itself is compact of various strands and figures; the epic, dramatic, and lyrical are interwoven with the dialogic, as are ancient history and tales of pagan heroes. Nonetheless, a significant conflict in this poem is indeed the thoroughly Platonic one, between rhetoric on the one hand and love of true wisdom on the other. Immediately, to return to the scene in the poem, the praise of Socrates mutes the apparent dismissal of classical learning, as does a move made later by the poet, at the climax of the poem.

Satan, his persuasiveness at an end, now tries fear (as if, for him as for the earlier Jesus, there are only two alternatives in moving people). Since Jesus has rejected all his offers, he wonders what Jesus is doing "in this world." To answer his own question, he resorts to what he can understand of prophecies, astrological signs, and spells, and predicts for Jesus a life of sorrows and violence and a "cruel death." A kingdom is indeed portended—"but what Kingdom, / Real or Allegoric I discern not." Again, there seem to be only two hermeneutical categories in Satan's thought, and both are lacking in wisdom, for he cannot imagine a "real" kingdom beyond a powerful one like Rome or an "allegoric" one beyond the classical learning of Athens. Allegory, however, becomes the keynote of his new attempt to heighten Jesus' fear of the life these signs portend: Satan will now try typological thought.

He returns Jesus to the wilderness and disturbs his sleep with a horrible storm and "ugly dreams." The following morning he advises Jesus that the preceding night was a "sure fore-going sign" of the life that awaits him. But Jesus is unmoved, and unafraid. Typology, like rhetoric, without true understanding is futile—and worse than that, is diabolic.

Satan is enraged, but continues his assault on the personal level. He reveals now that he knows all the details and actions of Jesus' life from his birth to the present moment and that all of his own efforts have been aimed at understanding this man, whom he calls his adversary. Above all, he is baffled by the otherness, by what "Son of God" means, for it "bears no single sence." Therefore, to find out what Jesus is that is *more than man,* he will use yet "another method." But Satan's aim is, as ever, wide of the mark. As noted earlier in our mention of Milton's typological use of the Sphinx for comparison in the following episode, Jesus *is* "Man"; the course of action he has resolved to follow is manly, well within human possibility, and not miraculous.

The answer to the riddle is before Satan, but the dramatic irony of the situation is that he cannot perceive it.

Therefore, he places Jesus on the pinnacle of the temple and presents him with a dilemma, a "double-proposition" (as Milton calls the dilemma in the *Logic*): here stand—stand up and take a stand against my assaults—if you can, which will require the greatest skill; or fall down, and so put your calling to the test (and allow me to understand it) for it is written that God will send angels to lift you up. In debate, the dilemma is also known as the "horned syllogism," for, as Wilson explains, either horn on a bull is equally dangerous: grab one and the other will pinion you.[48] The dilemma is, here, the last resort of the Tempter in his final effort just to get Jesus to debate, to "stand." Indeed, as Satan, or any debater, would know, skill in debate usually lies not simply in posing a dilemma but in escaping from one; if Jesus tries, like a debater, to escape from this dilemma, then Satan has at last forced him to debate—and on his own grounds. Later, as St. Luke shows us (6:1–11), Jesus, in his confrontations with the scribes and Pharisees, reveals considerable debating skill in escaping dilemmas, but here in Milton's poem, Jesus confronts unmixed evil; to use the techniques of escaping the dilemma—such as disproving both propositions ("taking the bull by the horns"), offering a third alternative ("going between the horns"), or posing a counter dilemma—would amount to taking or rejecting a "stand," and would be no better than, literally, standing or falling. Either way, Satan would have him at last where he wants him, amidst the thrust and parry of rhetoric.

Jesus' answer is the simplest and most dramatic of all his answers: "also it is written / Tempt not the Lord thy God." The answer may at first seem a response to the second proposition, but in its ambiguity it dehorns the dilemma; it makes it, in effect, pointless by fully revealing Satan's misestimation of his "opponent." Jesus' response gives, without Satan's fully realizing it, the answer to the latter's principal question, What does it mean to be the Son of God? It means, simply, that Jesus has placed his destiny solely in the hands of the Father, whose will alone he will obey. To accede to the adversary's will as expressed in the form of the dilemma would be an act of disobedience. It is, after all, "obedience" that we have been told at the outset is the subject and resolution of this drama. So closely, then, has Jesus aligned his will with God's that tempting one is tempting the other. Jesus' statement employs ambiguity but it is *functional,* unlike the confused and slippery ambiguity that Satan employs and tries to control. Throughout the attempted debate, Satan has been thinking like a dualist, trying to distinguish Jesus' godhead from his manhood, appealing to him now as the Son of God, now as the Son of David. But in Jesus' simple answer, two arguments come together in a statement whose ostensible ambiguity—I will obey God, I am God—means to the reader what it cannot mean to Satan: this obedience is at once manly and divine. Satan sees only the awesome power within Jesus' act, and so he falls.

The following passage is rich in repetition: "Satan smitten with amazement fell . . . his fall . . . fell . . . Fell . . . fall . . . fell the Fiend . . . So Satan fell." Within that repetition are the two epic similes mentioned earlier, which we shall recur to shortly. Jesus is then lifted up, ministered to by the angels—and, at the close of the poem, "Home to his Mothers house private returned." The quietness of the conclusion, by starkly contrasting with the violence and miraculousness of the preceding lines, strikes the keynote of Christian victoriousness, in its order, even in its ordinariness, but above all in its peace, and it strikes too the humble keynote of Jesus' forthcoming ministry. Perhaps, once more, the end is in the beginning, and vice-versa. For when the narrator prayed to speak of "deeds / Above Heroic, though in secret done" (I,l.15), "in secret" suggests not only "in private" but also (from its Latin original, *in secreto*) "in solitude, in a solitary place, in retirement," and so, as Louis Martz states in *Poet of Exile,* "the prologue foresees the final line" (p. 249).

Like all complex poems, this one is about a great number of matters. I have not even explored the complexity of its announced subject, obedience, through all its ramifications. But I have tried to suggest that among the poem's many subjects, rhetoric is an important one. We see Satan emerge as a kind of humanist rhetorician: his knowledge of the function of Ciceronian *sapientia* is suggested in his tempting Jesus with wisdom that will enhance his persuasive ability; further, his use of *controversia* is evidenced not only by the passage we examined, where as a mode of thought it dictates form. But it is at least implicit in all his dualistic efforts to find grounds on which to contend with Jesus. Moreover, Satan's lack of true wisdom pervades all his strategies, including his bungled use of typology and his final, frantic use of the dilemma. But, throughout, his behavior as an adversary is probable and at the same time humanistic, for it is grounded on his persistent efforts to resolve uncertainty or otherness by means of debate.

Recall the Miltonic hierarchy suggested earlier: reason, especially "right reason," form, and words. Wisdom, it would seem, does not depend upon form or words—as shown, again, in *Paradise Regained,* when Jesus rejects, not classical learning exactly, but the confinement of wisdom to the forms and words, the terms, of classical learning. Wisdom is confirmable by typology rightly used, as Andrew, Simon, and Mary show, and as Satan's attempt negatively shows. It is doubtful, however, that this wisdom could have anything to do with *controversia:* not only because only Satan uses it, but because controversial thinking is pointless in the presence of truth. Rhetoric, the word that names Satan's efforts in the first three books near their climax in the fourth, is not the "way" to or even the "method" of truth. Throughout the poem, the narrator calls Satan our adversary, and Satan calls Jesus his adversary. But, as noted, the adversariness in the latter case is all one-sided. Jesus never calls Satan his adversary, for he is not. Jesus, as the poem shows, demonstrates his obedience by standing outside, or rather above, adversariness, contention, rhetoric. He embodies wisdom, shown as much in his action as in his words. What about the form—that is, the poem—in which he appears? To what extent may we say that the form, like Jesus, embodies truth— and is thus the poet's way of dealing with *our* adversary?

In the first essay of this chapter, the thesis was proposed that discourse *as an embodiment of truth* rather than *as an action* marks a significant difference between Milton and Donne. Pursuing that thesis led to the conclusion that the way, then, to understand Milton is through contemplation, the operation of the intellect in surveying the total configuration of a discourse. For even discursive form in Milton is conceptual, a sum greater than its parts. The second essay advanced the thesis that there is little sense of opposition in Milton. That thesis has been further reinforced by our examination of *Paradise Regained,* where attempted opposition is overcome by noncontroversial means. As poetic strategy, these means are apprehended best by contemplation, because they lie in the total organization of a piece, not in the linear working out of an action. In this regard, Milton's "On Time" is a pattern for our reading. In this regard, too, the subject of *form* is at the center of our study. Rhetorical form, we noted, is a *doing,* thought

in action that proceeds—in humanist writing—by prolepsis or reconciliation to shape the emotions of the audience or the reader. But
Milton's view of rhetoric is not the humanist view, for he denied rhetoric its unique mode of thought. Form, then, in Milton must mean
something else, something nonrhetorical. It is toward *that* question
that the final part of this essay is directed. It may be proper to speak of
Miltonic form as an *embodiment* only when compared with the *active*
state of rhetorical form, but in another context such a statement may
be improper, even idolatrous. Let us pursue the subject of Miltonic
form by reference to the form of *Paradise Regained,* itself one of Milton's strongest rejections of humanist rhetoric.

"*Paradise Regained,*" states Cleanth Brooks,

> is a debate, a debate, I take it, over ends and means. But it is
> anything but a dry exercise in dialectics. It is dramatic; intensely
> so, and I suppose that wherever one feels intense drama, he
> properly suspects that metaphor is present and alive, even if
> there are no showy images to be seen.[49]

On the contrary, if there is one thing that *Paradise Regained* is not, it is
debate. Brooks's incomplete view of the form and intention of the
work leads him into an examination of its metaphors and "images"
and drama. But the poem itself, as I have tried to show, challenges our
understanding of comparisons (especially the juxtapositioning by example or by type) and of drama, in this case dialogic structure.
Though Brooks is one of our leading formalists—and though, as I am
attempting now to argue, formalist criticism offers our best approach
to Milton—another kind of formalism, one that incorporates a nicer
view of genre, is needed.

Twenty-five years ago, Northrop Frye observed about this poem
that, structurally, it

> is not only a success but a technical experiment that is practi-
> cally *sui generis.* None of the ordinary literary categories apply
> to it; its poetic predecessors are nothing like it, and it has left no
> descendants. If it is a "brief epic," it has little resemblance to the
> epyllion; its closest affinities are with the debate and with the
> dialectical colloquy of Plato and Boethius, to which most of the
> Book of Job also belongs. But these forms usually either incor-
> porate one argument into another dialectically or build up two

different cases rhetorically; Milton's feat of constructing a double argument on the same words, each highly plausible and yet as different as light from darkness, is, so far as I know, unique in English literature.[50]

The "double argument" of which Frye speaks concerns the two vastly different levels on which Satan and Jesus discourse. The plausibility of Satan's discourse does not make the work a *controversia* from the poet's perspective (in Frye's words, "two different cases" are not built up "rhetorically"), for the difference between the two is hierarchical, the difference between dark and light. The generic uniqueness of the work offers a starting hypothesis at least. We must try to understand the ways in which it might be unique.

In one respect, *Paradise Regained* is not *sui generis*. Plato is a predecessor, as are Boethius and the Book of Job. So, too, for that matter, is Cicero's *De officiis*. Job and Cicero offer an extradialogic presence, a third person, like Milton's narrator. But pressing these similarities leads us into a kind of satanic error: we may see only the comparatives and so diminish the uniqueness of the form we seek to know. Jesus is not the Son of God as Satan understands the term, nor is he the Son of David exactly—he is redeemed Man, a thing beyond Satan's understanding and beyond comparison with anyone but himself. *Paradise Regained* is not a debate, a dialogue, a drama, or an epic.

Nor does generic typology offer us much assistance unless it is coupled, as Milton in *Paradise Regained* shows all typology must be coupled, with understanding. Typology assumes fulfillment in time: Israel of the Old Testament becomes the Israel of the New Testament; the descendant of David, as prophesied in the Old Testament, inherits a kingdom of which earthly kingdoms are themselves only types; Hercules' labors prefigure the trials of Jesus.[51] But we cannot say that *forms* are fulfilled in time. An argument can be made that *Paradise Lost* carries the epic tradition as far as it can for the present, a present extending from Milton's culture to and possibly through our own—or that *Samson Agonistes* fulfills the aspiration and promise of Milton's entire poetic career.[52] But these arguments, which are not exactly typological, yet leave us with *Paradise Regained,* and the stark realization that it is the formally most unique and isolated example of Milton's creativity. To pursue the search typologically, and try to argue that *Paradise Regained* fulfills earlier debating, dialogic, dramatic, or epic forms, is to secularize the process. The wisdom with which typology must be joined is a sense of what for Milton was God's truth. Fulfillment of form lies in the service of that truth. To treat form in another way, as suggested earlier, would be idolatrous: it is not a thing in itself nor does it of itself fulfill its promise in time. This *detachability* of understanding or reason from form—in that hierarchy of values suggested in the preceding essay—separates Milton from modern formalists. He does share with them a monism on another level—the union of form and content. But that union is shaped to serve "some stronger impulse," some higher purpose.

Let us divide the remainder of our discussion into these two points. First, we shall examine Milton's literary monism, second, the detachability of reason from Miltonic form.

In his *De Doctrina Christiana,* Milton equates the term *form* with man's soul and argues that body and soul are inseparable. Since the term also means the structuring of matter in a discourse (as in his *Logic,* where he speaks of the formal cause), could it not also mean that "organic" (a word Milton uses for the arts of composition, in "Of Education") discourse is like a man, whose matter and form are so indistinguishable that taking away one amounts to taking away the other? Milton's theological doctrine of the firm union of body and soul was an extreme position, placing him among the "mortalists," specifically among the *thnetopsychists,* who denied the soul's separate existence.[53] The doctrine was a kind of "materialism," too, that from our perspective makes Milton "more scientific and rational than many of the scientists" of his own day.[54] The soul, man's form, realizes no life, not even life after death, until man's body does. The soul does not go to heaven, or hell, upon man's death but insofar as it may nominally be distinguished from the body, sleeps with it until the "two" are resurrected, together, at the last day. The "two" are eternally indistinguishable. Could a similar indistinguishability be applied to discourse?

Initially we are faced with Milton's own interest in *genre:* for example, his remarks prefacing *Paradise Lost* on English heroic poetry or, prefacing *Samson Agonistes,* on tragedy. These, I believe, are only further expressions of his confidence in form, confidence to the point of desiring a purifying or reforming of literary form. We are faced, too, with Milton's discussion of "equipollence" in the *Logic,* where he seems to claim that various verbal forms may express the same content (and therefore belong to "rhetoric"), or with his statement in the 1642 *Apology,* where he claims, un–Ramistically, that various methods may be used to teach various men, as if form depended on audience considerations apart from content. In sum, we may be faced with trying to find consistency where there is none, or trying—unrhetorically—to read polemics as if they were philosophical statements. But, allowing for these possibilities as well as for the necessity of a special brand of formalism, the fusion of form and matter *must* be a possibility in Milton, in view of the great lengths to which he goes in *Doctrina* to insist on the total fusion of body and soul, or in the *Logic* to insist that form (here let theologians awake!) is the product of matter.

There is one example that Milton himself seems to lay out before us. His Sonnet 12—"On the Detraction Which Followed Upon My Writing Certain Treatises"—begins,

> A book was writt of late call'd *Tetrachordon;*
> And wov'n close, both matter, form, and stile,
> The subject new. . . .

The "subject" was divorce, which was both new and shocking, and which Milton had justified in two earlier treatises and then documented in the *Tetrachordon.* My interest lies in what the poem says about the latter work. Its "form and stile" were "wov'n close" with its "matter." What Milton means is observable in the *Tetrachordon,* whose matter and form (and style) are announced on the title page:

Expositions upon The foure chief places in Scripture, which treat of Mariage, or nullities in Mariage

On
{
Gen.1.27.28 compar'd and explain'd by
Gen. 2.18.23.24
Deut. 24.1.2

Matth.5.31.32 with Matth.19 from the 3ᵈ v.
to the 11ᵗʰ
1 Cor. 7 from the 10ᵗʰ to the 16ᵗʰ
}

Wherein the Doctrine and Discipline of Divorce, as was lately publish'd, is confirm'd by explanation of Scripture, by testimony of ancient Fathers, of civill lawes in the Primitive Church, of famousest Reformed Divines, And lastly, by an intended Act of Parliament and Church of England in the last yeare of Edward the sixth.

The style of the pamphlet itself is "plain" and, like its form, fits the matter. The dichotomizing of Old and New Testament passages may echo Ramist "method," as does the plainness of the pamphlet's style, which is most appropriate for "teaching." His purpose, Milton says, is "to commun with reason in men." The form embraces that intention in its plain marshalling of evidence. The progression of the discussion follows the one announced on the title page: Milton discusses the Scriptures, testimony, and the "intended Act" in turn, with no introduction, no conclusion, no digressions. We see the operations of reason, following a method based on no more than its announced subject. The point is that here, in this pamphlet and the sonnet, we see that the meaning of *form* is indeed transferrable from theology to discourse—and its perfection in one is to be as carefully apprised as in the other. The point confirms the formalist's position: to know matter, know the form, for the "content" is the form and vice versa—a position subtly unlike the rhetorician's, for whom form is strategic and intentional.

What matter is closely woven with the form of *Paradise Regained?* An immediate and obvious answer is the one the poet seems to offer in the opening lines, the action of Jesus' obedience. The answer is satisfactory, as far as it goes, questions of "graven images" and Puritan iconoclasm notwithstanding. But the answer does not seem to go far enough in allowing for the presence of another voice throughout the work. The matter of this poem, I shall argue, is the action of another good man, the poet as prophet, whose "stronger impulse" is both to teach and to show contemplation by means of mythological thinking.

I do not mean, exactly, the construction of myth or plot, except in the Aristotelian sense of *mythos*. *Mythos* thinking, or mythological thinking, means giving thought a form or configuration by "imitative" rather than rhetorical means. The chief theorist of modern formalism, R. S. Crane, took the concept of *mythos* from the *Poetics*—the "plot" that Aristotle calls "the soul of tragedy"—and developed it into a general structuring principle for the sake of which every detail in a literary work functions, a principle of coherence.[55] In his superb study of the Bible, Northrop Frye has emphasized another dimension of the concept:

> History makes particular statements, and is therefore subject to
> external criteria of truth and falsehood; poetry makes no partic-

ular statements and is not so subject. Poetry expresses the universal in the event, the aspect of the event that makes it an example of the kind of thing that is always happening. In our language, the universal in the history is what is conveyed by the *mythos,* the shape of the historical narrative. A myth is designed not to describe a specific situation but to contain it in a way that does not restrict its significance to that one situation. Its truth is inside its structure, not outside.[56]

Both Crane and Frye have carefully distinguished *mythos,* or plot or myth, from what is usually meant by *myth,* especially in its archetypical force.[57] Frye's further distinction, that *mythos* actually *contains* its truth is, I believe, useful in considering Milton and the service to which he put his creative energy in the production of form. But my own work diverges from Frye's, as I believe a formalist view of Milton must diverge from the formalism both Frye and Crane represent. Milton's literary work is not its own end, does not contain truth quite in the way in which he believed the Bible contains truth. The didacticism, which is dismissed from consideration in modern formalism, and the extrinsic truth to which the work itself must correspond, also dismissed as heretical in modern formalism, are qualities no study of Milton should overlook.

"The two testaments," Frye writes, "form a double mirror, each representing the other but neither the world outside."[58] In one respect, the mirror comparison is applicable to "L'Allegro" and "Il Penseroso": each looks inward toward the other. The pairs do not look outward—except, as the Bible does, toward some anticipated future ("Even so, come, Lord Jesus," are the final words of the Bible, followed by a benediction), a futurity expressed conditionally at the ends of "L'Allegro" and "Il Penseroso." The mirror comparison by looking inward controverts the outward-looking faces of Janus, which we have used as our figure for controversial thinking. As we noted at the outset of the present study, with Milton we reach a brilliant understanding of humanism and a practice that controverts its chief mode of thought. The mirror comparison, as a figure for Milton's own work, or for a figure of a self-contained truth, denies the faces of Janus. Formalism denies rhetoric.

But a further distinction must be made, particularly when we consider pairing *Paradise Lost* with *Paradise Regained* as "mirrors." Mil-

273

ton's forms do not contain truth, though they are in the service of it. The Bible—the "inviolable Scriptures," as he calls them in *Doctrina*— is the only form that contains the truth. Consider Jesus' argument in Book IV of *Paradise Regained,* upon refusing the temptation to become learned in classical literature:

> Or if I would delight my private hours
> With Music or with Poem, where so soon
> As in our native Language can I find
> That solace? All our Law and Story strew'd
> With Hymns, our Psalms with artful terms inscrib'd,   335
> Our Hebrew Songs and Harps in *Babylon,*
> That pleas'd so well our Victors ear, declare
> That rather *Greece* from us these Arts deriv'd;
> Ill imitated, while they loudest sing
> The vices of thir Deities, and thir own   340
> In Fable, Hymn, or Song, so personating
> Thir Gods ridiculous, and themselves past shame.
> Remove their swelling Epithetes thick laid
> As varnish on a Harlots cheek, the rest,
> Thin sown with aught of profit or delight,   345
> Will far be found unworthy to compare
> With *Sion*'s songs, to all true tasts excelling,
> Where God is prais'd aright, and Godlike men,
> The Holiest of Holies, and his Saints;
> Such are from God inspir'd, not such from thee;   350
> Unless where moral vertue is express'd
> By light of Nature not in all quite lost.

How does one, then, write lyric poetry, or epic, or tragedy, or dialogue, drawing on classical models? To praise God "aright" one cannot rewrite the Bible. But one can use the classical forms in imitation of the biblical process of mythological thought, the very process that makes the Bible mirrorlike and self-contained. To follow the process means giving thought the configuration of myth built on typology. The character of the "one" doing this is, of course, crucial, for that one must be beyond personalism and individual voice, too. He should be not merely a poet but a prophet, whose "light" excels nature's.

    The uniqueness of *Paradise Regained* lies in its demonstration of this process as not simply the action of a good man, but the good action of a man. As such, it is indeed Milton's *De officiis,* but it is also an *imitatio christi.* Consider two passages from *Apology for Smectym-nuus:*[59]

> doubtless that indeed according to art is most eloquent, which returns and approaches neerest to nature from whence it came; and they express nature best, who in their lives least wander from her safe leading, which may be call'd regenerate reason. So that how he should be truly eloquent who is not withall a good man, I see not. . . .

> For me, Readers, although I cannot say that I am utterly un-train'd in those rules which best Rhetoricians have giv'n, or un-acquainted with those examples which the prime authors of elo-quence have written in any learned tongue, yet true eloquence I find to be none, but the serious and hearty love of truth: And that whose mind so ever is fully possest with a fervent desire to know good things, and with the dearest charity to infuse the knowledge of them into others, when such a man would speak, his words . . . like so many nimble and airy servitors trip about him at command, and in well order'd files, as he would wish, fall aptly into their own places.

Christ embodies the truth of the Bible; his character is what the Law and the Prophets come to. In Milton's terms, he is "regenerate reason" and the source of all eloquence. It is his "voice" we hear in the poet's. The doctrine ultimately places Milton closer to Augustine than to Cicero—and at a considerable remove from Donne.

Throughout this study, I have tried to argue that humanism di-minishes from Donne to Milton, an attenuation that is reflected in differences in their views of rhetoric and poetry as well as of truth and Christ. Christ for Milton is the embodiment of stable and enduring truth, and both Christ and truth are consubstantial with us. They are a manliness, within human possibility. The optimistic concept seems humanist, almost extremely so, except that it diminishes oppositions, our estrangement from each other, and the necessity to compromise and settle for provisional truths. Without these qualities there can be no rhetoric, and poetry will aim at different ends. Christ embodies truth *in Paradise Regained.* But it is the poet who embodies the truth *of* that poem—and not simply because form was born "naturally" of his

275

character, but also because in treating this subject he endeavors to pattern his actions on Jesus'—the very point of his invocation to the Holy Spirit.

The self-reference the poet makes at the opening of the poem guides our perceptions of him throughout, through all his inventive amplifications of the barest details of the biblical episode. At the climax of the action, at Satan's fall, the poet's use of typology in two masterful and complex similes offers a contrast with the comparisons employed by Satan in the latter's quest for knowledge.

> . . . Satan smitten with amazement fell
> As when Earths Son *Antaeus* (to compare
> Small things with greatest) in *Irassa* strove
> With *Joves Alcides,* and oft foil'd still rose,
> Receiving from his mother Earth new strength,   565
> Fresh from his fall, and fiercer grapple joyn'd,
> Throttl'd at length in th' Air, expir'd and fell;
>
> . . .
>
> And as that *Theban* Monster that propos'd
> Her riddle, and him, who solv'd it not, devour'd;
> That once found out and solv'd, for grief and spight
> Cast her self headlong from th' *Ismenian* steep,   575
> So strook with dread and anguish fell the Fiend,

If the poet's similes resemble the thinking of Andrew and Simon and Mary, they also work as a vindication of the classical learning ostensibly rejected by Jesus earlier in the book. For here the poet shows us the prophetic service to which classical learning can be put. He shows us this, too, in the creation of form, which in this poem is partly dialogic, partly epic, but wholly expressive of the action of one man. He refers to his own action at the first of the poem as "song"; throughout the poem he performs as narrator, at times as a chorus, or commenting narrator; but at the moment of Satan's fall, he reveals, in the shaping of these two similes, the true nature of his action, as inspired and learned prophecy, the regenerate reason that has given this myth its configuration. In a sense, character—a public, open, and prophetic ethos—is the matter closely woven with this form; but it is, itself, beyond form and words, it is truth, as Christ is truth, the *ratio* in *oratio*. It "brings forward reasons" and thus is beyond "testimony," too. This character is revealed in action, but not rhetorical action, for it is inher-

ent in modes of thought that are independent of controversy—matter
that this form "disposes" not so much to inform as to exemplify.

In the preceding essay, we found that Miltonic form, greater vision, and the poet's moral character are all consubstantial. But our
study of *Paradise Regained* has suggested that this consubstantiality
points toward an action that outlives the poem and remains a possibility, a pattern of "right reason." And like all patterns, it is impersonal.
Satan praises Jesus' skill in informing discourse with his character.
Satan's praise is, of course, woefully short-sighted. As we can see, he
lacks a knowledge that Jesus and the spiritually consubstantial poet
share: a sense of man's place in history, in time. Prophetic action and a
sense of man's place in history—that is, mythological thinking and a
wisdom based on typology—are the *intended* constituents, I believe,
of the character that truly informs *Paradise Regained.* From the outset,
the poet-prophet is meant to be more a mythic than a biographic reality: only an "I who e're while the happy Garden sung."

But often we read the poem, and treasure it, as I have done, because
that other (to us) who was John Milton wrote it—without our being,
for that reason, any more or less diabolic. The poem seems to me a
curious thwarting of controversy, and worth examining for that
alone. As such, it also reveals at least one significant context, the ongoing disintegration of humanism, here transformed into a manly
dignity that is independent of rhetoric. Moreover, just as the poem
may be a key to Milton's thinking about rhetoric, it may shed light on
all his work. Here I should like to conclude by recurring to the Janiform hermeneutic of my study. I have suggested some of the ways in
which *Paradise Regained* may clarify the work that preceded it. Let me
now suggest, briefly, some of the ways in which it may shed light on
the single work, perhaps Milton's greatest, that came after it.

Milton's final work, *Samson Agonistes,* would seem the most
overtly controversial of all. In this play no narrative voice guides us,
nor is the chorus exactly Milton's surrogate. The play seems structured by a series of debates leading up to Samson's decision to enter
the Temple of Dagon. Mary Ann Radzinowicz has argued that it is
through debate that Samson achieves both an integration of his personality and the truth that allows him to act: the high point of the
drama is Samson's debate with Dalila, for here the hero defines himself clearly and truly.[60] But if we ask the question posed by my
study—to what extent is all this debating an actual *source* of truth?—

277

the answer leads us toward another view of the play's structure and, consequently, of its intention.

The debate with Dalila, more than those with any other character, involves what I have called controversial thinking. Dalila and Samson clash directly: each recognizes the other's opposition and acts upon it by trying to appropriate or preempt the other's grounds for reasoning. And the debate ends with Dalila hastening toward Fame—which, she says, "if not double-fac't is double mouth'd." As for Samson, this single debate seems to produce less a change than a stage of growth, like the one marked by the *anagnorisis* in *Paradise Regained*. Samson begins to gain a renewed sense of himself, his ethos. It is the intuition subsequently possible to this newly integrated personality—the "rouzing motions" (l. 1382) Samson experiences at the structural climax of the play—that becomes the actual source of his truth.

In contemplating the structure, as we must do in thinking mythologically, we find these "rouzing motions" give Samson confidence: now he is able calmly to choose. We find, too, that these "motions" contrast with earlier intuitions, the impulses that led him to marry, confused as those earlier impulses were with an appetency that numbed his conscience. So viewed, the design of the play (its structure, form, and intention) can seem not at all dissimilar from that of *Paradise Regained:* to embody a vision beyond debate in the search for truth. *Controversia* produces not the climax but, in both works, a turning that prompts recognition and brings to full consciousness— in us certainly, and possibly in the hero as well—the true and truly submissive grounds for noble action. "In Samson's case," Camille Slights argues, "grace works through reason, as it usually does in Milton's view."[61] But sorting out one from the other, to prevent their too easy confusion, seems to occupy the artist in his final works. In this scheme, *controversia* is further set apart from the motions of that greater reason in us that is (as he tells us in *Areopagitica*) but choosing, or that is (as he tells us even more clearly in *Doctrina*) our conscience.

To claim that Milton never enjoins us to debate, or never reveals skepticism, or never uses irony and ambiguity—these claims are unwarrantable. Milton never denies our humanity. On the contrary, he strove continually for a certain very human possibility, but it was a singular possibility, something that he thought exceeded the limits of humanism's intellectual method and that was unattempted yet in prose or rhyme.

Conclusion:
Controversia *as* Inventio

James Shirley, in praising his fellow playwrights, offered an elegant and succinct observation on the art of reading in the seventeenth century. The observation appears in Shirley's preface to the first collection of Beaumont and Fletcher, in 1647—five years after the Puritans had closed the theaters, when plays had to be read if they were to be experienced at all. Shirley says,

> You may find passions raised to that excellent pitch and by such insinuating degrees that you shall not choose but consent, and go along with them, finding yourself at last grown insensibly the very same person you read, and then stand admiring the subtle tracks of your engagement.[1]

Consider the values expressed. The reader does not merely lose himself, he is charmed; he does not merely act another role, he becomes someone else—at least temporarily. Then another kind of experience supervenes. He becomes the critic, analyzing the strategies whereby the artist had induced his self-forgetful involvement and transformed him.

True, the *function* of Shirley's praise may be merely advertising, as was customary in such a preface, but that in no way diminishes the values expressed: the praise would not be praise if the implied hermeneutical action were impossible or out of fashion. Indeed, I know of no other statement that places in such short compass other observations on readerly attitudes scattered throughout seventeenth-century criticism,[2] and at least implicit in the trailing remnants of humanist education. Reading was still a rhetorical enterprise: readers were not only to identify with the speaker of a discourse but to admire the ways in which identification was achieved.

279

Figure 4. The beast of many heads. Holbein's illustra-
tion of Folly's line "hujusmodi nugis commovetur
ingens ac potens illa belua, populus" (by such toys [fic-
tions rather than philosophy or oratory] is that great
and powerful beast, the people, controlled). But note
that Holbein actually turns Folly's "beast" metaphor
into the conventional Horatian one for the multitude:
"belua multorum capitum." Viewed at this point in our
study, the emblem might recall the beginning of our
survey and the humanist attempts to deal with the
beast (within as well as without), emblematized in this
study by the Janiform (including *prudentia* and *controversia*). Our study ends at a period when (and with a
poet for whom) controversializing an audience's vision
seemed no longer a motive of discourse. Holbein's
emblem, thus, recapitulates.

Twenty years ago, when I first read the Shirley statement, I was intrigued by it as a possible perspective on the work of the two poets who move me most (by "me" I mean a teacher of composition, student of rhetoric, and lover of poetry who is necessarily most *self*-conscious at the points where those three interests converge). But I could see that to illuminate the writings of Donne and Milton, the statement needed further refinement. When you become, at first "insensibly," the "same person you read," that person is not quite the same in Donne as it is in Milton. There is a certain estrangement in the person we become when we read Donne, a restlessness regarding and alienation from the object of desire. There is simply more placidity, more "calm of mind," in the Milton we become. And there are two different kinds of "tracks": Donne's are like signposts on a path, Milton's like segments of a total configuration. That is, if we do in fact contemplate the literary strategies, as Shirley suggests, then it seems to me two kinds of contemplation inhere in the nature of our responses: when we contemplate a Donne piece, we are first charmed by its argumentative diversity, then amazed by its linear progression; when we contemplate a Milton piece, we are charmed first by its grandeur, then amazed by its difficult principle of coherence.

At any rate, these matters became the center of my initial study of these two poets, which has changed and, I hope, grown through the years, and the results of which are now before you. Rather than recapitulate the results of this study or suggest further avenues of research (two purposes of the final chapter of the usual scholarly book), perhaps I may reemphasize the single most important finding of my work by describing my own *inventio*. In my "prewriting," I had spent a considerable amount of time processing arguments without the aid of the most distinctive feature of rhetorical *inventio*. The story of how I found that feature is not suspenseful or, I admit, terribly interesting. But if it makes that feature, *controversia*, clear, then the story will have served its purpose.

As a reformed formalist, I determined to consider the "tracks" of our "engagement" first—to encounter my old bête noire and have done with it. For these "tracks" are actually elements of what we, rhetoricians and formalists alike, think of as literary form. So I studied first form, then (that other matter in Shirley's hermeneutic) the poet's personhood, or ethos, which in turn led me into the study of Renaissance humanism. All the while I was insensible to the real center of *inventio*—and it was, curiously enough, conspicuously present in the nature of the search I had undertaken, the *controversy* between the two poets in my imagination and between the two approaches—rhetoric and formalism—in my own critical temperament. But first I had to take my search through the three subjects I've mentioned: form, ethos, and humanism.

Form means a great number of things. I tend to distribute its meanings between rhetorical and formalist critical approaches. To the rhetorician, form is always verbal, and it extends from such local effects as figures of speech (metaphor, simile), to syntax, to schemes of sound (alliteration, rhyme), to schemes of reasoning (dilemma, syllogism, enthymeme), to the total organization of a discourse (*dispositio* in the general sense). To the formalist, form may be all these things, but in its most complex meaning *form* is less verbal than conceptual: it means *mythos*, plot, imitation of an action, the very "soul" of a discourse. A pseudo-Aristotelian comparison that is useful for understanding complex form in the formalist sense is this: if the eye were an animal, vision would be its soul; when discourse is "organic," then coherent action is *its* soul, its "formal cause," the product of its matter. All of these ramifications of meaning, whether rhetorical or formalist, pervade seventeenth-century critical thought. Criticism, which was at first largely rhetorical, began a subtle, almost imperceptible shift toward formalism in the sixteenth century when humanists rediscovered the *Poetics*.[3] (As always, in almost every instance, humanism itself provided the means of its own undoing.)

Then, too, all these ramifications are further complicated—and, I believe, clarified—by their connections with theological thought: can man's soul (form) and body (matter) be distinguished? Donne thought they could, and believed that their separation in ecstasy was a kind of death. Milton thought they could not and, significantly, said nothing about ecstasy. If Donne's notion of soul was ephemeral, Milton's was solid. But what about the poets' corresponding notions of form in discourse? Here I began to run into a confusing inconsistency, a reversal. Donne's notions of discursive form were more like the *body* than the soul; both—form and body—may be ephemeral, but the form of a discourse is useful for the "inherence" of ideas and arguments. The notions seem Platonic. However, ideas and arguments in Donne are not themselves permanent; they are, rather, temporary and provisional, as he makes plain in his often misread anti-idealist poems. Nonetheless, they remain as a kind of spiritual force, clothed in words necessary to its being, less than ideal but all we have. Without words—that is, verbal form—this spiritual force, ideas and arguments, would be, literally and figuratively, immaterial. Miltonic form is, by contrast, more like the "soul"—whether one thinks of the Aristotelian "soul" of a discourse or "soul" as in Milton's own theology. It suffuses its material, its body, and is inseparable from it. If this form-matter is all we have, in Milton's view it may be more than we have yet understood or realized.

In sum, I found two kinds of form. For Donne form is verbal; it is the body of thought, the air ideas and arguments must wear, like angels, else they could nothing do. For Milton form is conceptual, a principle of coherence—like a thought, or an action, or a special kind of character—that unites all elements of a discourse.

An option I faced at this point was the advisability of distributing these two notions of form into "outer" (Donne) and "inner" (Milton). But I rejected the option. The distinction would have only led me back into searching for similarities and differences with scholastic philosophy, and something more was needed, something that did not operate analogously but that directly fit the unique characteristics of the discourse I wished to study. I gradually began to see—though I had not as yet caught the more important distinction, which was virtually staring me in the face—that a strong difference between the two was related to the dualism and monism mentioned earlier. Donne, seeing dualisms but wishing to escape from them, is far more skeptical than Milton, whether the subject is discursive form or humane learning. Donne employs a variety of discursive forms, each designed for the needs of the particular argument, and seems to remain confident not that discursive form contains truth—what is truth?—but that discursive form communicates emotions, and that emotions are significant. Emotions are more present, more available, than intellectual certainty, and if not equally important, they will have to do. Milton, by contrast, is far less skeptical of truth's availability and far less diffident about form. Truth and discursive form are closer together. Thus, Milton gives considerable thought to such (outer and inner) forms as genre: English heroic verse, tragedy, elegy. Truth cannot simply inhabit form, but becomes form, if traditional forms are re-formed. That is, form for Donne is material shape, matter organized to serve a certain intention. For Mil-

ton form is material and shape and intent; all are one—at least, in a re-
formed, organic discourse. Form is separable in Donne; it is not in Milton. What was staring me in the face is that Donne is operating within
rhetoric, Milton within formalism. But I could not see that as yet—
partly because my past experience had conditioned me to quite the opposite view: the New Critics had made a formalist of Donne, and Eliot
had made a (failed) rhetor of Milton. But my search was leading me
inexorably into a reversal of that view, ever more swiftly so as I moved
on to consider the personhood of the two poets—at least, the "implied" authors.[4]

Ethos is probably the single most complex feature of any writing.
The difference between "real" and "implied" authors is like the difference between fact and fiction. Sanity requires that a distinction be
made. But every reader learns to be somewhat diffident about that
distinction: fiction can be more real than fact in that it can be deeper,
more significant, even more instructive. The Renaissance, moreover,
was a great age of self-fashioning, in which men consciously turned
their lives into a kind of willed fiction. Having an effective personhood was a prime requisite for moving and advancing at the court,
in the business world, in society. The revival of rhetoric in humanist
education suited that need perfectly: character in rhetoric is a thing
fashioned of words, all questions about "sincerity" to the contrary
notwithstanding. Ethos in rhetoric means a kind of proof added to
arguments, a proof that exceeds the logical and the emotional and
that inheres in the audience's perception of the speaker's moral character. Rhetorical exercises—particularly, *declamatio* and *imitatio*—
were designed to instruct youth in how to create a character, a persona,
on paper: rewrite Cicero's oration denouncing Cataline, imitate Erasmus advising a young nobleman to marry, argue *pro,* then *contra,* on
whether learning is preferable to ignorance.[5] These are parts of what
Stephen Greenblatt has called rhetoric's efforts to "theatricalize" education in self-fashioning.[6] Theater, too, of course, must have been a
factor. So, too, must have been the practice of writing "characters,"
along with a deepening interest in humoral psychology (the "hu-
mors" as a scientific cause of personality).

The Renaissance was obsessed with personality, and rhetoric was
at the true center of that obsession, as the single discipline that
showed how that obsession can be turned to advantage—these are
matters easy to prove. But the matters do not make the study of

Donne and Milton any simpler—particularly when one is, as I was, overlooking rhetoric as a possible *difference* between the two poets.

Donne's entire career seems like an effort—a failed one—to find himself. He tries on thin mask after thin mask in his poems. The masks are even thinner and subtler in his sermons, but remain varied. He divided his whole life into two masks, Jack Donne and Dr. Donne. Poor man, we say, all that restless energy with no center; or we accuse him of being a show-off. Milton, on the other hand, seemed to know from the outset who he was. He was to be a poet, with a great calling, and he spent years—and a considerable portion of his father's money—in training for that role. But the difference between the two poets, so far as their self-fashionings are concerned, can be put in another way. The difference is not that between self-doubt on the one hand and self-assurance on the other. It is, rather, more like that between skepticism and certainty. Donne's various roles may have been efforts to encompass *truth,* which was for him so complicated and so difficult to apprehend by human means that every possible avenue had to be followed—and, even then, access was uncertain and truth could be only glimpsed, if at all, partially and temporarily. Milton's single role was a stable avenue to truth—a traditional role, reformed and made serviceable for the apprehension of truth that had been present to our ancestors (though faintly to some). Ethos, then, the role that sums up each poet's career, might be expressed in the following way: for Donne it was a "manner,"[7] or a stance toward experience; for Milton it was itself an exemplary "form," a coherent character of integrity showing us how to live with truth.

The progression of my studies was becoming increasingly abstract. I had moved away from the texts of individual pieces to a survey of each poet's career. The next consideration moved me onto an even more abstract plane, but it was a level on which I found a turning point.

In light of what I had already seen, Donne appeared more the humanist than Milton. Yet how *could* this be? Donne, with his apparent delight in casuistry or other kinds of dialectical *controversia,* seemed to be late scholastic. Milton, with his breadth of classical learning and Ciceronian ideas about active virtue, had always seemed to be a humanist, if a late one. To begin with, Donne shows a greater degree of, and delight in, self-fashioning than does Milton. But, to put an end on it, that variety of self-fashioning in Donne is much more in accord with the northern humanism Erasmus fathered: in that humanism, there is little impulse to reform or change things, but much to increase diversity and human possibility within preexistent boundaries. Skepticism seems, necessarily, a motive of that effort, to live with a gap between what we see and what we can imagine, to live with uncertainty, to live an "unreformed" life because we are diffident about forms but to live that life as "abundantly," as Christ put it, as possible.

As I began a study of humanism, I discovered the inevitable: not all scholars agree as to what it was, though most acknowledge that whatever it was, Erasmus brought it of age in northern Europe. Increasingly, however, I did discover a large agreement on one score, that rhetoric is identifiable with humanism. Within that agreement, there seemed to be two notions about what rhetoric was; some think of it largely as philology and the study of Ciceronian style, others as a substitute philosophy. Nonetheless, one correlative argument seemed possible: wherever there was humanism, there was rhetoric; but the rhetoric that is truly associated with humanism is a rhetoric with its system of thought intact. Once rhetoric was deprived of that system of thought, humanism itself and rhetoric too changed, became something else. Some might say both died.

From classical times, rhetoric had always been a derivative subject, its various parts resembling, where they did not actually depend upon, knowledge in other disciplines—politics, ethics, architecture, gymnastics, grammar. But in no single one of its parts was its derivative nature more profoundly shown than in *inventio. Inventio's* purpose was to teach analysis and genesis, how to analyze an argument and fashion one to support or oppose it. But *controversia,* how to argue *pro* and *contra,* was also taught in logic, as were most of the forms of argument—the various syllogisms, for example. Logic also taught all the fallacies and many of the "places"—cause and effect, quantity and quality, distribution and definition—for generating arguments. The logic of which I speak is *dialectic.* Aristotle thought of rhetoric as the counterpart of dialectic, and was willing to allow for some overlapping: rhetoric was designed to teach argumentation as practiced in law courts and in deliberative assemblies; dialectic was designed to teach argumentation among experts. The real difference between the two, therefore, lay in the audiences of each. Aristotle's *logic,* by contrast, was concerned with valid, not necessarily verbal, forms of thought. But by the Renaissance, dialectic was thought of as logic—

and the older distinctions between verbal and conceptual were fuzzed over. Since this "logic" seemed to teach the more important modes of argumentation, the stage was set for an educational reformer, Peter Ramus, to insist that it is inefficient ("unwise" and "unjust" would be his terms) to teach the same subject in two disciplines. Since "logic" was the more noble discipline (it, after all, was traditionally concerned with truth), it alone, not rhetoric, should teach *inventio.* Rhetoric should teach only style and delivery.

The move may have started unscrambling the verbal from the conceptual, but it blurred one other distinction, that between truth and probability. Argumentation, in effect, became a means of asserting truth, not of winning a victory, a kind of science, not a mode of advocacy. Argumentative thinking was no longer controversial. Insofar as *controversia* was still present, it was only a kind of form in a larger science of assertion, one in which no distinction between audiences seemed important: thought was thought, whether practiced before a law court or in a treatise. Dialectical *controversia* was swallowed up. Rhetorical *controversia,* always the weaker sister, disappeared, and humanism declined.

The importance of having a system of thought *in* the discipline of rhetoric—and not simply *a* system of thought, but a uniquely rhetorical system of thought—cannot be overestimated. Consider again what rhetorical *controversia* means: it is the search for probability by imagining the possible cases of opponents in a dispute. This probability is itself conditioned by the nature of the audience before whom it is to be demonstrated: the judge and jury, or by extension, one's coy mistress, one's readers—not experts exactly but not necessarily interested parties either. So long as controversial thinking was part of the discipline of rhetoric, it was the central means whereby discourse was created. Once controversial thinking moved out of rhetoric, and to all intents and purposes vanished, once rhetoric became merely something added on to thinking done elsewhere, the very nature of composing discourse was altered radically.

With that historical observation, I had a basis for arguing that Donne, not Milton, was the rhetorician and therefore the humanist. Reading may have remained largely a rhetorical enterprise (as had most criticism) in the seventeenth century, but *poesis,* epistemology, writer's intention—the very principles of composition—were themselves shifting. All three parts of my search revealed the same set of circumstances, made concrete in the presence (or absence) of rhetorical *controversia*.

There are, of course, a vast number of differences between Donne and Milton. And Donne is not the perfect example of the controversial thinker: in much of his discourse the line between self-absorption and self-fashioning gets blurred, as does the line that divides the construction of a probability from the construction of a stance toward a given truth. Milton must have used some controversial thinking, but what there is seems muted, with little sense of opposition, as in "L'Allegro" and "Il Penseroso"—the result of an institutionalized *controversia*, perhaps, attenuated by its removal from the radical humanist attempt to subvert traditional philosophy and by its submergence in the merely academic. Rhetorical *controversia* thrives on skepticism—and on self-fashioning as well. It leads not simply to self-awareness (now I shall argue the *contra* case, now the *pro*) but also to self-parody: Donne in his sermons and poems sounds very like the Coscus he lampoons in an early satire; Milton puts his own arguments into Satan's speeches. But Donne hardly stands toward Coscus as Milton stands toward Satan. A key difference between Donne and Milton, something I wished to explore and understand, seemed ultimately a difference in degree of skepticism, in their use of oppositions and otherness, and even in their self-fashionings—in short, in their use of rhetorical *controversia* as an important mode of thought.

My case was finished, but how to begin presenting the results? Perhaps the beginning *is* in the end. But shall "end" mean a conclusion or a purpose—a formal closure that the beginning anticipates or an effect that the beginning aims at an audience? R. S. Crane has observed that we are not ready to write until we have some sense of the total conceptual form of the work—the plot, or *mythos*.[8] That, it seemed to me, is Milton's way, not Donne's. "It is characteristic of Milton's practice," A. S. P. Woodhouse has observed, "that having selected his subject, he should think of its treatment in terms of genre, that is, should reach out for a traditional form, which he would then feel free to adapt in whatever way subject and theme required."[9] By contrast, Donne's way is to use *controversia* not simply as a mode of analysis *(inventio)* but also as a means of organization *(dispositio)*— with one proviso: the organization must also produce an emotional effect on the audience, even if it does so only because the speaker has preserved the integrity of his perception of an urgent, all but inescapable otherness. Juxtapositions, thus, work differently for Donne than they do for Milton. For Donne they enhance variety, if only through perspectives by incongruity, and highlight whatever opposition is in the otherness. For Milton, juxtapositions are elements of a larger configuration, parts of a whole wherein otherness is dissolved. My plot would therefore be configurational in its progression from Donne to Milton—but the elements of that configuration would, I hope, retain something of their controversial nature.

Notes

PREFACE

1. It will become obvious that I use rhetoric and formalism as foils, as inherently contradictory of one another. Upon first conceiving this book, I was tempted to pose *structuralism* as the foil of rhetoric, partly to make my argument current (and fashionable) and no less accurate: humanist rhetoric is always anti-structuralist, or anti- any system of objectively specifying meaning, without thereby becoming deconstructionist (which is just as specifying). But formalism is the larger and more ancient critical concept, akin on the one hand to Aristotelianism and Platonism and on the other to structuralism and deconstructionism (to Saussurism, that is, and Derridaism). Formalism, in sum, displays its genealogy. The same is true of humanist rhetoric—which springs from quite different ancestors and has been kept alive by a restlessness with systems and philosophies, with almost every type of discursive thought but literature itself. In my characterizations of formalism, I have thought of such seminal works as René Wellek and Austin Warren, *Theory of Literature,* see esp. the first ed. (New York, 1942), and R. S. Crane, *The Languages of Criticism and the Structure of Poetry* (Toronto, 1953). Cleanth Brooks offers a succinct statement of the formalist position in "The Formalist Critic," *Kenyon Review,* 13 (1951):72–81. In listing other important modern formalists one would have to include T. S. Eliot, I. A. Richards, Robert Penn Warren, Bernard Weinberg, and Northrop Frye—only to discover that the list is impressive by its magnitude and distinction. Formalism remains the most influential critical approach of our time. An effort—in my view, a successful one—to meet the structuralists and other formalists on their own grounds and demonstrate the better efficacy of rhetoric in the work of interpreting texts is William J. Kennedy, *Rhetorical Norms in Renaissance Literature* (New Haven, 1978).

2. Kenneth Burke, *Counter-Statement,* 1931; rev. ed., 1953; rev. paperback ed. (Berkeley, 1968).

3. For the dramatistic pentad, see Kenneth Burke, *A Grammar of Motives* (Berkeley, 1969; first pub. 1945). For the clearest view of Burke's psychologism, see the concept of symbolic action in his *Attitudes Toward History* (Berkeley, 1984; first pub. 1937). Subjectivism, relativism, historicism, and psychologism are all generally (with no mention of Burke) discussed by E. D. Hirsch, Jr., who sees them as causes of hermeneutical skepticism, in *Validity in Interpretation* (New Haven, 1967).

4. See Milton's Seventh Prolusion, especially in the Hughes translation: Merritt Y. Hughes, trans., *John Milton: Complete Poems and Major Prose* (New York, 1957), p. 625. The translation seems to me closer to the spirit of Milton's argument than either Phyllis B. Tillyard's (in *Complete Prose Works of John Milton,* ed. Douglas Bush et al., I [New Haven, 1953], p. 297) or Donald Lemen Clark's (in *The Works of John Milton,* ed. Frank Allen Patterson et al., XII [New York, 1936], p. 267). "Oh, to vex me, contraryes meet in one"—so Donne begins Holy Sonnet XIX. That contraries can meet in one is a vivid expression of a rhetorical principle, however vexatious, which pervades Donne's mode of argumentation; it offers, too, a view of epistemology that changed little in his lifetime—e.g., for the obverse, see Donne's youthful "Satyre III," ll. 98–99. The seminal study of Donne's *use* of "contraries" is in Rosalie L. Colie, *Paradoxia Epidemica: The Renaissance Tradition of Paradox* (Princeton, 1966).

CHAPTER ONE

1. On Donne's sermonizing and techniques of delivery, see George R. Potter and Evelyn M. Simpson, *The Sermons of John Donne* (Berkeley, 1953–1961), esp. I, pp. 46–47; and R. C. Bald, *John Donne: A Life* (Oxford, 1970), pp. 406–407, 480–481. See, too, some of the funeral elegies written on Donne's death and printed in the first volume of his collected poetry (1633); and, of course, Walton's *Life of Donne* (first pub. 1640).

2. Potter and Simpson, *Sermons,* I, p. 99.

3. *The Works of Thomas De Quincey* (Boston, 1876), IV, p. 300.

4. De Quincey, *Works,* IV, p. 326.

5. The edition of the sermon employed in this study is in Potter and Simpson, *Sermons,* VII, pp. 257–278.

6. The third was his "Elegie on Prince Henry," printed in Sylvester's *Lachrymae Lachrymarum* (1613).

7. In Clement Barksdal, *Memorials of Worthy Persons: Two Decads* (1661) and eighty years later in John Wilford, *Memorial and Characters.*

8. The most complete discussion of this entire situation remains Astrid Friis's *Alderman Cockayne's Project and the Cloth Trade* (Oxford, 1927). For brief discussions, see *The Cambridge History of Europe,* ed. E. E. Rich and C. H.

Wilson (London, 1967), IV, p. 417, and Jan De Vries, *Economy of Europe in an Age of Crisis* (London, 1976), pp. 88–89.

9. Arnold Stein in "Handling Death: John Donne in Public Meditation," *ELH,* 48 (1981): 496–515, has eloquently treated a central strategy in this sermon and in one on Lady Danvers (discussed in Chapter Three): "No sins are mentioned, but potential flaws are brought up in passing, and careful discriminations answer and dissipate questions that are never quite formed" (p. 503). Moreover, Stein finds two voices in the reasoning of these sermons: an affirming voice and one "which exposes to doubt the positions of those who may imagine themselves to be certain but have not considered the grounds of uncertainty" (p. 514). Stein focuses on the "patterning" that the affirming voice asserts; I on both voices and the ways in which they ambiguate (later I shall call it controversialize) the reasoning.

10. The theme is an old one, though given one of its most famous voices a half century before Donne's sermon in Montaigne's *Apology for Raymond Sebond.*

11. The text I cite appears in *Complete Prose,* ed. Douglas Bush et al. (New Haven, 1959), II, pp. 485–570.

12. Ernest Sirluck provides an illuminating rhetorical reading of *Areopagitica* in his introduction to the volume in which our text is printed (New Haven, 1959); see esp. pp. 137–183. Sirluck distinguishes several possible audiences addressed by Milton: Erastians, Independents, Presbyterians, Westminster Assembly, the "nation." Milton's tactics, he argues, "may be defined fairly clearly. They consist of what may be called a negative and a positive maneuver. The negative maneuver is to define the opposition as restrictively as the most favorable reading of the situation will permit; then to isolate it; and finally to discredit it. The positive maneuver is to construct a coalition from all available elements, each appealed to on grounds of both principle and interest; and then to depict this coalition as being the nation" (p. 178). My own analysis, by concentrating on arrangement, focuses on a different though not incompatible intention.

13. See Don M. Wolfe, *Milton in the Puritan Revolution* (New York, 1963; first pub. 1941), p. 123.

14. Wolfe, *Milton,* pp. 121–122.

15. J. N. D. Kelly, *Jerome: His Life, Writings, and Controversies* (New York, 1975), p. 42.

16. Wolfe, *Milton,* p. 130. See Christopher Hill, *Milton and the English Revolution* (London, 1979), chaps. 8 and 10.

17. Wolfe, *Milton,* 135.

18. George Kennedy, *The Art of Persuasion in Greece* (Princeton, 1963), pp. 174–203. Kennedy's later work, *Classical Rhetoric and its Christian and Secular Tradition from Ancient to Modern Times* (Chapel Hill, 1980), makes a point about Isocrates closer to the one I seek to make about Milton—that in deliv-

ering his speeches in writing, Isocrates spurred the development of "secondary" (nonoral) rhetoric, one of whose purposes may be to "demonstrate the author's education, eloquence, or skill, and it often makes him more acceptable to his audience" (p. 5; see also p. 35).

19. See *The Complete Poetry of John Donne,* ed. John T. Shawcross (Garden City, 1967), p. 488.

20. Throughout this book I quote all Donne poems from Herbert J. C. Grierson, ed. *The Poems of John Donne,* (London, 1912), I. I have modernized the long *s*.

21. He actually uses "formes forme" and "soules soule" in "To Mr. R. W.," l. 32. To cite another and seldom noted example of metonymic complexity: in "The Canonization," Donne's speaker defiantly proclaims that he and his mistress will build in sonnets "pretty roomes," *room* being a literal translation of *stanza*.

22. *The Elements of Geometrie of the most auncient Philosopher EVCLIDE of Megara,* trans. H. Billingsley with a preface by M. I. Dee (London, 1570). For the place of this work in English intellectual history, see Charles Thomas-Stanford, *Early Editions of Euclid's Elements* (London, 1926), pp. 13–16, and J. L. Heilbron's introductory essay to *John Dee on Astronomy,* ed. and trans. Wayne Shumaker (Berkeley, 1978), esp. pp. 22–34.

23. See *Elements of Geometrie,* fol. 13, or this passage:

> A meruaylous newtralitie haue these thinges *Mathematicall*: and also a straunge participatiō between thinges supernaturall, immortall, intellectuall, simple and indiusible: and thynges naturall, mortall, sensible, compounded and diuisible. Probabilitie and sensible profe, may well serue in thinges naturall: and is commendable: In Mathematicall reasonings, a probable Argument, is nothyng regarded: nor yet the testimony of sense, any whit credited: But onely a perfect demonstration, of truthes certaine, necessary, and inuincible: vniuersall and necessaryly concluded: is allowed as sufficient for an Argument exactly and purely Mathematical.   [sig. ★★★★i]

24. The poem "does not attack poetic artifice or the rational intellect; it exposes the futility of relying upon them," argues Donald M. Friedman in "Memory and the Art of Salvation in Donne's Good Friday Poem," *English Literary Renaissance,* 3 (1973):442. Like Friedman's, my own reading centers on rhetorical instruments and produces an interpretation quite different from that of Barbara K. Lewalski, who in placing the poem within the tradition of Protestant occasional meditation finds Donne penitentially baring his back at the poem's end; *Protestant Poetics and the Seventeenth-Century Religious Lyric* (Princeton, 1979), p. 279.

25. Antony F. Bellette, "'Little Worlds Made Cunningly': Significant Form in Donne's Holy Sonnets and *'Goodfriday, 1613'*," *Studies in Philology*, 72 (1975):322–347.

26. A reemphasis, Martz might say, of the meditative structure that informs this poem. See Louis L. Martz, *The Poetry of Meditation*, rev. ed. (New Haven, 1962), pp. 54–56.

27. John Carey, *John Donne: Life, Mind, and Art* (New York, 1981), pp. 121– 122. In his review of this book, William Empson makes a point that confirms my earlier one: that the 1633 edition of Donne's poem remains the best guide to his rhetorical intentions. Carey's outrageous interpretations, Empson argues, are partly a result of his using a bad (Gardner's) edition of the poems; *New York Review of Books* (Dec. 3, 1981):42–50.

28. Text is from the London, 1645 edition. I have modernized the long *s*. Throughout the remainder of this book I quote all Milton poems from John L. Shawcross, ed. *The Complete Poetry of John Milton* (Garden City, 1963; rev. ed., 1971).

29. Rosemond Tuve, *Images and Themes in Five Poems by Milton* (Cambridge, Mass., 1957), p. 41.

30. This argument has been well presented by Raymond B. Waddington, "Milton among the Carolines," in C. A. Patrides and Waddington, eds., *The Age of Milton: Backgrounds to Seventeenth Century Literature* (Manchester, England, 1980), p. 341.

31. By different means I have arrived at an observation similar to one well put by Josephine Miles. Miles's observation will help me reveal the direction of my own argument: "Donne accepts and plays upon design as bondage enforcing the limitations of flesh; it is not emergent in Milton's way"; *Poetry and Change* (Berkeley, 1974), p. 13. With Donne and Milton we are involved in two totally different *uses* of form and, as I shall argue, two totally different *conceptions* of form.

32. Erwin Panofsky, *Meaning in the Visual Arts* (Garden City, 1957), pp. 146– 168. In his search for "tricephalous" traditions, Panofsky misses the relation of the Janiform Prudence, as represented even in Ripa's book, to Titian's *Allegory of Prudence*. He turns, therefore, to Ripa's *buono consiglio*, a representation of an old man holding a three-headed monster. Yet Ripa's *prudenza* is clearly a Janiform in the Renaissance mode, one head old, one young—as Ripa describes her, "Donna, con due faccie simile à Giano . . . L'eccellenza di questa virtu, e tanto importante, che per essa si rammentano le cose passate, si ordinano le presenti, & si preuedono le future" (a woman with two faces, similar to Janus . . . The excellence of this virtue, and its importance, is that through it past things are remembered, the present ordered, and the future seen) (Cesare Ripa, *Iconologia* [Rome, 1603], p. 416). Ripa's description bears an interesting similar-

ity to the inscription over the heads in Titian's painting: "ex praeteritio / praesens prvdenter agit /ni fvtvrā actionē detvrpet" (from the [experience of the] past, the present acts prudently, lest it spoil future action). The conflation of Janus with Prudence seems a Renaissance commonplace. For example, George Wither, in contemplating an engraving showing Janus as two heads of *equal* age, nonetheless found them offering "chiefly" a lesson about time—a lesson whose parts are, significantly, more like the *memoria, intelligentia, providentia* of Ciceronian *prudentia* than Wither's other descriptions of prudence (*A Collection of Emblemes, Ancient and Moderne* [London, 1635], p. 138; see also pp. 74, 142, 151). Edgar Wind discusses some of the relations between two-headed and three-headed Prudence in *Pagan Mysteries in the Renaissance* (New York, 1968), pp. 200–201, 231, 260. Raymond B. Waddington has a brief and insightful discussion of the Prudence tradition and its presence in Shakespeare's sonnets in "Shakespeare's Sonnet 15 and the Art of Memory," in Thomas O. Sloan and Raymond B. Waddington, eds., *The Rhetoric of Renaissance Poetry* (Berkeley, 1974), Chapter 5. Cicero's *prudentia* is in *De inventione,* II. lii. 160.

33. *Controversia,* as we shall see in Chapter Two, is the term Cicero uses for a process that is at the heart of rhetorical *inventio.* For students of rhetoric, *controversia* was the name of ancient Roman school exercises in which the mature boys were required to practice advocacy by preparing and delivering a speech at a mock trial. The *controversia* was the very apex of rhetorical education. It was a far more advanced and complicated (and career-oriented) exercise than the *suasoria,* the mock deliberative address, usually on historical events (e.g., deliver a speech advising or dissuading Agamemnon from sacrificing Iphigenia). What I call "controversial thinking" is true of both exercises; both required giving imaginary thought *pro* and *contra.* Because advocacy is the apex, the end, and outcome of rhetorical training, and because judicial oratory receives the greatest share of theorizing in Roman and humanist texts, *controversia* is a useful and shorthand way of characterizing essential rhetorical thought in its most practical and complex form. For *controversia* and *suasoria,* see Stanley F. Bonner, *Education in Ancient Rome* (Berkeley, 1977), chaps. 19, 20, and 21.

34. Though Milton calls our attention to the god—and his two controversial faces—he surely knew that opening the Temple of Janus signifies imperiling peace. In ancient Rome, the doors of the temple were opened only in time of war (see, e.g., Augustine's *City of God,* III.ix) and in the sixteenth century the temple with closed doors became a symbol of the *Pax Augusta* (see John Rupert Martin, *The Decorations for the Pompa Introitus Ferdinandi* [London, 1972; Part XVI of *Corpus Rubenianum Ludwig Burchard*], pp. 162–175). Milton's call to open the doors is not a call for war, exactly, though it might have been perceived by Parliament as disruptive of domestic tranquillity. Milton's call is for *intellectual* combat (by means of *controversia,* one might suppose, though I shall question

this later), that we may consciously join the discussion of "matters in agitation." For assistance in researching the Janus emblems, I am indebted to Mr. Keith Thoreen, of the University of California (Berkeley) Library.

CHAPTER TWO

1. Johan Huizinga, *Erasmus and the Age of Reformation* (New York, 1957; first pub. 1924), p. 39. All references to Huizinga in the text are to this edition.

2. Desiderius Erasmus, *The Praise of Folly*, trans. and with an intro. and commentary by Clarence H. Miller (New Haven, 1979), p. xi. I have been considerably aided in my thinking about Erasmus by Arthur F. Kinney's "Rhetoric as Poetic: Humanist Fiction in the Renaissance," *ELH*, 43 (1976):413–443. Professor Kinney states, "Without forgetting an inherent fluidity in language, [the humanists] nevertheless set about to use fiction as a means of exploring values and issues attendant upon humanism generally, as well as the problem of the relationship of rhetoric and fiction to truth; recognizing contradictory truths within a single tale, they couched their narratives in paradox and irony" (p. 419). Kinney analyzes the humanist fictions of Erasmus, More, and Gascoigne. A further treatment of More is present in Kinney's excellent *Rhetoric and Poetic in Thomas More's* Utopia, vol. 5 of *Humana Civilitas*, UCLA Center for Medieval and Renaissance Studies (Malibu, 1979).

3. I have drawn on two editions in my study of the work: the Latin edition published at Basel in 1515 and decorated with marginal drawings by Hans Holbein the Younger, as reproduced in facsimile with an introduction by Heinrich Alfred Schmid (Basel, 1931); and the English translation mentioned earlier. In the following discussion, page numbers in the text refer to the latter work.

4. *The Praise of Folly* by Desiderius Erasmus, trans. and with an essay and commentary by Hoyt Hopewell Hudson (Princeton, 1941); see pp. 131–142.

5. Like the one provided in the 1931 reprint of the *Moria*, II, pp. 18–19:

Exordium

  through "Genus, educatiõem, & comites, audistes" (I, Cᵛ)

Part I (definition; devinitas moriae)

  The nature of this divinity and the universal benefits conferred
  by Folly.

  Survey of all those made blessed by this dear delusion.

Part II (exposition)

  Examples from life and from literature.

  General folly of mankind.

  Folly of the learned.

  Examples from literature.

Brief peroration

6. See *Collected Works of Erasmus,* ed. Craig R. Thompson (Toronto, 1978), XXIV, p. 695.

7. See the frequent references, pp. 18, 19, 28, 45, 46, 54, 57, 89, 120.

8. See, e.g., pp. 17, 58, 71, 76, 78, 115, 117, 132, 138.

9. *Erasmus-Luther Discourse on Free Will,* trans. and ed. Ernst F. Winter (New York, 1961), p. 6.

10. John William Aldridge, *The Hermeneutic of Erasmus,* Basel Studies of Theology, No. 2 (Zürich, 1966), p. 62.

11. Erasmus apparently would have chosen *oratio* instead, except for its feminine gender. The storm of controversy that his translation provoked as well as the implications of the translation for understanding Erasmus are brilliantly reviewed by Marjorie O'Rourke Boyle, *Erasmus on Language and Method in Theology* (Toronto, 1977).

12. *The Antibarbarians: Antibarbarorum Liber,* trans. and annotated by Margaret Mann Phillips, in *Collected Works,* ed. Thompson, XXIII, p. 59. Page references in the text refer to this edition.

13. Phillips, *Antibarbarians,* pp. 27–28. The Latin text I have used is the one in Albert Hyma, *The Youth of Erasmus* (Ann Arbor, 1930).

14. "Antirhetoricians" in Phillips's translation (p. 41); *antirhetoribus* in the Latin; see Hyma, *Youth,* p. 270.

15. Aldridge, *Hermeneutic,* p. 16.

16. Margaret Mann Phillips, *The "Adages" of Erasmus: A Study with Translations* (Cambridge, England, 1964), p. 86.

17. *Erasmus-Luther Discourse,* ed. Winter, p. 92.

18. *Copia: Foundations of the Abundant Style,* trans. and annotated by Betty I. Knott, in *Collected Works,* ed. Thompson, XXIV, p. 302.

19. I am referring to Erasmus's "Plan of True Theology," *Ratio verae theologiae* (first pub. Basel, 1518), in which he says, "Adeo cum nostro Christo nihil sit simplicius, tamen arcano quodam consilio Proteum quemdam representat varietate vitae atque doctrinae" (p. 214). That is, Erasmus insists that "our Christ" is at once simple (nothing is simpler) and Protean in his curious embodiment of diversity in life and knowledge. Boyle, in citing this passage, goes on to state that Erasmus thought the text of Scripture "the perfect reflection of Christ's protean method" (*Erasmus on Language and Method in Theology,* p. 122; see also p. 242, n. 341).

20. A. R. Heiserman uses the Erasmian phrase to analyze More's irony in "Satire in the *Utopia,*" *PMLA,* 78 (1963):164.

21. Elizabeth McCutcheon, "Denying the Contrary: More's Use of Litotes in the *Utopia,*" *Moreana,* 31–32 (1971):107–121. McCutcheon notes—a point that substantiates her case as well as my own—that the Elizabethan critic Puttenham calls *litotes* "the Moderator." A further point, one that substantiates her case, mine, and Erasmus's idea of language, is that the Elizabethan rhetorician

Hoskins calls *litotes* "the most usual [figure] in the English tongue"; *Directions for Speech and Style* (c. 1599), ed. Hoyt H. Hudson (Princeton, 1935), p. 35.

22. William J. Bouwsma, "The Two Faces of Humanism: Stoicism and Augustinianism in Renaissance Thought," in *Itinerarium Italicum*, ed. Heiko A. Oberman with Thomas A. Brady, Jr. (Leiden, 1975), pp. 2–60.

23. Jakob Burckhardt's monumental work was the two-volume *Civilization of the Renaissance in Italy* (1860). The quoted phrase appears in his *History of Greek Culture*, trans. Palmer Hilty (New York, 1958), p. 300.

24. Ernst Cassirer, *The Individual and the Cosmos in Renaissance Philosophy*, trans. Mario Domandi (New York, 1963).

25. See Paul Oskar Kristeller, *Renaissance Thought*, I, *The Classic, Scholastic, and Humanist Strains* (New York, 1961). Kristeller has reasserted his position in a recent essay: "I never meant to say and I still do not believe that Renaissance humanism, let alone Renaissance thought and learning in general, is reducible to rhetoric alone. Rhetoric was only one of the five *studia humanitatis* cultivated by humanists"; "Rhetoric in Medieval and Renaissance Culture," *Renaissance Eloquence*, ed. James J. Murphy (Berkeley, 1983), p. 2.

26. Notably, Eugenio Garin, *Italian Humanism: Philosophy and the Civic Life in the Renaissance*, trans. Peter Munz (New York, 1965); Hans Baron, *The Crisis of the Early Italian Renaissance: Civic Humanism and Republican Liberty in an Age of Classicism and Tyranny*, 2nd ed. (Princeton, 1966), and *From Petrarch to Leonardo Bruni, Studies in Humanistic and Political Literature* (Chicago, 1968); Jerrold E. Seigel, *Rhetoric and Philosophy in Renaissance Humanism: Ciceronian Elements in Early Quattrocento Thought and their Historical Setting* (Princeton, 1968); Nancy S. Struever, *The Language of History in the Renaissance: Rhetoric and Historical Consciousness in Florentine Humanism* (Princeton, 1970); and the Bouwsma works listed below. A most important article on the subject is Hanna H. Gray's "Renaissance Humanism: The Pursuit of Eloquence," *Journal of the History of Ideas*, 24 (1963):497–514. Another truly monumental study, like Burckhardt's, is Charles Trinkaus, *In Our Image and Likeness: Humanity and Divinity in Italian Humanist Thought*, 2 vols. (Chicago, 1970).

27. In addition to the essay mentioned in note 22 above and in addition to his *Venice and the Defense of Republican Liberty: Renaissance Values in the Age of the Counter Reformation* (Berkeley, 1968), see in particular Bouwsma's "Lawyers and Early Modern Culture," *American Historical Review*, 78 (1973):303–327; *The Culture of Renaissance Humanism*, AHA Pamphlets (Washington, D.C., 1973; first pub. 1959); and "Changing Assumptions in Later Renaissance Culture," *Viator*, 7 (1976):421–440.

28. See, for example, Bouwsma on lawyers, cited in note 27; F. W. Maitland, *English Law and the Renaissance* (Cambridge, England, 1901); Guido Kisch, *Humanismus und Jurisprudenz: Der Kampf zwischen mos italicus und mos gallicus an der Universität Basel* (Basel, 1955); M. P. Gilmore, *Humanists and Jurists* (Cam-

bridge, Mass., 1963); Linton C. Stevens, "The Contribution of French Jurists to the Humanism of the Renaissance," *Studies in the Renaissance,* I (1954):92–105; R. J. Schoeck, "The Elizabethan Society of Antiquaries and Men of Law," *Notes & Queries,* n. s. I (1954):417–421, and "Early Anglo-Saxon Studies and Legal Scholarship," *Studies in the Renaissance,* 5 (1958):102–110.

29. R. J. Schoeck, "Sir Thomas More, Humanist and Lawyer," *University of Toronto Quarterly,* 26 (1964):1–14.

30. Cf. Elyot's *The Boke named the Governour* (1531): the study of law and the study of rhetoric are fused in the education of the man of wisdom; see esp. chap. XIV.

31. Bouwsma, *The Culture of Renaissance Humanism,* p. 14.

32. "Of Experience," in John Florio, trans., *The Essayes . . . of . . . Montaigne* (London, 1603), pp. 634, 637, 639, and 661. Italics are Florio's. I have modernized the spelling and punctuation.

33. Hannah Arendt, *Between Past and Future: Six Exercises in Political Thought* (New York, 1961), p. 225. The passage Arendt is commenting upon appears in the *Tusculan Disputations,* I. xvii. 39–40.

34. Richard Lanham, *The Motives of Eloquence: Literary Rhetoric in the Renaissance* (New Haven, 1976).

35. Trinkhaus, *In Our Image,* II, p. 663.

36. Mahood has described Marlowe's plays as a record of the disintegration of humanism: pride in man's potentialities is swiftly reversed to despair at showing that man, in the midst of that disintegration, once cut off from spirituality wallows in empty ambition (M. M. Mahood, *Poetry and Humanism* [New Haven, 1950]). A vivid exploration of Jacobean disparagement of rhetoric as a means of knowledge is provided by Mary Ann Bushman in her unpublished dissertation, "The Case Against Rhetoric: Problems of Judgment in Jacobean Tragedy" (Berkeley, 1982): *Hamlet,* for example, as Bushman shows, is set in a world of uncertainty, but the rhetorical method of arriving at some provisional certainty is a disastrous failure.

37. George Norlin, trans., *Isocrates* (Cambridge, Mass., 1963; first pub. 1929), II, pp. 337–339. Italics mine. See also George Kennedy, *The Art of Persuasion in Greece* (Princeton, 1963), pp. 178–179.

38. What Isocrates means by this distinction is implied in what follows as well as in a passage later, pp. 381–383; it is similar to a distinction Cicero will later make between different meanings of *utilitas,* expediency.

39. Peter Brown, *Augustine of Hippo* (Berkeley, 1967), p. 389.

40. John F. Callahan, *Saint Augustine and the Greek Philosophers* (Villanova, 1967), p. 94.

41. "Augustine himself was, in a certain sense, converted from rhetoric to Christianity." James J. Murphy, *Rhetoric in the Middle Ages* (Berkeley, 1974), p. 51.

42. The point is well explained by Brown, *Augustine,* p. 324.

43. R. S. Pine-Coffin's (New York, 1980; first pub. 1961). The later passage I cite from *Conf.* XI. xxviii. 38 is also Pine-Coffin's translation. Other citations in my text are my own translations, from the Latin edition by Joseph Capello (Taurini, 1948).

44. Burke's brilliant analysis of *The Confessions* pays particular attention to "turnings"—all the *vert* terms in Latin and the English words we have derived from them (conversion, controversy, perversion, adversary): Kenneth Burke, *The Rhetoric of Religion: Studies in Logology* (Berkeley, 1970; first pub. 1960), see esp. pp. 69, 81, 113.

45. See Elizabeth L. Eisenstein, *The Printing Press as an Agent of Change: Communications and Cultural Transformations in Early Modern Europe* (New York, 1979). Her earlier articles are also useful in this regard: "Some Conjectures about the Impact of Printing on Western Society and Thought: A Preliminary Report," *Journal of Modern History* (March–Dec. 1968):1–56; and "The Advent of Printing and the Problem of the Renaissance," *Past and Present,* 45 (1969):19–89.

46. Gerald A. Press, "The Subject and Structure of Augustine's *De Doctrina Christiana,*" *Augustinian Studies,* 11 (1980):99–124. Among the many interpreters who believe that Augustine does not discuss rhetoric until the fourth book is Stanley E. Fish, *Self-Consuming Artifacts: The Experience of Seventeenth-Century Literature* (Berkeley, 1972), chap. I. In Fish's argument, Augustine places rhetoric in a dialectical process, which demotes rhetoric and elevates dialectic. In my interpretation, Augustine shatters the integrity of rhetoric not by counterposing it with dialectic but by blinding it with the Light, with an unmistakable, *a priori* truth.

47. The quote is from Press, "Subject and Structure," p. 119. The examination is on p. 116. A more expanded outline is offered by Press in his "The Content and Argument of Augustine's *De Doctrina Christiana,*" *Augustiniana,* 31 (1981):165–182. In yet another essay, Press has thoroughly explored Augustine's use of the word *doctrina:* in that concept, Press argues, Augustine "retains the name and form" of a pagan ideal but Christianizes it, transforms it without discarding it, and so achieves a kind of "rhetorical coup" with his audience; see "*Doctrina* in Augustine's *De doctrina christiana,*" *Philosophy and Rhetoric* (forthcoming). Again, Augustine's habit of mind sets a pattern for later humanists.

48. This point is well explained by J. A. Mazzeo, "St. Augustine's Rhetoric of Silence: Truth vs. Eloquence and Things vs. Signs," *Renaissance and Seventeenth Century Studies* (New York, 1964), pp. 1–24.

49. The Latin text that I have used for this study is Volume XXXII of the *Corpus Christianorum, Series Latina* (Turnhout, 1962). I have also employed Sister Therese Sullivan's work on Book IV (Washington, D.C., 1930), and the

translations by J. F. Shaw, 3rd ed. (Edinburgh, 1892), and D. W. Robertson, Jr. (Indianapolis, 1958).

50. Augustine, argues W. R. Johnson, created on paper "a figure whose being is totally defined by the passion, the energies, and the logic of his will"; "Isocrates Flowering: The Rhetoric of Augustine," *Philosophy and Rhetoric,* 9 (1976):225. Johnson's description of the Augustinian ethos is incisive, and very useful, though I have some disagreements with other parts of his argument—in particular, that Isocratean rhetoric came to full bloom in the work of Augustine and that Augustine transmitted humanist rhetoric to later ages through *De doctrina.* My argument is that Isocrateanism and humanism were thwarted by Augustinian conversion.

51. Benedetto Morandi; quoted in Trinkaus, *In Our Image,* I, p. 287.

52. *De finibus,* II.xiv.45.

53. *Tusculan disputations,* II.xviii.43.

54. Richard McKeon, "Introduction to the Philosophy of Cicero," *Brutus, On the Nature of the Gods, On Divination, On Duty* (Chicago, 1950), p. 30.

55. Michael J. Buckley, S.J., *Motion and Motion's God: Thematic Variations in Aristotle, Cicero, Newton, and Hegel* (Princeton, 1971), p. 93.

56. Charles B. Schmitt, *Cicero Scepticus: A Study of the Influence of the Academica in the Renaissance* (The Hague, 1972).

57. To dismantle that rhetoric-centered philosophy, as Ramus and Talon did in the sixteenth century, even in the name of creating a fusion of wisdom and eloquence, is to completely controvert the nature and purpose of Ciceronian skepticism. Schmitt notes that neither Talon nor Ramus "ever rejected the rhetorical teachings of the great Roman statesman" (p. 98), a comment that seems to reflect an open acceptance of their *statements* about Ciceronianism. Schmitt is perceptive in his argument that Ramus and Talon found in the *Academica* a weapon to use in combat with their enemy, scholastic Aristotelianism. But Schmitt has not looked carefully enough at what Ramus and Talon actually *did* to that skepticism. Though Ramus vigorously attacked the stoics, as Schmitt notes (*Cicero Scepticus,* p. 80), for their failure to join eloquence with wisdom, Ramism itself depends finally on a stoical doctrine, the assent of the mind to naked, "natural" truth. Though Talon acknowledges in his commentary on the *Academica* that controversial thinking and the probable are keys to Ciceronian philosophy, the system of rhetoric and logic that Talon helped foster actually worked to the disintegration of Ciceronianism, the severance of mind from body, thinking from speaking, wisdom from eloquence, truth itself from mere words. The nature of Ramism is discussed in the next section.

58. Richard H. Popkin, *The History of Scepticism from Erasmus to Spinoza* (Berkeley, 1979). Philip P. Hallie, *The Scar of Montaigne: An Essay in Personal Philosophy* (Middletown, 1966). See also *Scepticism, Man, and God: Selections*

from the Major Writings of Sextus Empiricus, ed. Philip P. Hallie and trans. Sanford G. Etheridge (Middletown, 1964).

59. Too, the work contains the earliest statement of Cicero's status theory, how to determine the status of each question by classifying it so that the controversial matters rise to the surface: when the controversy is about a fact, the issue is conjectural; about a meaning, definitional; about the nature of an act, one of kind or quality; about the legal process, translative.

60. Or the techniques of praise and blame in epideictic, or demonstrative, oratory.

61. [Cicero] *Ad C. Herennium,* trans. Harry Caplan (Cambridge, Mass., 1954).

62. All five of the rhetorical tasks are discussed in the *ad Herennium:* Books I and II are on *inventio,* especially in connection with judicial oratory; III is on the other two kinds of oratory, and on *dispositio, pronuntiatio,* and *memoria;* IV is solely concerned with *elocutio,* style—a distribution that itself indicates which tasks are, if not most important for the orator, at least most susceptible to systematization by the *auctor.* Book IV meticulously and often tediously exploits the subject of style, and thereby sets the mode as well as the tone for a host of stylistic manuals that followed through the centuries, some endeavoring, especially in the sixteenth century, to impart into English usage the names and manners of Latin tropes and figures (of these, by the way, almost one hundred are listed by the *auctor,* a modest figure that had more than tripled by the sixteenth century).

63. *De inventione,* I.vii.9 (see passage I have quoted earlier) and *ad Herennium,* I.ii.3.

64. To keep our eyes drifting forward, to the English Renaissance, let us note that the hyperbole that Antonius creates here, in order to prove the impracticality of Crassus's ideas, was adopted literally by Sir Thomas Elyot in 1531: "fewe men in consultations wulde (in myne opinion) compare with our lawyars, by this meanes beinge brought to be perfect orators, as in whome shulde than be founden the sharpe wittes of logitians, the graue sentences of philosophers, the elegancie of poets, the memorie of ciuilians, the voice and gesture of them that can pronounce commedies, which is all that Tulli, in the person of the most eloquent man Marcus Antonius, coulde require to be in an oratour" (*The Boke named the Govemour* [London, 1907], p. 66).

65. Bonner echoes and confirms Cicero's reason: "In the course of time Roman listeners did become suspicious of orators who were thought to be using some kind of Greek craft *(artificium)* to persuade them, and this was why M. Antonius deliberately disclaimed any knowledge of Greek studies, and by so doing, made himself more acceptable as a speaker." Stanley F. Bonner, *Education in Ancient Rome* (Berkeley, 1977), p. 66.

66. E. W. Sutton and H. Rackham, trans. (Cambridge, Mass., 1979; first pub. 1942), Book II, pp. 273–275.

67. On this doctrine of arrangement, Antonius too seems to agree with the *auctor* of *ad Herennium;* see II.lxxvii.313–314.

68. See E. K. Rand, *Cicero in the Courtroom of St. Thomas Aquinas* (Milwaukee, 1946), p. 55.

69. According to Perry Miller, thought in the seventeenth century involved "a lessening sense of the sinfulness of man" and "a decreasing respect for formal logic. . . . One might say that these two changes were one and the same." *The New England Mind* (Cambridge, Mass., 1953), p. 428.

70. All Renaissance studies owe much to historians I cite in this essay. My own work, though derivative from them, necessarily disagrees with a few—Howell and Kennedy, in particular—disagreements that may further clarify my thesis. Wilbur Samuel Howell has given us the most detailed history of rhetorical theory in the English Renaissance: *Logic and Rhetoric in England, 1500–1700* (Princeton, 1956). But for Howell, the rhetorical study of poetry amounts to a conflation of two elements—rhetoric and poetry—that are best kept separate; indeed, much of his work seems devoted to the strenuous and ultimately impossible (for the Renaissance) effort of keeping those two arts away from each other. In that respect, a revealing study is Howell's "Peter Ramus, Thomas Sheridan, and Kenneth Burke: Three Mavericks in the History of Rhetoric," in William E. Tanner and J. Dean Bishop, eds. *Rhetoric and Change* (Mesquite, Texas, 1982), pp. 57–77. Rhetoric and rhetoricians have never stayed put, and one of the more detailed examinations of that unavoidably maverick quality is Brian Vickers, *Classical Rhetoric in English Poetry* (London, 1970). Howell's efforts to write the history of sixteenth-century English rhetorical theory were complemented by Ong's essay, "Tudor Writings on Rhetoric, Poetic, and Literary Theory," in his *Rhetoric, Romance, and Technology* (Ithaca, N.Y., 1971). Ong, without explicitly trying to, made a connection that Howell consciously avoided—but only for the sixteenth century.

George A. Kennedy's useful books on the history of classical rhetoric, *The Art of Persuasion in Greece* (Princeton, 1963) and *The Art of Rhetoric in the Roman World* (Princeton, 1972), accomplished the bibliographical research that is fundamental, like Howell's, to all subsequent studies. However, like Howell—like any of us—he has certain idiosyncracies. He slights sophistical rhetoric; he does not give due attention to the uniqueness of rhetorical modes of thought; and he relegates to a "secondary" position in rhetorical history all theory that veers toward the literary—characteristics prominent in his latest work, *Classical Rhetoric and Its Christian and Secular Tradition from Ancient to Modern Times* (Chapel Hill, 1980). So far as the sophists are concerned, I shall make no effort to resurrect them, nor is doing so necessary to my thesis. I would propose, however, that we stop looking at them through the eyes of Plato and Aristotle. The sophists originated controversial thinking. They also made rhetoric the center of their cultural ideal—*paedeia* in Greek, *hu-*

manitas in Latin. Few sophist theories have survived, unfortunately; see Mario Untersteiner, *The Sophists,* trans. Kathleen Freeman (Oxford, 1954) and Rosamond Kent Sprague, ed., *The Older Sophists* (Columbia, S.C., 1972)—the latter is a complete translation of Diels's *Die Fragmente der Vorsokratiker.* An important step toward looking at the sophists anew is taken by G. B. Kerferd in his *The Sophistic Movement* (Cambridge, England, 1981). However, the extent to which Cicero and humanism perpetuated sophistic ideals remains an open question, worthy of exploration. William J. Bouwsma has offered a polemical view of the sophists as the true founders of humanist education in "Socrates and the Confusion of the Humanities," *The American Future and the Humane Tradition,* ed. Robert E. Hiedemann (Tarrytown, N.Y., 1982), pp. 11–22. The gravity of my remaining two complaints about Kennedy's work is, I hope, sufficiently substantiated by my own approach to English humanist rhetoric.

71. Items in Wilson's *Arte of Rhetorique* with references to similar passages in Cicero (plus the *ad Herennium* and the *Institutio oratoria*):

Book I

Preface: Eloquence first given by God, after lost by man, and last repaired by God again (*De inv.* I.i–iv)
What is Rhetoric?
1. Its Matter: two sorts of questions (*De inv.* I.vi.8)
2. Its End: to teach, to delight, to persuade (*Orator,* xxi.69; *De orat.* I.xxvi. 118–119)
3. Its Means: nature, art, and practice, including painstaking imitation (*De orat.* I.xxxii.144–149, II.xxxiv.147–xxxv.151)
4. Its Parts: invention, disposition, elocution, memory, utterance (*De inv.* I.vii.9)
5. Parts of an Oration: entrance, narration, proposition, division, confirmation, confutation, conclusion (*ad Her.* I.iii.4)
6. The Four Causes (kinds of cases): honest, filthy, doubtful, trifling (*ad Her.* I.iii.5)
7. Circumstances of any matter in judgment (*Inst. or.* IV.ii.52, VII.iv.11 et seq.)
8. Three Kinds of Orations: demonstrative, judicial, deliberative (*De inv.* II.iii.12–13)
   a. Demonstrative (*ad Her.* III.vi.10–viii.15) (*Inst. or.* III.vii.1–28)
   b. Deliberative (*De inv.* II.lii–lviii)
   c. Judicial: status theory (*ad Her.* I.xi.18)
      (1) Conjectural (*ad Her.* II.iii.3–viii.12)
      (2) Legal (*ad Her.* I.xi.19–xiii.23; II.ix.13–xii.18) (abridges *De inv.* II.xlix.144–l.148)

305

(3) Juridical
   (a) Absolute (*ad Her.* II.xiii.19–20)
   (b) Assumptive (*ad Her.* I.xii.21–xvi.26)

Book II

Frame of an Oration, esp. Judicial Oratory
1. Entrance: direct and insinuative (*De inv.* I.xv.20–xviii.25)
2. Narration (*De inv.* I.xx.28–xxi.30)
3. Division (*De inv.* I.xxii.31–xxiv.34)
4. Proposition (*Inst. or.* IV.iv.1–9)
5. Confirmation (*De inv.* I.xxiv.34–xxvii.40)
6. Conclusion (*ad Her.* II.xxx.47)

Amplification (*ad Her.* II.xxx.47–49)
Moving Pity (*ad Her.* II.xxxi.50)
Delighting the Hearers and Stirring them to Laughter (*De orat.*
   II.lvii.234–lxxi.291)
Disposition (*ad Her.* III.ix.16–17; *Inst. or.* V.xii.14, II.xiii,2–5)
1. Artistic
2. Discretionary

Book III

Style: plainness, aptness, composition (*De orat.* III.x.37–40; for "colors"
   cf. esp. *Inst. or.* IV.ii.88–103)
Memory: natural and artificial (*ad Her.* III.xvi.28–xxiv.40) (*De orat.*
   II.lxxxv.350–lxxxviii.360)
Pronunciation: voice and gesture (*De orat.* III.lvi.213–lxi.227) (*ad Her.*
   III.xi.19–xv.27)

Wilson was also influenced somewhat by Richard Sherry, *A Treatise of Schemes and Tropes* (1550); see Howell, *Logic and Rhetoric,* p. 109. Useful studies of Wilson are Russell Halderman Wagner's "Wilson and his Sources," *Quarterly Journal of Speech,* 15 (1929):530–532, and "Thomas Wilson's *Arte of Rhetorique,*" *Speech Monographs,* 27 (1960):1–32. Why does Wilson divide his theory into three books? *Controversia* does not actually structure the work, as it structures, say, *De oratore.* Perhaps (the conjecture was offered by Kenneth Cardwell recently in a seminar at Berkeley) Wilson was following Aristotle's pattern for a philosophical presentation of rhetoric; certainly Aristotle's *Rhetoric* was studied at Cambridge during Wilson's time, and Wilson's distribution of material into three books is quite similar to Aristotle's. Thus, this first English rendering of Cicero may offer structural evidence of a humanist goal, to diversify within established boundaries.
72. A reprint of *The Rule of Reason* has been edited by Richard S. Sprague (Northridge, Calif., 1972). Page numbers refer to this edition. For the impor-

tance of Wilson's logic, see Sprague's introduction (pp. xi–xx) and Howell, *Logic and Rhetoric*, pp. 12–31.

73. Stephen Greenblatt has provided a most useful study of the subject in his *Renaissance Self-Fashioning: From More to Shakespeare* (Chicago, 1980).

74. Other humanist rhetorics in England before and just after Wilson include Stephen Hawes, *Pastime of Pleasure* (1509); Caxton's translation of *Mirrour of the World* (esp. the third edition, 1527); Leonard Cox's *The Art or Crafte of Rhetoryke* (1532)—all of which, as Howell has shown, are more a listing or catalogue of concepts drawn from Cicero than a full treatment—Sherry, *Treatise;* John Ludham's translation of Andre Gerhard's treatise published under the title *The Practise of preaching* (1577), a work stunning in its shallow efforts to put Augustine together with Cicero. Then there is the group Howell has incisively called "Neo-Ciceronians," for they made an effort to restore Ciceronianism after such ravages wreaked upon it as those by the Ramists: Thomas Vicars, *Manuduction to the Rhetorical Art* (1621); Thomas Farnaby, *Index Rhetoricus* (1625); William Pemble, *Enchiridion Oratorium* (1633); and Obadiah Walker, *Some Instrvctions concerning the Art of Oratory* (1659). My own study of these works—I have used Walker as a case study in the essay mentioned in note 83 below—prompts me to offer them in proof of the statement that English Ciceronians never managed to produce a coherent rhetorical theory. Too, *theory* was not a humanist desideratum in the first place.

75. Walter J. Ong, S.J., *Ramus, Method, and the Decay of Dialogue* (Cambridge, Mass., 1958), plus his comprehensive bibliography of Ramism, *Ramus and Talon Inventory* (Cambridge, Mass., 1958). For Howell's work, see note 70 above.

76. Forrest Robinson's book on Sidney has suggested what that radical principle might be: for Sidney, "thought is a form of internal vision" and thought's true rhetoric "is more deeply rooted in ideas than in words." *The Shape of Things Known: Sidney's* Apology *in its Philosophical Tradition* (Cambridge, Mass., 1972), pp. vii–viii.

77. These particular similarities are pursued much farther in Ong's book on Ramus (see note 75 above), not to show any necessary influence of the printing press on Ramus' thought but, rather, to trace a history suggested briefly in Ong's subtitle for that book: *From the Art of Discourse to the Art of Reason.*

78. See Richard Foster Jones, "Science and Language in England of the Mid-Seventeenth Century," *The Seventeenth Century: Studies in the History of English Thought and Literature from Bacon to Pope* (Stanford, 1951), esp. p. 157. Other helpful works on changing attitudes toward language in the seventeenth century include Barbara Shapiro, *John Wilkins: An Intellectual Biography, 1614–72* (Berkeley, 1969); and James Knowlson, *Universal Language Schemes in England and France, 1600–1800* (Toronto, 1975).

79. Ong, *Rhetoric, Romance, and Technology,* p. 102.

80. Francis Bacon, *The Advancement of Learning,* Book II (in *The Works of Francis Bacon,* ed. James Spedding, Robert Leslie Ellis, and Douglas Denon Heath [New York, 1869], VI, 297). To Karl R. Wallace's well-known work on Bacon's rhetoric (*Francis Bacon on Communication and Rhetoric* [Chapel Hill, 1943]) should be added Lisa Jardine's *Francis Bacon: Discovery and the Art of Discourse* (Cambridge, England, 1974) and Brian Vickers, *Francis Bacon and Renaissance Prose* (Cambridge, England, 1968). As these excellent studies have shown, Baconism remains a rich source of fascination for all students of rhetoric in the English Renaissance. The relationship between Bacon and Milton, in particular, deserves far more attention than it has yet received or than it can receive in the present study. Milton's respectful nod toward Bacon, which we noted in our review of *Areopagitica,* is one basis for exploring their possible intellectual affinity. More significant bases are Bacon's dismissal of Ciceronianism, indeed, all "contentious learning"—as he calls it in the *Advancement of Learning*—and Milton's distrust of *controversia,* or Bacon's search for truthful forms and Milton's similar literary quest. Milton's distrust of controversial thinking and his faith in form are reviewed in the final chapter of the present study, not for their Baconianism but for their contrast with Donne. In an illuminating article, Marc Cogan has suggested that Bacon's effort to reform rhetoric actually makes rhetoric more formalistic: Bacon would have reason to create a form that would make its argument more compelling by making it more present to the imagination; see "Rhetoric and Action in Francis Bacon," *Philosophy and Rhetoric,* 14 (1981), esp. p. 226. Milton's overt debt to the Ramists is easier to trace and to explore in terms of similarities and differences, but in influence the Ramists may actually be exceeded by a much more significant Baconianism.

81. Neal Ward Gilbert, *Renaissance Concepts of Method* (New York, 1960), p. 224.

82. Louis L. Martz, *The Poetry of Meditation,* rev. ed. (New Haven, 1962; first pub. 1954) remains the major work on this tradition.

83. See Thomas O. Sloan, "Rhetoric and Meditation: Three Case Studies," *Journal of Medieval and Renaissance Studies,* 1 (1971):45–58.

84. That we now may be ready for such a return may be signalled by the work of Chaim Perelman; see Perelman and L. Olbrechts-Tyteca, *The New Rhetoric,* trans. John Wilkinson and Purcell Weaver (Notre Dame, 1969).

CHAPTER THREE

1. John T. Shawcross, ed., *The Complete Poetry of John Donne* (Garden City, 1967), p. 92n.

2. This structure of Donne's argument is a matter I once tried to approach

through a difficult pairing of irony and Ramism: "A Rhetorical Analysis of John Donne's 'The Prohibition,'" *Quarterly Journal of Speech,* 48 (1962):38–45.

3. Clay Hunt, *Donne's Poetry: Essays in Literary Analysis* (New Haven, 1954), p. 14.

4. John Carey, *John Donne: Life, Mind and Art* (New York, 1981), p. 195.

5. Arthur F. Marotti, "Donne and 'The Extasie,'" *The Rhetoric of Renaissance Poetry,* ed. Thomas O. Sloan and Raymond B. Waddington (Berkeley, 1974), p. 144.

6. A. J. Smith, "New Bearings in Donne: *Aire and Angels,*" *English,* 13 (1960):52.

7. Edgar Wind, *Pagan Mysteries in the Renaissance* (New York, 1958), see esp. chap. III, "The Medal of Pico della Mirandola."

8. N. J. C. Andreasen is the most noteworthy exception. Although she does not interpret the angel's significance quite in the way I do, she does note the reversal of its ostensible meaning and captures the tone precisely: *John Donne: Conservative Revolutionary* (Princeton, 1967), p. 214.

9. *Summa theol.* Part I, Q.51, a.2.

10. Helen Gardner, "The Argument about 'The Ecstasy,'" in *Elizabethan and Jacobean Studies presented to F. P. Wilson,* ed. Herbert Davis and Helen Gardner (Oxford, 1959), pp. 279–306.

11. Earl Miner, *The Metaphysical Mode from Donne to Cowley* (Princeton, 1967), pp. 81–82.

12. Marotti, "Donne and 'The Extasie.'"

13. A passage in a letter Donne wrote in 1612 seems particularly clear on this point: "Our nature is meteoric, we respect (because we partake so) both earth and heaven; for as our bodies are allowed to partake earthly pleasure, so our souls demerged into those bodies are allowed to partake earthly pleasure. Our soul is not sent hither, only to go back again: we have some errand to do here; nor is it sent into a prison because it comes innocent, and He which sent it is just." Edmund Gosse, *The Life and Letters of John Donne, Dean of St. Paul's* (Gloucester, Mass., 1959; first pub. 1899), II, p.9.

14. Margaret L. Wiley used the phrase *The Subtle Knot* as her title for a study of skepticism in seventeenth-century England, including Donne's (Cambridge, Mass., 1952). Wiley's approach to Donne through skepticism is, I believe, illuminating. Skepticism and *controversia* work hand in hand in clarifying, as I shall attempt to show later, the movement of Donne's mind. This movement can be baffling even to a reader as perceptive as Mahood, who notices but does not quite know what to do about the curious inconsistencies "in an obscure verse-letter to the Countess of Bedford, of which the general tenor is that the body corrupts the soul. But the poem's labyrinthine reasonings reveal Donne's own uncertainty, and in one parenthesis he destroys his whole argument by granting the body a dignity denied the soul, that of re-

demption and not mere preservation from death"; M. M. Mahood, *Poetry and Humanism* (New Haven, 1950), p. 112. The structure of that letter is, I believe, uncovered by the rhetorical principles I am attempting to discuss.

15. Arthur F. Kinney, "Rhetoric as Poetic: Humanist Fiction in the Renaissance," *ELH,* 43 (1976):425. Moreover, the possibilities of connecting this forensic view with Donne's lyric voice were suggested in Arnold Stein, *John Donne's Lyrics: The Eloquence of Action* (Minneapolis, 1962): Donne "is also a poet deeply eager to break through the intellectual complexities, and to use them against themselves as a means of discovering, or rediscovering, the simple truths which the mind complicates. For in these matters mind is both ally and opponent, and finally judge" (p. 196).

16. See "Donne's Sources," in *Sermons* X, esp. p. 347.

17. Louis I. Bredvold, "The Religious Thought of Donne in Relation to Medieval and Later Traditions," *Studies in Shakespeare, Milton and Donne by Members of the English Department of the University of Michigan* (New York, 1964; first pub. 1925), p. 196.

18. Gosse, *Life and Letters.*

19. R. C. Bald, *John Donne: A Life* (New York, 1970).

20. Peter Brown, *Augustine of Hippo: A Biography* (Berkeley, 1967), p. 246.

21. Brown, *Augustine,* p. 123.

22. *Sermons* VI, p. 218. Further, Donne argues that salvation *is* "memory," in II, p. 73; another Augustinian feature, well explored by Stanley E. Fish in *Self-Consuming Artifacts* (Berkeley, 1972), chap. I.

23. A succinct review of *probabilism* and *probabiliorism* is in Camille Well Slights, *The Casuistical Tradition in Shakespeare, Donne, Herbert, and Milton* (Princeton, 1981), see esp. pp. 86–87.

24. Gosse, *Life and Letters,* I, p. 62.

25. *Biathanatos* (London, ca. 1646), sig. C2ᵛ.

26. Carey, *John Donne,* p. 253.

27. See A. J. Smith, "New Bearings in Donne."

28. Thomas Carew, in his elegy on Donne in the 1633 edition of Donne's poems, called him a king who ruled over "The universall Monarchy of Wit." J. B. Leishman called Donne the monarch of wit in his book by that title (London, 1951).

29. For the most part, Donne's use of the term *form* reflects certain theological concepts—particularly those of Thomas Aquinas. Form is that constituent of any being that animates it and impresses the creator's purposes upon it. When Donne's coins, for example, have been melted and re-formed into chains, he complains, "forme gives being, and their form is gone" ("Elegie XI," l. 76). Form is the body's soul, but the soul, too, as a created object has form, the impress of its creator: "My Soules forme," as Donne puts it in "Goodfriday 1613" (l. 10). Donne could use the concept in the most sexually conserva-

tive Thomist sense, in which the female supplies the material (the body), the male (through seminal force) the soul, or form:

> Hence comes it, that these Rymes which never had
> Mother, want matter, and they only have
> A little forme, the which their Father gave;
> ("To Mr. B.B.")

In Thomist / Aristotelian terms, the efficient and formal causes are usually male ("the 'ingendring force," "To E. of D. with six holy Sonnets"), the material cause invariably female ("our *Great-Grand-Mother*, DUST," "Elegie on . . . Prince Henry"). Further, soul is to life as spirit (the animal and vegetable spirits engendered in the blood; cf. "The Extasie," ll. 61–62) is to form, and conversely form is to life as spirit is to soul—in the nearly perfect mathematical equations Donne employs in his "Nocturnall" (ll. 19–20):

> All others, from all things, draw all that's good,
> Life, soule, forme, spirit, whence they beeing have;

Form, or soul, not only animates the body and impresses the creator's purposes upon it but also individuates the created object, by uniting its matter into a formal whole or shape—as in the extravagant praise he gives the dead girl in *The first Anniversary,* where he addresses the world (l.37): "Her name defin'd thee, gave thee forme, and frame"—or as in imagining a new world built out of her memory (ll.77–78):

> the matter and stuffe of this,
> Her Vertue, and the forme our practice is.

She, as he says in *The second Anniversary* (l. 72), returning again to extravagant praise, was the "forme" that made our old (before her death) world live.

So much can be taken for granted as the very "stuffe" of Donne's own poems. That is, he used Thomistic concepts as he used Neoplatonic (H.J.C. Grierson, in his comments on Donne's poems in volume II of his 1912 edition, has provided perhaps the most concrete guide to Donne's Platonism), Plotinian (see esp. Mary Paton Ramsay, *Les Doctrines Médiévales Chez Donne* [London, 1924]), Petrarchan (Donald L. Guss, *John Donne, Petrarchist* [Detroit, 1966]), and casuistical (in addition to Slights, *Casuistical Tradition,* see also A. E. Malloch, "John Donne and the Casuists," *Studies in English Literature,* 2 [1962]:57–76) concepts for the material out of which he fashioned—or, better, *formed*—poems that are yet animated with life and purpose and individuality.

30. For a succinct review of Augustinian and Thomist concepts of form, see Mortimer J. Adler, ed., *A Syntopicon of the Great Books of the Western World* (Chicago, London, Toronto, 1952), I, pp. 526–542. In the Augustinian view, Donne's use of *matter* in his poem about the Sidneys is metaphorical for a

composite work, matter that has been formed and re-formed, spoken by the Spirit through various forms.

31. See esp. T. S. Eliot, *Selected Essays* (New York, 1932), pp. 242–252, and "Donne in Our Time," in *A Garland for John Donne, 1631–1931,* ed. Theodore Spencer (Cambridge, Mass., 1931), p. 16.

32. See note 1 to the preface, above. One of the most penetrating formalist analyses of Donne's work is Antony F. Bellette's article; see Chapter One above, note 25.

33. Cleanth Brooks, "Milton and the New Criticism," *A Shaping Joy: Studies in the Writer's Craft* (New York, 1971), p. 331.

34. See L. Elaine Hoover, *John Donne and Francisco de Quevedo: Poets of Love and Death* (Chapel Hill, 1978), p. 9.

35. In my interpretation of this poem I am indebted to Nancy Mason Bradbury, "Speaker and Structure in Donne's *Satyre IV*," *Studies in English Literature* (forthcoming). But I must also note that Bradbury's reading does not veer into the Augustinianism I am trying out in this section.

36. N. J. C. Andreasen, "Theme and Structure in Donne's *Satyres*," *Studies in English Literature,* 3 (1963):59–75.

37. See C. S. Lewis, *English Literature in the Sixteenth Century Excluding Drama* (New York, 1954), pp. 468–470.

38. Louis I. Bredvold, "The Religious Thought of Donne," p. 226.

39. "For, as the well tuning of an *Instrument,* makes *higher* and *lower* strings, of one sound, so the inequality of their yeeres, was thus reduc't to an evennesse, that shee had a *cheerfulnesse,* agreeable to his *youth,* and he a *sober staidnesse,* comformable to her more *yeeres.* So that, I would not consider her, at so much more then *forty,* nor him, at so much lesse then *thirty,* at that time, but as their *persons* were made *one,* and their *fortunes* made one, by *mariage,* so I would put their *yeeres* into *one number,* and finding a *sixty* betweene them, thinke them *thirty* a peece; for, as twins of one houre, they liv'd. *God,* who joyn'd them, then, having also separated them now, may make their *yeres* even, this other way too; by giving him, as many yeeres after her going out of this World, as he had given her, before his comming into it; and then as many more, as *God* may receive *Glory,* and the World, *Benefit* by that Addition; That so, as at their first meeting, she was, at their last meeting, he may bee the *elder person*" (p. 88).

40. "Her *rule* was *mediocrity*" (p. 89). ". . . the *rule* of her *Religion,* was the *Scripture;* And, her *rule,* for her particular understanding of the *Scriptures,* was the *Church.* Shee never diverted towards the *Papist,* in undervaluing the *Scripture;* nor towards the *Separatist,* in undervaluing the *Church*" (p. 90).

41. Hiram Haydn, *The Counter Renaissance* (New York, 1950), p. 165.

42. Gosse, *Life and Letters,* II, p. 101.

43. Bald, *John Donne,* p. 328.

44. Nor was his Protestantism a dramatic alteration in his Catholicism—the point has been well made by Dennis Flynn, "Donne's Catholicism: I," *Recusant History*, 13 (1976):1–17. Part II appears in the same volume, 178–195. See also David Chanoff, "Donne's Anglicanism," *Recusant History*, 15 (1980): 154–167.

45. Gosse, *Life and Letters*, II, p. 124.

46. Ibid., p. 176.

47. See Donne's poem "To Mr. *George Herbert*, with one of my Seal(s), of the Anchor and Christ."

48. Donne's reference to Janus is in the third stanza of his *Metempsychosis*. For the Christianizing of Janus as Noah, see Wind, *Pagan Mysteries*, p. 251n.

49. The reference appears at the end of the prayer "for the whole state of Christ's Church militant here in earth," as the 1559 *Book of Common Prayer* has it: "Grant this, O Father, for Jesus Christ's sake, our only mediator and advocate. Amen."

50. Slights, *Casuistical Tradition*, p. 144. For a contrary interpretation of this work and an approach only slightly different from my own, see Rosalie Colie, *Paradoxia Epidemica: The Renaissance Tradition of Paradox* (Princeton, 1966): e.g., "*Biathanatos* depends upon the certain knowledge that life is uncertain, and that human interpretations of what happens in that uncertain life are themselves untrustworthy, that a given cause may produce a given effect, but that cause-and-effect explanation is liable to error, especially as a general law to which life—to say nothing of deity—might be bound" (p. 507). An excellent reading of both works is in Dennis Flynn's "Irony in *Biathanatos* and *Pseudo-Martyr*," *Recusant History*, 12 (1973):49–69. An absorbing analysis of Donne's satirical and lawyerly wit and a brief caution against accepting some of Flynn's conclusions are offered in Helen Conrad Mitchell Stroud, "John Donne and Gratian: The *Concordia Discordantium Canonum* in *Pseudo-Martyr*," Ph.D. diss., University of California, Berkeley, 1983.

51. Bald provides a succinct summary of the oath's features and analyzes its most controversial part; *John Donne*, pp. 212–213.

52. "Zealous" is a word used by Donne in *Biathanatos* to characterize St. Augustine's mind (see pp. 98, 99, 150, 200). This stance toward Augustine (whose zeal, Donne states, was a result of his conversion) marks an important difference, in both works, between Donne's rhetoric and Augustine's: to oppose zealousness, however eminent the source, is Donne's motive.

53. Bredvold, "Religious Thought," p. 213.

54. Gosse, *Life and Letters*, II, p. 16.

55. Herbert J. C. Grierson, *The Poems of John Donne* (London, 1912), II, p. 236.

56. Fish, *Self-Consuming Artifacts*, p. 56. Fish continues, "The distinctions and divisions that were to have marked the progress of our understanding

313

mark, instead, the extent of our entrapment" (p. 57). Our? The identification of Donne's audience is, I realize, almost as muted in my discussion as it is in Fish's. Yet I would argue that my observations always presuppose an audience familiar with Donne's homiletic characteristics; Fish's seem to presuppose on the one hand a general, "competent" (p. 406) reader and on the other an auditor with, apparently, the linguistic expectations of a Puritan at an Anglican sermon (I refer to Fish's own Puritan-Anglican distinctions; see pp. 70–77).

57. With this hypothesis, my reading contradicts Lewalski, who, with one eye on "the Protestant paradigm of salvation" within which Donne's holy sonnets may be arranged in sequence, finds that the "mindes white truth" is virtually synonymous with "true griefe" and offers the speaker the assurance that he has obtained repentance: Barbara Kiefer Lewalski, *Protestant Poetics and the Seventeenth-Century Religious Lyric* (Princeton, 1979), p. 269.

CHAPTER FOUR

1. "To tell the whole story and tell it rightly, Milton's imagination must work both backward and forward, and must draw on the deep conviction that trial is the will of a benevolent deity presiding over a universe that evolves toward ultimate good"; Arnold Stein, *The Art of Presence: The Poet and Paradise Lost* (Berkeley, 1977), p. 28. Among the many valuable arguments in Stein's book is that the poet-prophet himself is on "trial" in this poem. But the nature of this "trial," as described by Stein, is not the forensic battle it would be in Donne.

2. For a superb study of these conventions, see Joan Malory Webber, *Milton and His Epic Tradition* (Seattle, 1979).

3. This is, of course, the thesis of Stanley Fish's brilliant work on Milton, *Surprised by Sin: The Reader in Paradise Lost* (New York, 1967).

4. Christopher Hill has an incisive argument on this point in his *Milton and the English Revolution* (London, 1979); see p. 356.

5. William Kerrigan in *The Prophetic Milton* (Charlottesville, 1974) offers several interesting observations, set in a context of prophetic traditions; e.g., "Milton's poems are curiously anticipatory and, in a special way, incomplete. Often the reader is led, through proleptic ironies, to expect a fulfillment; but the fulfillment, when it comes, turns out to be yet another anticipation. The events of the poems move outside the temporal frames of art" (p. 228). But as rhetorical terms "prolepsis" and "irony" do not have the force in Milton they do in Donne, because in Milton they are more visionary than vocal; and in order to emphasize the difference I must move outside the prophetic (which can be vocal and even rhetorical, though not in a humanist sense) frame altogether.

6. Rosemond Tuve, *Elizabethan and Metaphysical Imagery* (Chicago, 1947). Walter J. Ong, S. J., *Ramus, Method, and the Decay of Dialogue* (Cambridge, Mass., 1958).

7. The following have advanced the most important arguments: Norman E. Nelson, *Peter Ramus and the Confusion of Logic, Rhetoric, and Poetry,* "University of Michigan Contributions in Modern Philology," no. 2 (Ann Arbor, 1947); A. J. Smith, "An Examination of Some Claims Made for Ramism," *Review of English Studies,* new ser. 7 (1956):348–359; George Watson, "Ramus, Miss Tuve, and the New Petromachia," *Modern Philology,* 55 (1958): 259–262.

8. Here I am compelled to offer (unnecessarily, I hope) a prolepsis of my own. True, Donne was trained as a lawyer; Milton wasn't. I have therefore, apparently, stacked the deck as Cicero does in the frame of *De oratore.* I could counter with this argument: lawyerly training—whether in studying Ciceronian rhetoric or in preparing for an actual career at the bar—was integral to humanism. Or I might counter with this argument: Milton, like Donne, was exposed to Ciceronian rhetoric, as were all educated men of his time; but, like other educated men of his time, he was also well grounded in certain non-lawyerly, even noncontroversial, modes of composition—in particular, Ramism—that mark the disintegration of humanist rhetoric. But this is the argument on which I will rest my case in this matter: my study is not aimed at tracking influences. My thesis is that the writings of both Donne and Milton reveal characteristics of humanist rhetoric in the period of its disintegration; the materials offered in proof should be mutually illuminating, both of Donne's and Milton's writings and of English humanism generally.

9. See the final section of Chapter Two above.

10. The psychological foundations of eighteenth-century rhetorical theory are commonplace. For a discussion of their nature, see Wilbur Samuel Howell, *Eighteenth Century British Logic and Rhetoric* (Princeton, 1971). A succinct review of this psychologizing of rhetoric is in Lloyd F. Bitzer, "Editor's Introduction," *The Philosophy of Rhetoric* by George Campbell (Carbondale, 1963), pp. ix–xxxi.

11. Fraunce, *Lawiers Logike* (1588), fol. 113ᵛ.

12. The point has been made many times, though few scholars have expressed the matter more incisively than P. Albert Duhamel, "Milton's Alleged Ramism," *PMLA,* 67 (1952): 1035–1053.

13. William Riley Parker, *Milton: A Biography* (Oxford, 1968), I, p. 51. Parker calls these methods of disputation "medieval" and "ancient," terms that are misleading because they do not discriminate finely enough. The most comprehensive studies of Milton's schooling are Donald Lemen Clark, *John Milton at St. Paul's School* (New York, 1948), and Harris Fletcher, *The Intellectual Development of John Milton,* 2 vols. (Urbana, 1961). In all these works the uniquely *humanist* nature of Milton's education in *controversia* deserves reexamination. Moreover, the educational contexts described in these works (and this is likely to remain true even upon reexamination) only enhance a view of Milton's ingenuity and strength of will as a student: his surviving prolusions

are clearly more than merely vapid exercises in the irrelevant. His fifth prolusion, for example, argues a position—one being, one form—that is pursued through other treatises, such as the two discussed in the present essay, and that is contrary to the attitudes toward form most humanist prolusionary efforts would inculcate.

14. The text used for this study is the translation by Allan H. Gilbert in *The Works of John Milton*, ed. Frank Allen Patterson, XI (New York, 1935). All page references to *Logic* in the text are to this edition.

15. *The Logike of the moste Excellent Philosopher P. Ramus Martyr, Newly translated, and in diuers places corrected, after the mynde of the Author. Per M. Roll. Makylmaneum Scotum* (London, 1574), cap. XVII.

16. The master himself had insisted that, after all, the final must work with the efficient (it moves him to create) and it is also a product of the formal cause. But the failure to group may have only been offered as a vague alternative to the opposition's, especially Aristotle's, complicated grouping of those causes that are external, the efficient and the final, and those that are internal, the material and the formal. Milton's position is closer to Fraunce (fols. 11–31) than to Ramus.

17. Quoted in Peter Brown, *Augustine of Hippo: A Biography* (Berkeley, 1967), p. 373.

18. *The Christian Doctrine of John Milton,* trans. Bishop Charles R. Sumner, 2 vols. (Cambridge, Eng., 1825), hereinafter cited in the text as *Doctrina*. Preceding quotations are from the preface; subsequent ones are cited by volume and page number. For an account of the composition and revisions of the original manuscript, see Maurice Kelley, *The Great Argument: A Study of Milton's De Doctrina as a Gloss upon Paradise Lost* (Princeton, 1941). Kelley, further, enthusiastically pursues the question of Milton's Arianism, a matter that has been well resolved by C. A. Patrides in the study cited in the following note. Arthur Sewell's *A Study in Milton's Christian Doctrine* (Oxford, 1939; reprinted Hamden, Conn., 1967) remains a useful overview of Milton's treatise, though as a contextual study Sewell misses important Ramist connections (see, e.g., p. 38).

19. "The Trinity as such is not rejected," C. A. Patrides has argued in *Milton and the Christian Doctrine* (Oxford, 1967), p. 16. They are simply not equal in terms of *essentia*. I would put the matter a little differently: formal, that is Ramist, logic requires that the precedence of the Father be acknowledged. The other members of the Trinity are subordinate. Professor Patrides, moreover, has shown that although Milton relies largely on Scripture for his evidence, biblical scholarship has clearly influenced his thinking.

20. *An Apology Against a Pamphlet Call'd a Modest Confutation of the Animadversions upon the Remonstrant Against Smectymnuus,* in Patterson, ed., *Works,* III, p. 312.

21. Robert Crossman, *Reading Paradise Lost* (Bloomington, Indiana, 1980): "The implication, unstressed and probably unnoticed, is that Milton's Hell is a tissue of words, and that words should be approached with a certain skepticism" (p. 48). The skepticism Crossman speaks of is more like suspicion than diffidence.

22. An adequate index of these terms is in the final two volumes of Patterson, ed., *Works.* See also Major's work, cited next.

23. A comprehensive review of Milton's attitude toward classical rhetoric is provided by John M. Major's "Milton's View of Rhetoric," *Studies in Philology,* 64 (1967):685–711. Major's discussion ends by noting Milton's overt hostility to rhetoric, which Major tends generally to equate with style and eloquence; I am trying to show that this hostility is actually a deep opposition to humanist *controversia.* That is, Milton's distrust of rhetoric was not acquired gradually, as Major argues. On the contrary, if one locates the center of humanist rhetoric in *controversia,* then it appears that, except for rare occasions, Milton never shows a trust in rhetoric. Major's effort to link Milton's view of rhetoric with Bacon is particularly illuminating, however; in this regard, see also note 80 to Chapter Two above.

24. This argument I have attempted in "Rhetoric, 'logic' and poetry: the formal cause," in *The Age of Milton,* ed. C. A. Patrides and Raymond B. Waddington (Manchester, 1980), pp. 307–337.

25. Bridget Gellert Lyons discusses the conceptual parallels between the two poems and their possible debt to Burton in the epilogue to her *Voices of Melancholy* (New York, 1971).

26. Both were, most likely, written in Milton's Cambridge years (1631 or 1632) and, according to E. M. W. Tillyard, *The Miltonic Setting* (London, 1938), chap. 1, follow the usual Cambridge undergraduate manner of developing themes—as, for example, the parodying of mythological descriptions, catalogs, and genealogies. The poems might recall for a Cambridge audience such idle debates as whether the pleasures of Day exceed those of Night—though they also show what a bright student can do with a hackneyed assignment.

27. Marjorie Nicholson offers an interesting discussion of the structural parallels between the two poems: *John Milton, a Reader's Guide to his Poetry* (New York, 1963), pp. 50–65.

28. A century later Handel, in giving these two poems a musical setting that intermingles one poem with the other, had apparently rejected a third poem written by a friend of his and entitled "Il Moderato," which was meant to fuse Milton's "opposites" of mirth and melancholy into a golden mean. But Milton's poems require no such fusions, for they are conceptually fused already in their forms, as Handel seems to have realized.

29. O. B. Hardison, Jr., has an illuminating discussion of the word *individual*

in this poem: *Texas Studies in Literature and Language,* 3 (1961):107–122.

30. For another view of the listing of "Chance" and an attempt to read Milton rhetorically but by non-Ciceronian means, see my "Reading Milton Rhetorically," in James J. Murphy, ed., *Renaissance Eloquence* (Berkeley, 1983), pp. 394–410.

31. Grierson reads the line "thou art so truth" to mean that "she is essentially truth as God is," II, pp. 33–34. This interpretation is justified by the function of excessive praise and all the pseudoeschatology throughout the poem, components of the poem's comic tone. But both the tone of the poem and the work's coherence are missed in Gardner's reading: she prefers "so true" (which appears in some manuscripts) because it is less awkward; *The Elegies and the Songs and Sonnets of John Donne* (Oxford, 1965), p. 209.

32. See Grierson's discussion, with reference to Aquinas, II, pp. 34–35. See also my discussion, in the preceding chapter, of Donne's Holy Sonnet VIII ("If faithful soules").

33. I do not hear the poem "halt" on line 5, as Tillyard does, thus finding it flawed. Rather, I hear in the prominent personal pronouns of the entire octave a conflation of myths. Tillyard's comparison of Milton's sonnet with Donne's "holy sonnet" on the death of Anne Donne is less irreverent than mine— though, interestingly, we come to something of the same point: Milton's poem "rests on a rhetoric of emotion, solidly grounded in reason and human nature, publicly ratified, and, in the best sense of the word, conventional"; *The Metaphysicals and Milton* (London, 1965; first pub. 1956), pp. 10–11. Tillyard's use of the word *rhetoric* is obviously not "humanist rhetoric," and thus it, too, enhances similarities in our views of Milton.

34. John Shawcross reviews the various arguments in *Notes and Queries,* n.s. 3 (1956):202–203. A comprehensive later review is presented by Douglas Bush in *A Variorum Commentary on The Poems of John Milton* (New York, 1972), II, Part 2, pp. 492–499. My own interpretation owes much to, besides Tillyard, Leo Spitzer, "Understanding Milton," *Hopkins Review,* IV, 4 (1950–51):16–27, and J. Huntley, "Milton's 23rd Sonnet," *ELH,* 34 (1967):468–481.

35. Keith W. Stavely, *The Politics of Milton's Prose Style* (New Haven, 1975), notes, "A reformed social order, Milton maintains, will be an imaginative social order, which is to say it will encourage true poets such as he hopes to become" (p. 1).

36. Kenneth Burke, *A Rhetoric of Motives* (Berkeley, 1969; first pub. 1950).

37. Stavely, p. 49. In another study of Milton's prose a similar observation is offered by L. C. Knights: "I am saying that in his political writings there is not the tension, the recognition of conflicting claims, that you find in Marvell . . .," *Public Voices* (London, 1971), p. 70.

38. Sidney's *Apologie* (1583) offers a good example of this critical commonplace. The commonplace, moreover, is the starting point of Don Cameron

Allen's study of Milton's poetry, *The Harmonious Vision* (Baltimore, 1970; first pub. 1954).

39. See *Paradise Lost,* IX, ll. 335–336, 698–700, 758–759, and the passages from the *Areopagitica* quoted in my Chapter One.

40. See Fish, *Surprised by Sin.*

41. Comprehensive reviews of these questions are available in Merritt Y. Hughes, *John Milton: Complete Poems and Major Prose* (New York, 1957), pp. 471–481, and in *A Variorum Commentary on the Poems of John Milton,* IV, by Walter MacKellar (New York, 1975). A particularly illuminating discussion of *Paradise Regained* as a choice of a certain style of life, a discussion that touches on myth and on what I refer to as otherness, is Irene Samuel's "The Regaining of Paradise" in Balachandra Rajan, ed., *The Prison and the Pinnacle* (Toronto, 1973), pp. 111–134. My view of the poem as a "drama of knowledge" owes much to Arnold Stein, *Heroic Knowledge: An Interpretation of Paradise Regained and* Samson Agonistes (Minneapolis, 1957). A most helpful discussion of the poem's structure is in Louis L. Martz, *Poet of Exile: A Study of Milton's Poetry* (New Haven, 1980), pp. 247–271.

42. As William G. Madsen states, "the Christian who says that earth is the shadow (that is, foreshadowing) of heaven is asserting the validity of history. The world is a stage on which the drama of salvation is enacted, and earthly things have meaning primarily in the context of history," "Earth the Shadow of Heaven: Typological Symbolism in *Paradise Lost,*" *PMLA,* 75 (1960):523. The point is further developed in his *From Shadowy Types to Truth: Studies in Milton's Symbolism* (New Haven and London, 1968); e.g., "Before the advent of Christ God did indeed veil His saving truths in shadowy types and ceremonies, but for Christians, who live in the full light of the Gospel, the purpose of types is not to veil but to illuminate and make 'lively' the truths that are already known. Their function, in short, is rhetorical and may be regarded as analogous to the function of figurative language in general" (p. 77). "Rhetorical," I must add, in the Ramist-Milton sense of "style."

43. See *Doctrina,* II, Chap. ix. The importance of this definition is pointed out by Hughes, *John Milton,* p. 476.

44. *In Reason of Church-Government urg'd against Prelaty:* ". . . that Epick form whereof the two poems of *Homer,* and those other two of *Virgil* and *Tasso* are a diffuse, and the book of *Job* a brief model . . ." (*Works,* III, Part 1, p. 237). For a discussion of the·tradition of the Book of Job as an epic poem, see Barbara Lewalski, *Milton's Brief Epic: The Genre, Meaning and Art of* Paradise Regained (Providence, 1966), pp. 10–36.

45. William Empson uses the term *analytic* for Satan's mind in *Paradise Lost;* see *Milton's God,* rev. ed. (London, 1965), p. 38. For perhaps the same reasons, Dr. Johnson applies the term to the "attempts" of the "metaphysical poets" in his life of Cowley (1783).

46. The only other use of the word is strikingly and dramatically similar: The lady refers to Comus's "Rhetorick / That hath so well been taught her dazling fence" in *A Mask*, ll. 790–791. The word appears frequently in Milton's prose, the significance of which was discussed in the preceding essay; see also note 22, this chapter, above.

47. In Milton's ideal scheme of education, expressed in his letter to Samuel Hartlib (usually referred to as "Of Education"), the *order* of the "organic arts" is somewhat different than Satan's. Boys are to learn logic before rhetoric, and then return to the art of poetry. Rhetoric serves the Ramist function, of making graceful and ornate logic's forms of thought. Poetry is encountered early, amidst other subjects, including grammar, and caps the education by providing the "laws" of genre, and imparts to the students "what religious, what glorious and magnificent use might be made of poetry, both in divine and human things." The passage bears comparison not only with Satan's review of classical learning but also with the discussion, later in the present essay, of genre: Milton never lost sight of what he considered the proper ends of things.

48. Wilson's rules for debating are mostly in *The Rule of Reason, Containing the Arte of Logique* (London: 1552); the passage referred to appears on fol. 173. See also fol. 70ᵛ and passim. Considering the nature of the conflict in *Paradise Regained*, it may be significant that to understand the use of the dilemma in debate we must turn to humanist writings rather than to Milton's *Logic*, where it receives only brief mention.

49. Cleanth Brooks, "Milton and the New Criticism," *A Shaping Joy: Studies in the Writer's Craft* (New York, 1971), p. 342.

50. Northrop Frye, "The Typology of *Paradise Regained*," in C. A. Patrides, ed., *Milton's Epic Poetry* (New York, 1967), p. 314. The essay was first published in *Modern Philology*, 53 (1956):227–238. Frye's work and Madsen's (see note 42 above) go farther in their use of typology and myth than does Lewalski's (see note 44 above).

51. Other examples: "Moses organizes the twelve tribes of Israel; Jesus gathers twelve disciples. Israel crosses the Red Sea and achieves its identity as a nation on the other side; Jesus is baptized in the Jordan and is recognized as the Son of God. . . . Israel wanders forty years in the wilderness; Jesus, forty days." See Northrop Frye, *The Great Code* (New York, 1982). pp. 172–173.

52. These arguments are made, respectively, by Webber, *Milton and His Epic Tradition*, and Mary Ann Radzinowicz, *Toward Samson Agonistes* (Princeton, 1978).

53. See Norman T. Burns, *Christian Mortalism from Tyndale to Milton* (Cambridge, Mass., 1972), esp. chap. 4.

54. Hill, *Milton and the English Revolution*, p. 321.

55. R. S. Crane, *The Languages of Criticism and the Structure of Poetry* (Chicago, 1953), see esp. pp. 42, 67, 153.

56. Frye, *The Great Code*, p. 46.
57. See esp. Northrop Frye, *Anatomy of Criticism* (Princeton, 1966; first pub. 1957), the third essay, "Archetypal Criticism: Theory of Myths." Moreover, though I pursue the concept of *myth* in Milton in ways different from Waddington's pursuit of myth in Chapman, I am deeply indebted to his insights—not the least, that Donne's poetry is "linear," Chapman's "iconic." Raymond B. Waddington, *The Mind's Empire: Myth and Form in George Chapman's Narrative Poems* (Baltimore, 1974), p. 13.
58. Frye, *The Great Code*, p. 79.
59. *Works*, III, p. 287, p. 362.
60. Radzinowicz, *Toward Samson Agonistes*. Radzinowicz's analysis is illuminating and satisfies the need, long urged in critical studies, to challenge the assumption that the play has no center (see pp. 55–66). But the precise function of "dialectic" needs more technical definition: Radzinowicz's analysis fuses *controversia* with an Hegelian movement toward synthesis. Nonetheless, the work itself, particularly her final characterization of Milton's role as poet ("to change men and make it possible for them to think the new and true," p. 363), is most instructive. For pinpointing the *controversia* in the play, I am indebted to Glen McClish.
61. Camille Wells Slights, *The Casuistical Tradition in Shakespeare, Donne, Herbert, and Milton* (Princeton, 1981), p. 284. Slights's argument characterizes Samson as a "hero of conscience," one who "is more radical than any models offered by conventional casuists" (p. 295). I agree.

CONCLUSION

1. James Shirley, "To the Reader," *Comedies and Tragedies Written by Francis Beaumont and John Fletcher, Gentlemen* (London, 1647), sig. A3ᵛ. I have modernized the spelling and punctuation.
2. That a reader would actually become the poem and simultaneously, or at a later moment, admire its craftsmanship is a desideratum not alien to our own age of formalist-dominated criticism. For the formalist, however, the reader's attention becomes directed and shaped by the poem's form (informed by the aesthetic ordering of the poem); correlatively, what the reader admires are the poem's principles of coherence. For the rhetorician, the reader identifies with the poem's voice and admires the poet's strategies of presenting that voice. Whether in our age or in the Renaissance, the rhetorician's view relies upon the reader's acknowledgment that poetry is a persuasive art, that the similarities between poetry and oratory are more significant than their differences— an acknowledgment that is anathema to formalists, who began their long ascent to critical dominance upon the disintegration of humanist rhetoric.

　　Throughout the humanist period the close union of oratory and poetry was casually assumed. DuBellay, for example, in his *Defense* (1549), Book II, chap. 1, called poetry and oratory the two pillars that support the edifice of literature. His friend Ronsard, in his *Abergé* (1565), made the poet an expert in the first three offices of rhetoric, *inventio, dispositio,* and *elocutio*—a distribution that was conventional and standard at least through Dryden (see his letter to Sir Robert Howard prefacing *Annus Mirabilis,* 1666). Characteristically, Puttenham in *The Arte of English Poesie* (1589) carried these casual resemblances to an extreme, in his argument that the poets were "the best perswaders, and their eloquence the first Rethoricke of the world" (chap. IV). But Ben Jonson was no less extreme in his well-known reversal of Cicero's argument: Cicero has Crassus claim (*De orat.* I.xvi.70) that the poet is almost the counterpart of the orator; Jonson (in *Timber, or Discoveries,* 1620–1625) claims that the poet is the equal of the orator in ornament and above him in persuasiveness.

The two pulls in critical allegiance in the rhetorical view—toward admiring craftsmanship and toward identification with the poem, its argument, or speaker—were resolved with dispatch by most Renaissance humanists. To begin with, in Cicero and in Quintilian there is ample warrant for arguing that the end of rhetoric—whether poetry or oratory—is on the one hand eloquence, or craftsmanship, and on the other persuasion. But most of the major critics of the humanist period strongly rejected the idea of eloquence *alone* as the end of poetry. Scaliger, for example, begins his *Poetics* (1561) with a forceful rejection of eloquence as the end for either poetry or oratory, insisting that both have only one end, persuasion—and the argument frames his revival of Aristotelian poetics. Later, when the Puritan attacks on poetry became sharper, the persuasive end of the art—in Sidney, Puttenham, Jonson—was strengthened and directed toward one goal, that poetry persuades toward the good.

In sum, poetry was written, theorized about, criticized, taught, and read by people for whom the central language art was humanist rhetoric. As a consequence, poetry was viewed as a persuasive source of knowledge, and one whose craftsmanship was to be admired; we learn from poetry as we learn from oratory, how to live virtuously and how to create voice on paper (or even, how to argue well). Of course, no humanist put the matter quite in those terms; nonetheless, for me, *persuasion* and *eloquence*—the terms actually used by these critics—are conveniently and accurately translated for our own age as "identification with voice" and "craftsmanship." For another, more Plutarchan view of these same issues, see John M. Wallace, "'Examples Are Best Precepts': Readers and Meanings in Seventeenth-Century Poetry," *Critical Inquiry,* I (Dec. 1974): 273–290.

A different order of craftsmanship and a different way to admire it began its ascendancy with Aristotelian formalism in the middle of the sixteenth century. See the following note.

3. A succinct review of the growing importance of Aristotle's *Poetics* to six-

teenth-century criticism is presented by Baxter Hathaway in *Marvels and Commonplaces: Renaissance Literary Criticism* (New York, 1968), pp. 9–10. Hathaway incisively refers to the growing importance of the *Poetics* as the ascendancy of "Aristotelian formalism."

4. The concept and term "implied author" I owe to Wayne C. Booth's *The Rhetoric of Fiction* (Chicago, 1960).

5. For the place of rhetoric in the education of Renaissance English poets, the standard works are T. W. Baldwin, *William Shakspere's Small Latine and Lesse Greeke*, 2 vols. (Urbana, Ill., 1944); Donald Lemen Clark, *John Milton at St. Paul's School* (New York, 1948); Harris Fletcher, *The Intellectual Development of John Milton*, 2 vols. (Urbana, Ill., 1961); and William Riley Parker, *Milton: A Biography*, 2 vols. (Oxford, 1968). To these should be added the brief but insightful work by John Mulder, *The Temple of the Mind: Education and Literary Taste in Seventeenth Century England* (New York, 1969).

6. Stephen Greenblatt, *Renaissance Self-Fashioning: From More to Shakespeare* (Chicago, 1980).

7. Wylie Sypher places Donne's work mainly in the "mannerist" stage of Renaissance art: *Four Stages of Renaissance Style: Transformations in Art and Literature, 1400–1700* (Garden City, 1955). "Mannerism," Sypher argues, was "a phase of formal disintegration" (p. 106), a phase through which Milton passed on his way to the formal reintegration that marks "baroque" style.

8. Crane says, "The process of literary composition has often been rather crudely divided, especially by authors of textbooks on English writing, into two stages: a stage of preparatory reading, thinking, planning, incubation, and a state of putting the materials thus assembled into words; and what happens in the second stage has usually been represented as a direct transference to paper of the ideas or imaginations which the writer has come into possession of in the first stage—as a simple matter, that is, of giving to an acquired content an appropriate verbal form." Having taught that doctrine himself, he further realizes that writing never goes well until the writer has achieved "a kind of intuitive glimpse of a possible subsuming form for the materials. . . . It is more than a general intention, more than a 'theme,' and more than an outline in the usual sense of that word; it is, as I have said, a shaping or directing cause, involving at the same time, and in some sort of correlation, the particular conceptual form my subject is to take. . . ." (pp. 140–141). R. S. Crane, *The Languages of Criticism and the Structure of Poetry* (Toronto, 1953). In the thirty years since Crane wrote that passage, we have devised many techniques of prewriting—though no one has put better the formalist technique of *inventio*, and no one has as yet revived the fully rhetorical technique.

9. A. S. P. Woodhouse, "Theme and Pattern in *Paradise Regained*," *University of Toronto Quarterly*, 25 (1956):168.

Index

Major discussions are noted in boldface numbers